Next Year
Will Be Better

D1353995

For Pauline

So when from hence we shall be gone
And be no more, nor you, nor I,
As one another's mystery,
Each shall be both, yet both be one.

"An Ode Upon a Question Moved,
Whether Love Should Continue for Ever"

Lord Herbert of Cherbury

Next Year
Will Be Better

A memoir of England
in the 1950s

John Lucas

Five Leaves Publications
www.fiveleaves.co.uk

Next Year Will Be Better:
a memoir of England in the 1950s
by John Lucas

Published in 2011 in paperback
by Five Leaves Publications,
PO Box 8786, Nottingham NG1 9AW
www.fiveleaves.co.uk

Cover illustration: James Boswell
courtesy of Ruth Boswell

Acknowledgements
Sections of this book originally appeared, usually in rather
different form, in the journals *Island* (Australia), *London
Magazine* and *Poetry Review,* as well as in *Starting to Explain:
Essays on 20th Century British & Irish Poetry* (Trent Books,
2003), and *Seeing Double* ed. C Kaplan and A Simpson (St
Martin's Press, 1996). Thanks to the editors and publishers
involved and to the Authors' Club, for an award that helped
towards the publication of the present book.

Five Leaves acknowledges
financial support from
Arts Council England

Designed and typeset by
Four Sheets Design and Print

Printed in Great Britain

Five Leaves is represented
to the booktrade by Turnaround
and distributed by Central Books.

Five Leaves is a member of Inpress
(www.inpressbooks.co.uk),
an organisation of independent publishers.

Contents

We go to work by bike and bus
In any kind of weather
And when we're late we call it fate
But next year will be better.

For we've a plan to build a van
From a scrap heap carburettor
And a chassis we found on old waste ground
So next year will be better.

Oh, we're the true-born optimists
Thumbs up, sing Hey etcetera,
And though this year may seem small beer
Next year will be betterer,
Yes next year will be betterer.

From "Next Year Will be Better," a skiffle number written and
sung by the Towpath Ramblers, 1954/55

"History leaves out so much. It leaves out the most
important thing: the detail of what being alive is
like," *J.G. Farrell*

Prelude

This book covers the ten years in which I grew from early adolescence to adulthood. I have written it in order to set straight the record about a much misunderstood and sometimes maligned decade. All too often the 1950s are casually dismissed as "the drab years", "the grey years", the "years of conformity", or "the dismal years", soubriquets accepted, even created, by people who never lived through the decade, or who, if they did, and for reasons I don't fully understand, have nevertheless chosen to accept as truth clichés which they must know are not merely misleading but plain wrong. But it makes for a good story. Day follows night. By contrast with the 1950s the 1960s was carnival time: a joyous release from post-war austerities and repressions. The 1960s was the time when sexual intercourse began. It was then we all stepped out of the prison-house of make-do and deference.

You could regard David Hockney's decision to receive the gold medal at the Royal College of Art in 1961 clad in gold lamé jacket rather than black-and-white as the moment when the keys, for so long rusted, could be heard to turn and locks to snap suddenly back. A good moment, certainly, a jazzy, genially contemptuous two fingers up to starch and sobriety. But those who lived through the 1950s, at all events the younger among us, could hear the locks being readied for loosening long before that moment came. In fact, we were the ones greasing them. Jazz, skiffle, Bill Haley and Elvis; Teds, the sack dress, jeans, duffle coats, desert boots; CND, The Goons, *Universities and Left Review, Look Back in Anger, Lucky Jim, Saturday Night and Sunday Morning....*

Still, what I have written is only incidentally social history. Peter Hennessy's magnificent *Having it so Good* provides a comprehensive, objective study of a decade which I inevitably choose to treat far more impressionistically. I am writing about *my* 1950s, and I don't doubt that for others the story

7

will be very different. They include those who belonged to the manual working class, for instance, which then made up 75% of the total population; or those youths — the majority — who did their national service, which I managed to avoid. Moreover, my 1950s were bound to be different from those of my sister and the various girls I knew.

One thing we did, however, have in common. We were all children who had been born just prior to the Second World War, we were all subject to the privations of rationing, and those of us who lived in towns and cities or who visited them — which must have been the overwhelming majority — took for granted the presence of as yet un-reclaimed bombsites: of weed-infested craters, some boarded up, others open to inspection and for play, of shattered houses and public buildings, which over the decade were slowly repaired or more often levelled in order to be replaced by new housing and, increasingly, large shops and "stores". And for many if not most of us, our fathers became presences in our lives only when those lives had begun to take shape. The shapers had been our mothers. Naturally, then, we were likely to be resentful of men who at war's end began to arrive in our houses, whom we thought of as strangers, and yet who came between our mothers and us, requiring us to do *their* bidding, to obey *their* commands. At the time we thought that this was our misfortune. Only later did we begin to understand that to a far greater degree it was theirs. A generation of fathers did not see their children for six years; many, those who were killed in action or whose wives found other loves, saw them fleetingly or never saw them at all.

For the men who survived and returned to married life, adjustment must have been difficult, sometimes unbearably so, both for them and their wives. Hennessy quotes a figure of 60,000 divorces for 1946-47 as "freakish"; but it is, I suppose, explicable if you consider the re-adjustment that married couples, whose prolonged enforced separations were bound to be problematic, had to try to make. It should come as no great surprise that some found the task beyond them. Nor was this merely because over a lengthy period they saw each other briefly, if ever. (Leave wasn't available to most soldiers serving overseas, and others were stuck in prison camps.) Inevitably, relationships frayed. Separation and divorce were by no means unusual. There was also the fact that in some cases returning soldiers were confronted by children they couldn't possibly have fathered. I spent the majority of the war years in a Leicestershire village called Burbage. Most of the men who occupied the houses along the road where we rented a small semi-detached house (owned by a local farmer), were away for the war's duration. One who had somehow escaped call-up took on the job of window cleaner. He had carroty red hair. By 1945 the road seemed to be swarming with small, carroty-haired children.

And there is a further matter. Men who had gone off to fight Hitler left jobs which in many cases they couldn't return to, either because the jobs had been taken or the businesses which supplied the jobs had themselves disappeared. And supposing they did get their old jobs back, they would find that while they were away fighting they had been passed over for promotion by men of their own age or even younger, men who because of ill-health or for some other reason had not been required to fight. In addition, male adults in "reserved occupations" had sometimes done spectacularly well out of the war, thank you very much. Farmers and market gardeners, in particular, filled their boots, while the families of those in uniform were forced to subsist on a pittance. This was especially galling for those, including my father, who had volunteered to fight. Where were the rewards for choosing to risk life and limb in order to save the free world from fascism? I never heard my father ask this question. He hadn't after all had a difficult war. As a tank instructor he spent his army years on this side of the channel, and though he was away for long spells he did occasionally manage trips home, sometimes on what was called "French leave", otherwise known as A.W.O.L.

But though he didn't ask the question, my mother did, and I suspect that resentment and his difficulty in finding work after he was demobbed played some part in his sudden, and, to me, inexplicable rages. Not that these were either frequent or prolonged. But they could come out of a seemingly clear blue sky. And men who had fought a far more dangerous war than him, or who had been away from home for longer, must have had very great trouble coping with what they would have considered the thoughtless ingratitude of the nation, to say nothing of the sulky resentment of their children and, possibly, the transferred affection of their wives. Hence, the remarks by Dr T.F. Main to a conference of the Royal Medico-Psychological Association in Birmingham in October, 1946, that in addition to ex-soldiers whose exposure to war have left them with psychiatric problems, there is "another newer problem — that of ex-servicemen who made satisfactory adjustments to civilian life before the war, and to service life during the war, but who are now in severe difficulties under the stresses presented to them by their return to civilian life." (Quoted by Hennessy, pp. 130-1).

By the beginning of the 1950s my father had to all appearances made the necessary adjustments to civilian life. He had work, he had a house, he even had a car — a second-hand, pre-war model, but a car for all that; and he had his family. As someone who was by nature an optimist, he resembled that friend of Dr Johnson, Mr Edwards, who would be a philosopher but who found that cheerfulness kept breaking in. My mother was much more of a worrier. Yet she loved laughter and always hoped that family occasions would prove to be times of jollity. For this reason, she both ardently and anxiously looked forward to Christmas. She yearned for the season of good will to be a "success", by which she meant, I think, a Dickensian romp, with plenty of games and good things to eat. (When she was growing up, her father, an elementary school head teacher and devoted admirer of the Inimitable, had at the appropriate moment each year read to her mother and herself the account of Christmas at Dingley Dell.) But at the end of 1949 most foodstuffs were still rationed. And laughter, too, could be rationed. Ardency and anxiety were therefore, as always, precariously balanced.

Chapter 1
Christmas Cheer

Christmas 1949 was a time of financial difficulties for my parents. Earlier in the year my father had been hit by a tax demand which related to the house he had acquired two years previously. The demand, it later turned out, was unjust, but at the time he was advised he should pay up. This left the cupboard bare and we were able to manage a holiday that summer only because some neighbours allowed us free use of a caravan they kept down at Pagham on the south coast. It was kindly meant, but the holiday turned out to be a cheerless affair. Just about every day there was rain. The caravan site, in a flattened, mud-caked field, was bare and unwelcoming, the nearby beach, of steep-shelved stone, was lashed by on-shore winds, the sea itself a thick grey soup. Still, it taught me to swim because one morning, as I shivered in its inhospitable murk, a wave knocked me off my feet. I went under, came up floundering, and, glory be, found that, no matter how ungainly my movements, I was able to keep afloat. But it was a brief moment of delight. That afternoon, despairing of the weather, we drove into Brighton to see a film about Columbus's discovery of America. Columbus was played by Frederick March in armour and frilled collar, there were shots of blue skies glimpsed beyond breeze-rippled sails, the mariners came ashore on a stretch of golden sand fringed by tall palm trees, and my father fell asleep in the middle of the film. I was glad to get home.

But it wasn't our family alone for whom 1949 proved difficult. Most people we knew had little money. Nobody said so, financial hardship was even more unmentionable than death, but its odour affected all our days. Work wasn't difficult to come by, but wages were low. Yet even if they'd been higher there wouldn't have been much to spend them on.

Four years after the end of the Second World War, severe rationing of food and clothes still limited what people could eat and how they could dress. A familiar epithet for the period is "grey": as in "the grey post-war world", "the grey fifties", "the grey decade". This is unfair, but dingy it certainly was, at least at the outset. How could it not be? Little re-building of the bombed cities had begun, the clothes people stood up in were mostly old or ingeniously crafted from whatever materials came to hand ("make do and mend" was the watchword of the time, and most women were prodigiously dextrous at handling both knitting and sewing needle), the dresses, suits and coats purchased with coupon allowance were usually unattractively severe or "practical". As for food, at best it could be called plain fare. There were few delicacies. The highlight of our holiday at Pagham came on the final, rain-splattered afternoon, when I and my sister, Jill, younger than me by sixteen months, raced our father along the beach in order to eat the knickerbocker glories he treated us to at a more-or-less deserted tea rooms.

Christmas was therefore a time of far greater cheer than can readily be imagined now, some sixty years later, when shops are full and the most exotic food and drink easily come by. Talk of how unimaginative English cooking was in those post-war years makes me angry. The fare may have been plain but if our household was anything to go by a good deal of effort and ingenuity went into making palatable meals out of the most unpromising ingredients. I grant that in the ubiquitous "British Restaurants" as well as most high street tea-houses and cafés, menus would be severely restricted and pretty unappetising. Egg on toast (for the most part scrambled and plumped-out with flour additive), beans on toast, sardines or pilchard on toast, rhubarb crumble (smothered in thick, lumpy custard), marmalade tart, rice pudding, sago, tapioca, semolina. Well, there will have been variations, but eating out wasn't an enjoyable experience.

Nor, despite my mother's best efforts, was eating at home. This didn't so much matter during the week. Breakfast was a rushed affair: a bowl of cereal, a piece of toast, and then I was off to catch the 216 bus, which would take me the six miles from Ashford to school in Hampton. On my return there'd be tea. Brother and sister ate together while my mother prepared the evening meal she and my father would sit down to when he got home from work in Slough. Perhaps because we weren't under parental gaze and certainly because the table would invariably hold one of my mother's expertly-made cakes or plates of tarts, and a pot of her equally well-made jam — marrow-and-ginger was an especial favourite — tea was a customary pleasure.

Not so the family's Sunday dinner. The execrable quality of such meat as could be bought was a problem. Every Friday my mother would queue for hours in order to buy a piece of beef or lamb or pork. She'd then spend Saturdays worrying aloud about whether she'd chosen wisely, and finally on Sunday, as she went about the task of roasting, the mood became more fraught and "a general infection of ill-temper", to use Dickens' great phrase, took hold.

It even, and despite my mother's best efforts, wormed its way into Christmas. Breakfast, dinner and tea on that day, all gave her licence to use her skills and imagination as no other moment of the year could. Breakfast, the table laid in the front room which for this day at least was warmed by a coal fire, featured sausage-rolls made from meat whose uncertain quality was cancelled by the crumbly, melt-in-the-mouth pastry in which it was encased. There was also egg-and-bacon pie. Baked in a deep pie-dish, this had a pastry base and sides which were filled with layers of raw egg mingled with bacon scraps and, having been baked on Christmas Eve, was eaten cold.

After the opening of presents our parents disappeared into the kitchen to prepare for the Christmas dinner, while Jill and I were left to "enjoy" our gifts and our grandmother sang carols in her sweet, quavering voice — "Once in Royal David's City" and "Away in a Manger" were her favourites. The wireless was tuned into the Home Service, I imagine because it was thought to be more dignified and therefore better suited to the day than the Light Programme.

Then it was time to make ourselves "look presentable" — my father's phrase — for attendance at the Shuters' "At Home". A childless couple, the Shuters lived at the top of our road in a small white-washed cottage which, perhaps because of its mullioned windows, looked far more distinguished than the two sets of semi-detached houses below them. Number 7 was home to the Furnells, father, mother and two daughters, then, at the adjoined no. 9, came the Grants. Mr Grant was a civil servant who always wore a dark-blue pinstripe suit. His wife, who had at some time trained as a nurse, was about the same age as my mother, and they became great friends, exchanging Christmas presents. (Mrs Grant's annual gift to my mother was a pair of salmon-pink knickers of generous proportions which, when unwrapped, caused titters). There was also a son of my own age. We lived at no. 11, next to the Collins's. The Grants, like us, had a grandmother living with them, the Collins went one better by having both grandmother and grandfather sharing their house with their daughter, Margaret, who was about my age, and her younger brother, Raymond.

Neither the Collins nor Furnells were invited to the Shuters'. I don't recall any explanation for this being either asked for or given. None was needed. Mr Furnell had manual employment at Heathrow and early every weekday morning set off to cycle the ten or so miles to work wearing overalls over which, in colder or wetter weather, a torn and stained raincoat flapped like a large, trapped and dismal bird. Bill Collins left the house at a similar hour, also in overalls, cloth-capped, and carrying his carpenter's tool bag. The rest of the road was decorously, even desperately, lower middle-class, or a little above that. The Frickers at no. 15 scraped in because although Mr Fricker was a self-employed jobbing builder his three daughters all attended the Welsh Girls' School, a local establishment which was part-boarding and wholly given over to training its pupils to be "young ladies", and in addition the family regularly attended church. Relations between "us" and the Collins and Furnells were polite, but a certain distance was maintained.

As we passed the Furnells on our short walk to the Shuters', the sound of a tune, faint but unmistakable, came from their house and a glance into their front room showed father, mother and the two fair-haired girls jumping up and down in approximate time to "The Teddy Bear's Picnic". "Fancy that," my grandmother said, her voice making plain her disapproval. "On Christmas Day of all days."

No such indecorous behaviour at the Shuters. The few families gathered there stood or sat about awkwardly in the long, low chintzy room that ran the breadth of their cottage. Sherry for the ladies, the possibility of beer or whisky for their men folk, and for the children, lemonade. Mince pies on doilied plates, slivers of sardine and hard-boiled egg on fingers of toast, and strained talk.

"Are you having anyone in for Christmas, Mrs Lucas?"

"No. Just the family. We like to be quiet. You know."

"Very sensible. Christmas is for the family, I always think."

My mother would smile fixedly when uttering or receiving these inanities. My father spoke in a manner I never heard him use at home, each phrase uttered as though by rote, civility teetering towards ingratiation: "awfully nice fellow," "jolly good show", "well done, that man", if someone rescued a drink from being knocked over, say, or took it on themselves to hand round more nibbles. Only my grandmother, seated in a deep armchair, behaved as usual, smiling sweetly if vaguely about her and ready to discuss with anyone who came within earshot the state of her bunions or of those occasions of "mild flatulence" or, more splendidly, "eructations", from which she had mercifully recovered in time to enjoy Christmas.

"That's the ticket," someone said.

After the best part of an hour of this exquisite tedium my father, always on edge lest his mother-in-law begin some embarrassingly intimate story of her current medical condition, would announce that it was time for us "to be on our way, rejoicing." And so, to a chaste chorus of "Merry Christmas", my grandmother was levered out of her chair,

15

we gathered up our coats, and left. Others remained, perhaps to "sink" another sherry or scotch, but "Never outstay your welcome" was one of my father's several watchwords, and I didn't at all mind our departure. Nor I suspect did anyone in our family, with the possible exception of my grandmother, to whom all occurrences were to be taken as proof of God's infinite mercy.

Looking back, I wonder whether anyone apart from her enjoyed those occasions. My parents never said that they did, though they always insisted that it was very kind of the Shuters to open their doors to the neighbours, that it helped "to make Christmas". I suspect that they took social obligations — the giving and receiving of ill-at-ease hospitality — so much for granted that it didn't occur to them to question whether they derived any pleasure from them. It was what you *did*. Perhaps the pleasure, thin and pallid though it was, came from having survived any such occasion without mishap: not uttering the wrong word, not picking up the wrong fork or spoon, not sitting too far back in your chair or too much on its edge, not this, not that, nor any of the endless others. There seemed to be limitless opportunities to commit the kind of solecism that would demonstrate your unfitness for "proper" company. But to come through unscathed, to be flawlessly decorous, restrained, above all "respectable", marked you out from those "who didn't know how to enjoy themselves without kicking up a racket." And though I suspect that deep down both my parents would have loved nothing better than to join those who kicked up a racket, how could they do that without putting themselves beyond the pale of respectability?

Even Christmas dinner was affected by a decorum that felt hostile to the day's spirit. There may have been a sherry for the grown-ups before we all sat down to eat, but there was certainly no wine with the meal, not even a beer for my father. On one occasion my grandmother drank what she referred to as a medicinal brandy — "to help my eructations" — which sent Jill and me into a fit of giggles; but that apart our meal was accompanied by water. Yet within the limits imposed by rationing and the scarcity of good foodstuffs we ate well that day. Chicken which, in those pre-battery times, was both succulent and rich in flavour, sage-and-onion stuffing (my mother would have scorned the packaged variety), giblet gravy, roast potatoes and, perhaps from our own garden, sprouts, which I loathed, although slathered in sufficient spoonfuls of gravy and bread sauce they could be forced down.

Plum pudding followed, rich with ingredients my mother had saved from rationed goods over the previous months. Sporting a sprig of holly, the pudding contained somewhere within it a silver sixpence that had once belonged to my maternal grandfather. Whoever found the sixpence in their helping could make a wish before handing the coin back.

Once that was done with, my mother was instructed to retire to the back room and put her feet up, while my father made her a cup of tea. And then, while she sat in enforced idleness, smoking a Weight, and, opposite her, her mother subsided into a gentle snoring, my father washed the dinner service which was rarely if ever on show for other occasions, while Jill and I dried up with increasingly sodden tea towels. Cleaning greasy plates wasn't easy. Into the bowl of hot water you plunged and vigorously stirred a kind of egg whisk which enclosed odd nubbles of soap. But no matter how hard you worked at stirring this contraption, the suds thus raised weren't enough to get the dirt off without powerful applications of wire wool, Vim and elbow-grease. Saucepans and baking trays needed several dousings and scourings before they were spotless, which was the only kind of clean my father tolerated.

At last we could stack the plates and return the cutlery to the front-room sideboard. "Well," my father said, kneeling to stow in its place the large meat dish which only ever made an appearance at Christmas, "that's that for another year". And with that remark, which he made every Christmas, all excitement seemed to drain away. Even now, as I write out his words, I can feel something of the desolation they caused me. It was as though he was deliberately, even forcefully, ruling out the possibility of continued pleasure. Christmas had disappeared with the meat dish into the dark recesses of the sideboard, the door closed and the key turned on it.

I can't suppose he meant his words to carry such a charge. And yet when we all gathered again in the lounge, the mood of the day had changed, brightness had fallen from the air. There was still Christmas cake to come (as rich as the plum pudding, it was expertly iced by my mother with small, wavy corrugations atop which sat a miniature robin on a log), there were mince pies, there were home-made sweets created from marzipan with bits of angelica and glacé cherry. My grandmother applied herself to a box of crystallised ginger.

Over cake which we were too full to eat much of, we played games. Card games. "Happy Families" — "have you got Mr Bun the baker?" — or Snap. Board games, but I loathed "Monopoly". Draughts, which I enjoyed, was ruled out because only two could play. Games with pencil and paper. Guessing games. My mother would want these games to continue. This was a family grouped together, at play, contented. This was all that a happy Christmas should be. But minute by minute the hoped-for feeling of togetherness waned, and despite the ardency of her desire to prolong her vision of Christmas spirit, by early evening there was little of it left. We drew the curtains on whatever promise the day had once held.

Now, as Jill busied herself with a jigsaw puzzle and I retreated to read a book I'd been given, the mood turned sour. "Why must you always have your nose stuck in a book," my father asked, "can't you see it upsets your mother." Without looking up, I said, "if I've got my nose stuck in a book I *can't* see, can I?" I must have been insufferable. Next minute the book was torn from my hands. "You're getting altogether too big for your shoes," my father shouted, while behind him my mother said, "Please, please don't let's have a row. Not on Christmas night. Don't spoil the day." But it was already spoiled.

Not long ago I heard Richard Eyre in a radio discussion about *King Lear*. How would he stage the king's first appearance? Well, Eyre, said, the general bad temper reminded him of his childhood Christmases, when his father had nearly always insisted setting up an argument with other members of the family. It was as though he was demanding their love for having provided them with the wherewithal to celebrate the occasion: the presents, the food, the drink, were all paid for out of his pocket. Didn't he then deserve their love? Didn't he warrant far more than they were prepared to show? Lear's interrogation of his daughters could effectively be set at Christmas.

I thought about this, but then rejected it as true of my own father, though he must have felt that he lacked for the love he surely deserved. By Christmas 1949 he had been back with his family for rather fewer than three whole years, and while during that period he had become a real person to us, rather than the shadowy presence to be inferred from photographs or the occasional, fleeting visit during the war, at some level of my being I must have resented his influence over my mother. He came between the two of us. From the time when I was a little over two until I was nine, she had overseen my life, had been the person to whom I looked for approval and for a love which I had come to take for granted. But with my father's arrival as more than a very occasional house-guest it became plain that she had somehow stepped aside from her former role and that from now on he would be the law-giver, the adult in the house with whom I would have to come to terms. Naturally I resented this fact. Naturally he resented my resentment.

My Oedipus Complex. But my father was no Murdstone. He was essentially a kind-hearted, genial man, and I suspect that his occasional bouts of ill-temper, especially in the period when he and I were getting to know each other, arose from the ungainsayable fact that the years he had spent away from his family meant that he had never seen, and could never now share in the experience of guiding Jill and me as we grew from infancy into childhood. Through no fault of his own we became as much strangers to him, our father, as he became to us, his children. This was his sadness, not ours. It occurs to me now that he was to see far more of his grandchildren in their early years than he ever saw of his own, and that this goes far towards explaining the delight, even joy, he took in those grandchildren, in being able to witness the various stages of their growth. In a sense, they were the children he never had.

Of course, this enforced estrangement of fathers and children must have happened — *did* happen — to countless thousands of other families. "And with the peace a stranger came to stay" I wrote in a sonnet after my father's death; and in another poem I tried to analyse how the gap those years opened up affected us all, how the word to which my mother

> pinned hope's star!
> "de-mobilised" — means "disbanded" as he knows
> "disband" means "cease to function as a group"

"he" being myself.

The words perhaps over-state the case. It wasn't so much that we didn't function as a group, or family, as that *how* we functioned often felt unfamiliar, unwelcome, under strain. And while this is common to all families, it was bound to be particularly so, or so in a particular way, for families whose men folk had been away on war service. So that just as what distinguishes men and women of my generation from later ones is that we could never in post-war years hear a fire siren whirr up — that weird, eldritch howl, long since discontinued — without a prickling sensation, a momentary return to war-time panic, the acceptance that an air-attack was imminent and that we must run for shelter, so, looking back, most of us must surely recall the disruptive arrival in the family home of a man who, without good reason, claimed authority over us all.

In my father's case, the claim was made more difficult by his failure to find work. Before the war he had sold insurance in Exeter, losing his post when the company closed down; then, after some months during which my mother, with one child to care for and another on the way, returned to her parents' house in Wimbledon, he found another insurance company in Coventry prepared to employ him. He moved us up to join him in the city and we had scarcely been there a month before Neville Chamberlain broadcast to the nation that "This country is now at war with Germany". My father at once volunteered for active service, and while he was waiting for his call-up papers the insurance company gave him the task of attending to its business in and around the small market town of Hinckley, in Leicestershire. Another move, this time to a rented house in the village of Burbage, some two miles from Hinckley. I have a vivid memory of sitting on bare boards staring out from between my father's legs at a garden visible through open French-windows, and of his voice saying "Well, it will do." Then he went to war.

By Christmas 1949, he was again in work, this time selling soft-drinks for a firm in Slough. But, while "respectable", the job wasn't well paid and there's no doubt that my parents were often hard up. Only once did I become aware of the struggle they must have had to put food on the table and keep us all reasonably well clothed and shod. The previous year, in the spring of 1948, when I was still at primary school, I had developed an interest in carpentry, no doubt prompted by the fact that next door Mr Grant and son John were endlessly to be seen and heard in their garage-cum-work shed, sawing, planing, hammering.

DIY is usually said to have sprung fully-formed from the TV programmes fronted by Barry Bucknell, which began transmission in 1957, but in my experience it began as soon as the war ended and demobilised men, many of whom had learnt manual skills during their war years, set about reno-vating or "improving" the homes to which they returned, or making "knick-knacks" — pot-stands, bowls, even small painted, wooden animals — either for ornamentation in those homes or for sale.

My route to and from junior school took me past a small iron-mongery, and one day I spotted in its window a fretsaw which I suddenly, passionately desired to own. I went in. How much was the fretsaw in the window? The shopkeeper, a small, faded man in a grey shop-coat, took his time about replying. Ninepence ha'penny, he finally told me. I had two pence in my pocket. If I offered him that amount would he agree to hold onto the fretsaw until I came back with the rest? "As long as it's before I shut up shop for the day."

My pocket money allowance was three-pence a week. Surely my mother would agree to lend me seven-pence ha'penny and I would pay her back over three weeks. At the end of school I ran all the way home. But she wouldn't do as I asked. I pleaded with her, I was near to tears of frustration. Why not lend me the measly sum, why *not*? I may have said something rude, I don't remember. But, herself driven at last to anger, she pulled out her purse, opened it, and spilled the contents onto the table. "That's what I've got to last the rest of the week," she said, "go on, count it." A three-penny bit, a penny, and two half-pennies.

I trudged back to the shop and, without speaking, the man handed me my coins.

"So little we had, and so gay, it is something to ponder," George Fraser wrote in his lovely poem, "For Tilly, Sick, With Love", remembering post-war years in bohemian London. But the words hardly hold true for lower-middle class outer London. Gaiety wasn't known only by its absence from our household and from thousands of similar households, of course not. But however desired it might be, it didn't regularly make its presence felt, not in those first, anxious years when the four of us were trying to learn how to live together.

Chapter 2
Shades

That we were in Ashford at all was for my parents a piece of great good luck, although for me it felt more like disaster. I had been happy in Burbage, how happy I realised only when, standing at the bottom of the garden behind our new house, I saw on the far side of a straggle of allotments, not tree-fringed fields tilting up the horizon, but a line of semis, bricky, obdurate, like a prison wall. I stared at those houses for I don't know how long, wishing them gone, trying to convince myself that some trick of vision hid the familiar green spaces, the thick, deep hedgerows, the minnow stream at the bottom of Farmer Bailey's field that I trawled with a friend and from which, though we mostly failed to net a fish, we would bring home clumps of watercress for our mothers. Gone.

We moved in the late spring of 1947. Jill and my grand-mother went first, most of the furniture and household goods going with them, my mother and I followed a day or so later. The reason for this delay was that I was sitting the Eleven Plus exams. Although not yet ten years old, I was in the top class at my village school, less through any display of intel-lectual precocity than because the school was so small, and the teaching so good, that I was able to be included in the class of fifteen boys and girls who were entered for the exam-ination that year. The exercise was purely academic. Suppose I passed, I'd not be going to Hinckley Grammar, because our move to Middlesex was by then assured, but my mother and teachers thought it "good practice".

Anyway, early on a Saturday morning in April 1947, my exams now concluded, I sat with my mother in the bare-board back room of the house we were about to vacate, feeding bacon rind through the hole in a box that contained

Sammy, our black and white cat, a ferocious mouser, and waiting for the arrival of the taxi that would take us to Hinckley station. The previous evening I'd exchanged presents with my friends John Masters and Frank Garner. Frank's father and an older brother who had been on Aston Villa's books had both been killed in the war, as a result of which grown-ups spoke to and of him in hushed tones, as though he must be wrapped in sadness, though in my experience he was an unfailingly cheerful boy and a terrific scrapper. Being known as Frank's friend guaranteed immunity from playground bullies. As we handed over our gifts, the three of us promised to write regularly to each other. In the event, I had one letter from Frank, telling me of life at Hinckley Grammar School where "we have to play at rugger, which I do not like." From John, younger than me but my closest friend, I never heard again.

"Will I like our new house?" I asked my mother.

"Oh, yes," she said, but her words didn't ring true.

Nor was the countryside we passed through on our way down to Paddington at all reassuring. The terrible iced-over winter of 1947 had finally slackened its grip, and the further south we went the greater the effects of the general thaw. Everywhere, fields were hidden under grey, standing water, and you only knew of lanes cutting between them when you saw lines of truncated street lamps poking up from the surrounding lakes. Telegraph wires sagged down to and sometimes dipped below the water line. It should have been dramatic, but to me it was all unutterably dreary.

Several hours later, by which time I'd glumly come to terms with the view — or rather, lack of it — from our back garden, the five of us sat down to lunch in the front room of our new house. The furniture was familiar, so too the plates and cutlery. We'd had to leave behind the steel Morrison table which served as indoor shelter during the war and under which we crawled whenever the sirens sounded the alarm for an air raid, but that apart everything was in its accustomed place. And the house, though of slightly more generous proportions than the one in Burbage, was the same design: front door leading to hall, stairs to left, two rooms off to right, kitchen at rear. Upstairs two large bedrooms with box room and small bathroom.

I imagine I was the only one at that lunch table who felt dismayed at the turn in our fortunes. For something like twelve months my father had chased jobs without managing to trap any. Burbage and its surroundings clearly had nothing for him, and so, dressed in his demob suit with overcoat and trilby, he went down to London, staying with friends and relatives while he answered advertisements, knocked on doors, walked the streets in the hope of seeing a hopeful sign. He tried for garage mechanic, but knowing little of electronics he never, as he said, "got a sniff", he applied for work as a salesman with numerous firms ("I always thought I could sell things" he told me, late in life), but with similar lack of success. At one especially low point he even thought of rejoining the army as a regular soldier. I know this because my mother, in tears at the prospect, broke the news to me one afternoon when I came home from the village school. They even, so I later learnt, briefly considered setting up a fish and chip shop.

The problem was partly that my father had no qualifications. As the younger of two sons, he was expected to fettle for himself. It was taken for granted in families of the sort he came from that parents would do all they could with whatever means available to ensure an education for the oldest boy — girls didn't get the same consideration — but that money would rarely, if ever, permit much for his younger siblings. I don't think it occurred to my father to complain about this. It was simply the way things were. But as a result, he left school in Torquay at the age of fifteen with only his wits to offer to prospective employers, and at once had to find work. Both before the war and afterwards, this wasn't easy, not, anyway, if certain work was considered to be beyond the pale. For, and this was a further problem my father had to cope with, his lower-middle class upbringing had left him anxious not to offend against its unwritten code. Central to this code was that certain jobs —

especially manual ones — were beneath consideration, and that no decent man would require his wife to work. She had to be kept according to the modest expectations to which her parents had accustomed her.

My father was a promising athlete and footballer. Soon after he left school he was playing on the right wing for Exeter City, although he wasn't contracted to them, merely receiving appearance money. Nevertheless, news of his sporting prowess had to be kept from his mother, who had made as a condition of her agreeing to marry my grand-father, also a footballer, that he stop turning out for Torquay United, even though he played as an amateur. The mere thought of his being tainted by contact with so vulgar a game as association football was more than his wife-to-be was prepared to accept. She herself came from a small family farm on Dartmoor and had been in service at the time she met her future husband. Being in service was respectable. Playing football in front of the paying public was not. Unfortunately, in the second game he played for Exeter, the sixteen-year old Len Lucas scored a goal and the local newspaper ran a headline *Have City Found a New Star?*, under which was a report of the match in which my father was mentioned by name. My grandmother was shown the paper by a neighbour and that was the end of my father's football career, at least until he escaped a year or so later to London, where he appeared on an irregular basis for Fulham and Millwall. Later still, he played in the same army team as Middlesbrough's Jimmy Gordon and the Wolves and England winger, Jimmy Mullen.

Amateur athletics was, however, a different matter. My father was not merely a promising footballer, he was a good sprinter and high-hurdler. He took part in local competitive races, represented Devon in the 3As at the White City; and he won numerous canteens of cutlery as well as cut-glass bowls and vases which decorated our sideboard during my childhood. His mother tolerated these events because they were free from the toxin of professionalism and because "proper" people took part in them.

It's easy to scoff at this, to feel a mixture of irritation and contempt for such absurd pretensions and the constraints they imposed; but my father and men like him deserve respect and, I think, admiration for the effort they made to live according to the code's dictates, to take care of their wives and families, and to ensure that those families could "hold their heads up" and therefore be seen as "decent people in the eyes of the world." The effort to achieve this must have cost my father innumerable petty indignities, not least those associated with what my mother called "money worries". But such worries would, I guess, have been absent or at least suppressed when we sat at the lunch table for the first time in April, 1947.

Because he now had work. And at almost the same time another, still greater piece of luck had come my mother's way. In early childhood she had become friendly with a girl of her own age, daughter of friends of her parents. Both fathers were teachers in London junior schools, and her father, Horace Kelly, and Arthur Reynolds had for several years before the first world war taught at the same school, Hope Walk, in Chelsea. That was where their friendship ripened and it was natural enough that their daughters, Joan Kelly and Hilda Reynolds, both of them their parents' only children, should also become good friends. When in the mid 1920s Arthur Reynolds moved to Ashford, my mother occasionally took the journey from Fulham and, later Wimbledon, to stay with Hilda. But then, when Hilda was seventeen, she fell suddenly ill and died, of pneumonia. The tragedy devastated her parents. I have seen a photograph of her grave: a plain white stone on which is inscribed the one word, HILDA. The grave itself, a vertical slab of white marble, is surrounded by a low wall, as though by such means her parents hoped to keep her isolated, safe from further harm. Much of their love for their daughter they transferred to my mother, who at regular intervals still went to see them and as a result came to know and be on friendly terms with several of the families who lived in the same road.

What she didn't know was that the Reynolds had made their house over to her. But at the end of 1946 the two died within months of each other, and when their Will was opened my mother discovered that, in addition to the £200 they had left apiece to Jill and me, she had become the owner of a house which, in her "wildest dreams", as she would say, she could never have been able to buy. Not that 11 Exeford Avenue was a sizeable house. To repeat, although a tad larger than the one we rented at Burbage, it was nevertheless a smallish semi-detached, and although it had a long back garden, the space in front was, compared to the generous one I was used to, pocket-handkerchief: just enough to play host to a few rose bushes about which ranged borders of crazy paving and gravel. But my parents had absolutely no money. Without this unlooked-for bequest, my father, now he had work, would no doubt have tried to find rented accommodation for us in or near to Slough. But accommodation in those post-war years was hard to find, and especially hard in the South-East, the most heavily bombed part of all England. Prefabs apart, building and rebuilding of the shattered housing stock had in 1947 scarcely begun. It was the Labour Government's failure in this respect that partly accounts for its defeat in 1951: Macmillan, incoming Minster of Housing, promised to build 300,000 new homes a year and in the first years of the Conservative administration he made good his promise.

So there we were, the four, or rather five of us, for my mother's mother was as a matter of course living with us. This was common practice at the time. Their husbands' deaths usually left women of her generation with little to live on and no means of earning money apart from selling up. The death of my maternal grandfather occurred a few months before his 60th birthday. As a result the pension fund into which he had paid all his working life was withheld from his widow. He died in February, 1940, having been evacuated from London together with his school. Left without any money, my grandmother sold their house in Wimbledon and installed herself at Burbage. "She should

28

never have let the house go. Not at that time," my mother would mutter whenever her mother's presence riled her. It wasn't that the sweet-tempered old lady went out of her way to upset my parents, more that whereas during the years at Burbage she'd been a useful presence and, no doubt, welcome and even comforting companion to my mother during night-time vigils when enemy aeroplanes rumbled overhead, in peacetime Ashford, and with my father now at home, the relationship between the two women was bound to suffer. My father saw his mother-in-law's presence as an irritant. That wherever you looked you saw other families with grandparents in residence, most of them grand-mothers, didn't lessen my parents' sense of grievance.

It wasn't vast, it wasn't constant, this sense of being put upon, but nor did it give promise of disappearing, although there were periods of respite, when my grandmother, who came from a large family and whose late husband was one of thirteen children, several still living, herself disappeared by train to stay with various of her relatives. Even then, irritation could surface. My grandmother was normally the most unflappable of people. However, fear of being late for a railway journey customarily prompted the old lady to arrive at the station far earlier than she needed, so that on more than one occasion she climbed aboard the wrong train. My mother dreaded phone calls that might begin, "Joan, I am at Rugby. Why am I not at Cirencester?"

Inevitably, she came with us to Ashford. The money the sale of her house in Wimbledon brought in was far too little to allow her to buy or rent one in post-war England, always supposing one could be found. Still, her continued residence chez Lucas provided at least one benefit.

My parents persuaded her to use some of her capital on buying a car for my father. Second-hand, of course, partly because in 1947 the car industry had barely swung into action again, but also because a new car would have been beyond my grandmother's purse. As it was, the stylish 1938 Morris 10, complete with cracked green-leather upholstery and running boards, of which my father became owner

29

(registration number DJ02 — you always remember the first one) cost £213. That it came with various faults didn't especially worry him, not even when he found that the petrol tank leaked and he had therefore to siphon the newly-filled tank out by means of a rubber hose on which he sucked.

"Man's heart expands to tinker with his car" Louis MacNeice wrote in his 1933 poem, "Sunday Morning". Most Sunday mornings my father would leave the breakfast table to don a pair of blue overalls and then go out to the space beside our back door where the car was housed. Once there, having prised up the car's bonnet — though bonnet always struck me as an odd word for a piece of metal that looked more like the wing of a giant beetle — he would spend hours bent over the engine in order to fine-tune sparking plugs or, legs poking out from under the chassis, inspect the car's underside, its wiring, suspension, brake linings. Because petrol was rationed we rarely used the car for family outings, but he sometimes drove it to his work in Slough, on cold mornings having first to bring in the sparking plugs and warm them under the grill before they would guarantee to fire up the engine. After a year he built a garage at the back of the house, using the ubiquitous sundeala with which everything in those days seemed to be constructed, but while that protected the car from the worst of weathers, it did not solve the problem of frozen plugs.

* * *

My arrival at Ashford coincided with the Easter holidays. For three weeks therefore I was free to wander up and down the road, peering in at houses, being introduced to neighbours by my mother, several of whom she knew from her visits to the Reynolds. There was the old lady across the road who was reputed to have lost no fewer than three fiancés in the Great War and who had never married. She lived alone in a bungalow more or less hidden behind tall briar hedges, her only companion an aged Airedale called Barney, who usually lay in the middle of the road and was greeted by most passers-by, including the early morning milkman, newsboy and postman. Cars rarely used the short, curving avenue, and most of those that did knew about Barney, so nobody feared for the dog's safety.

Not so Sammy, who clearly resented our new cooped-up life as much as I did. He fought with the Grants' tabby, he brought in the occasional bewildered-looking mole, but he must have felt his hunting days were over. Life had turned sour, and in revenge for his new enforced idleness he took to launching himself, spitting and scratching, at members of the family, on more than one occasion drawing blood. Eventually he had to be "taken away".

The Grants' tabby was a large, placid creature with an air of soporific benevolence. It slept on the bonnet of their immaculately preserved Austin Seven from where it was dislodged whenever — which was not often — Mr Grant decided to take the car out "for a spin". One Saturday afternoon, he drove his wife, son John, and Jill and me to see the floods at Runnymede. Here, the Thames had overflowed its banks to such an extent that it was impossible to know where the river was supposed to run. We crept down a lane until stopped by a sign propped on a chair that said WATER AHEAD. HALT. Washing-water grey, swirling, and as always that spring equally supportive of water birds and the mantles of street lights that seemed to float on its surface as though they were glass buoys, stretched in every direction like an inland sea. The son, who was about my age, I thought of at first as dauntingly intelligent. This was partly because his hair was slicked down with oil, which, together with black-rimmed glasses, a smart school blazer — blue with yellow piping — and his remote air, gave him the appearance of the kind of boy who, in Captain Cuttle's words "would sink one of my tonnage soon." Only later would I come to understand that the blazer signified a private fee paying school to which he was sent because he had no hope of passing the eleven plus.

There was another boy living down the road with his parents whom I would know less even that I knew the

31

Grant's son. I discovered that he was called Ian, because on one occasion when we met in the street I asked his name. But this did not lead to friendship. Whichever school he went to required him to wear grey uniform with an outsize cherry-red cap under which was concealed a head of hair he apparently wasn't allowed to cut. As a result, the cap bulged around his head rather like a rubber inner-tube. His parents, bare-headed, short, always in shapeless woollen clothes my mother asserted they themselves put together, would from time to time make forays up and down the road. But they were more regularly to be seen working in their garden. They were vegetarians, living off the produce they grew. The man had a beard that extended greyly to the waist, as did his hair; and his wife, too, had waist-length grey hair. Each morning and evening they sang hymns to the accompaniment of an harmonium which was kept in the cottage's front room, so that anyone passing by could peer in and see the three of them together, mother seated, father and son on either side, backs to the road, absorbed in their singing. I suppose they must have gone to a chapel some-where. Or maybe not. Perhaps they conducted their religious life entirely at home. They didn't socialise and I don't think either adult went out to work. How they came by money to pay their bills was a mystery to us all.

Beyond them lived a couple of whom my mother was espe-cially fond. The Coxes had built their own substantial house, "Hurst Cottage", in a rustic style, including thatched roof, white-washed walls and mullioned windows, when they moved to Ashford as a newly-married couple soon after the Great War. Mr Cox worked for Coutts Bank in which he had, by the time I came to know them, a senior position and was reckoned to be comfortably off. He was a genial-looking man who at weekends exchanged the pin-stripes of his working week for a rough, gingerish suit, down which spilt ash from the Golden Flake cigarettes he smoked in great number. Mrs Cox, large, square-faced, wore floral dresses, and looked, I later came to realise, as though she had stepped from a Stanley Spencer painting of Cookham. She had a deep, almost bass voice, and was a benign, reassuring presence, who, my mother told me, had been a great comfort to the Reynolds in the fraught, grieving years after their daughter's death.

She herself had known great sadness. She was the mother of three sons, one of whom had died in adolescence of leukaemia, while another, a fighter pilot, had been killed in action in the war. Only David, who had also been a war-time pilot and subsequently followed his father into the banking business, now remained to her, and there were rumours that an air accident had left him, if not impotent, then quite possibly sterile. I don't think I was aware of those rumours until some years later when, although he'd been married for some time, he and his wife had still produced no offspring. But their childlessness added to the aura of loss, or incompletion, which I sometimes fancied hovered about Mrs Cox, although — or perhaps because — she was rarely without a smile, and she welcomed Jill and me into her house and garden whenever on the least pretext we went to visit her. There'd be a glass of barley water which we would drink while standing in her red-tiled kitchen. We liked to breathe in the oven scents — she seemed always to be baking — along with the sweet, waxy smell of floor polish, and then, once she'd put on the broad-brimmed straw hat without which, and no matter what the weather, she never left the house, we would wander with her among the fresh-leaved red currant and gooseberry bushes, and follow tippy-toe the narrow grass paths beside raked, crumby earth from which each spring tiny threads of greeny white protruded which would in due course become peas and beans. Broad beans were staked out in rows, runners grew round a circle of cane rods whose tops were drawn together like a latticed wigwam. Most intriguing of all was a square of earth, about twenty feet in each direction, in which were carefully spaced rows of floppy-leaved plants that looked like the palm leaves with which the church was decorated on the Sunday before Easter. What were they? Sweet corn, she told us. Neither Jill nor I knew what sweet corn was, but I could see at a glance

33

that Mrs Cox's plants bore no relation to the wheat that grew in Farmer Bailey's fields at Burbage.

It comes to me now that Mrs Cox treated Jill and myself as the grandchildren she lacked, and although I had no inkling of that in the days when we first met her, we always felt at ease with her. I never, though, thought of Mr Cox as a surrogate grandfather, and on the only occasion I spent any time with him the talk between us was stiff and came at infrequent intervals. Not that it much mattered. Knowing of my passion for cricket, he once volunteered to take me to a crowded Oval to see Surrey play Lancashire and I remember that the young PBH May scored 96, although what most thrilled me was a diving catch that Lancashire's Ken Greaves took at second slip. Absorbed in the game itself, I didn't at all mind that Mr Cox had little to say, though I recall being mildly shocked when, on the way home, he said that he didn't think Greaves's catch really "counted", because Greaves was an Australian. I put that down to the fact that he was a Surrey supporter. I was for Middlesex, and had been ever since my father, not yet demobbed but in immediate post-war England temporarily on leave, took me to Lords to see the last day of a county game between Middlesex and Kent. Middlesex were batting and were being destroyed by Kent's Doug Wright, a leg-break bowler with a fast bowler's run up. Only one batsman played him with any ease. Denis Compton. From where we sat, side on to the wicket and just below the famous "Tavern", it was possible to see the extraordinary speed and grace with which Compton really did skip down the wicket (cricketing fable true, if true, here only) before choosing either to drive or late cut. At cover, in front of us, was a deeply-tanned fielder my father told me was Les Ames, England's former wicket keeper, though then supplanted by Godfrey Evans. I noticed that from time to time both Ames and Evans would be driven to a kind of head-shaking, laughing wonderment by one of Compton's more outrageous strokes. In the end he scored 56 not out, and Kent won easily. But from then on Compton was my hero.

I tried explaining this to a boy rather older than me whom I met soon after the move to Ashford. On a large patch of open ground on the opposite side of the road to the Shuters' cottage, a newly-built house was nearing completion, and one day as I was walking past I saw a family, father, mother, two boys and a girl, the three children roughly my age, standing on the unkempt grass in front of the house, looking up to where two men in blue overalls were sliding and hammering some last corrugated roofing tiles into position.

I paused to watch and as I did so the taller of the two boys turned to look at me. He had dark, wavy hair and as he came towards me I saw that he was in fact older than me and that he looked friendly.

"Hello," he said, "do you live locally?"

I pointed towards my house. "Number 11," I said.

He nodded. "Good," he said. "I'm Michael. Michael Hill. When we've moved in you must come to see us." He seemed socially far more at ease than I was. "Where do you go to school?"

I explained that, having only just arrived in Ashford, I as yet had no school to go to, although I'd be joining the local junior school in a few days' time. "Where do you go?"

"Hampton Grammar," he said. Something in the way he pronounced the name, a kind of deprecating, off-hand pride, suggested that Hampton Grammar must be the kind of place that Frank Garner would have called "posh". In Frank's eyes to be "posh" wasn't a recommendation. "Perhaps you'll come to Hampton, too," Michael said.

"It's not *that* easy, darling," the woman who was presumably his mother said, coming to join us. Dark-haired, handsome, taller than Michael, round whose shoulders she now hooked an arm that was sleeved in what I instinctively knew to be an expensive material of green cloth, she looked me over with intense, glittering black eyes and a smile that was as much taunt as it was challenge. She looked witch-like and I took an immediate dislike to her. "Now, say goodbye to your new *friend*," she said, putting a mocking stress on the word, "because we must be going." And then,

35

to me, "Though Michael is rather too old to be friends with you, isn't he."

* * *

A few days later I saw the school I would be going to after Easter. If the house in Exeford Avenue had been a shock after the green freedoms of Burbage, Echelford Primary was a still greater shock after Grove Road Junior. In the first place, I wasn't to be in the main building at all, but in a wooden-hutted annexe some streets away. In the second, where I had been used to mixed-sex classes I now found myself among boys only. And where I had left a class of fifteen I now joined one of no fewer than fifty-six. Last, and for me the most humiliating of changes, whereas at Grove Road I had been in the senior class I was now, because of my age, still not yet ten, required to join the third years.

Of course, this worked to my eventual advantage. It gave me a further year to prepare again for the Eleven Plus, which I passed with enough marks to enable me to go to Hampton Grammar School. I was one of five boys from Echelford who did so. The other successes went to the local grammar school, Ashford County. That more than half the boys in my class passed the Eleven Plus was almost wholly due to our teacher, Miss Newton. Not only did she keep fifty-six boys in order, without as far as I can recall ever losing her temper, she was loved by us all. On an occasion when she was ill and in hospital we saved up to buy her a present. We also left for her flowers picked from our gardens, and when she reappeared in class we clapped and sang "Onward Christian Soldiers", which she had once told us was her favourite hymn.

Miss Newton was an archetypal-looking teacher. She cycled to school on an old "sit-up-and-beg" bicycle, attached to the handlebars of which was a wicker basket into which her books were crammed and from which one or more occasionally spilled. Under an unvariable shapeless grey, belted overcoat she wore a variety of blue-and-white spotted

36

dresses, her grey hair was tied back in a bun, and behind her tortoiseshell spectacles her grey eyes looked steadily out at us. Many years later, when I came across Joan Downar's lovely poem, "Lying Deep", I thought at once of Miss Newton. The speaker of the poem is a teacher who has to tease a confession of theft out of one of her pupils:

> Delicate, bijou,
> With aquamarine eyes and gold cropped
> Hair, he knew I knew his guilt — an expertise
> Much practised — but my questions stopped,
> Drowned in the blank blue of those eyes an analyst
> Would have found quite pure, while the sound
> Of No and No curved the classroom walls. I missed
> The old noise of truth, which now unnerved
> Even the believing, and wondered whether somewhere in the boy's
> Depth, a coelacanth would splash in surprised birth.

Miss Newton's much practised expertise lay not merely in seeing into our depths, but in persuading us into behaving well, and of knowing the sting of shame whenever we failed.

There was nothing "preachy" about her, nothing smug or self-righteous. Children are quick to see through the kind of adult who comes over as in any degree unctuous: who, like Chadband in Dickens' phrase, is intent on "shedding train oil". And of course we trusted her because, faced with the fifty-six of us, she nevertheless managed to pack into our heads sufficient knowledge of the basics of grammar and the rules of arithmetic, including mental arithmetic, to ensure that a large number of us succeeded in getting into grammar school.

Even she had her failures, though, above all with a boy called "Nobby" Clarke. On the morning when the results were to be announced the class was in a state of tense fear. So much depended, we knew, on success or failure. Shortly after eleven o'clock, the headmaster arrived in our classroom, list in hand. He read out the names of all those who had passed to go to Ashford County. My name wasn't among them but then I'd been entered for the special grade exam for Hampton. Five names now: Baker, Boulton, Lewis, Lucas

37

and one other I can't recall. I was in a daze, as much relieved as excited. Then I heard a muffled sound behind me. The sound became a howl, a choking cry of grief. A few rows back Nobby Clarke, head buried in his arms which were propped on the desk in front of him, was being watched by those sitting nearby, on their faces a mixture of embarrassed consternation and shared pity. As I stared, his head came up. Mouth open, he looked about him as though unaware of where he was, then plunged back into the protective shelter of his arms, still sobbing.

Suddenly Miss Newton appeared by Nobby's side. "Class dismissed," she said to us, "Go on, boys, take yourselves off."

Silently, we shuffled out. The headmaster was nowhere to be seen.

I don't want to say that that moment made me realise the iniquity of selective education. Of course it didn't, I was far too young, and anyway my excited relief at discovering I'd passed with good enough grades to go to Hampton occupied most of my mind that morning and for the following days, especially as my reward for success was to be bought an adult bicycle. (An Elswick, and the only bike I ever owned, it would accompany me to university and beyond, though in its early days the saddle had to be adjusted to the lowest possible position, and even then I regularly fell off.) But in later years, when I came to recognise the stinking injustice and social divisiveness of the Eleven Plus exam — and even before the revelation of Cyril Burt's skewing of intelligence tests in order to bear out his thesis that class and intelligence went together — I had only to summon up Nobby Clarke's appalling cry to know why no civilised society should want to expose its children to such a vicious ordeal. As Douglas Brown, a fellow-lecturer at Reading University said to me in 1963, at a time when, with a new Labour government in the offing, the proper promotion of comprehensive education seemed inevitable, "if all those who defend selective education had to live by its consequences, they'd end it tomorrow." But of course their children could be bought out of having to go to secondary modern schools.

Nobby Clarke and millions like him couldn't.

There must have been some attempt to promote the cause of comprehensive education in Middlesex while I was still at Echelford. I know this because some weeks after I had first met them, the Hills moved into their brand-new house and Mrs Hill, who at once introduced herself to my parents, soon made plain her fierce opposition to any proposal to threaten the selective status of Hampton, the single-sex grammar school which Michael attended, or Lady Eleanor Holles, the posh girls-only school next door, which her daughter would be starting at, so she made plain, the same time as I was to go on to secondary education. Within weeks she had involved my mother in a pressure group she set up to "Save our Grammar Schools".

Why on earth did my mother join her? Perhaps she was flattered. Perhaps she was simply caught up by the arrogant force of the other woman's personality. This seemed of a piece with the house the Hills lived in. The largest by far in our road, it had a long through lounge that ran from front to back and included a television, the first one I'd ever seen (a walnut cabinet with two doors behind which the screen lurked), and on the opposite side of the large square, parquet-floored hall, a dining room separated by serving hatch from a spacious kitchen, larger than our front room and with a tall fridge from which I once saw Mr Hill take a sizeable wedge of pale cheddar cheese and cut himself a slice which he ate in leisurely fashion while sitting at the scrubbed kitchen table. Our cheese, like most people's in those times of rationing, was orangey, smelt of soap, and sweated unpleasantly in its grocer's wrapping.

Beyond the house itself was a garden big enough to take a tennis court as well as a chicken shed with plenty of scratching ground for the dozen or so chickens the family kept, plus a wild area where you could play games of hide and seek. Mr Hill had been excused war service. A market gardener, his was a "reserved occupation", which resulted in him making good money out of helping to feed the nation. My mother resented this far more than my father did. He was soon on friendly terms with Mr Hill, also called Len, with whom he played tennis, as well as helping with heavy work in subduing areas of the Hills' garden that still needed attention.

My mother would mutter about the unfairness of the Hills having "more money than they know what to do with, while others have to rub along without two ha-pence to call their own". And yet she helped Ruth Hill make posters for the campaign to "Save our Grammar Schools", helped book halls for meetings, helped get speakers for them. One such meeting, she told me, had been addressed by a "Mr Jago. He teaches French at Hampton and spoke very well. He's passionate about the need to protect the grammar schools. If you go to Hampton you're bound to come across him and I'm sure you'll like him." In fact, I would loathe and despise the man.

I told my mother about Nobby Clarke's tearful collapse and added that it seemed unfair because he had done well in all class tests and in the mock exam we'd had to take earlier in the year. Perhaps stirred by guilt, my mother got Ruth Hill to accompany her in a visit to Nobby's mother, who lived on the other side of Ashford, I think on a council estate. They planned to suggest that Mrs Clarke might challenge the authorities over the marks her son had been given, and that, should this fail, not all was lost, because there might still be some alternative to the local secondary modern. This had a fearsome, and quite probably unjust, reputation as a place from which fifteen-year old boys emerged well educated for a future in crime. But they didn't get beyond the front door. Mrs Clarke shouted at them to go away. They'd done enough damage already, she told them, and they could take themselves off. My mother was shamefaced when she told me this.

* * *

A few days after the results came out I left school with Lionel Farmer. Lionel was a bright, witty boy, whose tawny skin and a wild canopy of orangey-yellow hair gave him a leonine appearance. I asked him whether he hadn't thought of putting in for Hampton. "What and have to get up early on a Saturday morning?" he asked incredulously. Because Hampton — this was part of its image as an out-of-the-ordinary school — gave up Wednesday afternoons to sport and compensated by having Saturday morning classes. "I don't mind," I said, though the prospect didn't greatly appeal. Even if the school had been local I might have resented losing Saturday mornings, but as Hampton was six miles from Ashford and required a bus journey followed by a long walk, I would have to leave home six days a week at an early hour. I didn't of course say this, but then I didn't need to. Lionel stared at me, then shook his head and grinned. "You must be fucking mad," he said. It was the first time I'd heard the word, but I knew at once that it was wildly improper and that anyone using it would cause my mother to say that he should wash his mouth out with soap.

Lionel, however, was unaware of any shock he might have caused. "Anyway, I won't be going nowhere," he said, "not in England. We're emigrating. Rhodesia."

That seemed just right. Leonine Lionel, bound for Africa. In the next few years scarcely a week went by, or so it seemed, without one or other of my schoolmates announcing that he was off with his parents to Africa, or Canada, or Australia, or even New Zealand. Off to start a new life, one that featured sun, swimming pools, even the promise of servants. I was headed for the town's library, Lionel for the smallholding on which his father raised pigs. We said goodbye outside the library's main door and I never saw him again.

The library, though, I would continue to visit. I loved it. In winter its deep yellow lights, like the lights of church at evensong, gave it the atmosphere of a special, even sacred, place, although unlike the church I associated it not with a lowering but heightening of spirits. And now, in early summer, light, cool and grey, drifted through its dusty windows, fingering row after row of books, as though pointing them out for my special consideration. But it was the smell of books that most thrilled me. It combined the oily odour of Rexene (in which most of the books were bound) with dust and the faintest suggestion, or so I persuaded myself, of printer's ink. "The must of books". That redolent phrase, coined by my friend, the poet Matt Simpson, exactly captures how I felt whenever I crouched to inspect the lower stacks of Ashford's library, where books for junior readers were shelved.

There was nothing elevating about the books I chose. I read whatever came to hand, read voraciously and indiscriminately. An "as told to" Life of Geoff Duke (famous as the regular winner of the Isle of Man motorbike TT races) would be followed by one of Henty's adventure stories or a novel by Felix Aylmer. There was the boy detective Bunkle as well as various heroes from history, both factual and fictional. Not Biggles, though. For some reason I never especially enjoyed Capt. W.E. Johns, and I'd been bored to tears by *Swallows and Amazons* (which the Hill children professed to like — I didn't believe them, any more than I could credit Michael's indifference to cricket). Arthur Ransome's book must have been one of the very few books of that period which, to use Johnson's words about *Paradise Lost*, I laid aside and forgot to take up again, though in my case there was no pretended admiration for what seemed to me a tedious novel.

But for other authors I had admiration in plenty, above all perhaps Arthur Conan Doyle, whose great detective I confidently believed to be the genuine article, as much flesh and blood as the well-known footballers and cricketers whose no doubt ghost-written biographies I swallowed before testing my father's own formidable knowledge, especially of footballers, with information taken from them. Who did Peter Docherty play for before he joined Doncaster Rovers? How many times did Strudwick keep wicket for England? Why was Spofforth called the Demon Bowler? Name the Arsenal forward line that last won the Cup. He could and did.

Chapter 3
Smells

I was sixteen when I first came across the writings of George Orwell. A television production of *Nineteen Eighty-Four* had caused a huge stir, both before and after its transmission. Some Conservative MPs had tried to prevent adaptation of Orwell's dystopic fable from being broadcast, I think on the grounds that it was too horrific, and perhaps because Orwell was a known leftie and must be trying to smuggle through a message about the superiority of one-party socialism, although how that could have been read into Orwell's novel goodness only knows. But it was a time when otherwise sensible people became convinced that their lives were being secretly undermined by enemy agents. These didn't step out of UFOs, though belief in aliens, and the endless reported sightings of spacecraft, made for regular headlines in the popular press, nor did agents give themselves away by the snow on their boots. Nevertheless one of the effects of the Cold War was to induce a commonly-shared fear that the enemy was everywhere. Some of this paranoia must have been a hangover from the Second World War, when posters warning that *Dangerous Talk Costs Lives* were prominently displayed in all public places. At war's outset some communities were issued with passwords. Locals were to challenge any stranger they met with a request to speak the password. If you didn't know it you were in all probability an enemy agent who had been parachuted onto England or, at a pinch, dropped offshore by U-boat and left to find your own way inland. The inhabitants of Princes Risborough, where my maternal grandfather and grandmother were evacuated with his school, were given the password Pied Piper to use. Most of them immediately forgot it.

Rather more than a decade later, when the Cold War was at its height, when in the USA reds were being found under many beds and in the UK some were convinced that Soviet Russia was poisoning the wind that blew direct off the Urals onto the Cambridgeshire fens, there was on both sides of the Atlantic a wide-spread belief in the "hidden messages" which could be communicated on air and through the cathode tube. An American called Vance Packard produced a book called *The Hidden Persuaders*, about "subliminal" messaging which corporations and governments could introduce into, say, harmless-looking TV adverts; and in this country questions were asked in Parliament about the possible subversive politics of The Goon Show. Wasn't it secretly an agency for Communist propaganda? The BBC was sufficiently rattled by this to forbid Peter Sellers from further imitations of Churchill, an edict he revealed on the following week's show, using as I recall, his impeccable Churchill voice in which to make the announcement. From that moment on The Goon Show became our favourite programme.

Radio was an immensely popular medium during the 1950s. Virtually every household owned a wireless and all but the stuffiest listened to the half-hour comedies which were regular features of the Light Programme. (The Home Service was altogether more staid.) Many of these comedies had begun during the war and some, such as Much Binding in the Marsh and The Navy Lark, were chiefly for the armed services. They featured officer types as silly twits and Other Ranks whose resigned cheerfulness in the face of pettifogging authority was leavened by verbal displays of mild insubordination. It was all very English and it was undoubtedly licensed by the fact that the Second World War was fought in a good cause. You couldn't laugh at the jolly old cards who led thousands to their death at Ypres and the Somme. You could, though, laugh at those who contributed, no matter how ineptly, to opposing fascism. (The popular belief that the Germans had no sense of humour must have been linked to this: we after all could laugh at our authority figures.) Hence not only much radio comedy of the time but a number of long-running West End farces, among them *Seagulls Over Sorrento, Worm's Eye View,* and *Reluctant*

Heroes. They took for granted that Hitler's professionals were seen off by servicemen (and very occasional women) who more or less blundered their way to victory. They also exuded a certain complacency about the social system — or was that resignation? If, as Orwell said, England was a family with the wrong members in control, then so what? Our rulers were loveable rather than dangerous. The effect, as C.S. Lewis later wrote of Addison's Sir Roger de Coverley, was to trick us into admiring an old ruin. As far as I know nobody has pointed out the extent of the debt owed by the TV series *Dad's Army* to farces which during the 1950s played to packed houses up and down the country.

The Goons featured blunderers but there was an edge to the programme's humour that felt different from even the best of its rivals. Take it From Here and Hancock's Half Hour were blessed with excellent scripts and comic acting but they endorsed the social status quo. Our parents listened with pleasure to those two shows, but they left The Goons to us. "Can't see what you find so funny about it," my mother once said to me, mystified by my near-hysterical response to Eccles, the Crums, Colonel Gritpipe-Thynne and the rest.

She was equally mystified by my advocacy of Orwell. He was such a depressing writer. I read as much of his work as I could get hold of. After *Nineteen Eighty-Four* came, in no particular order, *Animal Farm, Down and Out in Paris and London* and *The Road to Wigan Pier*. It was there I read Orwell's statement that "The working class smells." In years to come, this remark would cause his reputation some difficulties. I merely thought it odd of him to single out the working class, because in my experience *everybody* and *everything* smelled.

When we are young we see the world afresh. "Look, the sun is melting" my small granddaughter said in wonderment to her mother when they were out for a walk late one afternoon. This, infancy's "visionary gleam", all too soon fades into the light of common day. Perhaps the intensity of smells fade too. But smell is a sense you can trust, even if

45

sight lets you down. Years ago I used to watch women in Nottingham's old fish market haggling with stall holders over their weekly buy. Was that mackerel fresh? Of course. And to prove his point, the fishmonger would balance a fish on his outstretched index finger. If its tail drooped then it hadn't just come in from Grimsby. Tail straight out and the mackerel, gleaming gun-barrel silver with blue streaks, had been in the sea not a day since. But this test rarely convinced a potential buyer. The fish would be lifted off his finger and passed back and forward under her nose. Only if it survived that test would she buy.

At my first school, the Church School for Infants at Burbage, we were given place mats to cover our desks when we ate. The mats featured nursery rhymes printed in large black letters and were gaily illustrated. I especially liked one of Tom, the Piper's son, who had red hair, a green suit with yellow stockings and highly-polished black buckled shoes, and who came running towards me with a small very pink pig under his arm. The pig, its face tilted up to Tom's, seemed to be enjoying the experience. I was sure it was grinning, perhaps because it was pleased to get away from the grey-haired men in the village square, mouths open in shocked disbelief as Tom legged it from market. One of them reminded me of the local postmaster, a man I detested because he'd made a song-and-a-dance about my difficulty in fitting the gas-mask which he'd been given the responsibility of handing out to our end of the village, and had shouted at me when I clawed it off. "You're not to do that. Do you understand? Suppose the enemy were overhead at this instant and dropped a gas bomb?"

I stared at his watery-blue eyes, the bulbous nose whose ginger sproutings of nasal hair seemed to confirm his bad temper. Was the man mad? The Germans *weren't* overhead. There'd been no siren to warn of an air-raid.

"*I* would have to shoulder the blame, you do realise that."

I said I couldn't breathe, which was true. I certainly couldn't tell him that I feared and loathed a smell I associated with the dentist and — I think now — at a deeper level

46

with the hospital where I'd been operated on for a mastoid. The gas-mask, in its cardboard box with strap, accompanied me to school, banging uncomfortably into the small of my back, but although it sometimes served as a goal-post, I never wore it. It and all the other gas-masks were for a while hung in the school cloakroom then, gradually, the children began to leave them at home.

But every day the place mats came out, and although I didn't always get my favourite, I was always able to snuff up the rich, warm, waxy scent. It was almost as enticing as the scent of tomato plants my mother grew in our back-garden greenhouse, in which, despite sandy soil and several lost panes of glass, she nurtured a number of flowers as well as the tomatoes whose leaves, if you rubbed them and then sniffed your fingers, gave off an acrid, pungent, warm smell that hinted at a mysterious world you could gain access to through scent alone. Years later, when I read Theodore Roethke's "greenhouse" sequence, "The Lost Son", about childhood memories of helping his father, a gardener by profession, it puzzled me that although he evokes both the feel and look of plant-life, of blossom, leaf, tuber and soil, he has nothing to say about odours. Even in "Flower Dump", where Roethke sees "Cannas shiny as slugs,/Slug-soft stems,/Whose beds of bloom pitched on a pile", he doesn't tell you what they *smelled* like. Whereas when Edward Thomas writes of the plant "Old Man", also and paradoxically called "Lad's Love", and sees his daughter sniff "that bitter scent", then sniffs it himself and thinks "I cannot like the scent,/Yet I would rather give up others more sweet,/With no meaning, than this bitter one./I have mislaid the key", I think, yes, that's it: scents have meanings whose significance you can't always track to source but which do, invariably, lie somewhere in your consciousness. Such smells are my madeleine.

* * *

To get to Hampton I had to take the 216 bus. A single-decker, its route took me past a featureless stretch of suburbia and small factories to Sunbury Cross. (A clock-tower, in the early fifties a local feature, but long since hidden under a tangle of flyovers.) After that the bus turned right in order to reach lower Sunbury, a small village running along beside the Thames. We followed the river for maybe a mile before a sharp left took us up to Kempton Park racecourse on our left — in those days another racecourse, Hurst Park, long since gone, could be seen to the right beyond the sewage works — and next stop, an educational establishment beyond the end of the racecourse and also on the left. This three-storey building, of London brick, hand-some if severe, had earlier in the century housed the grammar school, although when in the 1930s Hampton developed a new site some distance away, the building became home to a Technical Grammar school. (Nobby Clarke was one of its pupils and caught the same bus as me though we were awkward with each other and didn't talk.) Finally, some half an hour after I had clambered aboard, the bus arrived at Hampton station where all of us who were Hampton-bound dropped off and the bus continued its journey to Kingston, while we walked the mile to school.

I grew used to most of the sights along that bus route and after a time took little interest in them, although one spot always thrilled me, at least in anticipation. It was a point where a backwater of the Thames ran alongside the road, separated from the main stream by a grassy bank and a line of poplars. Poplars interspersed with weeping willows also lined the river's further bank, so that as you made the morning journey you could look from the bus to your right and see what in full-leaved summer was like a tall, glinting, flickering screen, now green, now silver as early sun tangled among the leaves, and, at its base, beer-brown river water.

At some point, a single diving board had been positioned high above the water. Metal steps, rather like the steps you used to see affixed to railway signal-boxes, ran up to it. I imagine the board had been put up during the 1930s, that decade of outdoor sports activities when, especially in the southern counties, open-air lidos became all the rage. The contraption looked dilapidated and abandoned. But one morning, as the bus trundled along towards it, I saw that a man, dressed only in black swimming trunks, was poised on the board, ready to dive, and at the very moment we passed him he sprang upwards and outwards to touch his toes before straightening his body and arrowing down into the water. His movements seemed so exactly timed to coincide with the bus's passing that it was as if he had chosen to put on an exhibition for us. Perhaps he had. The sight of that white body disappearing into the water with scarcely a ripple to show the point of entry became a permanent part of my consciousness. Like Bede's sparrow, it was an image of breathtaking grace and of transitoriness. "Man is in love and loves what vanishes." I can't swear that when I read Yeats's words I thought of the man on the diving board, but I know it was the vision of his white body outlined in summer air that filled my head when in 1960 and courtesy of Argo records I first heard Auden recite "As I Walked Out One Evening": "Into many a green valley/Drifts the appalling snow;/Time breaks the threaded dances/And the diver's brilliant bow."

The diver's brilliant bow. I imagine that in the 1930s, and especially when he was with Isherwood in Berlin, Auden, self-rejoicing endomorph though he was, would nevertheless have taken the chance to watch plenty of athletic young men performing acrobatic feats on and from diving boards.

* * *

On the journey to school, the boys who joined the bus had it more or less to themselves. We were too late for workers on morning shift, too early for shoppers going into Kingston. But the return journey was a different matter. We left school at 4.20pm. This was to ensure that we didn't meet any of the hoi polloi who went to the secondary modern school on one side and who were let out at 4pm or, even more dauntingly, girls from the Lady Eleanor Holles school on the other, whose school day ended at 3.40pm. This is what Squeers might have called practical knowledge: along with its more formal education, Hampton taught segregation of class and sex.

But it didn't succeed. Our late dismissal meant that even on those evenings when I chose not to stay behind for extra activities I was never able to catch a bus home before 5pm. At that hour, anyway by the time we reached Sunbury, the 216 was filling up with working men and women who, their own days over at the various small factories that lined the route from Sunbury Cross all the way back to Ashford, were waiting in "long, uneven lines./As if they were stretched outside/the Oval or Villa Park." I've no idea what every last one of the factories manufactured, but what they had in common was a working population which, the day's toil over, scrubbed up in carbolic soap, its raw, gritty smell reminding me of chilblained hands I had in winter to hold under cold water. It was as off-putting as the stink of Brylcreem which the men, especially the younger among them, slicked onto their hair. Brylcreem came in tubs the size of jam jars and its soft, thick whiteness stank like rancid lard.

Then there were the women. Unlike the ones my mother knew or who attended church, these wore vivid lipstick and gave off perfumes that were heady with allure. As both men and women crowded onto the bus and stood wedged against each other, they talked and laughed, loudly and unabashed, the men in brown or grey gabardine belted raincoats, the women, a few with headscarves, more often than not clad in woollen coats under which you could catch a glimpse of white blouse and, at ear and throat, what must have been fake gold but which, like their perfumes, had a charge that was unmistakeably sexual.

Wet weather washed away this allure. The men's hair smelled even worse then, rancid lard turned to silage; and as the Brylcreem forming a water-resistant shield, rain drops stood proud on their gleaming heads, so that you could fancy they wore beaded hairnets, while their coats gave off a smell like wrung-out floor cloths. As for the women, they seemed shut up in themselves, steaming quietly, their scents now tainted by sour body odours. These smells were braided

50

through with the dusty acridity of cigarette smoke. They all smoked, men and women alike. Most of them had a cigarette on as they climbed aboard the bus, they smoked en route, they lit up as they forced their way past the standing line in order to get off. "T'ra". "See you tomorrow". "If you're lucky". *Park Drive, Woodbines, Weights,* more rarely *Gold Flake, Dunhill, Senior Service*, rarest of all *Churchman's Number One* and *Kensitas*. To produce a packet of these last was to be the object of comic derision: "Goin' up in the world, then? Won't want to know us next week." And if it was a woman, "What favours *you* doin' for the boss?" Cigarettes were commonly offered around, and I enjoyed watching the casual grace with which one man in particular would put three, sometimes four cigarettes in his mouth, light them from a single match, then pass them on to mates who'd accepted his offer of a *Park Drive*.

As far as I could tell, only one woman never smoked. Young, pretty in a pale, June Allyson manner (her hair, worn shoulder-length, curled over the tawny coat with faint red squares and large, brown buttons she had done up even on the warmest days), she got on two stops past Sunbury Cross with a man who was clearly her boyfriend, and whose arm she clutched whenever the bus swerved or came to a sudden halt. Sometimes another, older man was with them. I'd see him emerge from a builder's yard on the front wall of which was a half-painted out sign declaring KNACKER'S YARD. He wore a trilby hat and dark-blue overalls from the top pocket of which poked a wooden folding rule. Even in winter he went without an overcoat, though he habitually wore a black-and-white check sports jacket, and he smoked his own hand-rolled cigarettes. The other two came from a single-storey brick building next door, over the green-painted glazed front door of which a tacked-up board announced SURPLUS SUPPLIES. Surplus supplies of what? If they stood near to where I was sitting I listened to their talk in the hope I might find out, but the two murmured to each other, indifferent to and perhaps unaware of the surrounding hubbub, and while they

51

murmured they gazed into each other's eyes as though work was the last thing on their minds. They intrigued me because from the way the older man stared fixedly at the girl, and hardly ever let his eyes wander to the other man, I fancied that he was in love with her, although she had eyes only for her lover. Young, broad-faced, his thick black hair worn unusually long for a period when most hairdressers could manage no more than regulation "short back and sides", something about his dark, round eyes, the way they flickered over his fellow passengers, candid, openly curious, amused, made me think him gypsy-like. He reminded me of the Traveller (though everyone called Travellers gypsies then) who, with his shawled wife and small scamper of children, was a frequent visitor to a spinney near us at Burbage, their red and yellow painted caravan and piebald horse which they tethered to a stake in the grass an endless attraction to John Masters and me, for all that our mothers tried to warn us off. After they had gone, we would rake through the ashes of fires they had made, finding small bones which I claimed were from birds, most probably pigeons, and John said were those of rabbits or, perhaps, hedgehogs. Did the young man on the bus ever eat hedgehog pie? But no. I liked him, and even more I liked his girlfriend, the softness of her face, her perfume, which was less insistent than most, as her clothes had subtler touches, like the variety of scarves she wore to set off her tawny coat, pale yellow or maroon, and the plain round silver brooch pinned to her left lapel.

"The nylon gloves and jewellery-substitutes, The lemons, mauves, and olive-ochres". Larkin's observation of young women decked out in wedding finery belongs to a slightly later moment, but it pays homage to that craving for colour, for stylistic dash, that so often went unappeased in the immediate post-war years. When I look at photographs of that period, especially photographs of street-scenes, I'm appalled by how ugly, graceless, and shapeless people look. Those bulky coats, seemingly held together by their belts, the women's thick-heeled shoes, their puddingy hats

52

clamped over cardboard perms, the men's baggy trousers with turn-ups enveloping all but the toe-caps of what I think will have been brogues, the trilbies worn at a slight angle — the only rakish touch as they move about smoke-shrouded streets invariably glazed by rain water. Did it rain so much then, or did rainy weather attract photographers? Looking at such photographs it's easy to imagine you are face to face with scenes of some province of a defeated state under the grip of a pitiless oppressor.

Which was the case. Although the oppressor wasn't a foreign power, it was rationing. In the post-war years of my boyhood there was rationing of food, of furniture, of household goods, of petrol, of houses. Hitler's bombs had destroyed over a quarter of a million homes and not much replacement stock had yet been built. And although clothes were freed from rationing in 1948, the shops had at first little to show for this new freedom. As the 1950s got a toe-hold, so "ready-to-wear" became both affordable and universally fashionable; Peter Hennessy reports Israel Sieff, brother-in-law to Simon Marks of Marks and Spencer, noting that "women would want light, comfortable clothes, the cheapest of which would not be greatly different to look at from the most expensive. Shop girls were going to expect to look like duchesses". Twenty years later, of course, duchesses were trying to look like shop girls, but at the outset of the '50s people were by and large still pretty well restricted to the few garments their wardrobes held, augmented by the limited pickings that dress shops and "Gentlemen Outfitters" — a largely bespoke profession — could provide. Some years ago my wife found in a second-hand bookshop a book of advice to young men setting out on their own. This *vade-mecum,* which had been published not long after the war, included tips on how to make your clothes last longer. When you retired for the night you should take care to place inside your left shoe the sock you had that day worn on your right foot and vice versa. Big toes would not so readily make holes in socks worn turn and turn about. As for trousers, they should be folded and placed under the mattress. This would renew the edge of their creases. At a time when hardly any man owned more than two suits (while one was being worn the other was being "saved" or sponged and pressed at one of the innumerable laundries in every town) and women's wardrobes were similarly circumscribed, these tips made perfectly good sense, especially as men in white-collar jobs were expected to be "properly attired", that is, besuited.

But the paucity of choice inevitably meant that the clothes people wore made them look like each other. Out of this necessity came a claimed virtue. "Standing out in a crowd" so far from being a term of praise, meant "making an exhibition of yourself". Only Debs were dressed to look like dolls created from icing sugar and only Debs' Delights wore the kind of suits of which Edward VII was supposed to have disapproved. "Mornin' Harris", he greeted his friend (he of the tweed) when the man dared to turn up at Ascot wearing a three-piece suit of the material. "Goin' rattin'?"

And yet those photographs that agree on making the post-war years into a time of unremitting drabness don't by any means tell the whole truth. According to Hennessy, a friend of his recalled the period as one of utter greyness. No, it wasn't. True, the clothes people had to wear were for the most part drab and shapeless. But there was colour and style, too, and as a reverse foot will do more to enliven a pentameter than the wildest rhythmic flourish in a line of free verse, so a flash of colour against dull greys and browns makes an impact that a coat of many colours can't. That "instinct for shapely beauty" which Lawrence found in every creature was present in my fellow-passengers on the 216 bus, in their determination to use colour to offset the poor quality of those clothes they were forced to wear. Lawrence remembers watching while a young miner, striding home from his shift, stooped in his pit clothes to pick up a pheasant's feather which he stuck behind his ear. (In Greece until very recently, young men going courting would place a sprig of basil behind an ear and, when they greeted their loved one, would produce from their back pocket a wayside flower they'd picked on the walk to her house.) The young woman I silently admired had surer taste than the others who crowded onto the bus, so anyway I thought, but perhaps this was because I preferred the implications of her withheld sweetness to the more obvious gaiety of the rest. But I liked to watch them all, liked listening to their bantering talk, their raucous cheerfulness, the explosions of laughter that would sometimes follow remarks I didn't always catch or understand, laughter in which neither she or her partner joined, although from time to time they would look smilingly at each other when a more than usually loud burst of hilarity swept through the bus, as though what they shared was worth more than such companionable cheer.

Then, one evening, as she stood some rows ahead of me on the more than usually crowded bus, I saw there was something different about her. Her face, never as vividly made up or as red-cheeked as most of the young women, was markedly pale, there were violet hollows under her eyes, as though she had not slept, and when her boyfriend leaned to whisper in her ear she seemed not to attend to what he was saying, didn't turn to smile at him, although she nodded absently. The bus jerked to a sudden stop, and when she put out a hand to grab hold of his arm I noticed the gold that gleamed on her ring finger. That had not been there before. Then, as she turned sideways to allow someone leaving the bus to press past, I noticed something else: the faint but unmistakable bulge beneath her tightly-buttoned up coat. I knew what that meant and, without understanding why, I was aware of a desolating sadness.

For perhaps a further two months she and her boyfriend — or, as he must now be, husband — boarded the bus each weekday evening, though of the older man there was no longer any sign. Then came an evening when the young man got on alone. It was a warm summer's day, and his raincoat was draped over the sleeve of a brown-and-white checked jacket under which was a white shirt set off by an electric-blue tie made of some satiny material and kept in place by a gold tie-pin. It was knotted so as to show off the head of a white horse. He must have worked hard to get the horse's head in place. He shuffled up the aisle to near where I was and his face looked set, even hard, and I saw that without the customary smile his lips were unpleasantly thin. "She alright", someone — a man — asked, and he nodded without speaking. A young woman standing beside him offered him a cigarette, and as he cupped his hands around the flame she held out to him, the look he gave her was at once guarded and open, as though he was enquiring something of her, and I no longer liked him.

And then, a few weeks later he, too, was no longer in the queue of those waiting to board the bus at SURPLUS SUPPLIES, and from snatches of overheard conversation I gathered that he had switched his place of employment. Nothing unusual about that. By the early 50s, work was in plentiful supply, and especially in what became called blue-collar work it was an employees' market. On the evening journeys I'd frequently hear talk of how so-and-so, fed up with the foreman's attitude, had asked for his cards and simply walked out of the current job to find a better-paid one elsewhere. Perhaps Flash Harry, which was how I now dubbed him, and his girlfriend — I couldn't bear to think of her as his wife — had left the district altogether? At all events, I never saw them again, although some years later, when the older man unexpectedly re-entered my life, I heard more about them, and what he had to say justified the earlier sadness I had felt on her behalf.

* * *

I say that work was easy to find in the years when we first arrived in Ashford and I began life at Hampton Grammar, and so in the main it was. But at least one section of the male population found suitable employment less easy to come by. Lower-middle class men without qualifications but wanting "respectable" occupations were at a disadvantage. The work was there, but for the most part it was poorly paid, required long hours and was a monotonous grind. For his work my father had to leave home shortly after 7 o'clock each morning, and he was rarely back before 6 in the evening. Sometimes, but not often, he would go by car. Petrol rationing eased but the price of petrol was high. More often, therefore, he travelled by bus, as most people did. (The alternative for those who lived too far from their place of work to be able to walk was of course the bicycle.) He was always well-dressed. It was expected of him, but anyway he took pride in his appearance, and at the end of each working week he would get me to deliver to the local laundry the suit he had been wearing for the previous five days, and which I would then collect at 5 o'clock on Saturday, "sponged and pressed".

Like most men of his class, he had two such suits. One was of brown material, the other blue, and both came in an odd "bird's eye" pattern which had numerous tiny flecks of white among the wool. At weekends he wore a sportscoat — I remember a rather handsome brown-and-white check — and grey flannels. And he never went out without a tie. The suits had been made by a bespoke tailor, other clothes were off-the-peg, and although he smoked he seldom drank. The money he spent on clothes was in a way his one indulgence, although it certainly wouldn't have been seen as such. "Smartly-dressed man needed for..." advertisements for employees invariably began. My father's suits were his work uniform.

My mother's way of keeping up appearances involved rather more guile. Like her mother she was a prodigious knitter, although she never knitted the egg-cosies that were my grandmother's *chef-d'oeuvres* and which for many years I and other members of our family would find stuffed into the back of rarely-visited drawers, many of them in the Christmas wrapping paper in which she had enclosed them and then forgotten to send to various relatives and friends of hers, of whom there were a large number. But socks, sleeveless sweaters, balaclavas for winter (a protection against chilblains on the ear), pullovers, cardigans, scarves — they seemed to cascade off my mother's knitting needles. When these and other clothes needed to be darned, out would come a wicker box in which she kept a supply of coloured wools and thick needles, plus her darning mushroom for sock heels that had worn through ("spuds", such holes were called), and for anything out-at-elbow. There was another, smaller, box for more delicate needle-work requiring cotton thread. This was kept for stockings and other women's wear, and shirts. ("Turning" a collar and even cuffs of a shirt was common practice.)

As a seamstress, however, my mother was less than adept. To make a garment for Jill or herself — a skirt, or blouse, or, more rarely, dress — she had first to cut out in tissue paper the design taken from some pattern book or women's magazine, then pin the paper to the material out of which the garment was to be created, cut round it, assemble the pieces and sew them together. For this, she had a Singer sewing machine, one of those handsome but heavy table-models which I had to lift onto the table for her, after she had first placed a protective cloth over the table's polished surface. (A scratch counted as a sin against the Gods of Domestic Care.) Then, when the skirt, say, for Jill had been sewn up, Jill herself would be required to stand on the table wearing the almost finished article while my mother walked round checking that the hem, which had still to be sewn, was evenly pinned. It was at this point that difficulties most often arose.

"Stand straight."

"I *am* standing straight."

"Then why is the hem drooping *there*." An impatient tug, and the skirt would slide unevenly off Jill's hips. "*Now* look what's happened. I knew I should never have bought this material."

Or followed that pattern. Or used that stitch.

Sometimes the instruments were to blame. "These scissors cut all they can see."

Or it was the place's fault. "This machine has never been right since we came to Ashford."

Or it might be the electric light: "I'm blessed if I can see my hand in front of my face."

If she was making something for herself, my mother would call in Mrs Grant, who would be required to pin the hem while my mother stood on the table, "like patience on her monument" she'd say, though nobody could be less patient than her on these and many other occasions when she found it all but impossible to keep still. Her sudden, darting movements, characteristic of many short people, as though by such means they can gain an advantage over those who are taller and, perhaps because they have a complacent sense of the benefits their height brings them, move to a steadier, more regular rhythm, were bird-like, her eye robin-bright like her father's, whose face I know only from photographs. Mrs Grant would try to keep my mother calm during these fittings.

"Now, Joan, just hold still while I pin the back up."

"Oh, lummee" — one of my mother's favourite expressions, especially at times of stress — "this business is enough to try the patience of a saint." And despite her friend's soothing murmurs, she'd jitter and fret, with the result that very often the work had to be re-done.

Yet in our pokey kitchen she was all absorbed concentration. An excellent cook, she made savoury stews and casseroles out of the scraggiest ends of lamb or beef, with sliced carrots, parsnip and celery eked out by dumplings, flavoured with sage, their firm, even crisp outsides yielding to succulently moist interiors; and her pastry, whether intended as casings for meat dishes or for tarts, was a marvel of textures, of flaky, crumbly sweetness. There were fish-pies, in which plain white fish was turned into something altogether finer by the addition of chopped hard-boiled egg, sliced onion, white sauce, and, over the topping of mashed potatoes, a thin crust of grated cheese which when baked lost its repulsive greasiness. Then there were the puddings: steamed (figgy duff, treacle, chocolate), oven-baked (potato, made from remains of mash with a sprinkling of currents and caster sugar, apples cored and stuffed with brown sugar and currants, treacle or jam tart). And cakes: simnel, fruit, sponges, maids-of-honour, rock-cakes, current buns, scones to be sweetened by home-made jams (raspberry, strawberry, marrow with ginger), and trifles and jellies and junkets, decorated with strips of angelica or sweet, powdery "hundreds and thousands" which, when shaken over the prepared dish turned to a Technicolor mist, a sort of angel-exhaust like the exhalations that Disney's more sanctified characters trailed behind them.

For the most part cooking smells were fine. We were even free of the stink of boiled cabbage that afflicted so many kitchens. But two other smells were foul. My mother suffered from heavy head colds and catarrh, for which a prescribed remedy was something called Friar's Balsam. I think this came as a powder which my mother emptied into a large bowl before pouring over it a kettle-full of boiling water. Then, bending above the bowl, and draping a towel over her head so as to cover both her hair and the sides of the bowl, she inhaled the mixture for as long as the vapours continued to rise from the cooling water. From time to time she would come up red-faced, blinking and watery-eyed, then once more plunge her tented head back into the steam, like a traveller in some shady haunt, among Arabian sands. The smell of the Balsam was of rotting prunes with something more fecal. Whether it did my mother any good, I've no idea; but after she had poured the water away, my father, having closed the door that led from kitchen to hall, would open both the back door and kitchen window in an effort to dispel the stink which hung around the house for days.

But the stink of Friar's Balsam was as nothing compared to the one given off by the shampoo which my mother bought for herself and, increasingly, Jill. One of the more popular advertising gimmicks of the time, to be seen on billboards and in newspapers and magazines, showed the heads of twin sisters smiling broadly beneath their helmets of permanently-waved hair. Above — or below, I don't remember — ran the caption "Which Twin Has the Toni?" Women's hairdressing was a luxury not all in those years could regularly afford, yet women were encouraged to wave their hair, to crimp it so rigidly that it looked like corrugated metal. This was how models looked, or those with the Desperate Dan chins who featured on the front of fashionable magazines, especially any Deb whose engagement to the Hon. Chinless Diphthong was being announced. Home shampoos promised to put the wave into your hair as successfully as the priciest salon, and for a fraction of the cost. Millions of women bought these shampoos, together with the attendant paraphernalia of curlers and crimpers and tongs.

Friday night was Toni night. Not every Friday, but with the weekend coming up women were expected to ready themselves for whatever entertainment might be on offer, as well as Sunday attendance at church, which in our family, as in most others on Exeford Avenue, was a *sine qua non*. Hence, the ordeal of home shampoo. I doubt that my mother enjoyed administering these, and as I always tried to keep to my own small back bedroom while the process was underway I've little idea what was involved, beyond the fact that once the shampoo had been applied she and Jill would adjourn to the front room where they'd sit rigidly on dining chairs, heads swathed in chiffon scarves under which were shapes that made the two of them look as though they had netted a collection of sprockets and penile sheaths.

"Beauty in waiting" my mother would say, laughing dismissively, all a-twitch about the mouth and fingers. But the smell of the shampoo itself, as of rotting eggs opened up by the dozen, penetrated to all corners of our house, its foul odour still discernible when we sat down to Saturday breakfast. Besides, as the shampoo rarely managed to bring my mother's stiff mass of hair into line, or lines, she was seldom in a good temper. "Drat the thing," she'd say, "I'd do better without."

And she did. The Toni shampoo was given up after a few months. But its stink hung on in my imagination. People who don't remember the smells of the 1950s suffer the same degree of sensory deprivation as those who persist in seeing it as the grey decade.

61

Chapter 4
The Way We Lived Then

1951 was the year of the Festival of Britain. In our household this proved to be a non-event. My father simply wasn't
interested in taking us to any of the sites, or "traipsing
round the Embankment in order to get your pocket picked",
as he put it. The nearest we got to the excitement was one
evening when the four of us went up to Waterloo and shuffled along among packed crowds, looking briefly at the
lights. Then we went home again. I can recall nothing of the
occasion except for my sighting of a couple of spivs in regulation gear: brown trilby, heavily padded camel-hair belted
coats that came down to mid-calf, circumflex moustaches,
and that strange, rapid rolling shuffle which required an
exaggerated forward thrust of shoulder in time to leg movement. They were selling trinkets from card-tables set up on
the pavement at the foot of Waterloo Bridge. I'd previously
known about spivs only through Arthur English, a then
popular radio comedian who appeared on alternate early
Sunday evenings in the Light Programme's "Variety
Bandbox". He was turn-and-turn-about with Frankie
Howerd, my favourite, and although I found English funnier
than Derek Roy, a kind of poor man's Bob Hope with routine
stand-up jokes whom I think he replaced, his cockney wide-
boy patter was both more predictable and less bizarre than
Howerd's.

A small amount of Arthur English went a long way. "A
lady come up to me and she sez 'how much are them apples?'
I sez 'ten for a bob, love'. She sez, 'I'll take a bob's worth
then.' So I gives her a bob's worth and she sez, 'ere, there's
only eight apples in this bag.' And I sez, 'I know love, only
two was rotten, so I left 'em out. I didn't want to rob yer'."
English's stage gear dress featured a wide-lapelled, double-
breasted suit, complete with trilby and tie, gaudily

patterned and with huge knot. This, together with the camel-coat was standard spiv dress, and is worn to great effect by the young George Cole in comic film roles of that period. Cole also had off to perfection the walk that went with the dress. I've no idea though why that style was *de rigueur* for a spiv any more than I know where the word itself comes from. The *O.E.D.* doesn't help, admitting that the word's origin is "uncertain", although defining *spiv* as "A man who makes a living by dishonest or unscrupulous dealings *esp* one who dresses in a flashy manner." Spivs were a left-over from the war, men who, like Parolles or Autolycus, were prepared to brazen out an image as shameless tricksters. Simply the thing I am shall make me live. They were black marketeers, whose range of dodgy goods included just about everything that was officially rationed. You weren't supposed to buy from them but at one time or another everyone did. Even my father, who went in fear of law-breaking — both my parents did — once came home with a pair of brogues that he'd bought for me off "the back of a lorry" in Slough. But he then became so appalled by what he had done that he never let me wear the shoes out of the house. It wasn't that he feared I might be nicked for wearing stolen goods, if that's what they were, but some deeper conviction that the shoes carried with them a subliminal message of disreputability, one that could communicate itself by radio-wave or aura to the most inattentive passer-by, troubled him. Many years later I discovered that the phrase "back of a lorry" came from a test case in Berlin in 1929, when two boys were accused of stealing coal from a lorry which had partially shed its load. The court judgement was that once the goods had fallen into the street they became public property and that the two boys were therefore free to keep the coal. But I doubt that legal decision, even if he'd known about it, would have done much to assuage my father's sense of guilt.

By the time the Festival of Britain opened, the Labour government which had masterminded it was out of office. Herbert Morrison in particular had wanted the Festival he said, because after the war and with the austerity years still plaguing the land, people deserved to be cheered up. Whether he was aware that his words echoed those of the circus-owner Sleary in *Hard Times*, who tells Gradgrind that "people muth't be amuth'd", I don't know, but Morrison certainly didn't mean them lightly. Nor did he intend any condescension. The Dome of Discovery, the wondrous Skylon, the South Bank complex, all testify to an entirely serious as well as joyous vision, as does the range of sponsored cultural activities in, for example, art, opera, drama. You have only to think of the ghastly, vacuous pointlessness of the Millennium Dome to see how splendid the Festival of Britain must have been, though, as I say, at the time I knew none of this, and by the time I did become aware of what had been achieved, much that was finest had been wiped away by the incoming Conservative government.

Would such acts of vicious philistinism have troubled my parents? I'd like to think so, but I doubt they did. Like most lower-middle class people, they voted Conservative. To vote Conservative, and even more to be known to vote Conservative, was proof of respectability. In the run-up to the election, most of the houses in our road carried posters in their front windows urging everyone to vote for the Tory candidate, who rejoiced under the name of Beresford Craddock.

Only the Furnells had a red VOTE LABOUR poster, while the Collins had no poster at all, which according to my mother meant that they voted Labour but were ashamed to admit as much.

As to the Festival of Britain, it wasn't for the likes of us. I don't mean to suggest that my parents lacked an instinct for pleasure or fun. My mother in particular loved to laugh, had a keen sense of the ridiculous, and a sharp eye and even sharper ear for any occasion when it showed itself. She once told us of listening to a woman in the queue outside the butcher's explaining to another why a mutual acquaintance would no longer speak to her. "Just because I said she shouldn't wear yellow, it made her look bilious. She called me every name under the sun, including quite a few I'd never heard of." Then, indignantly, "I was off my food for days." And she often repeated a story she'd heard at second-hand, of a local junior schoolteacher rewarding a pupil who'd correctly answered a brain-teaser by telling her that "You may go to the top of the class and give out the pencils." When, a year or so later, I was able to report that an especially stupid teacher of French at Hampton had announced to us that "I am in charge of blotting paper at this school", she was overjoyed. It became one of her favourite sayings. Over the years she gathered a large number of these sayings, which were augmented by recalled incidents of comic happenings in the family, including holiday incidents, as when a cousin leapt over the promenade wall at Paignton and landed in the lap of a woman dozing some dozen feet below in her deck-chair, thus flattening both chair and woman, or when her own mother, who had been sitting on the end of a bench with some friends while they watched cricket, was deposited in the picnic hamper when the others suddenly stood up. I realise now what I didn't then, that these tales, stored in her memory, were a way of cementing family history, and that my mother, who had a deep love of her family, was its unofficial historian.

My father, though rarely a source of comic tales himself, enjoyed these stories and would join in the laughter. But they were for indoors. Once beyond the front door we were expected to present straight faces to the world. We had also to be "properly" dressed. For me, school uniform or, at best, blazer and grey flannels with white shirt and school tie, for Jill, blouse, skirt and, in winter, buttoned-up coat. Suit or, more rarely, sports coat for my father, and, for my mother, endless self-doubt about whether she was wearing the clothes that best fitted her. Her fretting about this often meant that whereas about the house she looked relaxed, outside she was bundled into dresses or skirts that made her look even shorter than she was.

And then there were the hats. Nowadays when women wear hats it's with dash, and the hats themselves are fun.

Not then. Working women wore either headscarves or the inverted pudding bowl I associate with Bessie Braddock or the grandmother figure in Giles's famous cartoons. All other women went to the milliners for headwear that was intended to be at once fashionable and yet usable on a daily basis, and which as a result proved an uneasy compromise, one made worse by the fact that whatever royalty wore set the pace, and the taste for hats among royal women was appalling. It may have aimed for "chic" but it regularly hit "frump". My mother's hats, the choice of which caused her prolonged anguish, weren't frumpish but they were more often than not bizarre. I have seen photographs of her, taken during the 1930s, wearing berets set at a rakish angle, and in these she looks good. But in the early 1950s something more formal, "respectable", was required — or anyway supplied — and because she was short these seldom suited her.

The time for buying new hats was in the run up to Easter. Easter Sunday was when church-going families such as ours marched to Matins in new suits and dresses, and, of course, hats. On Easter Saturday my mother, with Mrs Grant to advise her, would set off early for London's West End, grimly determined to buy herself an Easter bonnet or its equivalent. There was no sense of fun about these jaunts. At breakfast the atmosphere would be tense, my mother fretting to be off, glum in the certainty that by the time she could bring herself to show us the hat she'd bought after "hours of traipsing about, trying on this and that", it would prove to be a disastrous mistake. Home again, tired, down-in-the-mouth, she would reluctantly unwrap the hat from its clouds of tissue paper and we'd see that what she had bought was indeed a disaster, and Jill and I would look at each other, trying not to laugh, and my father would say nothing, which made matters worse.

I remember one hat above all others. It was shaped like a small, rimless, cinnamon-coloured oval bowl, and had a single, brown-and-white feather pinned lengthily to its side, making it look rather like a poorly-plucked game bird. Its first and last outing came next day. Easter morning. An old lady in the pew behind ours, Miss Parnes, in leaning forward to congratulate my mother on her choice of headgear, somehow snared the feather in a brooch pinned to her own coat, with the result that as she sat back the hat was jerked off my mother's head and landed in the old lady's lap. As soon as we returned from church the hat was thrown on top of my mother's wardrobe and never seen again. It amazes me that in the novels of one of my favourite contemporary writers, Stanley Middleton, the women he writes about are customarily given to selecting and wearing hats with a matter-of-course panache. Not in our household, they didn't. I've no doubt that when women of my mother's class could at last appear in public hatless they felt a delighted release. But in 1951 that was hardly possible.

Two pieces of evidence. The Guide to *The South Bank Festival of Britain* has both fore and aft a large number of advertisements for, among other things, cigarettes, drink (sherry and whisky), cars and toothpaste. These mostly include *soignée* women with cigarette-holders, gleaming smiles, and, without exception, hats. And the special "Exhibition Number" of *The London Illustrated News* includes a photograph of holiday crowds at Battersea on Whit Bank Monday. The caption runs, "The Scene at four o'clock in the afternoon, showing some of the thousands of people who, undeterred by the bitter weather, waited outside the turnstiles, hoping to join in the fun of the fair." A few of these women are bare-headed but many more wear hats or headscarves.

Naturally, we didn't experience the fun of that fair. A little later in the year, though, we were at a garden party given by the successful Conservative candidate for our Spelthorne constituency. I don't recall which hat my mother wore on that occasion, but I do remember having my hand perfunctorily shaken by our MP when I was introduced to him as a successful Tory candidate in my school's mock election.

There was no great cause for pride in this success. Each year-group had to select candidates to represent the major parties who would then "in public" — that is, in front of as many of their mates as could be bothered to waste half an hour of lunch break — debate the issues on which the General Election was being fought. My chief third-year opponent was a boy called Pitman who had dirty finger nails and a spectacularly ripped and stained school blazer. He had wanted to stand as Communist candidate but as this was forbidden he stood instead for the Labour cause. In our one debate he startled me by knowing much more than I did about world affairs. He argued with impassioned eloquence that the Korean war revealed the imperialist ambitions of the west, its determination to stamp out the proper nation- alist aspirations of North Koreans who were being helped to achieve victory by the heroic Red Chinese army. My answer, culled from headlines in the *Daily Mail*, that the West was trying to prevent the nightmare possibility of world-wide communist domination, that we were fighting to preserve our own freedoms, was scornfully dismissed. Why were Americans and their British "lackeys" fighting a war on the far side of the world? What had that to do with "our" free- doms. Later, I would come greatly to respect Pitman. He not only had for elder brother a professional journalist whom he denounced when that brother became a feature columnist on the *Daily Express*, he lent me his heavily-marked copy of *The Great Gatsby*. But in 1951 it was enough to call him a "commie in disguise" to be assured of a thumping victory. I deserved the reward of having my hand briefly clasped by an MP whose party, in a fit of philistine sacrilege, was soon to tear down as much of the Festival as it could, including the magically beautiful Skylon, that slender steel structure which rose some hundred or so feet into the air from its place on the South Bank. And then to boast that Skylon had been turned into ashtrays!

* * *

Ashtrays were a feature of virtually all households at the time. For a period that may have lasted for as long as two years, my parents went turn-and-turn-about with the Coxes on Saturday nights, entertaining or being entertained over Canasta, a card game involving the use of two packs and played between pairs. Although I have never taken an interest in such games, I enjoyed helping my mother prepare for the evenings when she and my father played host. Food comprised bridge rolls with fish-paste and egg-and-cress fillings, together with home-baked sponge and, usually, flapjack. (An oatmeal and treacle mix baked until it's biscuit hard) Coffee — instant, of course — was drunk from acorn size cups, intriguingly designed with sharp corners and decorated with red and black flashes. These were wedding presents and may have been designed by Clarice Cliff or one of her epigoni.

An hour or so before the Coxes were due to arrive, my father would vacuum the front room where they were to play while my mother arranged the food, together with plates and cups and saucers, on the trolley that had accompanied her from house to house through her married life. Years ago now, the socialist historian Raphael Samuel wrote an essay for *New Society* in which he anatomised social life during the 1930s. Tea trolleys, he pointed out, provided a brilliantly effective solution to the problem of how to entertain at home when there wasn't much to eat but you wanted to give your guests the impression of largesse. Dinner parties were out. Anyway, "dinner time", when the main meal was eaten, meant the middle of the day; so an evening of cards was broken for "supper", supplied on a trolley which was wheeled in and then out and which by means of careful arrangement — cups, plates, milk, coffee-jug and sugar bowl on top, plates of goodies on the lower shelf — could be made to look as though it was laden with delicacies. When I was young, those trolleys were still an essential part of home entertainment.

Alcoholic drink wasn't. There may have been a glass of sherry at half time but that apart the Canasta evenings were alcohol free. Cigarettes were a different matter. When the four of them sat down to play, a packet of Gold Flake would be at Mr Cox's elbow, and, at my father's, either Senior Service or Player's. By the time they broke for refreshments both ashtrays would be full and I was expected to take them out, empty them and replace the wiped ashtrays on the table, ready for when the game re-started. Apart from that I was free to spend the evening as I chose. Since I had few friends in the area — one of the consequences of going to a school some six miles off was that you became estranged from those your own age who lived locally — I had to rely on Michael and Anne Hill. I got on well enough with both of them, but our increasingly divergent interests meant that we grew bored with each others' company. Saturday night was in consequence the loneliest night of the week.

Not for friends at school. One in particular would each Monday tell me about how on the previous Saturday evening he had dressed himself in check shirt with silver-grey gabardine trousers, white socks and casuals (step-in shoes also known as "loafers" or "moccasins" and much favoured by those who had seen Gene Kelly wear them in the film *An American in Paris*), and thus accoutred had strolled about the back lanes of Hampton or Twickenham with his latest girlfriend, sharing kisses and cigarettes. I had no girlfriend, I still hadn't tried cigarettes, I didn't even have a pair of gabardine trousers — that cheap, then fashionable material, whether brown, lovat green, steel blue or, sharpest of all, silvery-grey. And my only shoes were black lace-ups plus the brogues I wasn't allowed to wear beyond the front door. As for entertainment, I had access to an old wind-up gramophone on which I played a selection of 78rpm shellac records contained in a record-album which my parents had bought not long after their marriage and which I still possess, although most of the records I then played, like the gramophone itself, have long been broken: the pre-pubescent "Master" Ernest Lush singing "Oh, For the Wings of a Dove", Harry Lauder barely audible through the static of a cracked and wobbly 12-inch rendition of "The Road to the Isles", an even scratchier record of "The Skater's Waltz". This had been bought either by or for my grandmother, who in her childhood and youth was a keen skater on the frozen ponds and streams around Kenilworth, and who would hum along to the tune and sing, in her wispily fragile voice, the words of the pretty waltz on the other side, "After the Ball": "Many the promise that's spoken/If you could hear them all,/Many the heart that is broken/After the Ball."

Having exhausted the records, which I played in my own bedroom, I either read some geological text-book — geology was then my passion — or briefly rejoined the card party downstairs as it proceeded on its placid way to ten o'clock. The game didn't interest me, but the gossip did, especially when delivered by Mrs Cox in a voice deeper than any other woman's I have ever heard and made the more fascinating by her Sussex "burr", so that the sounds she produced seemed those of some softly rumbling engine. I never knew either her or her husband's Christian names. Perhaps in deference to their greater age, my parents always called them Mr Cox and Mrs Cox, while they called my parents Len and Joan. But their friendship was genuine, although on one occasion Mrs Cox became slightly flushed while pleading the cause of the former church organist who had been sent to prison for stealing some trifling sum of money from the offertory plate and who on release begged for his job back. "I can't see what harm it would do," she said, "he's done penance and he's a good organist." This was a touchy subject, as both Mr Cox and my father served on the church committee which had to decide the organist's fate, and it was known that a majority of the congregation was opposed to re-hiring him. The two of them muttered something about the bad feeling that might follow were the organist to be re-instated, though I don't think they believed what they were saying. Mrs Cox certainly didn't. "Nonsense," she said, and it was the only time the engine threatened to break free of its casing. "Go to church and not know the meaning of charity. They need a lesson in Christian love, that lot."

***

71

The Canasta evenings went on for at least a year, maybe longer. But increasingly my parents were caught up in other forms of entertainment, either on Friday or Saturday evenings — rarely on both. Although picture-going was no longer the mass attraction it had been, and anyway my father wasn't greatly interested and always claimed he went to sleep during most of the inferior B features (usually shot in black-and-white with dubious scenery and actors of no great worth) and, often, during the A feature as well — a claim my mother confirmed — they managed to see most of the better-known films that came to our local cinema, the Astoria. And they went to dances.

For a brief period, this meant Barn Dances or "Hoe-Downs". These were held in the parish hall on a regular basis. I never attended any but I was told that they were for couples only, that the music was provided by an accordionist, sometimes accompanied by a violinist, and that there was a Caller, whose function it was to stand at the end of the hall and shout instructions as to the steps or manoeuvres required of the dancers; "Take Hands", "Dozy Doe", "Link Arms", "Promenade": that kind of thing. The barn dances were, I was told, "fun", but in my parents' social calendar they were soon replaced by ballroom dancing.

As far as dress went, these were altogether more elegant affairs. For Barn Dances you dressed down. Casual trousers and open-neck shirts for the men, for the women, blouses and skirts. But for ballroom dances the women wore long dresses, jewellery and, if they had one, a stole, while the men went in black-and-white. The refreshment at Barn Dances was limited to sandwiches and soft drinks; but at ballroom dances there might be a sit-down supper and, even, a glass of wine. I doubt that this was the case in 1951, but as the fifties wore on and my father's career took several turns for the better, these dances became part of his and therefore my mother's life. Company dances, golf-club dances, Masonic dances.... They happened with greater frequency, were increasingly lavish. Dances at famous London hotels, at well-known restaurants, at the more exclusive golf-clubs, and dancing to orchestras with national reputations, who had been hired for the occasion: Joe Loss, Ambrose, Cyril Stapleton.

At first though, the dances they went to were held at local hotels and the more up-market public houses, which had a hall attached to the rear of the premises. My father loved to dance. A tall man, he was light on his feet and, as befitted a good sportsman, he had a fine sense of balance. And both of them enjoyed dance music. They had grown up at a time when stage and film musicals were newly glamorous, as a courting couple spent many an evening in what Auden called "the fug of talkie houses" or, more rarely, at a West End show (my mother seemed to know the scores of *Showboat, White Horse Inn* and other stage musicals by heart), and now, given the chance to spend an evening dancing, were, I think, not merely re-capturing their youth but making up for the lost, wartime years.

So were their contemporaries. Any excuse for a dance was good enough. There were dances for charitable causes, for church funds, for local schools, for the hell of it. As the fifties went on these were increasingly called dinner-dances, although at the beginning of the decade this would have been next-to-impossible. Peter Hennessy points out that in 1951, at the height of the Korean war, meat rationing, which ended three years later, was at its most severe, and such commodities as butter, cheese, cooking fats and sugar were all still rationed. But at least my parents, along with many thousands of others, were able at a time of such enforced privation to put on what my father called their "glad rags" and go "to a hop". They'd return from these occasions flushed and happy and the good mood would often last through the remainder of the weekend.

In the years that followed I came to know some of the musicians who played at the local "hops". Among them were ex-service bandsmen who in the post-war years supplemented their weekly wages by turning to good advantage their musical skills. The groups they formed were mostly quartets: piano, bass, drums, and a single front-line instrument — trumpet or tenor sax. Any more and the shared pickings would be too slim. Dressed in black-and-white or, more rarely, a jacket with the band's initials on its breast pocket, the groups played what they privately called "ricky-ticky" music for the dances. Many were jazz aficionados. One tenor sax player I got to know well, a passionate admirer of Lester Young, would inject a phrase from "Lester Leaps In" or "Seven Eleven" into a standard foxtrot, though I doubt if any of the dancers noticed. This obliviousness to the music's finer points would much later produce a routine sneer from Benny Green. During the 1980s and 90s, Green, a part-time jazz musician turned radio presenter and over-rated journalist — his columns on cricket were as opinionated as they were block-headed — ran a Sunday afternoon record show on Radio 2 in which he played recordings from, or anyway of, the great period of popular music. These featured composers — Gershwin, Porter, Berlin, Kern etc — orchestras (Green routinely and unloveably groused about Bennie Goodman's unloveable-ness and never mentioned Goodman's supreme talent as a clarinettist) — and singers. His hero, Sinatra, was forgiven far greater sins than those for which Goodman was condemned. At some moment in the programme Green would be sure to reminisce sourly about his time playing in dance bands when, no matter what delectable musical fare was spread before the dancers, they failed to register any pleasure in this, musical illiterates that they were, fox-trotting with the same indiscriminate enjoyment to "Clap Hands, Here Comes Charlie", say, as to "Body and Soul". "Why did I bother?" was his implied question. Answer: because you were getting paid.

When for a brief period in the mid-1950s I played in a dance band, I realised that one of its pleasures was that you were invisible to the dancers, who were far too wrapped up in each other to care about those dispensing the music to which they quick-stepped or waltzed. As a result, from your elevated position on stage you could notice all that the dancers themselves didn't notice, about themselves and others. There will be more to say about this. Here, I want merely to remark that when I first read Larkin's lines about how, thinking it will be spring soon, he feels like a child: "Who comes on a scene/Of adult reconciling/And can understand nothing/But the unusual laughter/And starts to be happy", I at once thought of my parents returning home from a dance. Not that they were in need of reconciling, but their gaiety on these occasions warmed us all.

I say "all" and realise that my sister doesn't much feature in my memories of our early years at Ashford. We went to different schools, had different friends and different interests. Her passion at the time was for dance, though not the kind my parents followed. Like most girls of her age, she was attracted to ballet, and attended a "School of Dance", where she learnt tap dancing as well as some ballet steps. The School, together with others in the area, took part an annual show that in 1951 was held at Kingston Empire, a large variety hall which on this occasion had for audience parents of the dancers together with siblings and hangers-on. The girls of the school Jill attended wore black dresses with salmon-pink sashes and her contribution seemed to be over very quickly.

When we left the theatre we stepped out into a fog which had thickened from earlier mist into one of those intense pea-soupers, "smogs", as they were called, that limited vision to a few yards at most. Problem. My mother, Jill and I had crammed into the Hill's car, driven by Mrs Hill who was ferrying Anne — in the same school of dance as Jill — and Michael to Kingston for the show. Now we had to get back to Ashford, but how exactly? Michael and I volunteered to walk in front of the car, holding out handkerchiefs so that his mother could see us in the sulphurous yellow gloom that blotted out all other signs. It took us nearly three hours to cover the six or seven miles from Kingston to Ashford, following the route that the 216 bus took. A year later, in December 1952, "the great London smog", rather like the "great stink" of nearly a hundred years earlier, caused the government of the day to begin the process of cleaning up

75

the air. Deaths from bronchitis that could be attributed to smogs climbed to alarming levels in the early 1950s, just as in mid-nineteenth century Britain deaths from cholera caused by foul water reached epidemic proportions.

In view of the damage they caused, to humans, to transport arrangements, to everyday business, I probably shouldn't say that I found the smogs exciting, even magical; but I did. Walking through one, you would find yourself suddenly confronted by mysterious figures that emerged out of the yellow curtain in front of you and as suddenly disappeared. A car lamp behind you threw your shadow forward, so that like the Brocken spectre which excited Coleridge you appeared to be walking towards a shape that kept a constant distance between you and it. And if the smog developed while you were on the bus, you became witness to a marine underworld sliding silently by, the fog not only blanking out sounds on the far side of the window, but stilling conversations within, as passengers turned from their neighbours to stare absorbedly at bug-eyed monsters pushing slowly through glutinous yellow fronds and billows.

"Like inter-planetary travel" the boy sitting beside me on one of these journeys whispered in my ear. Bruce Mellors was a year ahead of me at school, a reserved, lonely youth, who at the start of my second year began to join me at the stop where I waited for the bus. He and his parents had recently moved to Ashford, he told me, and he qualified for Hampton because of the school he'd previously gone to, somewhere in the Portsmouth area, and which he said was "where nobs hang out, just like a public lavatory." He had a pendulous nose and a wide mouth from which words slipped sideways, so that I imagined the most mundane of his remarks carried a humorous, even satiric edge to them. I think he had few if any friends among his own year group, and whenever I came upon him in one of the school corridors, waiting for admission to a classroom, he would be standing apart from the other boys, his bony frame, from which arms far too long for the school blazer he wore poked rawly, propped against the wall, and almost always a smile, not malicious but implying self-containment, on his long, thin lips. It took me some while to realise that his pose of apartness was one of self-defence, a way of shielding himself from a loneliness that began at home and extended to his school life.

I learned little of his parents. His father was some sort of an engineer who had been employed in naval work during the war and now worked on maintenance at Feltham's huge railway sidings. As to the middle-aged woman I once saw when I went to the rented flat Bruce lived in just off the high street, I learned only that she wasn't his mother. "The dame in slacks," he called her, a phrase which not only indicated a certain dislike but that he was an avid reader of American crime fiction. On that occasion, I saw on the table, which was of blond wood like the chairs the man and woman sat in, an open copy of *The Cruel Sea*, a novel which my parents had read but which they told me wasn't "suitable" for someone of my age. Since they'd made no objection to my reading other best-sellers of the time that they'd either bought or borrowed from the local library — I remember *The Robe* (a wholly boring novel by an American called Lloyd C Douglas which I gave up on after a hundred or so pages), *The Kontiki Expedition, London Belongs to Me, A Town Called Alice* — I was naturally curious to know what made Nicholas Montserrat's novel forbidden fruit. But Bruce couldn't tell me. "Ah, it'll be boring clinches," he said, "lovey-dovey staff."

We were off to see a feature film which he had persuaded me would be well worth the one-and-nine pence we'd each be spending on a seat in the stalls. Wrong. The film, an adventure in space travel, was shot in black and white, and though I can't recall its plot, nor even its name — I think, but can't be sure that *Planet X* came into it — I do remember it being almost laughably incompetent. Cardboard rockets wobbled through grey drapes of space, men in sagging tights exchanged meaningful looks, and the planet on which they eventually landed and from which they would never return resembling nothing so much as some stray allotment filmed on a murky evening when the stalks of Brussels sprouts and runner-bean tendrils could do service as alien growths. As we left the cinema after the obligatory playing of the National Anthem, even Bruce, devotee of science fiction though he was, admitted that what we'd seen was, as he put it, "crap".

Science fiction, crime fiction. In addition to Micky Spillane, Bruce read Leslie A. Charteris, whose debonair sleuth, the "Saint", he much admired, and as a result of which he decided that you should always smoke a cigarette every half an hour and that the only car worth driving was a Bentley. So when he told me he was writing something on which he needed my help I naturally assumed it must be one of those forms of fiction. He wouldn't tell me what it was however, merely asked me to go round to the flat the following Saturday afternoon when his father and the dame in slacks would be away for the day. "But," he said, "you'll know how to handle it." His confidence in my ability as a writer came from the fact that a recent essay of mine in which I'd satirised both teachers and classmates had gained a kind of *samizdat* notoriety, and boys I hardly knew would come up to me to ask for more of the same, only next time I was to include — and they'd name some member of staff or a classmate against whom they bore a grudge. Flattering, but I had no intention of making needless enemies. Assisting Bruce in writing a crime story was a very different and far more exciting proposition.

When I got to his flat, though, I found he had a different kind of writing in mind. He ushered me into the living room. There, on the blond wood table, was a stack of lined paper, across which were laid four sharpened pencils. Bruce motioned me to the chair where I'd previously seen the dame in slacks sitting. He took the chair opposite.

"You get two pencils OK? One's a 2BB. That's for initial thoughts. Then, when we get what we want, we use an HB. And here," he reached down and produced some sheets of paper on which I could see lines of writing, "is what I've written so far."

"What is it?"

"A pantomime."

"A *what?*"

"Pantomime. It's the way to make money."

In answer to my bewildered look he explained that in the back of one of the magazines he read he'd found an advertisement for a Correspondence School of Writing, had sent off for More Information and, having enclosed as requested a recent piece of writing together with required payment — how much, he didn't say — was given the advice that his natural "metier" was for pantomime scripts, which were, he was assured, in demand "the length and breadth of the country." A further shelling out of money had brought a kind of do-it-yourself sheet of tips from "an expert with years of experience" on how to write this particular form of entertainment, including the advice about using lined paper and two kinds of pencil.

"But why not try crime fiction?"

"Too obvious. Everyone's at it. But for pantomime you need special gifts." He read from the sheet he'd been sent by *Our Expert*. 'Imagination, an appreciation of the fantastic and a sense of humour.' "I'll do the fantasy, you supply the humour," he said. Then he pushed over as much of the pantomime as had so far been written. It was called *Jack and the Space Ship*.

The dialogue, such as it was, contained numerous gaps, and after each gap, in brackets, were the letters WFL.

"What do these mean?"

Bruce tapped a forefinger on the Advice Sheet. "They're to help the actors. It says here that we need to put them in, like stage directions. I write the serious stuff, your job is to fill in the gaps with comic dialogue and then, after the actors deliver it, they Wait For Laugh."

I don't think *Jack and the Space Ship* got further than its opening scene. You could say that it never left the ground. And soon afterwards my developing passion for geology took me away from any desire to write pantomime dialogue. As for Bruce, he left school a year later, having decided to sign on, so he told me, as a telegraph operator in the Merchant marine. "A good way of listening in on any messages transmitted from outer space," he said with that odd, side-of-the-mouth delivery, his lips puckered in a smile whose meaning I couldn't decipher.

He came to mind when, in the late 1990s, I first read *Wireless Operator*, Simon Darragh's translations from the Greek poet Nikos Kavvadias. Himself an operator in the Greek merchant marine, and self-taught as are or anyway were so many Greek poets, Kavvadias writes with a direct, stark power about the lonely lives of his fellow sailors, and I thought of Bruce Mellors in particular, painfully and discomfortingly, when I came to Kavvadias's account in "Coaliers" of how

> The Flemish sailors laugh; they say the English can afford
> To weep for no more than a single day for those who drown:
> If they wanted longer, there wouldn't be the time;
> For every ten who go to sea no more than five return.

A few years after that, I took the chance offered me to publish under the Shoestring Press imprint Darragh's translation of Kavvadias's autobiographical novel, *Sea Dog*. Though it would be untrue to say that memories of Bruce Mellors partly impelled my decision, it *is* true that, having the image of his lonely, queerly sardonic face once more in my imagination, I wanted to hope that in the years after I knew him he found some sort of fulfilment in the life he'd perhaps chosen, and, supposing he himself had become a salty sea-dog, that he was able to steer clear of the "dark harbour" Kavvadias writes of in another poem, where suicides and failures end up, while the sun, "as always, flaming and gay" describes "its usual orbit."

Chapter 5
"Open the Windows"

In the spring of 1952 I was confirmed and nothing happened. This was a severe disappointment. I'd been promised, especially by my mother, that when at the confirmation ceremony the bishop placed his hands on my bowed head and blessed me I would be filled with a — well, I can't in all honesty remember exactly what was supposed to happen, but it must have had something to do with a new certainty of existing in a stage of grace. Not a blinding light, perhaps, no sudden revelation, but a conviction — a *confirmation* — that the Christian faith was real, knowable, that it would be "felt in the blood, and felt along the heart". When I first read the lines in *Tintern Abbey* from which that phrase comes, it seemed to me, and in a way still does, that Wordsworth was describing precisely the experience for which I had been prepared but which that spring evening in my fifteenth year failed to deliver.

The formal preparation was undertaken by the vicar, the Reverend Jaggin. A group of adolescents, and one adult, a history teacher at my school whom I greatly admired and who must have been deeply embarrassed to find himself in my company, met once a week for an evening hour's instruction in the church's side chapel. Jaggin was a mild-mannered man, on the short side, a chain-smoker, with a feisty wife whose crop of blonde, straggly curls and frequent shouts of laughter on public occasions made me think of Gracie Fields. They had two daughters, younger than me, the senior of whom I'd seen smoking with friends in the local park. There was general agreement among the parishioners that it was Mrs Jaggin who wore the trousers and an equal agreement that the Reverend's mind was on higher things. He was also held to be a man of encyclopaedic knowledge, though I already had reason to doubt this. Not long before the confirmation classes began, I was puzzling over some feldspar embedded in rock I'd picked up on one of my archaeological jaunts, and whose exact composition I couldn't determine. "Take it to the vicar," my father advised, "he'll know, he's an authority on rocks." So a few evenings later I marched round to the vicarage with my piece of igneous rock. Jaggin greeted me on the doorstep, and in response to my query turned the crystals over in his hand, peering uncertainly at them. "It's quartz," he said at last, handing me back the feldspar.

He no doubt made a better job of preparing us for confirmation, though I can remember nothing of his instruction beyond his telling us not to bother our heads too much with the 39 Articles and that works mattered more than arguments about the nature of faith. I recalled this when, at a later date, I came across Attlee's reply to an interviewer who asked him whether he considered himself an Anglican: "Don't mind the ethics. Can't stand the mumbo-jumbo." As for the confirmation service itself, I remember only my immediate sense of deflation when the bishop's blessing failed to bring about the transformation I believed would occur. No blinding theologies of flowers and fruits, and the celebratory party, held in the vicarage, was also a let-down. A cup of tea, a sandwich, a token handshake from the bishop whose manner combined aloofness with switch-on smiles, and who was soon chauffeured away — "a busy man" my father said, placatory — and that was that.

I did not tell my parents of my disappointment. I don't think it would have much bothered my father, whose Christianity was of a purely conventional kind. He attended church because that was that people did. He wasn't being cynical in behaving this way, indeed my father was probably the least cynical man I've known. He always hoped that people were good, and even when evidence to the contrary piled up he'd do his best to ignore it. "A nice enough chap," he'd say of some absolute shit, not because he was entirely blind to the man's nastiness but because at some level of his being he wanted to believe that speaking well of a person could make it so. He was an optimist who lived by good deeds, and to the extent that Christianity *is* works then he was a

Christian. Had he known it, he would almost certainly have concurred with Attlee's view of the matter.

My mother, on the other hand, who had a more pessimistic cast of mind, was more truly religious, and she would have been hurt, perhaps even dismayed, had I revealed that the bishop's laying on of hands was of no more consequence than the attention I received from my once-a-fortnight visit to the local barber's. Her love of laughter was the obverse of her horror of cruelty. Laughter dispelled the dark, or at least pinned it back. But the dark always returned. I once asked my parents if they could remember how they felt at the moment of Chamberlain's announcement that "this country is at war with Germany." "Alright," my father said, "I knew we were going to win." "Terrified," my mother said, "I had you two to care for" — meaning my sister and myself — "and I thought we'd probably all be killed." And she then told me a story that explains much about her and, I suspect, about countless others who have found themselves helpless in time of war or of violence about which they, the innocent, can do nothing. In September 1939, we were living in Coventry, and although we left for Burbage before the dreadful bombing of the city, German bombers would drone over our midland village on their way to industrial centres. One night the number of enemy aircraft overhead was so great that my mother became convinced that either we were to be bombed or that the invasion of England was about to begin. So she ran to the mirror, made herself up, then dressed in her best clothes and, with Jill and me, settled into the Morrison shelter — a steel structure that would have withstood very little — and waited for the end. Why had she done that? "I couldn't think what else to do," she said.

To dress gaily in defiance of imminent, pulverising death! This is the pure, unsaving grace. Towards the end of Theodore Roethke's lovely poem "Meditation at Oyster River" the poet finds himself watching small shore birds skirting dangerous waves and thinks "How graceful the small before danger." Because I think — no, I'm sure — my mother found the world a threatening and, sometimes, a truly frightening place, I love that story, one that she only ever told me late in her life, drawing it from the depths where over the years it had been overlaid by family events and histories of which she made herself the unofficial custodian, so that her mind was as crammed with the bric-à-brac of anecdote and reminiscence as the cupboard of Rimbaud's sonnet, with its

Fragrant must of crumpled linen, lace,
Yellowing shawls, cravats, cuff-links.....locks
Of white and brown hair, sepia snaps, a box
Whose wispy scent tells of roses and lime

Anecdote was for her was a hook by which to draw up memory, to clothe it and set it before her and her listeners, it was the past not so much made present as given enduring life, it testified to continuity, it was her stay against the ultimate cruelty of erasure. And so she knew the names and more often than not important dates — birth, marriage, death — of the most distant cousins and forbears, could tell me of incidents relating to each, the significance of which lay not in their momentousness, because these incidents were mostly trivial, but in the individuality conferred on the person to whom it belonged. I have a spoon of tarnished silver which my mother inherited, so she told me, from the grandfather of her own mother's father on the occasion of his converting from Catholicism to Anglicanism. This happened at the beginning of the 19th century, when the young man crossed from Ireland to England to look for work, found it, and married into the family from which my maternal grandmother would eventually come; and it occurs to me that my mother's life-long commitment to the Anglican faith was a form of family piety, and that this was why she mourned my early abandonment of that faith.

I don't mean that her piety was hollow, any more than it was "pi-jaw". She believed, but she would have agreed with Dryden that "The things we must believe are few and plain." She wanted a simple faith, she once said, one in which good works meant more than theological niceties — to that extent she and my father were at one — and though she wouldn't have agreed with Lord Melbourne that prayer in private was going a damned sight too far, public protestations of belief ran counter to her nature. For her, religion was an ever-present, unshowy but vivid and restorative reality: "Church-bells beyond the stars heard, the soul's blood./The land of spices; something understood," as the greatest of all Anglican poets puts it.

At Burbage I'd sung in the church choir, which I loved, and Jill and I had been sent to Sunday school, which we both loathed. With the move to Ashford we became a regular church-going family, and our Sundays were given over to the kind of stiff, knobbly sobriety which Protestantism grafted onto the painfully-acquired version of "respectability" that afflicted the lower middle-class. It wasn't as bad as that New England perverseness which Edwin Arlington Robinson catches in his account of how "Conscience always has the rocking chair,/Cheerful as when she tortured into fits/The first cat that was ever killed by Care", but it was certainly a way of squeezing all pleasure out of the Day of Rest, as my grandmother, entombed in the lounge, called it. There was Matins, comprising prayers, readings, hymns and more prayers, which went on for about an hour-and-a-half, followed by a dash home to finish the preparation of the Sunday roast, followed by an afternoon of sullen sitting around — on rare occasions my father would take us out in the car but as we had always to be dressed in our "Sunday Best" and could do very little except study from car windows the changing views of ribbon estate and tatty fields, we never volunteered to go on these — followed by tea, followed by our required attendance at Evensong.

This was where the day had been heading, or, as I used to think, had been tilting inexorably down as into a world of stifling gloom from which we might never escape and which was epitomised by the church's dingy yellow lighting.

But the dismalness began earlier in the day. Dinner in particular was liable — was virtually guaranteed — to be a fraught affair. Everyone was edgy, my mother fretting that the over-priced meat would prove not worth the money she had paid nor justify the care with which she had roasted it. And all too often her worst fears were borne out: the meat would be grey, gristly, with lumps of yellow fat, and threaded through with strands of white tendon or narrow pipes that couldn't be cut, much less chewed. This would make my father tetchy, either because Jill and I weren't observing "table manners" or because we weren't eating with sufficient gusto and, therefore, "gratitude" for what we'd been given. And while Jill and I sulked, our grandmother would chatter on, her innocent inanities winding up the tension until something in itself fairly insignificant — a dropped fork, a piece of meat pushed aside — would cause my father to snap and there'd be a row which might end with my mother leaving the room in tears.

"There," he'd say, "now see what you've done."

"Sunday, the fathers make the children cry," the American poet Ralph Robin wrote, who must have experienced some of the effects of Sunday which I knew in my early days. I met Ralph in Washington DC, when I spent a year as Visiting Professor at the University of Maryland in 1967-8, and at once took to his poetry. He blamed his father for oppressing his youth and, he implied, wrecking his mother's life. I don't blame my father. Short of money, with work cares and aware of an emotional distance between himself and his children, both of whom saw in him an authority figure rather than someone they could easily love, it would have been odd if he hadn't occasionally felt resentful at their sulky resistance to his taking over a role they had assumed would always be their mother's. Robin's bleakly witty villanelle, which I published in 1969 for the Byron Press in his collection *Cities of Speech*, ends,

> Open the windows and enjoy the high
> Sounds of the sport before the sky is starred.
> Sundays the fathers make the children cry,
> Having remembered that fathers die.

Although he went regularly to watch Brentford, my father's own footballing days were behind him, as were athletics. The only two sports which were now available to him were the only two which he didn't much like: cricket and tennis. He turned out on a few occasions for his works' cricket team but, being neither batsman nor bowler, he didn't greatly enjoy the experience, and as for tennis, which he played even more reluctantly against Mr Hill across the road, he saw that as a duty owed to companionship rather than a pleasure. But anyway, to play either cricket or tennis on the Sabbath was unthinkable. And so, Sunday after Sunday, a pall of tedium descended on the house from which even the thought of a return to school on Monday seemed to offer some relief.

Very occasionally, an old friend of my mother's was invited to dinner. The two women had known each other since the late 1920s, when they worked together for a chocolate-making business, my mother as book-keeper, the other, Dorothy she was called, as a typist. I never could see what they had in common. Dorothy had faded, heavily ringletted blond hair, painted her fingernails scarlet, wore rather girlish clothes, and seemed to exude perfume from all parts of her body. Her conversation was breathtakingly banal, consisting for the most part of reports about a variety of gentlemen encountered on the tube whose intrusive glances she felt compelled to turn away from, although one, I remember, insisted on looking over her shoulder as she tried to read her newspaper while strap-hanging, until he suggested turning the page for her and she retorted that he could jolly well buy his own newspaper or pay for hers. My mother would smile, my grandmother would say "Fancy", and my father would remain stonily silent. Such fun we had.

Was it really that bad? I fear it must sometimes have come close, because I know that when I first read Dickens's account of Arthur Clennam's return to the London of his own childhood, of his walks through the city's deadened Sunday streets, it was as though I was seeing my own boyhood brought to life, as Orwell said he thought of *his* childhood when he read of David Copperfield's early schooldays. Not only that: "The mental atmosphere of the opening chapters was so immediately intelligible to me that I vaguely imagined that they had been written *by a child*." What I encountered at the beginning of *Little Dorrit* was a piece of writing that both defined and excoriated the English Sunday of post-war Ashford quite as much as mid-19th century London, as though in a hundred years little, if anything, had changed.

> In every thoroughfare, up almost every alley, and down almost every turning, some doleful bell was throbbing, jerking, tolling, as if the Plague were in the city and the dead-carts going round. Everything was bolted and barred that could possibly furnish relief to an overworked people. No pictures, no unfamiliar animals, no rare plants or flowers, no natural or artificial wonders of the ancient world — all *taboo*....Nothing to see but streets, streets, streets. Nothing to breathe but streets, streets, streets. Nothing to change the brooding mind, or raise it up. Nothing for the spent toiler to do, but to compare the monotony of his seventh day with the monotony of his six days, think what a weary life he led, and make the best of it — or the worst, according to the probabilities.

Actually, the cinemas were open on a Sunday evening. But they showed only old and poor-quality films, not the regular features, and the almost entirely male queue that stood outside the Astoria as we walked up to church looked somehow furtive, as though ashamed of themselves.

We walked home by a different route, one that took us past a pub called the Kings Head which my parents affected not to notice, and then, as we turned into Exeford Avenue, we came to a long wooden hut on the corner. Every Sunday evening accordion music skirled out from the hut's wide-open windows and we could hear the pounding of heavy feet, boots perhaps, in some sort of dance, laughter, shouting. After the boredom of Evensong, the vicar's tepid sermon, the enervate singing, the air of stunned, mildewed lethargy, this sense of life happening elsewhere made me want to jig in frustration. Why wouldn't *we* have such merry-making. But I knew the answer. The hut was the social centre for the nearby Roman Catholic church, and it was well-known by all god-fearing people that Catholics had made a pact with the devil. The pounding of their feet, which seemed to the unwary a signal of innocent pleasure, of joyous abandonment, was precisely that: abandonment of the true way. Those heavy boots concealed cloven hoofs. And though I wasn't literally required to believe this, of course I wasn't, my mother in particular did seem genuinely wary of, even frightened by, people she knew to be practising Catholics, as though to get too close to them was to risk being infected by some subtle corruption.

* * *

Yet for both my parents, the church opened the way to social and cultural possibilities that sweetened their lives. My father, I now discovered, had a love of music which came out in organ recitals he took me to. One, held at the parish church, had a special significance because it was given by the organist and choir master who, despite months in clink for filching from the offertory plate, was pardoned by the vicar. To mark his return to the fold he gave a well-attended recital at the parish church St Matthew's, intended as an act of expiation for his sins. I was vaguely thrilled at the prospect of seeing a criminal in the flesh. In the event, the man looked much the same, and when he shook hands at the end of the evening my covert glance at his wrists failed to discover any of the tell-tale signs of reddening or bruising which the detective stories I'd read told me were the sure tokens of manacled incarceration.

Another recital, given by a visiting organist at St Hilda's, the sister church at the other end of town, was of Stainer's Crucifixion. At one point during this recital I glanced sideways at my father and saw his eyes were shut. Assuming he was asleep, I nudged him and he frowned slightly and shook his head. Afterwards, he told me, "the right way to listen is with your eyes shut", and for once he wasn't speaking as an upholder of respectable behaviour.

He also enjoyed singing hymns and to my mother's embarrassment would dominate the congregation's feeble warbling at evensong. This was especially so once he became People's Warden. There were two such wardens, one — Vicar's Warden — nominated by the incumbent, the other voted for, or so I assume, by parishioners. Whether my father put himself forward for this point I doubt; more likely he was persuaded by others to act on their behalf, to be a people's tribune, alerting the vicar to lay concerns. I know he interceded for the disgraced organist because I remember half-overheard telephone conversations that seemed always to occur on weekday evenings when he and my mother were trying to eat, conversations that for his part invariably required him to soothe the outraged feelings of parishioners at the pardoning of this "evil man", as one of them called the organist. My mother would fume at the constant interruptions to their meal but I don't recall him ever being anything but good-tempered with the callers, no matter how long-winded or preposterous their diatribes.

"Who was it this time?" she'd ask, when he could get back to his food, and, when he told her, she'd say "I might have guessed it would be his [or her] rigmarole. They'd talk the hind leg off a donkey, that lot. I don't know why you put up with it, they make me mad."

But she was proud of his diplomatic skills, his ability to soothe the most ruffled of feathers. Even the postmaster, a blustery, choleric man whose hairy suits seemed fit covering for his generally boar-like behaviour, could be calmed by my father's good humour. This was important because not long after my father became People's Warden a group of parishioners decided to set up an amateur dramatic society which they proposed to call The Ashford Parish Players, and the postmaster, who had managed to persuade everyone that he was a man of considerable dramatic experience, became either president or chairman or anyway, in my father's phrase, "chief cook and bottle washer." He got to choose most of the plays, he was often the producer, he carpentered and painted the stage sets, and he usually had a leading part in whichever comedy — and it always was a comedy — took over the parish hall for a week's run twice a year. The productions played to packed houses — that is, to about a hundred a night — and at the last-night party, and in the best tradition of amateur luvviedom, the postmaster invariably threw a tantrum. Either he hadn't had sufficient support for all the work he'd done, or someone had cut him off in the middle of his big speech or hadn't come in on cue and so wrecked a special producorial effect, or he'd detected a slighting reference to his set design or lighting (because, yes, he rigged and plotted the lighting, too), or, always supposing praise had been heaped on the production, he knew it wasn't meant, that it was shallow pretence, and when all was said he really didn't know why he was throwing his best years and endeavours away on such an ungrateful lot.

I witnessed these tantrums because I was part of the regular backstage team. My father, who had been pressed into taking a minor role in one of the first productions, discovered in himself a talent for comic acting and as a result became a regular player, although he rarely accepted major roles, partly because he was genuinely modest, and partly because he had difficulty learning his lines. My memory was by contrast strong — without much effort I could learn the entirety of any play he was in — and so he recruited me as personal prompt, which meant that once rehearsals reached the stage when scripts were supposed to be set aside I stood in the wings ready to whisper lines he might forget or stumble over. What made learning his lines additionally difficult for him was that the play text was always liable to excisions and re-writing. This wasn't so much at the whim of the producer — who was strongly resistant to any attempt to alter or, worse, cut lines, especially his own — but because the Mothers' Union was required to vet each text before it could be declared suitable for use by a Christian drama group.

My mother belonged to the Mothers' Union, but in view of the fact that her husband acted in the plays she was declared an interested party and so couldn't be one of those who pored over each play-text, blue pencil in hand, alert to hunt down and strike out possible obscenities or anything that might bring a blush to the cheek of a young person. But she was also a member of the Ladies' Working Party, whose major function was to find suitable ways to raise funds for the parish, and as the plays undoubtedly raised funds and as the Ladies' Working Party were involved in the productions — they prepared and dispensed the profitable interval teas — they insisted on having a representative on the vetting committee. My mother was elected to serve and by this Machiavellian ruse she was enabled to bring home news of the latest absurdities, which included an attempt to block the use of "the bottom of the garden" because it was liable to misinterpretation (objection overruled), and the phrase "Oh, my God" (objection sustained). "Oh, my Gawd" was to be substituted on the grounds that working class speech, being that of the largely uneducated, couldn't be thought of as intentionally blasphemous.

It was accepted that emendations and excisions could go on being proposed until dress rehearsal. I wasn't present at a very late rehearsal of a Ben Travers farce when one of the actors, a greengrocer who had very reluctantly accepted a walk-on part as greengrocer — "go on, Roger, you *must* know how to act a greengrocer" — lost his only line. The line was "Strewth, if I'd known you was a lady, I'd have charged you double." He was all set to deliver the words when a cry of "stop" came from the producer's chair. Apparently, a member of the vetting committee, which had hitherto failed to pick up the word "strewth" in its trawl for improprieties, was now, in the nick of time, at hand to prevent it from befouling the stage.

"Leave out 'strewth' will you, Roger?" the producer asked.

Roger saw his chance. "If it goes, I go," he said.

The lady from the vetting sub-committee, who was standing by the producer's chair, was appealed to but remained adamant. It was her duty as a good Christian, wife and mother, to insist that the offending word be not spoken. So the production went ahead without the greengrocer who, I have to report, was anyway thoroughly unconvincing in the role of greengrocer.

My presence at rehearsals inevitably led to my being given a number of menial tasks, such as adding licks of paint to the flats and climbing ladders to hang drapes. From these I graduated to sound effects. (Assistant, I should note. The Chief

Sound Effects Man was, you will be surprised to hear, the postmaster.) There wasn't much to do as Assistant to the Chief Sound Effects. The occasional use of a thunder sheet, some persistent door-banging in the middle of one play to indicate an off-stage argument, and, in another, the simulation of bird song, although I never got to sound my piercing whistle over the microphone rigged up at the side of the stage because each night the postmaster/producer, lead actor, set designer and Chief Sound Effects, then briefly off-stage, swiped me aside and did the whistling himself. As he had badly-fitting false teeth, this meant that the audience was treated to susurrations rather like a breeze in the willows and as a result could make little of the on-stage cry, "Ah, the lark. It must be morning."

My consolation was the last-night party, when my father was regularly called on to congratulate everyone who had in any way helped with the production. Naturally his words had to be managed with great tact because of the need to thank last and most fulsomely the postmaster, producer etc. who, while others were being given their due, would be growing increasingly agitated, shifting from foot to foot, his already red face deepening from cinnabar to maroon, muttering under his breath, sweat standing on his forehead, eyes rolling wildly behind his thick, horn-rimmed spectacles, until, when my father at last turned to him, he was in no condition to hear the generous words of praise, would brush them aside and begin his denunciation of all who had done their best to wreck the days and weeks of labour he had devoted to his production which was definitely the last he would ever offer to mount and the sooner they got themselves someone to replace him the better for all concerned though where they could expect to find such a person he couldn't think because frankly the task was becoming beyond even *him* though he had endless patience with their excuses and demands.... On and on he went, while my father, unflurried, also went on, and gradually the storm of words began to weaken and fade to whimperings and then a change would come and he'd be listening to my father, would begin to smile, first at him and then at all who stood around hardly daring to meet his eye, as though he forgave them their peccadilloes, they were after all friends together in this great enterprise, and at last he would raise his glass as in benediction to those whom a short time before he had been vehemently denouncing.

Although this happened after every production, I was never less than amazed by behaviour which I now think was genuinely deranged. Years later, when I read some of the Norse sagas and was introduced to shape-changers and berserks, I thought of the postmaster, and it was his face that would sometimes come to mind when I was at work on my versions of the poems of *Egils Saga*.

Fortunately, most of the others who formed the production teams of the Ashford Parish Players were less eccentric, and the actors resisted what I later heard was known in the profession as the curse of amateur luvvies: a delusion of adequacy. They were there to have as good a time as they could manage, and if they remembered most of their lines, came on and exited at roughly the right moments and avoided colliding with the scenery and each other while on stage, they could account their contribution a success. The audiences were tolerant — they knew all of the cast and helpers — and the local newspaper unfailingly courteous in its post-production review. Everyone was mentioned by name, even the tea-ladies were thanked, and although an occasional actor was tempted to believe the compliments paid his acting, for the most part the reviews were taken with a pinch of salt.

There was one exception. The owner of a toy-shop on the high street, a man with dowdy wife and two daughters, all of whom were regular attenders at Evensong, took his acting very seriously indeed. He didn't quite go to the extreme of enquiring from the director what the motivation for each of his lines or moves might be, but he certainly let it be known that, had circumstances permitted, he would have preferred life on the professional stage. He usually had a lead part in any production — postmaster willing — and there was a widely-expressed conviction that being on stage with him brought out the best in other actors, which in practice meant a great deal of raising and extending of arms in gestures vaguely reminiscent of a traffic policeman and the shouting of lines that would have been better delivered *sotto voce*. On the one occasion I found myself in stage dialogue with him I was determined not to go the way of the others.

The opportunity arose because early in 1954 I was persuaded to take the juvenile lead in a production being mounted during my father's prolonged business absence in Canada. It was put to me that by playing the part I was carrying on the family tradition, and so, very reluctantly, I agreed. My opening line, which had to be delivered as I lifted the lid of a chafing dish conveniently placed on a table near the door through which I emerged onto stage, ran "Heck, devilled kidneys for breakfast again." "Heck" had replaced the blue-pencilled "Damn", although on the last night I rebelled and used the censored word. I don't think anyone noticed. But then they would have had difficulty noticing much about my performance. I spoke so fast that nobody could pick out more than an occasional phrase as it bobbed momentarily on the ever-rolling stream which bore all my words away. My crucial scene with the toy-shop owner, who played the father of the girl I was intending to marry, therefore became a confrontation between an irresistible force — my torrential delivery — and an immovable object — his determination To-Make-Each-Word-Count. To try to calm my nerves, I decided to push my hands deep into my trousers pockets.

"You can't do that," I was told at rehearsal. "It's all wrong. You can't afford to look as though you're being insolent to the man whose daughter you're asking permission to marry." I explained that I was intending to convey an appearance of careless grace, a phrase which I had come across Jeeves uttering when he attempts to instruct his young master in the art of arranging for his trouser bottoms merely to "lap" the instep.

"Well, it looks rude."

Rude or not, I stuck with the gesture. It seemed to provoke the toy-shop owner to an unusual degree of vehemence in his stage scorn for my prospects, my social position, and my general unsuitability as a future son-in-law. Disconcertingly, the vehemence carried over into the last-night party, when he refused to shake my hand and noticeably sneered at the conventional words of praise I received. I noticed, too, that my stage fiancée, a young teacher at a local primary school, kept well away from me. A week or two later the pair of them ran off together. "I always had my suspicions," my mother said. "He was too much the actor. All that mopping and mowing." Presumably the man's hostility had been fuelled less by my incompetence as actor than from jealousy of the on-stage kiss I had to give his real-life lover. Either that, or he suspected that I knew what was going on between them and was worried I might spread the news. He could have rested easy on both scores. The teacher was at least ten years my senior and I was as little attracted to her as she to me. And as for the closet romance, I hadn't a clue.

The abandoned wife soon sold the shop and she and the two daughters disappeared from Ashford. But getting on for twenty years later, when my wife and I were on holiday in Norfolk with our two then very young children, we visited Blickling Hall, a fine Elizabethan house set in the Norfolk countryside. As I paid for our car-parking tickets I glanced at the attendant, who looked quickly away. But it was him all right. Older, shabbier, defeated-looking.

* * *

By the time I made my one and only stage appearance as an Ashford Parish Player I had lost all interest in the group's theatricals. During spring and summer cricket took up many of my evenings and my Saturdays. And as the fifties wore on, so, too, I increasingly freed myself from the grip of Sundays, as, I noticed, my parents also began to do. Their church-going continued and I often went with them to Evensong, but there was now less of a funereal, oppressive atmosphere about the house. Meal times in particular were no longer a strain. For one thing, the foodstuffs with which my mother had to work improved. Rationing had finally ended. There was more in the shops and the quality of goods was higher. Besides, my father, free of Slough and now working in London on an improved salary, was more relaxed, liked to talk and joke over dinner, so that when I was there for the Sunday meal I could enjoy rather than fear it.

But in the summer I was more often out than in. County cricket wasn't of course played on the Sabbath, and a good many local clubs refused to open their grounds or field a team on that day. Nevertheless, Sunday was becoming a day for the game I loved almost to distraction. At school I played in the first-year team, then the Minor XI, the third-year Junior XI, the fourth-year Colts, then leap-frogged into the school Second Eleven and, soon after, First XI.

I once went with my father to the sports ground at the far end of Ashford where the town's very good cricket team played, in order to watch a charity match in which my hero, Denis Compton, turned out for the Guest XI. He scored 22 then gave an easy catch to mid-on and sauntered off to the pavilion. I was sad because I wanted him to bat for longer, but it was explained to me that the function of these matches was to draw in large crowds on the promise of seeing "star" names from the world of entertainment as well as sport, and that everyone had to have a turn. This seemed to me a very improper way to play cricket and I never again went as spectator to such a game, though in the mid-fifties I sometimes played for a team called "The Stage XI", run by the radio actor Gary Marsh, and featuring, among others, John Slater and Sam Kydd, (both of whom regularly featured in British films of the period), Abraham Sofaer, and, once, Trevor Howard.

This team had an annual fixture against Hampton, and after one of these all-day games, always played on a Monday at the very end of the school year, I was asked if I would deputise for a member of the Stage team who wasn't available for the remainder of what was a week's tour of local clubs. I soon discovered that I was expected to do most of the bowling and fielding while the rest stood around nursing hangovers from the previous night's carouse or retired for long minutes at a time to the Visitors' Changing Room — "Call of Nature, old man" — where the captain had stashed crates of beer. When it came to batting, I was number 11, which I didn't at all mind because so drunk and incapable were most of the team by the time their innings became due (if he won the toss Marsh always put the opposition in) that none of them lasted more than a few balls. As a result, number 11 was all that stood between defeat and disgrace. The opposing captain would by then have taken pity on his hapless opponents and given the ball to "occasional" bowlers, whose long-hops and full tosses were easily dealt with. We actually won one of these fixtures by putting on over 80 for the last wicket, my partner being an at-first comatose actor who, as the stand progressed and I forced him into taking first singles, then twos and, even, threes, gradually came to his senses and, once he could focus, proved to be a more than capable batsman.

By then, I was also playing on Sundays for Laleham, a good club side whose excellent ground was near to Ashford, and when I wasn't playing I was watching. Lords could be reached by train and tube in under an hour, and in the early fifties my father and I always went for Middlesex's August Bank Holiday game, played against Sussex. On one especially warm Saturday, Sussex, having batted first, were all out soon after tea for well over 200, and by close of play Jack Robertson, a most elegant opening batsman, the grace of whose late cut I have seen equalled only by Tom Graveney, had scored 97 not out. Unfortunately, play for the day ended before Compton could bat.

He was my greatest sporting hero, his handsome face staring down from countless advertising hoardings where he featured in Brylcreem ads. But I had others, including for a while, Charlton's goalkeeper, Sam Bartram, famous for his flaming red hair and his ability to kick the football, in those days made of leather and often by the middle of the game sodden with rain and mud, direct and on the full from his own into the opposing penalty area.

My enjoyment of sport, and in particular my love of cricket, was bound into or perhaps it's more accurate to say was time and again set off by smells. Football meant the sweet, waxy smell of the dubbin you applied to boots to keep the leather supple. This was rubbed across all parts of the upper except for the toe-cap, which had to be kept brick hard. Football also meant the dark, peaty scents released by the gashed earth as you tackled an opponent or fell under his challenge. It meant the dark, dank scents of rain and sweat, washday-warm, that clung to the thick yellow-and-black quartered school-team shirt. As for cricket, two smells above all stirred my emotions. One was the rich, thick odour of linseed oil. In those days every newly-bought bat had to be first knocked-in, which meant hours of bouncing a cricket ball against the white, satiny-smooth and unblemished blade, after which it was repeatedly banged with a round-headed mallet. The bat was then left to stand upright in a shallow container of linseed oil — an empty sawn-in-two paint can would do — until the oil had thoroughly impregnated the blade, at the base of which a small hole had been drilled to allow the oil to seep upward. Only when the bat had lost its ivory white purity was it considered ready for use. Over winter, older bats, some dark as teak, several bound in twine to protect their splintered edges, were also stood in oil, so that walking into the dark sports shed where the bats were stored was like entering a world of night in which smell alone would guide you, a pungent, odoriferous, promissory scent.

The shed also housed the mowers used to cut the grass: and the late April chirr of the mower and, far more, the sappy, *green* scent of newly cut grass drifting through classroom windows, meant, quite simply, joy-in-waiting. "Cut grass lies frail", Larkin wrote, "Brief is the breath/Mown stalks exhale,/Long, long the death."

But not that brief, and anyway, even if it implies transience, exhalation doesn't *have* to suggest expiration, not for as long as summer lasts.

Yet while I was becoming more and more committed to cricket, whose joys are inseparable from the vulnerable frailties of fortune — that one unplayable ball, the one missed catch, the uncertainties of the weather — I was also becoming increasingly passionate about a form of study which dealt in matters of age, continuity and permanence. Geology was offered as a possible area of interest at the Natural History Club, one of the many after-school activities encouraged at Hampton. I joined the club in my second year. At first this was because the local gravel pits, where I sometimes went to trawl weed that festooned the many ponds, produced a reliably rich harvest of water beetles, snails, newts, small fish, even leeches; and having taken these home in jam jars before transferring them to a small aquarium from which the newts in particular regularly escaped (my mother often discovered them dozing on cushions or nestling in vases on the sideboard), I was encouraged to give them to the school's natural history laboratory cum aquaria. Item by item my collection was carried to Hampton. This included a grass snake. I found the foot-long snake one Saturday afternoon sunning itself on common land not far from our house, lifted it into a narrow biscuit tin that, with straps I'd attached to either end, now served as a herbarium, and briefly kept it in the Anderson shelter at the bottom of our garden, charging a penny a time for anyone interested in seeing it. Nobody was.

My interest in flora and fauna never amounted to much. Geology was a different matter. Not that I was either especially thrilled or appalled to discover the earth's great age. My Anglicanism was of so vaporous a kind that it wouldn't be dispelled by the keen winds of pre-historic evidence. At the end of each verse of the Bible, Ruskin mournfully said, he could hear the clink of the geologist's hammer. The clink of my hammer — which I bought at the age of 13 and still have — was a tool by which I could literally bring to light objects beautiful in themselves and confirmation of what I read in books: that fossils *were* most often to be found in limestone country, that the various, gorgeous colours of quartz — smoky, amethyst — *did* come with igneous rock, that garnet *did* occur in areas where gneiss was to be found.

I never went to Pegwell Bay, scene of Dyce's mid-19th century sombrely powerful painting, where those who stoop to discover fossils under a sullen sky bear witness to the "melancholy, long, withdrawing roar" of the sea of faith. But, my head full of much reading on the subject, I went on a number of school expeditions to parts of the country which delivered up different rock specimens that over several years grew into a sizeable collection. From Derbyshire came Blue John fluorspar, its magenta cubes turning phosphorescent when heated. And on that same trip, which included a magical walk beside the river Dove where we saw otters tumbling, I was chased up Castleton High Street by an enraged householder as I tried, unsuccessfully, to liberate an ammonite from a piece of rock that formed part of his front wall. Never try running when you have a knapsack full of rocks. From North Wales, to which I was transported in a motor-bike side-car driven by a botany teacher with an older boy, a keen botanist, riding pillion, and where it rained the entire five days we were there, I brought back, as well as rocks in which were embedded evidence of silver, lead and iron, useful knowledge on the formation of glaciated valleys and of the moraines, like gigantic smoothed down mole-hills, that formed at valleys' lower ends. Gloucestershire produced haematite ("kidney ore"), red-brown, glossy, rounded, as well as fossilised stems and leaves in coal, and agate, though how it got to May Hill I have no means of knowing. (I love the story Auden tells of Goethe stepping down from his coach in order to inspect a stone and, as he turned it over in his fingers, saying, "Well, well, what are *you* doing here.") And from Scotland came perhaps the richest trove of all: banded gneiss, a hunk of basalt, the hardest of rocks, on which seemingly nothing could make a mark, nodules of granite glittering thickly with mica and quartz flakes, and garnets, some of them translucent and red as rubies, others rough-edged and more gingery in colour, vaguely reminiscent of those "grog-blossoms" that used to grow on the noses of dedicated drinkers.

The Scottish trip, which took place in the summer of 1952, is memorable for other reasons, too. I had gone with Michael Hill and his French pen-friend. This was at a time when schools encouraged their pupils to find such pen-friends from other European countries because writing letters and occasional visits to each other's homes was held to be useful, as I've no doubt it was, in increasing international understanding and command of a foreign language. I never had a pen-friend, probably because I was too busy with cricket and geology, but plenty of my class mates did. Michael, being two years older than me, exchanged letters with someone who, at the age of 17, seemed an immensely sophisticated Parisian. On our drive up to Scotland — Michael, having recently passed his test, was allowed to take the family car — Jean-Louis smoked, his English proved well-nigh perfect, and though I could talk more easily in French than could Michael, I realised that compared to Jean-Louis I was wet behind the ears. The following year he came to Ashford accompanied by a girl friend who was *chic* rather than pretty. She fascinated me because her presence caused what at first seemed a puzzling constraint in the atmosphere at the Hills' house until it suddenly dawned on me that she and Jean-Louis were sharing a bedroom. So this was what was meant by a "mistress".

On our way down from the north of Scotland we stayed for a night in a farmhouse in Dumfries. That evening we went to the cinema and saw a John Wayne film of no great interest. At its conclusion, Michael and I automatically stood up as the opening bars of the National Anthem began to sound through the auditorium. In those days the anthem was always played as the curtains closed and the lights came on. In England audiences accepted this, and although one or two might slink out, the vast majority stood silently to attention until the final chord died away. Not here. Amid the hubbub of tipped-up seats and conversation, the audience mostly thronged noisily to the exits, and those who stayed behind did so in order to heckle the music, throw objects at the screen — ice-cream cartons, empty cigarette packets, balled-up paper bags — and instruct us either to sit down or get out. We got out.

The next morning, over breakfast, the farmer's wife, a pretty, red-headed woman, told us that there was a good deal of anti-Royal sentiment in the area, a matter to which I'd never given a thought, and this despite the fact that two years previously, at Christmas 1950, some Scottish nationalists had got into Westminster Abbey, removed the Stone of Scone, and carried it back to Edinburgh, from where it was taken to Arbroath Abbey and placed beneath the high altar under the flag of St Andrew. I remember reading about this and my parents' mild condemnation of the act, but at the time I thought of it as some sort of joke. Perhaps it was. But the contempt for England's monarchy which the three of us had witnessed, though not lacking in humour, was no mere joke. Far more than my confirmation, that moment marked an initiation for me, was liminal, involved me in stepping over into an entirely new awareness that "world is various, and more of it than we think."

I learned something else that morning. During the war, the farmer's wife told us, she had been in the WRAFS, and had been stationed at an airfield in Norfolk, where she served in the canteen for both British and American airmen. This had been at the height of the daylight bombing raids into Northern Europe. "They were lovely lads," she said, "though you couldn't really keep them in order." And then, in reply to our enquiring look, she said, "not much point, anyway. The average life-expectancy for them was three weeks." Perhaps a year earlier I'd seen a black-and-white film featuring Gregory Peck, called *Twelve O'Clock High*. It was about the wartime bombing raids from Eastern England at the very time our hostess had been working there, framed by the memory of a man who now looks over waving fields of corn where the runways had once been. Had she seen the film? Yes, she said, she had seen it. A good film. She paused. "I've been back to have a look at where I was stationed," she said, "and it's farm-land right enough, just as though the war hadn't happened. But," she paused again, "for me it was full of ghosts."

I thought of her words when, some twenty years later, I stood with Pauline and our two small children on the almost grown-over runway of one of Norfolk's wartime airfields. Parked there were rusting combine-harvesters which seemed monstrously symbolic of the deaths that had not so many years previously been associated with the place. Hence the poem, "An Abandoned Airfield in Norfolk", which I originally wrote in 1974, and later revised for publication.

Something that's more than wind troubles the wheat:
squadrons of leaves hurl past under a sky
grey with apprehension of a near storm:
the noon sun's blotted out. *Twelve o'clock high.*

On this cracked, brambled runway, grim machines
rust where they stand, idle. Once, like fate,
they toppled fields to appease hungry cities:
now these metal reapers are out of date.

But a Nissen hut nearby fills with echoes
as its door bangs and bangs; hurrying feet
pound the concrete floor when a thick hail burst
drills on its iron roof. *The flyers meet*

and scramble for their planes while sirens howl
as telegraph wires do, and bushes bend
in the squall's thrust, and over forty years
my mother asks me "will it ever end?"

"Will it ever end?" was the question my mother had almost despairingly asked as she and I listened to a wartime news broadcast not long after D-Day. When I re-wrote the poem to end with that question, Thatcher and Heseltine had just approved the siting of cruise missiles at Greenham Common.

Chapter 6
Hampton

In 1953 Stalin died, Elizabeth was crowned queen, my new headmaster began to show his real face, and I passed my O Levels and bought a trumpet. Some of these events were famous.

I read about Stalin's death in the *Daily Mail*, which my parents still took, though they soon would move to the *Daily Telegraph*. The change meant that I was deprived not merely of "Rip Kirby: Special Agent", but, far more of a loss, "Flook", the highly entertaining cartoon strip attributed to "Trog", which, though I didn't then know it, was the shared pseudonym for Humphrey Lyttleton's clarinettist, Wally Fawkes, and George Melly, a not very good jazz singer but engagingly anarchic spirit. I have no recollection of what the *Mail* had to say about Stalin's passing, but I can remember feeling a moment of bone-chilling fear when I looked at the image of his successor, Malenkov, no doubt some sort of official photograph: grim, flat-faced, chin riding above his military collar. Cold War rhetoric affected me and all of my friends. We took almost for granted the likelihood of a third world war, but this one would be different from its predecessors because no-one could win. Or rather, by the time some side or other declared itself victor, the vast majority of us would be dead. Years later, I came across a novel by Edward Hyams, *A Perfect Stranger*, first published in 1964, which dealt with political and social matters of the time. At one point the protagonist tells his father that "'with paranoid politicians brandishing H-bombs at each other, our expectation of life had been cut.' My father said, 'my dear boy, before it was these bombs it was the Lord of Hosts and before that it was sabre-toothed tigers. Our footing has always been precarious. You young people are too sorry for yourselves.'" Perhaps self-pity played some part in our dread of the future, but why not, dammit. It was our future which was being threatened. I think it must have been sometime then that, quite by chance, I heard a performance of Holst's "Planet Suite" on the 3rd Programme and was left quaking by "Mars, The Bringer of War".

News of the Americans' H-bomb test had been available since November of the previous year, and one evening I overheard my parents and some friends they had invited in for coffee discussing the event in a near whisper, as though it wasn't a subject to be voiced aloud. The bomb, someone said, had more power than all the explosives used in the last war. It could destroy entire cities. Or nations, someone else suggested. Looking at Malenkov's potato face on that morning in early 1953 I probably did feel sorry for myself, and, though I don't remember this, I imagine I felt even sorrier when in August Malenkov announced to the world that Russia had successfully tested a hydrogen bomb. I doubt I'd have felt much better had I known that, as Hennessy reports, the bomb was in fact "a 'hybrid' not a 'true' H-bomb — a boosted fusion device." Apparently it took the Russians a further two years to come up with a 100% H-bomb.

Malenkov didn't last long. Soon, the newspapers were referring to Mr B and Mr K (Bulganin and Khrushchev), and then Khrushchev alone. But the faces and names seemed interchangeable, although Molotov was a constant. So, too, was the sense of some vast, joyless half-world of bleak uniformity from which laughter and pleasure were banished on pain of death, and whose triumphs were all somehow a victory for impersonal will over individual freakishness. Zatopek's grimace as he ground out his victories in middle-distance races at the 1952 Olympics, Puskas's power as he bashed goals against the gallant English team at Wembley, causing the first home defeat by foreigners of the national side (and such a defeat — 3-6 was the final score): what were these but images of grim determination in defiance of creaturely delights. I would soon enough outgrow these clichés, but for us all in the early 1950s, whether young or old, they gripped hard and pinched deep.

America, by contrast, was all light and colour — the colour or rather colours of Hollywood. It was the land not merely of plenty but of jazz, the music I was beginning to listen to with increasing excitement and, yes, love. America meant glamour, laughter, snazzy clothes, its musicals, whether on film or the West End stage, threw up endless memorable songs, it was *desirable*. In the autumn of 2007 an old and committed Marxist couple told me how, as students at Bristol in 1947, they and others had demonstrated against Churchill, who was the Chancellor of the local university, when he installed the then American ambassador to Britain as an honorary Doctor of Letters. Had I know about that at the time or even later I would have been not merely astonished, but incredulous. The USA was surely the Great Good Place.

Moreover, it was where, in the late summer of 1953, my father was heading. Well, not *exactly*. His destination was Vancouver, but a quick glance at the atlas confirmed that Vancouver was within spitting distance of the American West Coast, and indeed by the time he returned to us in December he had driven down into California where he loaded up with gifts for us, including, for me, American sports shirts, a "windcheater", as the long-sleeved woollen pullovers with filled-in v-necks were called, brightly-coloured socks, and most prized of all, a 10 inch LP of the 1940 Ellington orchestra playing such classics as "Jack the Bear", "Concerto for Cootie", "Harlem Air Shaft" and "Cotton Tail".

* * *

By then, Coronation Day had been and gone. The chosen date was June 2nd. The nation was to unite in celebration. No work that day, no school. We at Hampton had each been given a Bible and a booklet of the Royal Family, both paid for by Middlesex County Council, Twickenham Education Committee, so presumably the Committee provided funds for all schools in their charge to have the same, a tidy sum

107

to fork out. Prayers for the day's success had been offered the previous Sunday at St Matthew's Parish Church, Ashford, and led to an unfortunate argument between my father and myself. At lunch he rather rashly said, or perhaps implied, that God so loved the English that Coronation Day was sure to dawn bright and fair. I said that even if the weather turned out to be good I didn't think that would prove conclusively either God's existence or his love of the English. On the other hand, if the day happened to be rain-affected then that was bound to knock my father's assertion on the head.

June 2nd began wet and got wetter. Our neighbours across the road, the Hills, offered to let us and sundry others watch the events on their TV. Quite early on I got away, though I recall that a dust cart which had presumably been sent out to clean the last vestiges of litter from the streets around Westminster Abbey collected a huge cheer when one of the dustmen imitated a royal wave from the cab's open window. A commentator showed the front pages of all the national newspapers wishing the royals well, except for the *Daily Worker*, whose banner headline was UP WITH THE PEOPLE. I also remember the announcement that Everest had been conquered by Sir Edmund Hillary, although it later turned out that the true conqueror may have been the Sherpa, Tenzing, and that the conquest had been achieved some days before and news held back to coincide with the coronation. Besides, Hillary was from New Zealand. Still, New Zealand was Commonwealth, and the leader of the expedition was an Englishman, Colonel John Hunt. So that was alright.

By mid-morning, both bored and irritated by the tedium of watching and by the hushed, crape reverentiality of Richard Dimbleby's voice, I was walking round Ashford's wet, empty streets. Everywhere was shut up. Cinema, pubs, shops, all closed. It felt unutterably dreary. This was celebration English style. In the intervening years I have read numerous accounts of that day, including those compiled by historians and social commentators, nearly all of whom insist on the sense of national "togetherness" which the coronation somehow both celebrated and epitomised. Perhaps. I can only say that I *know* that for me June 2nd 1953 watered republican roots which my experience in a Dumfries cinema had first stirred to life.

But in England, approval of the new monarch was not merely official, it seemed widely shared. Some weeks after the coronation, Ashford staged a pageant as part of its own celebrations of what was often labelled the "New Elizabethan Age". Similar pageants must have been held in other towns and villages, but I want to think that the one I saw was unique in its comic ineptitude. I don't know whose idea it was, but suspect the postmaster. At all events, he took the role of Sir Francis Drake, who seemed to be here, there and everywhere as the story of the "Glorious Reign of Elizabeth I" hirpled its way through various episodes, several of which were impossible to understand, in part because the actors couldn't be heard above the noise made by an increasingly derisive audience which had gathered in considerable numbers at Clock House Lane recreation ground one warm Saturday evening in late summer.

There were difficulties from the start. As the young queen presented herself for her crowning, trumpets were supposed to ring out. Unfortunately, they were late on cue with the result that, having been silent when they should have been heard, they suddenly blazed upon the words of the Archbishop of Canterbury, identifiable to many of those present as the grocer on Station Road. Cries of "Service", "Shop", and "Three pound of sugar, please", petrified him into forgetting his lines. As he left the grassy area where the pageant was being played out and made for the anonymity of the changing rooms, he was, however, given a reasonably sympathetic round of applause.

Mary, Queen of Scots, had no such luck. The moment she arrived, in chains, being led to the block, there were a number of wolf whistles and a cry of "Give us a song", followed by suggestions as to what the song should be, "I've Got a Loverly Bunch of Coconuts" emerging as clear favourite. The hooded executioner meanwhile had to endure public guesses as to his true identity and the promise of a prize (unspecified) for the most plausible. "John Wayne" brought a round of applause, "Stalin" was booed, and "Johnny Ray" (a briefly popular American crooner who was rumoured to cry on stage) treated with contempt. The eventual winner was Stanley Matthews.

By the time Sir Francis Drake appeared, strolling across the grass arm-in-arm with Sir Walter Raleigh, a tall, lugubrious and friendly enough Latin teacher at the local grammar school, the crowd had taken control. Quite apart from the inevitable questions, "Who's your fat friend?" and "Who's a lovely boy, then?", there were demands to "show us what you're hiding in them tights," delirious yells of "Roll 'em, Pete" and "missed" (for, yes, Sir Francis did attempt to play bowls), and, as the two pointed towards where the Armada was supposedly advancing beyond the putting-golf course, a falsetto cry "Behind You".

Given his recently-discovered appetite for acting, I suppose it's possible that had my father been available he might initially have agreed to take some part in the pageant, although I suspect that his shrewd good sense would soon have told him to stay well clear. But anyway, by the time "The Glorious Reign of Elizabeth I" was made flesh, he was on the other side of the Atlantic, learning how to be a timber broker.

For this, he had to discover as much about timber as could be packed into two lengthy spells of work-and-study in the far west of Canada. With a month off for Christmas, these kept him away from home for almost twelve months. Later, there would be trips to Norway, Sweden, Corsica and Sardinia. Suddenly, my parents had some spare money in their pockets. Not much, perhaps, but the more noticeable because this change in their fortunes, modest though it was, coincided with the end of rationing. More and better food was on show, more clothes, too. People began to eat better, and, though these things are comparative, to dress more stylishly. Shops advertised goods and gadgets "New In." On Saturday mornings Ashford would be thronged with people window-gazing and buying. Not the bare essentials only, but extras. Conspicuous consumption, maybe, though on a very modest scale. People bought fripperies and gewgaws simply because they had gone for so long without having money to spend or anything to spend it on. Now they had both. The goods might be inferior but at least they were available. And so people bought doorbell chimes and wrought-iron flower-pot holders to go beside the door and wrought-iron boot scrapers to set before it; they bought trios of plaster ducks to be displayed winging their way from right to left along the dining-room wall and, for hanging, beaten copper plates which carried views of Windsor Castle, and swizzle sticks and coasters and brass candlesticks and ashtrays which mimed the bellpushes found on the posher hotel reception desks — press to make ash disappear; they bought metal egg-timers and whistling kettles and beaten pewter sugar bowls and plated silver tea-pots whose handles were far too hot to hold, but never mind; they bought new tea-caddies and new tea-strainers and new tea-spoons and new and mostly inferior this, that and the other, and oh, how easy it would be to deride such a frenzy of spending on what was mostly tat and little of which would last. But it was one in the eye for those watchwords "scrimp and save" and "make do and mend" which for so long had dictated how they must lead their lives. By the end of the year my parents, like many of the neighbours, acquired a television, though not before they had sought advice as to the correct level of lighting and height from the floor the set should be placed in order to obviate eye and neck strain.

By then, having passed my O Levels, I was about to become a sixth-former, and my life, though I had no way of sensing this, was to change decisively. For most boys, and probably girls, the ages of 11-16 are difficult. You're no longer a child but you're not yet an adult. Odd and frequently unwelcome things over which you have no control are happening to your body. Why won't your voice stay under control, why do spots suddenly erupt on your face, why are you in a constant sweat? Why? Why? Why? Why do your parents want you to conform to their outlook and patterns of behaviour at the very moment when you're becoming resistant to both and are beginning to doubt the adequacy of either? Why, even when you're not at school, do you have to wear school uniform when you go out, whether to church or to visit your parents/friends or to social occasions you'd anyway rather not be at. Why do you have to suffer the indignity of a regular, fortnightly visit to the hairdresser, so that just at the moment your hair is becoming an acceptable length scissors and clippers return you to the shaven look of an inmate of Wormwood Scrubs or some poor unfortunate doing his National Service.

And then there was the school itself. My parents were inordinately proud of my being at a "superior" grammar school. Neither of them had been given the chance to continue with their schooling after the age of fourteen or fifteen, but by passing the Eleven Plus with high enough marks to go to Hampton, a name they spoke almost reverentially, their son was somehow vindicating the family honour. It was as though my success was theirs, or so it seemed to me at the time. Looking back, I can see how unfair my ingratitude was. Because I *was* ungrateful. I didn't want them to waste money, as I saw it, on my school uniform, on the sports gear I had to wear — the quartered gold-and-black football shirt, the new cricket flannels; I may even have resented my mother's trips up to London to buy French and Latin dictionaries and other essential text books which the school didn't supply but which it insisted we all possess. Whenever I complained about Hampton they would remind me of what it cost to keep me at it. "Then let me go to the local grammar school," I said, "I've got no friends at Hampton." This wasn't strictly true, but certainly I had very few friends in our neighbourhood and not many at school. Moreover, I didn't even like the damned place. That dislike, which at first had me taut with loathing, to some extent slackened as I grew older; and even in my early years there I was instructed by one or two unusually gifted teachers. Jack Hobbes, for one, whose geography classes were always informative and, as in the case of his telling us about geo-politics, eye-opening, and for another, "Bouncer" Cook, from whom I learnt a "bottom up" version of English history that in later years I realised must have come from his principled socialism, but at the time simply seemed exciting narratives of people taking on their oppressors, even if the oppressors invariably came out on top.

But during my first years at Hampton I crept unwillingly to school. The headmaster when I arrived was a genial old cove called "Bossy" Mason, whose chief fault was probably that he didn't bother to curb the excesses of several ill-tempered and sadistic teachers, among them a history teacher called Garside, whom I once in my first year watched with appalled fascination as he chased a classmate round the classroom and, when he caught him, thumped the boy's head against the nearest desk, bloodying his nose and blacking his eye. Another, a French teacher called Jago, he who had extolled the grammar-school system to my mother, relished handing out detention notices to any boy who offended against minor and very often obscure rules, ones that, for all anyone knew to the contrary, he himself had there and then dreamt up.

Mason's replacement was a man called Whitfield. If it's true that teachers acquire nicknames because this in a sense humanises them and gives a measure of vicarious control to those over whom they exercise actual control, so that a sort of sympathetic if undeclared bond exists between them and their charges, then it says much about Whitfield that to the best of my knowledge he never had a nickname. He discour-aged familiarity. I was in early middle age when at some university occasion I recognised sitting across from me a man, by then a distinguished professor of mathematical education, who had been a young, much admired maths teacher at Hampton in my time there. During a break in proceedings I introduced myself to him and asked what he recalled of Hampton, and especially Whitfield. "Oh, a terrible man," he said. "I'd not been there for more than a month, I imagine, when he came into the staff room, and I wanted to ask him something. So I called out 'Headmaster, could I have a word?' Silence. You'd have thought I'd sworn in church. Then, in front of everyone, he said 'I may be addressed as Sir or Mr Whitfield. I am *not* to be addressed as Headmaster.' And off he went. The most joyless man I've ever met."

"And one of the vainest," I said, and told him of an occasion I had witnessed in the school hall one afternoon, when house boxing was going on. Boxing, we were given to understand, was a manly sport and one in which we should be willing take part. A boxing ring had been fitted up at the front of the hall and volunteers plus conscripts took it in turns to bash each other or, more sensibly, pat the air that circled their opponent's head until the bell clanged to signal the end of the three-round contest. The honour of the school houses — Pope, Garrick, Walpole, Blackmore — was reputedly involved, and all four houses had to find representatives from each year to fight for points. Some boys and quite a few members of staff, for whom terms like "backbone" and "true grit" were seldom far from their lips, took it all seriously. On this occasion a boy called Kelly Braden was due to fight. He was the son of Barbara Kelly and Bernard Braden, then well-known television and radio personalities and comedians, who lived in nearby Shepperton, home to the famous film studios and various stars. Shortly before their son's bout was called a large Daimler smoothed its way up the school drive. As it happened, Whitfield was in the hall when news was brought to him of the Bradens' imminent arrival. He left in hurry but not, as we thought, to greet the distinguished visitors. They were ushered in looking suitably glamorous, she in furs and sparkling earrings, with carefully styled blonde hair, he in sharp suit and soft brown leather loafers. Having been shown to seats halfway down the hall, the pair settled to wait for the relevant boxing match. Only when the bell had rung for the first round did Whitfield re-appear. He now had on his gown and academic hood, and, without looking at the pair for whom he had obviously dressed himself in full canonicals, walked self-importantly up and down the hall's aisles, ostensibly on the look-out for signs of pupil misbehaviour. After two or three of these turns and turn-abouts, and still without any suggestion that he knew who was present, he paused dramatically at the front entrance to the hall, cross-gartered, as it were, gazed slowly round, then withdrew. There were some subfusc titters and someone near me clapped, but very quietly.

Whitfield was often the cause of quiet. We had a school song, one of those ridiculous instances by which grammar schools of a certain vintage aped the public schools. The first verse proclaimed that Hampton was founded in days "of haughty Tudor rule", then went on to invoke the honour of former boys, "For some were men of worth and some" (and here we were expected to drop our voices to a mere whisper) "For love of England died". But they were uplifted for the chorus:

Then let us join our school to praise,
The bond that none shall sever,
Hamptonians all a chorus raise,
HAMPTON the school for ever.

I put the name in capitals because under Bossy Mason we were positively encouraged — well, anyway, permitted — to shout it out. Naturally the shout became a kind of football roar. Not only that, for the name Hampton many boys substituted others. *Arsenal, Chelsea*, even *Brentford*. This last was the football club nearest the school, and quite a few Hamptonians were supporters.

There were other, even more adventurous cries. A friend of mine, who had a crush on a girl called Brenda, called out her name at the appropriate moment, and, spurred on by this inspirational decision, other boys were moved to declare equal love for *Barbara, Alice* and *Marlene*, although this last was probably a reference to a fictitious radio personality made famous by Beryl Reid. Reid was a comedienne who had a spot in the BBC comedy show, *Educating Archie*, during which, in Brummie accent, she referred to Marlene as her great friend whom she nevertheless hated. Peter Brough, the dummy's manipulator and an almost uniquely incompetent ventriloquist, was thought to be ideal for radio comedy

115

because on the wireless you couldn't see his lips move. A radio ventriloquist! It reminds me that a friend of mine, knowledgeable in such matters, once told me that the first BBC radio outside broadcast from Halifax Palace of Varieties, I think in 1936, featured a mime act followed by a woman tearing a telephone directory in half.

Naturally, Whitfield put a stop to all this. He also insisted on the wearing of school uniform at all times when we were travelling to and from school, a rule that provoked the anarchic spirit of many of the boys, for whom their blazers became an experimental site for the testing of wool's, or more rarely linen's, resistance to, among much else, powders and liquids collected from the chemistry labs., food stuffs (school gravy was especially favoured as possessing, so it was rumoured, more bite than hydrochloric acid), ink, and bicycle paint, while caps were tortured into shapes ranging from gothic to faux-primitive by way of the baroque. My friend Peter West quickly became adept at removing the cardboard stiffener from his cap peak, sewing the peak back up, and appearing in public with a kind of black half moon clinging to his forehead.

"West, what on earth has happened to your cap?"

"I can't imagine sir, and it was bought only yesterday. Bad workmanship, perhaps, sir?"

It was Peter who on another occasion wonderfully discomforted Whitfield in the only class that he taught. True, the headmaster from time to time took it upon himself as an expert in English literature to announce from the assembly platform that the morning's hymn was worthy of his dissection. Herbert was more than once opened up by Whitfield's version of textual analysis, though I don't think he ever gave classroom displays of these skills. Then, one year when I was in the sixth form, he undertook a series of classes in "Philosophy and Religion". These were built round twenty minute talks on the old BBC Home Service for Schools, which were broadcast during the middle of the morning. A large floor-model radio was brought in by one of the school caretakers and placed at the front of the class. Lo and behold, it transpired that he himself was a contributor to the series. Why, he had even written a book called *Philosophy and Religion*. Copies of this book were made available at each class, but Peter brought his own. He arrived with it under his arm in good time for one class and as Whitfield entered, Peter, sitting at the back of the class, raised his hand.

"Yes, West, what is it?"

"Sir, I was lucky enough to be able to buy a copy of your book in Twickenham yesterday afternoon. Would you mind signing it for me, Sir."

Whitfield, for once in his life smiling, but becomingly reluctant. "Very well, West. Bring it here."

Peter advanced to the front of the class, holding the book in front of him. Everyone could therefore see that on the front cover was stamped the legend REMAINDERED STOCK.

Whitfield encountered further difficulties when one morning he announced at school assembly that the hair of far too many of the boys was over-long. He proposed therefore to institute, class by class, a series of close inspections of heads, and woe betide any boy whose hair was deemed to exceed the regulation short back and sides. The following morning at least half the boys came to school sporting that appallingly brutalist, shaven-head style known as a crew-cut. It felt like a victory for wit.

Nevertheless, Whitfield managed to subdue and depress most of us. A new joylessness took over. He was helped in this by National Service. National Service had been set up at the end of the war. There was to be conscription of every fit and able eighteen-year old male into one or other of the armed services for an eighteen-month period. (Later raised to two years.) Attitudes to this tended to split along class lines. Working class boys didn't on the whole mind conscription. Many used their time in uniform to learn a trade, or, more usually, to profit from skills they had already acquired, some who were leaving home for the first time found themselves in exotic locations (Malta, Cyprus, Malaya), others

117

developed a taste for the services and signed on as regulars. As for the gentry and aristos, given that they'd been at public school where in all probability they had been recruited into the OTC, it was for them business as usual. Early morning waking, cold showers, bad food, and the chance to order inferiors about.

But for most middle class boys National Service was anathema. They dreaded the prospect and loathed the reality. Tales of the malign pointlessness of it all filtered down to us. The ridiculous demands for brass-buttons and leather-belts to be polished and re-polished and then polished once more, the requirement that blankets be folded with no overlap, the yelled, nonsensical orders from red-faced NCOs: to cut the grass with scissors, to paint lumps of coal white, to scrub floors with brushes that lacked bristles. There were punishments for infringement of rules that weren't even known to exist until it was said that you had offended — Jago could have taken the NCO correspondence course — including the dread order to run round the parade ground with your knapsack full of bricks, or stand to atten-tion for hours on end, or languish in the glass house, and always, but always, to discover that for some tiny misde-meanour you had been refused the days of leave to which you were entitled. Old lags recommended as a way of keeping out of trouble never to be seen in public without a bucket in hand. "That way you look as though you've got a job on." But buckets were in short supply.

Whitfield played on our fears. Boys could be threatened with expulsion from Hampton, and being booted out of the school meant that you couldn't take the A Levels without which you had no hope of going on to any form of higher education. Expelled boys would therefore have to make do with whatever work they could find while awaiting their call-up papers. Even those who passed A Levels and were accepted for university wouldn't be able to avoid National Service, but they could at least defer it. Moreover, they could expect a better time if, prior to conscription, they joined the Combined Cadet Force. Then, once they arrived at university, they would be fully mature, seasoned people. This, anyway, was Whitfield's claim. And he added that universities typically preferred would-be students to have completed their National Service before they were registered as undergraduates, and that some even insisted on it. All this was by way of making the CCF an essential part of life at Hampton.

You could join as soon as you were sixteen, and although joining was voluntary Whitfield let it be known that only those who volunteered were likely to become prefects or captains of any of the sports teams. It was also noticeable that a number of teachers who on days when the CCF was active squeezed themselves into old army and air force uniforms — the Senior Service didn't feature — became bullyingly brisk with those of us who refused to join. Whitfield didn't himself wear uniform, nor, we discovered, had he fought in the war, but he was soon extolling the virtues of service discipline. He also took it upon himself to read out letters purporting to come from boys who, having left school for their two years' conscripted service, couldn't wait to put pen to paper in order to tell him how pleased they were that they had done time in the CCF. "Dear Headmaster, I never realised until I came here how grateful I would be to school for giving me a taste of army life. It has stood me in good stead as knowing the ropes takes the pressure off one and gives one the chance to offer a helping hand to the less fortunate. The map-reading skills one obtained through CCF have proved especially useful." I suspect Whitfield wrote the letters himself. At all events, he never gave away the name of any correspondent — it was always "I have a letter here from a former pupil" — and I never came across a former Hamptonian who admitted to having written one.

Chapter 7
Jazz and Jane

One of the few teachers at Hampton I admired taught English. He did so without any noticeable enthusiasm although with a dry attentiveness. And he was good at mnemonics. From him I learnt how to remember who lined up against whom at the Battle of Philippi. BOAC. British Overseas Aircraft Company. Brutus facing Octavius, Antony facing Cassius. Useful for O Levels, which tells you something about O Levels. During the war, he himself had fought in the far east, where he was captured and tortured by the Japanese, and his tall, lanky figure was always shrouded in a black suit that hung off his bony frame. A keen cricketer, he liked to coach the first XI of which I was a member, but he never changed into his cricketing gear with us. Some time after I had left, I bumped into another teacher who, over a pint, told me why. "Scars all over his body," he said. "He didn't want anyone to see them."

He chain-smoked Kensitas, and although he never said a word about the CCF, I sometimes caught him glancing at boys in uniform as they strutted across the playground-cum-parade ground under the command of one of the dressed-up teachers, a look on his face from which a faint derision wasn't absent but which was mostly one of quizzical distaste. He spoke in an unemphatic monotone, whether he was talking to us about the "Lotus Eaters" or cricket. Of the opening of Tennyson's poem, he said, "It is held by some to be the equal of Keats at his most sensuous", though he declined to give us his own view of the matter. And once, when I was batting pretty well against Kingston Grammar School and he, as always, stood as umpire, he muttered to me as I stood at the non-striker's end, "we're going to lose this unless you stay in." A few minutes later, when I was four short of my half-century, he gave me out LBW. "Pity

120

about that," he said afterwards, as we brooded over our defeat. "Ball was probably going to miss leg stump, but I don't like to be accused of bias."

I admired him very much, and I have an especial reason to be grateful to him because it was he who took a group of us to see the film version of *Julius Caesar*, with John Gielgud as Cassius and Marlon Brando as Antony, a performance which, for all its faults, was powered by such smouldering energy I could almost ignore Gielgud's dreadful woodenness, epitomised by a moment when he was required suddenly to turn and the camera's unsparing scrutiny revealed the marionette-like lack of ease with which he moved. I suppose on stage his mellifluous voice over-rode his physical awkwardness, though I have to say that on the occasions I saw him act I found the voice an irritant: it seemed arbitrarily switched on and rarely if ever persuaded me that Gielgud had much understanding of whichever part he happened to be playing.

Our visit to *Julius Caesar* was the first time I experienced Shakespeare "live", as opposed to reading the words on the page, and when, soon afterwards I saw a TV performance of *The Merchant of Venice* and heard Lorenzo invite Jessica to "look how the floor of heaven/Is thick inlaid with patens of bright gold", the words hit me with the force of a sudden, violent blow. That is how it is when you are young. Wordsworth's image of his mind being "turned round" as with "the might of waters" comes as close as any words can to capturing this experience.

Not long before his death, Gael Turnbull, that lovely man and endlessly, joyously inventive poet, phoned me for a chat, as he did with all his friends, and during the course of our conversation he mentioned a recent essay of mine where I touched on my first experience of listening to jazz. This occurred not long before I saw *Julius Caesar*. More out of curiosity than interest I had gone along to a meeting at school of the after-hours "Rhythm Club" — presumably "jazz" was a term too outré to be permitted on the premises. There, I heard Dizzy Gillespie's "Cognac Blues" which, to repeat the words of a poem I wrote some years ago, went through me "like a needle of white light", a phrase which also seemed the best way to describe my later discovery of a poem by John Heath-Stubbs, "The Unpredicted". Gael and I agreed that such moments "seem to belong exclusively to youth", as I put it in a piece I wrote about Gael for the Scottish magazine, *Zed 20*. The essay appeared in 2007 and in its turn stirred my friend, the poet and painter, Huw Watkins, to rebuke me for my confident generalisation. Huw, who at the time of writing is 84, told me that a few years previously he and his wife had gone to a performance of Shostakovitch's Fifth Symphony at the De Montfort Hall, Leicester. It was the first time he'd heard the symphony, and, he said, "That night, still intensely moved by it, I got up from bed at one o'clock, pinned a sheet of paper to my fixed painting board and worked furiously... to try to capture in colour the *emotional* impact the music had made on me...[the painting] has been on display at the City Gallery, and then, with a few other paintings, ended up on show, in of all places, the De Montfort Hall. So, you see, not only young men are affected by that 'needle of white light'".

A lovely letter. And yet I still believe that nothing that happens in later life can equal the intensity of certain early experiences, ones that dazzle you with previously unguessed-at possibilities, that open roads you may travel by. They happened for me, as I'm sure they happen for most, in a bewildering rush. It's as though you're being invaded by blasts of energy that hit you far too suddenly for you to be able to withstand them. Early one morning in 1954, having cycled over to the Thames at Twickenham, I sat beside the river as it poured slowly to Richmond, looking across to the substantial eyot called Eel Pie Island. It was June, the sky was flawlessly, tenderly blue, smells of the previous night's fags and beer drifted across to me from the nearby "Barmy Arms", a pub which fronted onto the tow-path, and suddenly a great wave of emotion rushed through me, a flood of warmth from feet to the top of my head. I suppose the feeling was one of happiness, though I don't feel much inclined to give it a name.

* * *

That feeling must, however, have been in some part connected to my discovery of jazz. Not merely the music, but also the way of life it symbolised. "Everyone making love and going shares," Larkin writes with mock solemnity in "For Sidney Bechet." Yes, there was that. But, more important, the music cut through to deep emotions, joy mostly, but sometimes, too, a piercing sadness or melancholy, and though some of the people who played it and were its most ardent aficionados could, in their tight-lipped devotion to "authenticity" be irritating — those "scholars manqué" who nod around unnoticed, "wrapped up in personnels like old plaids", to quote Larkin again (the term "anorak" came later) — you could ignore them and get on with the drinking and the dancing. Jazz jive was easy enough to learn and it was so exuberant, especially when compared with the decorous and routine-dominated ballroom dancing alone permitted at school "hops" and outside social occasions, it's no wonder that those of us who became proficient at it scorned the other sort.

Opportunities for demonstrating our expertise were at first limited. But in other ways jazz was the new world wide open for exploration. I found my way, heaven knows how — and heaven knows how it came there — to a corner of the school library that housed the biography of Spike Hughes. Perhaps the name alerted me. In jazz argot "Spike" is a familiar soubriquet for a bass-player. A public school, Oxbridge educated man, Hughes had fallen in love with jazz in early manhood and during the inter-war period played professionally with various bands as well as accompanying a number of American jazzmen when they visited the UK. From his book I learned something about these luminaries. He had a special regard for the music of Duke Ellington and soon I was marvelling at such 78s as I could find of the Duke's Cotton Club days. A friend turned out to have a collection of jazz records and I would make regular trips to his house at Woking, where I'd spend hours listening to

Ellington, Billy Banks and his Rhythm, Muggsy Spanier, Jimmy Noone, Artie Shaw, Bessie Smith, Henry "Red" Allen, Jelly-Roll Morton, Fats Waller and, above all, Louis Armstrong. I took myself several times to the cinema to see *The Glenn Miller Story*, not so much for the sound of Miller's band as for the brief moment when Armstrong was featured, playing "Basin Street Blues". That was when starlight lit my lonesomeness.

I began to buy the *Melody Maker*, in those days devoted to dance music and jazz. I listened to radio whenever I thought jazz might be played. Not that this was a frequent occurrence, but as the *Radio Times* carried not merely information about which orchestra would be broadcasting on any hour of the day but the programme they would be playing, I could more or less know when to switch on for, say, the Squadronaires' version of "Sophisticated Lady" or Geraldo's "Caravan". And the early morning record request programme, "Housewives' Choice" invariably concluded with a Fats Waller number, either "My Very Good Friend, the Milkman" or "When Somebody Thinks You're Wonderful".

* * *

"You'd think *someone* would have taught me to play the piano," Randall Jarrell said fiercely, and to no-one in particular, on an occasion when he had been listening to Debussy. Jill had been sent to piano lessons which I think she didn't much enjoy. But such lessons were for girls alone. I doubt that it occurred to my parents to send me to them. I don't at all blame them for this. I imagine they felt that an ability to play a musical instrument was a skill that might recommend a girl to a future husband or in the event of prolonged spinsterhood enable her to teach what she had learnt. (In later years, when I was at work on the biography of the Sporting Gunns [the great Nottingham family], I was amazed to discover how many women in the period 1870-1930 listed their professional occupation in the national census as "piano tutor".) But my discovery of jazz brought with it a desperate desire to play the music I now loved. And

124

so, in the summer of 1953, after I had passed my O Levels, I bought my first trumpet, a cheap, second-hand, valve-clanking but usable instrument, from a shop in Hounslow, and, armed with a paperback "Trumpet Tutor", set about teaching myself to play. It is often said that skiffle was the first "do-it-yourself" music of the post-war period. Certainly skiffle was almost childishly easy to perform. Cheap guitars were easily come by and I can't imagine anyone took more than a week to master the invariable three-chord routines of most skiffle numbers. Once you'd done that, you persuaded a mate to set up on tea-chest bass (the tea-chest was inverted, a broom stick was propped at one corner and thick string or thin rope stretched from its top and secured to the corner opposite), you found another tyro guitarist, and you were away. There were several skiffle groups at Hampton, some of whom managed to secure gigs at local youth clubs and even as "interval bands" at dances, but those of us who chose to buy "proper" instruments took a dismissive view of such amateurish goings on. There were enough of us to be able to form two bands of contrasting styles. The Hamptonaires featured piano, guitar, saxophone, accordion and drums, and found work playing for dances in church halls and the back rooms of pubs. The VIKings — so called because we saw ourselves as the 6th form Kings of Swing (how wrong can you get) — comprised piano, drums, alto saxophone doubling clarinet, and trumpet. We, too, played for dances but we prided ourselves on having "in the book" a number of jazz standards, including the inevitable "Saints" with which we ended each gig.

Dress was another matter that separated us. The Hamptonaires had band uniforms. In fact, they had two sets. Black-and-white for formal occasions, and white jackets and black trousers for others. The jackets came from a "cast-off" shop and had originally been intended for waiters. We would have no truck with this. We sported check shirts and gabardines. These required some hunting down because in 1953/4 clothes of the kind we favoured were still far from easy to come by. But the Army and Navy Stores which sold what were styled "Canadian Lumberjack Shirts" of various check patterns, and duffle coats in sand-brown or the less popular grey or blue, supplied our needs. There was a good deal of making-do with grey flannel trousers and shirts, uniformly dull and often uncomfortably starchy; but colour wasn't absent.

Gabardines were a particular joy. I am speaking here exclusively of the trousers. (Gabardine as material for raincoats is a different and altogether staider matter.) These trousers came in a variety of colours of which the most popular were ice blue, lovat green, chocolate brown, and silver grey. And then there were the shoes. Early in the 1950s it became possible to buy what were called "Desert Boots", as worn, so legend had it, by soldiers in the Middle East. These had suede uppers and, for soles, a peculiar white rubbery material, and they were much favoured by art-school students. The alternative was a brogue with thick crepe soles which had to be treated with ox-blood polish in order to produce the desired colour, a kind of liverish dark red which looked good while it lasted, although unfortunately the polish soon transferred to socks and trouser turn-ups.

I had a pair of ice-grey gabardine trousers, ox-blood brogues — though I shortly switched to Desert Boots — a red-and-blue check shirt and a duffle coat. The dress code was inevitably a way of identifying yourself, your tastes, your dislikes. Most of us disliked Hooray Henries. Henries wore cavalry twill trousers, Austin Reed shirts and ties. Their partners were habitually garbed in twin-sets and pearl necklaces, and both male and female said "Gosh". A perfect foursome of Henries turn up in Karel Reisz's short documentary *Momma Don't Allow*, filmed at the Wood Green Jazz club in 1955 and featuring the Chris Barber band. The film's title comes from a stompy late-night number of that name in which each member of the band is featured ("we don't care what Momma don't allow/Gonna play that trumpet/banjo/trombone etc, any old how") seems to me easily the best of the documentaries that were being made at that time and which were intended to promote the work and chances of young British film directors. Other worthwhile documentaries of the period include *We Are the Lambeth Boys*, unfortunately marred by poor editing, and *Every Day Except Christmas*, a lovely film about Covent Garden when it was still a huge vegetable, fruit and flower market, which an infuriating voice-over commentary fails to wreck. All were in black and white so you can't see the colours of the Hoorays' outfits. But their shirts invariably had thin brown and orange markings and they wore woollen, mustard-coloured tie under sage green or brown sports coats with leather buttons and a double vent at the back called a bum-freezer. The females' twin sets would have been in green or burnt umber, and they wore dark-blue or grey pleated skirts. The Henries who appeared at jazz evenings turned their elbows out when they danced, and always, but always, asked the band if they knew a number called "The Saints". "No, sorry. Never heard of it."

They rarely, though, came to more conventional dances, or if they did, it was to dances where the VIKings weren't contracted to supply the music. We got the number three jobs: tennis clubs, Church "Hops", the occasional office "do", even the odd garden or birthday party. One of the incidental pleasures of being in the band was that you were in effect wallpaper, invisible. You supplied the music and nobody ever looked at you. You were therefore free to look at the dancers: to note momentary flirtations, developing romances, strained or breaking relationships, secret and possibly illicit tendresses. All the little signals which couples sent each other as they danced, looked into each others' eyes, wrapped their arms round each other or kept a demure or disdainful distance, and which they assumed were shared only with and by their partners, were witnessed by the four youths who were paid to play and who, as they played, watched.

There were those we liked, those we didn't. If you fell into the latter category you never won the Elimination Dance. This was a foxtrot for which two parallel lines were drawn in chalk across the floor. As dancing couples came to them the man had to lift his partner and carry her across the "river". Any couples caught in the "river" when the music stopped were eliminated. It always amazed me that as far as we could tell the dancers never suspected foul play, even though the band had made up its mind at the outset who was going to win: either a friend of the band or a woman to whom we'd taken a fancy. And losers included anyone we suspected of being a "boss", or who took himself too seriously as a dancer (readily identifiable because such people brought "pumps" — patent leather dancing shoes — into which they changed before the dancing began), or whom we marked down as a Tory, or without the slightest evidence took to be a supporter of either Arsenal or Chelsea.

The evenings followed more or less the same ritual no matter for whom or where we played. Quickstep, foxtrot and waltz would be interspersed with "novelty" dances: rumba or samba, which as far as any of us could tell were interchangeable (certainly the music was), Barn Dance, Dashing White Sergeant, Palais Glide, and finally the conga, a tedious but harmless bit of fun which signalled that the evening was coming to an end. Once the conga was over lights were lowered and we played the last waltz, usually Irving Berlin's "Always" ("I'll be loving you, always/With a love that's true, always...."). After which the National Anthem struggled into life, the lights came up, and we all went home.

As the VIKings became more proficient at playing for these dances, our repertoire increased, although it was never very extensive. On one early engagement we found ourselves having to play "Whispering" several times during the course of the evening. It featured as quickstep, foxtrot and, even, with time signature altered, as waltz. We got away with it, too. At all events, nobody complained. But we realised we'd have to do better. We bought the sheet music of some popular numbers of the day, among which I remember especially "All Dressed up in a Sky-Blue Shirt, And a Rainbow Tie" — quickstep, "Walking my Baby Back Home" — foxtrot, and "Cara Mia Mine" — waltz; we made rudimentary arrangements of standards; and gradually we learnt tunes that could be played to the novelty dances. "MacNamara's Band", "You Are the Honeysuckle, I am the Bee", "One Note Samba".

But our hearts weren't in it. We wanted to play jazz. At the end of one evening, after we had played the National Anthem and were packing away our instruments, a man came up to us. He was someone I vaguely recognised, a local businessman, I think, whom I'd seen in church. "I just want to tell you," he said, "that I think you are an absolute disgrace. To play the National Anthem sitting down, as you did, is to show such contempt for her Gracious Majesty that I intend to lodge a formal complaint with the Management." The management in question was the youth leader, who had invited us to play for his club's monthly dance and who had acted as amiable MC throughout the evening. Whether he was given an ear-wigging by that pompous ass I doubt, but for us it was a decisive moment. As I put it in a poem many years afterwards, "We knew jazz came from the wrong side of town;/We played the National Anthem sitting down."

Jazz for me was almost from the first linked to radical politics. It was the music of protest, of the oppressed, and it licensed a breaking free from those restraints that too much governed my parents' lives and the lives of others like them. So I thought, so we all thought, and this gave us a particular, heady motive to abandon commercial music. Such idealists we were.

* * *

But first, we had one more dance engagement to fulfil. The following Saturday we were booked to play at Hounslow Drill Hall. It was a new venue for us. As we were setting up, we noticed that the place was beginning to fill with Teds. Drape suits, frilled white shirts and bootlace ties, brothel-creeper shoes with deep, ridged soles for the men, and, for the women, similar shirts and ties or, alternatively, frilled white blouses, pencil-tight skirts, black stockings with

129

seams and/or decorations (butterflies, clocks), stiletto-heeled shoes. They stood around in clusters, smoking, not so much talking as nodding to each other. The mood didn't seem especially friendly. Then one of the males detached himself from the group he was with and came up to us.

"Who's the leader of this outfit?" he asked.

As I had got this particular booking, I indicated that I was.

"Know The Creep?"

"Yes," I said, "I know The Creep."

He nodded. "Give us The Creep, you'll be alright," he said, and went back to rejoin his group.

"The Creep" was a ridiculous number. 32 bars of slow, slurpy saxophone riff, it had been composed by Ken Mackintosh, whose big band was "resident" as the term went, at Wimbledon Palais. After the Ted Heath Band, the Mackintosh orchestra was probably the best band of its kind in the country, packed with excellent musicians and playing music that ranged from hits of the moment through standards to swing. Presumably its leader had dreamt up "The Creep" as a way of catering for the tastes of the local Teds. Even now I can remember the tune, can recall some of the words. "Caterpillars do it soft and slow... You shuffle in your shoe, a one and then a two. And that's the way you do The Creep." In fact you did The Creep, if you were the man, by being propelled backwards by your female partner, using waltz steps but going in a straight line from one end of the dance floor to the other, where you turned and shuffled back to the end from which you had started. There was no variation. Moreover, although the woman placed one hand at the back of her man's neck, the other, clamped in his, was held rigidly down, while his free hand rested at the base of her spine. Smiling and talking were not allowed. Each couple simply trod up and down the hall more or less in time to the rudimentary tune, the women chewing gum, the men as likely as not smoking. All in all, it was a devastating parody of "polite" dance hall mores.

Did we have the tune in our book? Of course not. But it was so simple that we knew we could busk it without difficulty.

And so we did. During that evening we probably played "The Creep" more often than we had played "Whispering" on that earlier, rather more fraught occasion. True to their word, the Teds caused us no bother, though from time to time scuffles would break out in far parts of the hall and once a chair was thrown in the general direction of a group who, unmoved by this, simply went on combing their hair, smoke drifting up from lips that seemed never to be without a cigarette.

Before we played the final set, I went over to the youth who had interrogated us while we were setting up. "Will you want a last waltz?" I asked.

"Just give us The Creep," he said.

"The Saints?"

"Balls to that. Just give us The Creep."

So we did.

* * *

At the end of that evening the VIKings Dance Band disbanded and thirty seconds later reformed as the Vikings Jazz Band. Bound for glory? No such luck. There were a number of reasons for this. In the first place, we had the wrong personnel. We lacked a bass player and a trombonist, thought to be essential to jazz bands, anyway those which played the music we preferred. On one or two of our gigs, we did have a stand-in bass. The school's music teacher, a dear man with wild blond hair and a hairy, ginger suit, whose passion was for Bach, lugged his string bass to where we were playing, and his ability, enthusiasm, and overall appearance were all godsends. He not only played driving and sometimes slap bass but he *looked* the part. And when it was discovered that he drove a clapped-out Morris (could the tyres have been patched with sticking-plaster?) he quite rightly became the star of the show.

But he didn't play on every job, far from it, and although we talked of advertising for a trombonist, we never did. I myself couldn't see the need for one, but the empty trombone "chair" undoubtedly lost us a number of gigs. Those were the days when jazz fans were self-styled purists, which meant that if you belonged in the "traditional" camp, as we more or less did, to turn up without a trombonist was positively sacrilegious. How, some purist would want to know, could we possibly play either "Tiger Rag" or "Ory's Creole Trombone"? If we replied that there were literally hundreds, probably thousands, of numbers that didn't require that particular front-line instrument, we'd be met with a dismissive curl of the lip. And if we added that some of the finest groups, like Jimmy Noone's, didn't use trombone, the purist would shake his head and turn away. We were clearly a lost cause. Which, though for a different reason, we were. We were now all studying for A Levels. It followed that our commitment to jazz began to tug against commitment to our studies. We all wanted to go on to university and none of us wanted to do National Service. Something had to give. I can't remember who was the first to blink, but gradually, if reluctantly, we decided that for a while, at least, we'd have to stop playing. Once A Levels were out of the way, we promised ourselves and each other, we'd re-form. I was especially keen to do so. I had a notion that at some future time I might become a professional jazz musician. I wouldn't call it a conviction but then again....

* * *

By the time the band called its last number I had acquired and lost a first girl friend.

She was called Jane Brown. She came into existence because one afternoon in the late spring of 1953 I wanted to go to the local cinema, the *Astoria*, to see a film which starred Dan Dailey and June Haver. It was made on the cheap, but I didn't mind. I craved the chance to gaze on June Haver from the one-and-nine pennies. "When June Haver sang 'Deep in the Heart of Texas/Love burnt bright deep in my solar plexus' as I put it in a poem called "Hollywood Nights". It did, too. For her, I would dress my best. And so, in my one and only sports coat, grey flannels, Fair Isle sleeveless sweater over white school shirt, I was leaving the

132

house when my mother said, "Where on earth are you going?"

"To the flea-pit," I said, knowing what was coming next and trying to get out of the door before it did. But I was too slow.

"And why are you dressed up like that?"

"I'm meeting a girl friend," I said. Which, in a way, was true. I don't know how many times I'd declared undying love for June Haver, and she hadn't once turned me down. It was simply that as yet she was unaware of my adoration. As to how she would get to know of it, well, I was working on that.

"What's her name?" my mother asked

And, in a flash of non-inspiration, I said "Jane Brown". ("Jane Brown I want you to meet John Smith.")

But that wasn't enough to end the questioning. "Where does she go to school?"

I could have said "She doesn't. She works in Woolworths." But I knew better than to risk the enquiries that would follow that revelation, beginning with "How did you meet?", and no doubt ending with "and what does her father do?" — implying that whatever it was it couldn't be a suitable occupation and certainly not one that could be mentioned on future social occasions which Jane Brown was to be expected as attending.

So "The Welsh Girls," I said. And with that I was off.

It didn't seem such a bad choice. The Welsh Girls School had been established in the 19th century as a boarding school for the daughters of Anglican vicars whose livings were in the Principality, although how Ashford became the chosen spot for it I've no idea. The school itself, at the far end of our town and near the station, was a long, grey stone, neo-Gothic building, and the daughters of several Ashford parishioners, including some I knew at least by name, went there as day girls.

But as it happened, I could hardly have chosen worse. During my absence my mother had scanned the local newspaper, *The Middlesex Chronicle*, and found there a fairly detailed report of the Welsh Girls' Annual Speech Day, which had occurred the previous week. The report concluded by printing the names of all girls who had won scholarly and sporting prizes, and then added further lists of all those who, not having won prizes, nevertheless deserved commendation for coming second or third or simply for taking part. Jane Brown had not only failed to win a single prize, she had apparently not even taken part. Nor had she been in the school play, she hadn't helped at charity events, sporting occasions had without exception passed her by, and as to scholarly attainments, she proved to be an unmentionable disaster. In short, only the most abject or gormless of boys would want her for a girlfriend. What struck me was less the unfairness of my mother's scorn for the sporting, artistic and scholarly incompetence of a girlfriend who, had she existed, would undoubtedly have shown herself to be a star in class, with paint brush, and on the running track, than the fact that among nearly two hundred girls *not a single one was called Jane Brown*. I scanned the lists of names my mother thrust at me. One girl was called Carmen Ruggiero, another rejoiced under the nomenclature of Hildegarde Swithin, a third admitted to being Jennifer Burkett-Seymour, and there was a wide-ranging supply of homelier, off-the-rack *prêt-a-porter* names, something to suit virtually every taste: Valerie Lee, Jenny Roberts, Kate Bourne, Pam Fricker, Diana Evans, even Susan Smith. But where was Jane Brown when you needed her? Absent without leave, that's where.

"She's been ill," I said.

My mother sniffed derisively. "Not too ill to take herself off to the cinema whenever she feels like it. Who paid?"

"We paid for ourselves," I said.

And with that she had to be content.

Not for long, though. In the following weeks Jane Brown's name was repeatedly brought up, often when I least expected it. So, for example, I once announced that I no longer wanted sugar in my tea. "I suppose that's the influence of your blessed girl friend," my mother said. On another occasion, after tea and as I was spreading my books out on the dining room table to begin an essay, she put her head round the door and said, "I was talking to Mrs Lee today."

Valerie Lee was my own age, a day girl at the Welsh Girls' School.

"Oh."

"She says Valerie has never mentioned Jane Brown."

"Well, why should she?"

"Didn't you say she was in Valerie's class?"

"No."

"Then which class is she in?"

"Don't know, I've never asked."

"A likely story," my mother said, shutting the door more firmly than usual behind her.

* * *

Soon after that the romance died. "Aren't you going to meet your girl friend?" my mother asked me one Saturday evening as I sat over a book. No, I said, we'd decided to end our relationship. "I hope you haven't hurt her feelings," my mother said. As this would have been impossible, I said merely that the decision had been mutual and got on with my book. I was reading Tawney's *The Acquisitive Society* which Bouncer had lent me in tandem with a collection of Orwell's essays, including his wondrous analysis of Boys' Comic Papers. Tawney and Orwell between them persuaded me that socialism not only had all the best arguments, it also produced the best polemicists, and before long, in late evening prowls about Ashford's deserted streets, smoking cigarettes which I'd bought from slot machines — Dunhill was the cigarette of choice — I began to consider whether I could combine the life of a jazz musician with political journalism. Paradise for a sect.

Chapter 8
Discovering Cool

Fears for and of the future were part of the mental atmosphere of the 1950s, to be breathed in as regularly as the smoke-hazed air of Ashford's wintry nights or the brighter blue of summer glimpsed through the town's asphalted, plane-tree avenues. In particular, fears of mass annihilation were, like the odour of death, discernible if unmentionable. I can't believe that anyone took much pleasure in the reports of a "successful" detonation of Britain's nuclear bomb inside HMS *Plym* in October, 1952, off the Australian mainland. It was hardly likely to reduce Britain's vulnerability to Russian nuclear attack. If anything, this proof of what nuclear bombs could do merely increased the sense of dread. And this will have been still further intensified when, a month after the British bomb went off, the Americans exploded on a south Pacific atoll a device which was apparently equivalent, so we were told, to "twice the amount of *all* the explosives used in the Second World War", and in the process vaporized the coral island of Elugelab, leaving a crater 200 feet deep and scorching trees and brush fourteen miles away. Very reassuring.

The only remark I can recall my mother making at that time which may have referred to her fears for the future was "it makes you wonder why we bothered." She uttered the words, intendedly to herself I think, as she glanced at the headline of the day's newspaper, but I have no memory of what that headline was. For all I know it might well have been about continued food shortages or the unavailability of motor cars for the home market, or any of a dozen or more things which between them indicated that victory over Germany and Japan had still not brought to most of the population much by way of material benefit. I can place the moment in so far as I was finishing my breakfast before having to go out into the cold, wet, wintry morning to catch the bus for Hampton; and her words seemed to concentrate and deepen the gloom I felt about my inability to master the previous evening's physics homework, a failure which I knew would invite the sarcasm of the teacher whose own failings as a transmitter of information and explanation, so I told myself, had made the subject virtually incomprehensible to me.

Not that my mother was an habitually gloomy person. But she undoubtedly saw the world as a frightening place. *Mutatis mutandis*, I could apply to her some words of that excellent poet Matt Simpson in his poem "Explaining Things": "My mother half-lived a half-sized life:/Not understanding, did what she bravely could." True, as the fifties advanced and my father's material prospects improved, my own mother at least became adept at spending money that previously she would have hoarded. And she relaxed in other ways, too. She went out rather more, to the theatre with my father (their fondness for musicals took them up to London to see, among other west-end shows, *Oklahoma, Annie Get Your Gun, Carousel, South Pacific, Kiss Me Kate*) and she found friends with whom to watch various films on show at the *Astoria*, though my father certainly accompanied her to showings of *The Third Man, The Blue Lamp* and *The Cruel Sea*. And with these same friends she instigated trips to "Royal Ascot". I think they did no more than watch from afar the comings and goings of royalty, people with titles, and those who made the fashion pages and gossip columns of the dailies, for various sightings were later discussed over coffee and home-baked cake in one kitchen or another.

Then there were the dinners. In the mid-50s, by now a city businessman, my father was increasingly required to attend semi-formal occasions at posh London hotels where he and other businessmen and their wives would wine, dine, dance and no doubt arrange business deals. I don't know whether my parents much enjoyed these events, which involved a good deal of dressing up and downing of rich fare. We'd be shown the menus they brought back with them, five or even six-course affairs, which seemed to Jill and me impossibly lavish. Some time later, when I first read *The Wild Duck* and came to the moment of Hedvig Ekdal's disappointment over her father's failure to bring home the detailed menu from a grand dinner at which he's been a guest, I thought of the menus that for a while knocked about our house: fake parchment affairs with the dishes written out in almost indecipherable curly italic script, each given a French title. In the mid 1980s, while Basil Haynes and I were at work on our biography of the Sporting Gunns, we discovered that even professional cricketers, poorly paid and peremptorily treated though they might customarily be, were, if on tour with the MCC, allowed to take their places at sumptuous banquets held in honour of the touring party of which they were part. The menu for the Melbourne Cricket Club dinner for the touring MCC side of 1901-2, for instance, featured among its seven courses *Sole d'Agneau à l'Anglaise, Punch a l'Impériade, Gelée Maçedoine au Vin de Champagne, Gâteau Helvian Garnier, Petite Soufflé au Fromage,* and *Crème de Vanille.* These menus would be passed among the diners and signed by all present to be framed and displayed on wall and mantelpiece, though heaven only knows whether the food was as grand as the names it went under, let alone what such names could have meant to players (not the Gentlemen) who at home subsisted on a diet of meat and two veg. For a while, similar menus — unframed — were propped on the mantelpiece of our front room.

So were invitations to Masonic Balls. Shortly after his career in the timber trade began, my father was persuaded to become a Freemason, membership of which was thought to be terribly good for business. He took his induction seriously and was for a while punctilious in attending lodge events. He even went so far as to purchase an item of headgear about which I wrote in my poem "The Death of the Hat", where I recall how he "hurried indoors a round, posh-leather box",

> which, undone, free clouds of tissue paper
> and so disclosed to our astonished gaze
> a vast black cabochon. My mother

bit her lip, hard, as the bowler
wobbled on his usually level head.
Next day the Drama Club gained one more prop.

"Next day" may be poetic licence, but the bowler hat was
never worn and before long found its way into the Ashford
Parish Players' prop cupboard. His feverous ardour for the
Masons soon abated, although during the time he went to
meetings he was sometimes called on to make speeches
which he asked me to write. They were well received, so he
told me, partly because of the jokes they included — most of
which I'd picked up from school — and partly because of the
occasional quotation from Shakespeare, introduced with
some such formulation as "Shakespeare does well to remind
us...", which, given that to the best of my knowledge my
father had never once seen, let alone read a Shakespeare
play, he must surely have found difficulty in delivering
straight faced. No doubt the actor in him helped to keep his
voice steady. At all events, he paid me well for every speech
I wrote.

* * *

I refused, though, to help him with a speech he was asked to
give to the local Conservative fête in the summer of 1954.
This was not long after someone on the government benches
had queried whether The Goon Show might not be a secretly
subversive programme.

By then I had become friendly with someone in my year at
school who, although he lived round the corner in Ashford
and sometimes caught the same bus to Hampton, more often
cycled the six miles there and back, so that I'd not in earlier
years had much to do with Laurie Fincham. One day I volunteered to try for a place in the newly-formed school tennis
team. Laurie also turned up, which surprised me because I'd
heard rumours that he was even more hostile to the school
than I was, as well as being a determined non-joiner of
sports, social activities, and the dreaded CCF. As soon as he
began to play, he showed himself to be a highly skilled

performer. Afterwards, he suggested to me I might like to join the lawn-tennis club at Ashford of which he was a member, and so the following week I went along and was registered.

It might not have happened. Lawn tennis was after all a bit vicarage tea-party for someone keen to display his newly found radical credentials. The very fact that tennis clubs were identified with suburbia's ways, as indeed they had been since their inception at the end of the 19th c., counted against them. But for those of us with rebellious instincts tennis became acceptable with the sudden rise to sporting pre-eminence of two young Australians, Lew Hoad and Ken Rosewall, who were still under twenty when they began to smash their way through the Wimbledon rankings. So, at least, we could tell ourselves. Besides, there was an undeniable sexiness about tennis. "What strenuous singles we played after tea." Or more often in our case, games of mixed doubles. Warm summer evenings, the allure of deepening twilight, and the erotic enchantment of brushing against a girl's bare arm as she and I ran for the same ball. I could never understand why this didn't count for more with tennis-playing poets, of whom I don't think Betjeman was one. He merely fantasised. It may be implicit in some of William Scammell's poems but Donald Davie mewls over its absence from his life when he comes upon the courts "Where children of the local magnates played", and as for Theodore Roethke, for several years tennis coach at a posh American women's college, and Randall Jarrell, whom I imagine to have played with the elegant ferocity of his compatriot, Budge Patty, I don't think they wrote about tennis at all.

It wasn't only tennis that brought us together. There was also jazz. Not that Laurie shared my passion for the roots of the music. He was a modernist, a keen admirer of the Modern Jazz Quartet, always known as the MJQ, of Dave Brubeck, of Stan Kenton, or anyway such sidesmen as Zoot Sims and Lee Konitz, and he also worshipped Charlie Parker and West Coast cool. He was learning to play bass, would take his instrument by bus and train to lessons from

140

professionals, among whom in later years was Red Mitchell, and was himself an exemplar of cool.

From this distance it's difficult if not impossible to summon up those images of cool that distinguished followers of modern jazz in the mid-1950s. Crew cuts and button-down shirts were *de rigueur*, dark glasses and berets useful aids. Gerry Mulligan's piano-less quartet, the leader's baritone sax playing off against the lyrical melancholy of Chet Baker's trumpet, epitomised the sound I thought of as somehow chastened into still, almost marmoreal calm. I heard Mulligan's music a good deal at that time because the school tuck shop, open at break and lunch hour, was managed by a boy called Barry Cripps, who brought his wind-up to school with him, and who regularly played Mulligan 78s: "Walking Shoes", "I'll Remember April", "My Funny Valentine", and others. Barry contrived to narrow his school tie so that it looked like one of the Italian ties the Mulligan combo favoured and when he smiled, which was seldom, there was a grudging, down-turned, sardonic edge to it.

As for his neatly-trimmed dark hair, it was said to have been cut by Reg Pountney, a name to be reckoned with because Pountney's Hounslow salon was advertised on the District and Piccadilly Lines. Barry's hair was fashioned in the DA style "as worn by Tony Curtis", so the adverts said. DA stood for "District Attorney" though it was more familiar to us under the soubriquet of "duck's arse". This made visual sense, given that the style required the hair on each side of the head to be somehow combed round to the back, where the "wings" met above the nape of the neck. Men and youths who adopted the DA were forever taking a comb from their breast pocket in order to draw it vertically down the backs of their heads, intent on keeping the wings apart, and they would do this, quite unconsciously it seemed, while walking along a street or, of course, in class. Others spent time fussing over their quiff, a curl crimped and trained to lean stiffly over the forehead like a Hokusai wavelet, though again Tony Curtis was the aimed-for model.

Hairstyling was by now becoming far more than a matter of short-back-and-sides. Most hairdressers, to be sure, could offer little else, a limitation to be accounted for by the fact that the majority had learnt their trade in the armed services. This was certainly true of the barber I went to in Ashford. Known to habitués as Uncle Joe, he had recently retired from long years of cutting squaddies' hair. His technique was simple and unvarying. Having scissored off what he could locate on the top of your head, he then got to work running clippers up and down each side until you were left with little but bristles starting out of raw, pink flesh. And as the flesh was minutely beaded with blood from pimples through which the clippers had ploughed their way, by the time his ministrations came to an end you looked as though your head had been newly plucked and ought really to be hung in a butcher's shop. When in 1976 I was helping to curate at Nottingham University an exhibition by the artist, James Boswell, I studied several sketch-books he had filled with drawings of army life during the Second World War. Savage caricatures for the most part, a number of them showed men hunching in a barber's chair, wrapped in a sort of winding sheet as their heads were shaved into approximately bald lumps by fellow soldiers, Uncle Joes, all of them.

But in the mid-1950s a new class of barber began to emerge. Hair stylists, they called themselves. Reg Pountney was king of the stylists for men, while young women I knew swore by "Mr Teasy-Weasy", otherwise known as Raymond, although I've no idea what his actual name was. I do, however, recall that on some Christmas-time TV show he went through his routine of "styling" the hair of a young woman who was supposedly going to a ball as Cinderella. After what seemed an eternity of teasing and weasing, she was pronounced ready, a carriage drawn by two horses appeared, one of which promptly raised its tail and deposited a mound of horse-shit on stage, while Cinderella, gathering her skirts gamely about her, clambered aboard. "And there she goes," Raymonde said, as the carriage lurched away, "off to the ball and looking absolutely ravenous."

Laurie was cool, not so much in dress — even at weekends he seldom wore anything other than school blazer and grey flannels and his hair was regulation short-back-and-sides — but in his manner. Light grey-blue eyes glinted behind spectacles, their gleam the only sign of a wit that was otherwise perfectly concealed by a chiselled mouth that rarely relaxed into a smile, let alone laughter. In fact, for the most part his face was immobile, Buster Keaton-like, his gaze inscrutable. He was, though, an acute observer. Like me, he had his hair cut at Uncle Joe's, and he always insisted on going on Friday afternoons. Why choose the busiest time of the week? Because, he explained, that way you could find out which men who went there planned on sex for the weekend. Hadn't I noticed that below the wall mirror facing the barber's chair, Uncle Joe kept a large cardboard box into which he sometimes dipped a hand when a customer was paying him, and that money and whatever he'd withdrawn from the box were then swiftly and silently exchanged. Not really, I admitted. Then I should have, and Laurie knew, although he didn't say how, that the box contained packets of contraceptives. "Something for the weekend, sir?" he said, in passable imitation of Uncle Joe's rasp, canting over and whispering in my ear. I'd sometimes heard the words, but never guessed their meaning. Well, well. Of course, most of the men to whom Joe put the question were married, and though it at first seemed odd if not downright improbable to imagine them actually having sex with the starchy, unappetising wives you saw accompanying them to church or walking along the public highway, watching Joe smuggle into their hands a small packet from his box, as under Laurie's tutelage I now did, had a certain interest.

But it turned out that it wasn't these men whose needs Laurie monitored. He was as near as he ever came to being delighted when, late one Friday afternoon, a local schoolmaster, who was also a lay-preacher, accepted a packet from Uncle Joe. The man was unmarried, although there was a "lady friend" as my parents called her, another schoolteacher, whose stupendously bony ankles seemed to click as

143

she strode about town on highly polished court shoes. She had an unyielding, distant, unapproachable look. But now we knew better, as we did in the case of the man who ran an electrical goods shop in the high street, another regular church-goer, and a widower, who, so Laurie reported, was spotted accepting one of Uncle Joe's packets. "Must have a woman somewhere," Laurie said. A few weeks later the man ran off with the wife of a local bank manager, himself a tall, droopy figure who continued to have his hair cut at Uncle Joe's as he continued to show up at church, until one Sunday evening he went absent and the next day staggered into the bank drunkenly weeping and had to be taken to a mental hospital.

* * *

Laurie had a girl friend. At least I think he did, though as with most things to do with Laurie you could never be sure. There were several attractive girls at the tennis club, most of whom were or had been at the Welsh Girls' School, and among them was Kate Bourn. She was almost heart-meltingly beautiful, blonde, blue-eyed, with an oval face, peaches-and-cream complexion, slim, lithe, and she was obviously deeply attracted to Laurie. Was he to her? Together they went to the pictures and Laurie was often at her parents' house. Her father, a genial, somehow absent-minded man was rumoured to be a research scientist, and the Bournes lived in a detached house with a straggling garden large enough to allow space for an impromptu tennis court where from time to time some of us played. Donald Davie's poem "The Garden Party" mourns the social disadvantage of not being one of the "children of the local magnates" who, alone in the speaker's Black Country, could afford to play tennis. "Theirs was all the youth I might have had", the poem whimpers at its close. But none of us was the child of such parents, none had the "monied ease" whose absence from his own life the poem's protagonist whinge-ingly laments. The Bournes were, as the phrase goes,

144

"comfortably off", but they certainly didn't keep themselves apart from the rest. Good with his hands, Laurie made frames for the pictures Kate was beginning to paint in a small, tumble-down, back-of-the-house shed she called her studio. That apart, he never gave anything away about the nature of their relationship.

But soon after I'd joined the tennis club he suggested we go together to a concert at the Welsh Girls' School. Kate would be singing, he told me, as would other girls I was getting to know. The "concert" turned out to be Speech Day, an event I associated with the depths of winter, because that was when Hampton's occurred. The afternoon was warm, heady smells of fresh-cut grass drifted through the wide-open windows, and after the handing out of prizes and awards, and a speech from the headmistress which I remember included the claim that "At this school we train our girls not to be scholars but to be young ladies", the choir sang. What they sang is gone from mind, but I have the most vivid recollection of how they looked, of honeyed sunlight that poured through the high-arched embrasures and gave the girls a radiance all their own, and of Kate among and yet somehow apart from the rest, her face ardent with delight as she sang. It's an image of youthful beauty that haunts me to this day. But if Laurie felt anything of that, he gave no sign. "Well, it's one way to waste an afternoon," was all he said.

Chapter 9
Soho Etc.

Because Laurie wasn't interested in traditional jazz, I relied on another friend to talk to about the music that so thrilled me. Peter West was a classmate whose major interest — obsession might be the better word — was art. Dissatisfied by the poor teaching he got at Hampton, he had started going to Saturday morning life-classes at Ealing College of Art, where he was soon drawing with what seemed to me great dexterity and wit. He showed me notebook after notebook filled with pen-and-ink drawings of the nude model whom the college employed for these life classes and with whom he occasionally went for a drink when the session was over. She was, I learnt, herself an artist who modelled to get some extra, much needed cash, and — "this should interest you" — she lived somewhere in Clapham with a professional jazz musician. Who? "Can't remember his name," Pete said, "but he plays bass with several bands, so Sue tells me." I asked him to get the name from her and he said he would, but when he next went to Ealing Sue had gone, to be replaced by another, older model. So I never did find out the name of the bass player.

Perhaps by way of making amends, Pete suggested that we take a trip to London one Saturday. He wanted to look around various art galleries and thought I might like to go with him. "And we can see if there's any live jazz on."

At midday of the appointed Saturday Pete and I met at Waterloo. From there he took control. I was marched over Hungerford Bridge, up Villiers Street, across the Strand, through Trafalgar Square and into St Martin's Lane, where we passed a large, glass fronted and handsome pub called the Salisbury Arms — "interesting place", Pete said airily, "but not what I want to show you" — veered onto the

Charing Cross Road — "there's a good coffee bar near here, called Bunjy's, we might drop in later" — across the head of Shaftsbury Avenue, sharp left into Old Compton Street, then, some way down, left again, where we entered what seemed to be a narrow one room public house, jammed with men and women. "This," Pete said offhandedly as he paused before shouldering his way through to the bar, "is called The French Pub."

I waited by a window until he came back with drinks. A half-pint of beer for me, for him, a double whisky. "They only serve beer in halves," he said, "and I wasn't sure you'd want anything stronger." I took a sip and glanced about me at the bohemian-looking crew who thronged the small space, among them a florid-faced man with handle-bar moustache at whose sallies those able to hear him were laughing. "Gaston Belmont," Pete said, "it's his watering hole. That's why it's called The French Pub. Although I've heard he's Belgian." He spoke casually, as though he was a regular.

How on earth did he know about it? How, come to that, did he move so easily about this area of London, as though he was an habitué. Perhaps he was. But if so, how come? My comparatively few previous visits to the capital city had mostly been on school trips or with parents. Sightseeing tours to the Tower of London, Buckingham Palace, the Houses of Parliament .... But Pete seemed entirely at ease with an area of the city I knew only as legend, and which was mentioned at home, if at all, in whispers. Because I sensed that I was now in Soho. The famous square mile: home of vice: of criminals, prostitutes, night clubs, of foreign restaurants and drinking dens, including, it appeared, the bar where we now stood clutching our glasses. But then, wasn't this the kind of atmosphere which jazz musicians ought to breathe? From the *Melody Maker* I knew that Denmark Street was where musicians met to exchange talk and tout for gigs. I had no idea exactly where Denmark Street was, but I knew it was in Soho. I began to relax.

And then, quite suddenly, to feel an uprush of pure elation. It wasn't the drink that did it. Though still some six

147

months short of my eighteenth birthday, I was fairly used to going into pubs. In my Everyman *Selected Johnson* I had come across the great man's remark that "A tavern seat is the throne of felicity" and was beginning to share his opinion. The mere smell of hops drifting from a pub door signalled the promise of earthly delights. There were the back or upstairs rooms of pubs where the VIKings had gigs, there were pubs into which I had been taken after the cricket XI had played away games versus local club teams, and there was one Ashford pub in particular where the land-lord was known never to question your age and where, as a result, several of the younger members of the tennis club would congregate and, while the girls mostly settled for Babycham or fruit juice, the boys ordered half-pints or even pints of beer, Fullers in this instance, although Watneys and Manns were the dominant breweries of the neighbourhood.

So, no, it wasn't the beer. It was the fact of being *here*, in this place, in a bar which, as I began to look around me was, I saw, packed with the kind of people who, for all I knew, were writers, artists, musicians, actors, all talking loudly, their faces, some bearded, many of them hinting at ravage or hard living, blurred by thick veils of cigarette smoke, their clothes worn with a kind of casual — or was it deliberate? — indifference to the proprieties I took for granted. The general impression was of louche grubbiness: men in out-at-elbow jackets, pullovers holed and stained, shirts with buttons missing and ties askew, one or two of them sweating in army or camel-hair overcoats; women for the most part of an indeterminate age, their faces either garishly painted or without any make-up at all, some looking as though their rats'-tail hair was never washed, others sporting berets or, in one case, a man's cap, sweatered and trousered. A couple of the younger ones were encased in black-beaded ball gowns, suggesting that they had come from or were on their way to a party. "Darling heart," I overhead one of these say to a man in a dark-blue roll neck sweater who was leaning over her and whispering in her ear, "do fuck off, there's an angel." He laughed and moved away and as he did so she glanced in my direction, then, with a slight smile on her dark-red lips, raised an eyebrow, shrugged, and turned back to her companion. "Sorry about that," the shrug said, "but what's a girl to do."

I looked at Pete to see whether he had registered any of this, but he was staring non-committally into his now empty glass. "A refill?" I asked, and, no doubt mindful of the fact that he was older than me and "legal", he said, "I'll get them. You pay, of course." He took my glass and as I watched him head back to the bar it came to me that although he greeted nobody in the pub he seemed to belong naturally to its ambience. I was wearing my duffle-coat, under which was a grey polo-neck sweater and grey trousers. I had thought that in this outfit I could pass muster as — well, as an art student or at least as someone who was beyond schooldays. But now I felt acutely self-conscious, out-of-place, at least until the young woman's smile and shrug suggested that I might not be such a gawk. Pete, on the other hand, wore a suit that looked at once new and old. It was tweedily grey, its pockets fat with papers and a sketchpad, and round his neck he had draped a red, ravelled, knitted-wool scarf, which emphasised his face's pallor and the rope of black hair that fell over his forehead. An inch or two shorter than me, a difference in height increased by his slight stoop which had become more pronounced as soon as we'd entered the pub, he nevertheless looked both bigger and broader. He was a second-row forward in the school's first XV, and on the field his Welshness came out in the ferocity with which he chased and tackled opponents. He had played Hotspur in a school production of *Henry IV Part I* with a similar ferocity.

"The curse of my blood," he said once, grinning sardonically, when I asked him whether he enjoyed playing rugger. "My dad brought me up to it." This was as much as he ever told me about his family circumstance. The rest was speculation and rumour. According to one such rumour he lived alone with his mother. His father, who was either dead or had left the family home, so the same rumour ran, had worked on the railways and was an important union official.

149

This would help to explain Pete's politics, his commitment to socialism — he seemed to know the Communist Manifesto by heart — and his contempt for Hampton, where he was, so he said, "immured", although the school was otherwise useful in that it enabled him to identify the enemy which in later life he would have to fight. As to his art, someone claimed that in homage to one of his heroes, Soutine, he had on one occasion bought a large leg of lamb and hung it in his bedroom window in order to paint its successive stages of decay. After some weeks neighbours complained about the bad smell and his mother made him throw it out. I wasn't sure I believed this, but as I accompanied him from gallery to gallery that Saturday afternoon the certainty grew that Pete knew his way around London as none other of his schoolmates did and that there was an aplomb in the manner with which he commented on various pictures we stood in front of which was both enviable and deeply impressive, the more so as he certainly wasn't trying to impress me. He was quite simply engrossed in *looking*. It came to me then that he'd suggested I go with him because he sensed in me someone who, like him, chafed against the intellectual limitations which Hampton by and large not only fostered but in which it seemed to rejoice. So, at least I told myself, and for that solicitude I was grateful, although gratitude is a word too weak to account for what happened towards the end of that afternoon.

We had gone into Roland, Browse and Delbanco, where Pete wanted to see some drawings of Welsh miners by an artist he especially admired. The artist's name was Josef Herman and Pete told me that Herman was an escapee from Hitler who had first settled in Glasgow and who now lived and worked in South Wales. The name meant nothing to me; the drawings did. They reminded me a little of Millet, at least in the anonymity of the miners' faces, Herman's refusal to provide any detail for them. Heads were mostly turned away or bent to the ground. But the manner in which shoulders slanted, the firm grasp on pit prop or pickaxe, the curve of thigh or arm visible through thick, shapeless clothes, told

150

you all you needed to know about the men, their stoical acceptance of work, and although the viewpoint from which they were seen didn't sentimentally heroise them, it did, insistently, require that you attend to them. The men dominated in all the drawings; there was nothing to distract the eye from concentrating on what they inescapably *were*.

The impact of Herman's drawings on me was immediate, powerful, and lasting. Nearly twenty years later, when in 1975 he published his *Related Twilights: Notes from an Artist's Diary*, I came to know something of Herman's life. He had been born in Warsaw, in the Yiddish-speaking quarter where he began to discover himself as an artist but where he was increasingly harried by the state, partly because of his opposition to fascism, also because of his Jewishness. "Anti-Semitism was part of State policies...." As a result, "for well over a year I never slept twice under the same roof". In 1938 he left Poland for Brussels, and then, two years later, when Belgium became over-dangerous, he managed to get across the Channel where he fetched up in Glasgow. He stayed there for three years, then moved on to London, and then, in 1944, took himself off to a Welsh mining valley, Ystradgynlais, where he stayed for 11 years. "Every artist knows when he experiences something new, something he has never experienced before," Herman writes in *Related Twilights*. "What he may not know is the effect the experience may have on his life, or how it may shape the course of his destiny." And then, in italics: *"This image of the miners on the bridge against the glowing sky mystified me for years with its mixture of sadness and grandeur, and it became the source of my work for years to come."* Of course I knew nothing about any of this when I found myself transfixed by Herman's drawings and sketches on that late autumn afternoon of 1954, though I must have sensed the strength of his response to the "sadness and grandeur" of which he writes in *Related Twilights*. But the experience of looking at those drawings was certainly to have a decisive effect on my own life.

As we left the gallery we were approached by a short, stocky, hirsute man standing on the pavement, looking a bit like a genteel tramp, although the bundle he carried under his arm wasn't of clothes, but magazines. Somehow he managed to force a copy into my hands, intimating as he did so that I must surely want to buy it. I was about to hand the magazine back when I found myself staring at the cover image. A miner in pit helmet and boots, head and shoulders bent in concentration, was in the act of fixing a long wooden stake into a hole in the ground, watched attentively by a small dog. The dog's back was to the viewer but it was plainly part of the man's life, shared in his workaday world. I was looking at a drawing by Josef Herman. The coincidence was uncanny. I paid my shilling and walked away clutching my first copy of *Stand*.

Before I could do more than glance at the contents, Pete suggested we go for a coffee and sandwich to Bunjy's, the place he'd mentioned as we swung towards Soho. We sauntered back to the Charing Cross Road, where Pete ducked into a double-fronted art shop called Zwemmer's. Here, he spent perhaps half-an-hour trawling the stacked shelves and tables, noting in the back of his sketchpad the names of authors and publishers of any number of monographs and period studies because, he explained, he could then order them through his local library. Finally, having bought a handful of postcard reproductions of paintings by Van Gogh and Cezanne, he said "Right. Coffee." And out we went.

Bunjy's was in the basement of a building just round the corner. To get to it you had to corkscrew your way down a steep, twisting staircase on the walls of which were hung a half-dozen small paintings, thickly layered, the pigment looking as though it had been laid on with a trowel or fingers or even squirted direct from the tube, the wet, vegetable smell so vivid I imagined that the paintings had been completed and hung that very day. "Auerbach," Pete said, as he led the way downstairs. "Good artist. Takes a lot from Bomberg." How on earth, I have often wondered since, did he know that the paintings, which for all I could see bore no recognisable signature, were by the artist he named, a name which, like Herman, meant nothing to me? And how did he know about Bomberg? After all, Bomberg, who died in poverty in 1957, was, I later discovered, entirely neglected at the time of his death. I wish now, as I so often find myself wishing, that I had questioned Pete about his knowledge of these and a host of other matters. I must have been so dazed by the easy certainty with which he threaded his way about parts of London of which I knew nothing and which were made the more mysterious by their boarded-up bomb sites, by streets of gapped vistas where buildings had been flattened or survived as roofless walls buttressed by timber props, that I thought of him as part of the mystery, to be accepted rather than questioned, not to be included in the dull catalogue of common things.

The coffee bar, which was really no more than a small, square cellar, was divided by brick pillars into sections, barely large enough to take a couple of tables and chairs. Groups of men and women, most of them student age, sat hunched in discussion in front of glass cups of coffee. Pete greeted one or two, then, after we'd got our coffees from a gleaming, hissing machine and he had chosen for us each a liverwurst sandwich on granary bread, he steered us to a vacant table. "St Martin's art students come here," he said, nodding in the direction of the occupied tables. "They'll know which jazz gig is worth going to." And with that he stood and loped over to one of the groups. "There's a choice," he said when he returned. "Cy Laurie's on at Windmill Street, just down from here, although you have to queue to get in and it's pricey. Or there's a dance at the college, even nearer. Eric Silk and his Southern Jazz Band. Never heard of them but I might try that. Fancy it?"

But I was more or less out of funds. "I need to get home," I said.

Half an hour later, when I emerged into the evening air — Pete had chosen to stay behind — I bumped into a man who was in the act of propping his bicycle against a gas-lamp just outside the entrance to Bunjy's. I watched as, with the aid of a long pole, he reached up and drew down a metal chain that hung from the gas mantle. There was a flutter of blue flame and then a soft light began to expand and glow. The man, who was wearing a dark polo-necked sweater under his baggy sports coat, stared up at the now fully-lit lamp for a few moments, nodded in satisfaction, then, holding the pole vertically like a church-warden's wand, reached for his bike, and I saw that he was not much older than me. A student, or perhaps an artist needing the money from lamp-lighting to help pay the rent on his studio? He seemed an agreeable element in the mystery of my suddenly expanding world.

Soon I was on the southern electric train heading for Ashford, fifteen miles and a world away from where I had spent the afternoon. I took the copy of *Stand* from the duffle-coat pocket where I'd thrust it, opened the magazine and began to flick through. Poems by Thomas Blackburn, James Reeves, Emmanuel Litvinoff, and, in a translation made by Stanley Chapman, Jacques Prevert's "Whale Hunt". If any of them made an impression, I can't recall what it was. Then I came across this.

> The goddess Fortune be praised (on her toothed wheel
> I have been mincemeat these several years)
> Last night, for a whole night, the unpredictable
> Lay in my arms, in a tender and unquiet rest —
> (I perceived the irrelevance of my former tears) —
> Lay, and at dawn departed. I rose and walked the streets
> Where a Whitsuntide wind blew fresh, and blackbirds
> Incontestably sang, and the people were beautiful.

The author's name was given as John Heath-Stubbs, although I may have decided that he was translating from some foreign language. Not that I cared. I read the poem again, then once more, and by the time I stepped off the train I had it by heart, as I still do. Why it made such an impact I can't be sure. My friend the poet Helena Nelson has suggested that the lines "Last night, for a whole night, the unpredictable/ Lay in my arms in a tender and unquiet rest" are especially likely to appeal to a lover of jazz, that the "tender and unquiet rest" captures something about both the music and poetry. There is a restlessness there, a beautiful abstraction, a moment of falling in love — and of course a sense of delighted surprise. She may be right, although "delighted surprise" hardly does justice to the emotion I then felt, which was one of dazzled, breathless exultation. And I do recall that the word "Incontestably", waiting round the line-ending as a kind of emanation, lanced through me as powerfully as the sound of Louis Armstrong's trumpet.

Coming at the end of a day of revelations, I may have over-reacted to Heath-Stubbs' poem. I don't know. I've never really wanted to know. It's enough that the poem flicked a switch that changed me. In a sestina of the 1980s recalling my discovery of jazz as a fourth-former, I wrote "Love found me out in a bare-bulb classroom." (Which was where meetings of the after-school Rhythm Club were held.) Poetry found me out on a southern electric train. Love again. Of course, I'd had to read poems at school, but I'd not found the experience in any way exciting, let alone revelatory. For O Levels we studied "Michael" and "The Lotus Eaters", and though I quite liked the dramatic opening of Tennyson's poem, "'Courage', he said, and pointed toward the land," and enjoyed its descriptive opulence, especially of the streams which "through wavering lights and shadows broke,/Rolling a slumberous sheet of foam below", (you could have a good deal of fun in class with those long "os"), Wordsworth's poem, which I now think of as one of the great poems of the language, seemed prissily dull, even silly. It wanted us to believe that young men shouldn't go to the city where they were sure to be corrupted. They should remain at home, content to work for their fathers. But I *wanted* to be introduced to what Wordsworth called "the dissolute city", I *wanted* to hear more about those "evil courses" to which Luke gave himself. Nor was I alone. To give "Michael" to teenagers is asking for trouble. We proposed a class trip to London in order to look out for evil courses, and when this was turned down we fell back on Twickenham or, as a truly evil course, a visit to Kempton Park.

The experts on the London Examining Board who came up with those poems for O Level students excelled themselves for A Level. Book One of the *Fairie Queene*, Masefield's *Reynard the Fox* (quite jolly if truth be told and

155

decently anti-fox hunting, but not especially alluring), Housman's *Shropshire Lad* (which seemed unbelievably lugubrious) and, by some happy mistake, the first two books of *Paradise Lost*, although the discovery of Milton had to wait until we began life in the upper sixth. True, there was Shakespeare, but he seemed to me in a special category, a world of his own. If Spenser represented poetry, as we were assured he did, then Shakespeare wasn't a poet. Unfair to Spenser, of course, as I would later discover when I read "Epithalamium", but in 1954 all I had to go on was what seemed then, as it still does, the unending, remorseless tedium of *The Fairie Queene*.

But my reading of "The Unpredicted" changed everything. Looking back, I realise that I must have been ready for it to do its work, and that my reaction to the poem was the culmination of much I couldn't have predicted about that Saturday, a day that had *licensed* me to be interested in, take for granted a right to care about art, literature, non-prudential living: things that the suburbia in which I grew up sneered at or giggled over or shuddered away from. Of course, these responses belonged to or were acquired by people terrified of over-stepping the line drawn for them, so they must have felt, by circumstances about which they could do nothing. The result was that they conspired in their own abjectness.

But I was over that line now, and I was never going back. Within days I had found in the Staines branch of W.H. Smiths a copy of the Everyman *English Poetry, 1900-1942*, edited by Richard Church and Mildred Bozman. Soon, I was buying other such anthologies: the Penguin Centuries' Poetry, and, in the same series, selections of individual poets, including D.H. Lawrence and C. Day-Lewis, all of them in beautifully designed buff covers with leafy, fern-green borders. There were the stiff-backed green or blue-jacketed Everymans. (*Minor Poets of the Seventeenth Century* with an introduction by an H.G. Howarth, proved a treasure house of the bawdy and erotic, including Suckling's "A Candle", Lovelace's "Ellinda's Glove," above all "A

Rapture" by Thomas Carew.) From Church and Bozman's generous anthology I discovered Hardy, Yeats, although with the exception of "Sailing to Byzantium" none of his great poems was included, Auden's "Lay Your Sleeping Head" and "As I Walked Out One Evening", MacNeice's "Meeting Point" (three more poems I almost at once had by heart), and, a favourite for a while, Thomas Sturge Moore, whose name I later found the American poet-critic Yvor Winters invoking when he claimed that Elizabeth Daryush was the greatest English poet since T.S.M. There was as well work by poets reputedly so difficult as to be not understandable, T.S. Eliot and Dylan Thomas chief among them. The egregious Whitfield had once remarked to the sixth-form class he took on "Religion and Philosophy" that "if I wanted, I could explain Eliot's *Waste Land* to you", thereby giving us to understand that the poem fell some way short of deserving the time and effort he might have to spend in enlightening us. Church and Bozman didn't include *The Waste Land*, although "Gerontian", which they did, was quite enough to be going on with.

Or at least I thought it was. But soon afterwards I read and was entirely bewildered by Eliot's great poem, even though certain passages thrilled me, "thrill" being perhaps too abject a word, even in its meaning of "pierce", to account for my reaction to a passage in "What the Thunder Said"

A woman drew her long black hair out tight
And fiddled whisper music on those strings
And bats with baby faces in the violet light
Whistled, and beat their wings
And crawled head downward down a blackened wall
And upside down in air were towers
Tolling reminiscent bells, that kept the hours
And voices singing out of empty cisterns and exhausted wells.

The insistent, insoluble mystery of those lines came back to me when, some months later, I saw for the first time reproductions of work by Max Ernst and de Chirico, and vaguely thought of them as illustrating if not some scene from then the atmosphere of *The Waste Land*, though they didn't affect

157

me as Eliot's lines did. They didn't "break through an enemy line", which is another meaning of "thrill" given in the *O.E.D.*

Still, I wasn't an enemy. I might be bored by Spenser and largely indifferent to *The Shropshire Lad* — I have since made amends to Housman's poetry — but "The Unpredicted" had opened me up to an overwhelming desire for more. Why that didn't include wanting more of Heath-Stubbs I can't explain. Perhaps I feared that more of him would mean worse and lead me to doubt my response to "The Unpredicted"; perhaps I thought of him as a one-poem poet, a latter-day Chidiok Tichborne. In all likelihood, I saw "The Unpredicted" as unique, talismanic, and sufficient unto itself. And now that I had read *The Waste Land* I wanted to read more *modern* literature.

It was Bouncer who helped me out. That principled socialist from whom I became aware of the significance of such names as John Ball, Kett, Rainsborough, the men of Pentridge, the Tolpuddle Martyrs and others, was so nick-named because there was such a spring in his stride that you felt he might at any moment defy the laws of gravity and take off from earth to where the lawless auroras run. He had on his shelves copies of *Tropic of Cancer, Ulysses* and the unexpurgated *Lady Chatterley's Lover*, all of them banned books which he'd smuggled past Customs on return journeys from France. I knew this because he had lent them to Pete — who else — and Pete reckoned Bouncer would do the same for me. So he did, though swearing me to silence and insisting I should return direct to him, all books he lent me. I understood his nervousness. If it came out he was circulating banned books among boys in his charge, Whitfield, who plainly didn't like him, would use that as grounds for dismissal. First came *Ulysses*, which I convinced myself I admired, then Miller, whom I found tedious. This was followed not by Lawrence but by the unbanned Turgenev's *Fathers and Sons,* then Dostoyevsky's *Crime and Punishment* and *The Brothers Karamazov*. All of these I thought wonderful, and said so. Bouncer told me in that case

158

to get hold of Chekhov's stories. "The greatest of all writers of short stories," he insisted.

I was lent an Everyman copy of these by a fellow sixth-former, David Pitman, the boy who had stood as Labour/Communist candidate against me in the school's 1951 mock election. Scruffier than ever, he believed that the end of capitalism was nigh, and from him I borrowed not merely Chekhov, but *The Communist Manifesto* as well as *The Great Gatsby* and *Tender is the Night*, which, he assured me, were the two greatest novels of the century and which between them exposed "the hollowness of the American dream". I was prepared to believe him.

* * *

By the spring of 1955 I was taking regularly Saturday trips to London, sometimes with Pete, when we would drop into The French Pub, sometimes on my own, when I didn't. Bunjy's, though, became a regular port of call and a source of information, not merely about which band worth listening to was playing where, but about which art exhibitions should be seen. One name cropped up more than any other: not an artist, but a critic. John Berger was regularly and almost reverentially quoted by the art students whose conversations I overheard or, more rarely, joined. Where were Berger's words to be found? In the *New Statesman*, I was told. He was that journal's art critic and the only one worth reading. What of Eric Newton? I had not long before read Newton's *Pelican Guide to Modern Art*, and thought it bland stuff, but undoubtedly knowledgeable. The students treated the name with derision. Only Berger's views counted.

Not long after that I saw Newton, whose face I recognised from the photograph on the back of his book, signalling for a taxi in Trafalgar Square. He was wearing a camel-hair over-coat and carried a black, silver topped cane. The uniform, I decided, of the bourgeois art critic. I began to buy the *Statesman*, where I read not only Berger's pieces but the

159

regular jazz column by Francis Newton. I mentioned this at school to the bass-playing music teacher who said "well, that's not his real name. Francis Newton is the pseudonym of Eric Hobsbawm. He's a Marxist historian."

"Why doesn't he use his real name?"

"No idea. Perhaps he doesn't want anyone to think he's 'slumming'. It might damage his reputation as a serious historian."

At the time, this explanation satisfied me but when, some years later, I became aware that the official Communist line on jazz was that it was "decadent" music — Stalin and Hitler had that much in common — it occurred to me that Hobsbawm might have felt the comrades would have been less than tolerant of his enthusiasms. Certainly the great Marxist classicist George Thomson in his book *Marxism and Poetry* instructs young Marxist poets to listen to folk songs and encourage others to do likewise. Jazz music he dismisses as commercialised pap, the fit product of a decadent society. Presumably, spirituals and blues didn't count as authentic folk song.

Goathead, who loved jazz as intensely as he did most forms of music, would have seen through such claptrap. He once got me to play at a school concert the trumpet obbligato to an arrangement by Nancy Bush of "Soldier's Song", her version of an Hungarian folk song. Like her husband, Alan, Nancy Bush was a life-long Communist, and at the outset of the Second World War Alan Bush had been banned from broadcasting because of his political sympathies. It was only after a mass meeting at the Conway Hall on 17th March, 1940, at which E.M. Forster read out a letter from Vaughan Williams protesting against the victimisation of Bush, that Churchill announced to the House of Commons the lifting of the ban. Forster campaigned not only against the treatment of Bush and other well-known artists and performers, but on behalf of "the smaller people. Because when important people are thrown overboard they make a big splash... But the smaller people don't make a splash; they vanish silently and the injustice never comes to light." His reward for this

160

in the immediate post-war period was to be pilloried in the Communist arts magazine *Our Time* as a panicky liberal clinging, like all his sort, to the rotten tree of state.

Had I been aware of the Party's attitude to Forster — but for that I would have had to know about Forster — I might well have identified with its condemnation of him. Because by then I was becoming headily committed to a belief that the society I lived in *was* rotten. Although I didn't know Auden's remark that the best reason he had for opposing fascism was that at school he had lived in a fascist state, I had decided that Hampton reproduced the structure and effects of totalitarianism. One leader ruled, his commands were always to be obeyed, the regime was marked by uniform, and there was even a military caste to reinforce his authority — the CCF. And with a bit of ingenuity Hampton could be seen as a microcosm of English society, where deference to authority, whether Church, government or throne, seemed so unquestioned, and unquestioning, that anything done in the "good name" of the state had to be accepted, had indeed to be celebrated, as on all public occasions royalty was celebrated by the playing of the National Anthem. To show our contempt for this "bovine acquiescence", Pete, I and several others, made a point of heading for the exit of any cinema we were in during the playing of the Anthem; and as we deliberately chose to sit in the middle of a row, we could guarantee to be hissed at, tripped, or half-heartedly slapped as we pushed past those who were standing to attention, which gestures of displeasure we received as marks of honour.

Goathead's choice of Nancy Bush's setting of the folk song was almost certainly a way of putting one over on the witless Whitfield, who sat in the front row, his glauberite cod's eyes staring solemnly ahead as the music rang out. Goathead was a man of wit, of good taste — he once gave Pete and me an impromptu lecture on the poor architecture of the school building, which had been put up in the 1930s and whose asymmetrical tower in particular was, he said, a botched attempt to imitate the style of Mies van Rohe — and it was

161

easy to see that he detested Whitfield. He was delighted when some of us decided to infiltrate the debating society and turn it from a forum for pompous would-be rhetoricians hoping for a parliamentary career into one that took on controversial issues. Pete preferred other forms of cunning, even though the few of us who joined did so with the active connivance of the only openly Marxist member of staff, a chemistry teacher called Harrison. Harrison wore natty suits and a bow tie, and each morning, having taken up his position at the front of the stage with the rest of the staff, made a point of exiting left as soon as the religious part of assembly began. We occasionally saw him in public with his wife, tall, elegantly-dressed, and looking sufficiently like Grace Kelly for us all to lust after her. They were off to concerts or the theatre or, more rarely, political meetings, so they gave us to understand.

***

In May 1955 Eden called a general election. Naturally, the school held a mock election, and naturally David Pitman wanted to stand as a sixth-form Communist candidate, an ambition a few of us enthusiastically backed. Whitfield forbade it. "I will not have the popular press visiting this school to question even one boy's loyalty to our constitution," he announced at assembly. Pause. "Especially as I believe that boy to have been misled or prompted by others too cowardly to expose themselves to scorn." Who did he have in mind, the few of us wondered who met that evening in a Twickenham coffee bar, called, of all things, The Swiss Chalet. There was general agreement that it was less likely to be any of us than Goathead or Harrison or Bouncer, or all three, though to our certain knowledge Pitman, who was a loner and had no contact with any teacher, had come by his decision himself. We decided to spoil our votes and persuade as many others as possible to do the same. In the end, the winner was the Tory candidate, a hapless figure who refused to debate with his opponents on the grounds that he didn't understand politics and had only agreed to be put up because he'd been promised 20 Dunhill if he took part and 50 of the same if he won.

In the weeks before the election, which was held on 26 May, Beresford Craddock held a number of public meetings. Pete and I decided to go to the one at Ashford Grammar School where Craddock was due to give an eve-of-election address. Pete had on a beret, red scarf and his suit; I was wearing my father's old, oil-stained overalls which I had unearthed from the back of the garage. When we arrived we found the assembly hall so crowded we had to stand at the back. At the end of his speech Craddock asked for questions. I put my hand up.

"Yes?"

I had wanted to ask what the government proposed to do about Cyprus, the island which was then much in the news and which had been the birthplace of the father of a school friend, Rigas Doganis. Rigas was a declared socialist and school dissident. He told me that his father wrote for a Greek Communist newspaper which paid him very little, but that he earned good money from regular work as a free-lance journalist in England. One evening Regis took me to the flat they lived in down by the river at Twickenham. The room I was shown into doubled as sitting-room and study. A desk under the window looked out onto the Thames, on it was a typewriter half buried under a scatter of books and papers, more books spread across the floor, one wall was completely lined with books, and on other walls hung oil paintings and framed cartoons, among which I recognised signed drawings by the famous *Daily Mirror* cartoonist, "Vicky", as well as some which were, I was told, by an equally famous Greek cartoonist, who went under the pen name of "Papas". The talk was dominated by Doganis senior in his thick, guttural, smoker's voice. He was affable and irate by turns, cursing the British for their two-faced treatment of Greece, then pausing to laugh at some absurdity of the government before returning to his tirade against its perfidy. Rigas must have mentioned that I was planning to attend Craddock's meeting because Doganis senior said "then you be sure to ask him about Cyprus."

"What should I say?"

"Ask him why you British don't leave us alone. You did enough damage after the War, forcing the damned fascists back on us. Now, get out of our land. You ask him." I said I would.

But it wasn't that prompting alone which made me determined to ask my question. By 1955 British soldiers stationed on Cyprus were being regularly killed by members of EOKA, the Greek Cypriot nationalist organisation, and among those being sent to the island were older contemporaries from Hampton, now in the army, where they were serving either as regulars or, more often, national servicemen or short-term commissioned officers. Novices in the art of guerrilla warfare at which the Greeks had become masters after long centuries of fighting first Turks, then, more recently Germans and, even more recently themselves, the British were repeatedly ambushed on patrol or attacked in supposedly "safe" quarters of the island. Just how expert the Greeks were I learnt something of not long ago, when talking to a Greek acquaintance who now lives on the island of Aegina. George was born on Cyprus in the mid-40s, and he told me that as a boy he heard stories of how EOKA members, as soon as they knew of any army patrol in the offing, would swiftly rig a wire to stretch across the road which, when driven into, activated a bomb. "They worked quick, so they never got caught." Then there were bombs hidden in piles of melons left temptingly at the roadside, others buried under sand to be set off by passing foot patrols. "And John, we always knew what the British plans were. We worked in their kitchens, we ran their bars, we served their food. We listened." Hearing George's stories brought back memories of Eden's insistence that Cyprus must remain under British control, and of the needless deaths brought about by that insistence.

I think it was only a day or two before Craddock's meeting

that I heard a BBC news broadcaster announce the death in ambush of a young Army Captain stationed on Cyprus. Much was said of the man's outstanding abilities, of the grief of his parents, of the loss to the army, all of it no doubt true. But then the announcer added, "his batman, who was with him at the time, was also killed." End of story. The grief of the batman's parents was not thought worthy of mention. After all, as Steerforth says, "they are not to be expected to be as sensitive as we are. Their delicacy is not to be shocked, or hurt so easily... They are not easily wounded." The unctuous, rounded tones of that BBC announcement of the two deaths, so differently treated, exploded in my head. Although the numbers of deaths that came about as a result of the Mau Mau insurrection in Kenya were far higher than in Cyprus, the violence far worse (according to official figures, between 1952-6 over 14,000 Kikuyu were killed, 1,000 by execution), and the evil of African colonialism was a matter a group of us sixth-formers talked about much more often that we did about Greece, it was Cyprus I was determined to ask about on that May evening.

Unfortunately, when I tried to put my question I was so nervous that instead of asking how the government proposed to deal with Cyprus I asked how it proposed to deal with Corfu. But it made no difference. "The government is considering its strategy with regard to Corfu," Craddock said smoothly, "which when announced will, I have no doubt, prove acceptable to all concerned. Next question, please." Much applause and looks of satisfaction from nearly all present. That's how to deal with would-be trouble makers.

At the time I was unaware of my slip, and when Pete mentioned it as we sat afterwards in a corner of a nearby pub, I was mortified. Rigas's father had asked for a report of the meeting and I would have to confess my humiliating blunder. "Still," Pete said, "for all you know, you may have got Craddock worrying about the Corfu crisis. He's probably asking all his friends what it is."

"That shouldn't take long."

"Don't you believe it," Pete said, "people like him always have plenty of friends."

As usual he proved right. I think it was in the next New Year's honours list, after the Conservatives had been returned to office and Ruth Ellis hanged, that Craddock's knighthood was announced.

Chapter 10
Getting Clear

In the summer of 1955 I passed my A Levels with good grades and failed to get into Leeds University. Leeds was the only university I had applied to because it had the only geography degree that offered a course on forestry. Choosing such a course pleased my father, who had suggested the timber trade as a suitable career for me. He would have been delighted if I had followed him into the trade because it would have been a sign that I valued his advice and to some extent at least modelled myself on him. My sixth-form years were the closest we ever came to an untroubled relationship. He watched me play cricket and, occasionally, rugger, and afterwards would take me for a pint to one or other of the attractive pubs which were a feature of Laleham, the riverside village just down from Ashford. Laurie was often with us. Both my parents liked him — "he's so *sensible*", my mother would remark in part praise of him and part reproof of what she saw as my rebellious tendencies, though I was hardly the Rimbaud of Exeford Avenue. But I never invited Pete. He belonged to a quite different side of my life. Still, my new absorption in socialist literature and ideas led to arguments with my father, although I don't think they rankled, and he proved nimble in discussion. We both enjoyed what my mother called our "slanging matches".

She was far more disappointed than I was that Leeds turned me down. Having herself been denied much by way of a formal education, she wanted her children to take all the advantages she had never had. Her father's salary as an elementary school headmaster gave him no chance to pay for her education beyond any the state provided. I don't think she resented the fact that she had to leave school at fifteen and find work — initially as a bookkeeper — but she yearned for her children to do better. University was an unheard-of achievement for men and, even more, women of her class and generation, but in 50s Britain it was becoming suddenly attainable to a growing number of eighteen-year olds. Jill, who wasn't academically-minded, by now had secretarial work in London. But I was to go to university.

University was for my mother less an actual place than a romantic image. A world of dreaming spires, peopled by eccentric dons and undergraduates who sprawled in their rooms at languorous ease, of musty libraries and of learning effortlessly acquired and dispensed. While I was a young boy she passed onto me novels she had been given as a girl and which she'd kept for her own children. Not, as you might think, stories of girls' but of *boys'* public schools. Among the titles I remember are *The Fifth Form at St Dominic*, and *Cock House of Garth*. Each featured rotters brought to book, manly types to be revered, and an *esprit de corps* whose essence was released on the rugger or cricket pitch. Neither, however, was as truly weird as *Play Up Queens*, the one book my father kept from his boyhood. This extolled the virtues of the public school spirit during the Great War, which the novel treated as a time of great adventure. The novel's closing words record the death of Manton, one of the school's sporting heroes, of whom we are told, "The men of his company, who were proud of him, related that he died with a whimsical smile on his lips, and the words, 'Play up, Queens', on his lips". *And this was published in 1922.* Perhaps my father's owning such a book as a boy was to be expected. But why on earth did my mother read such tripe? I think, sadly, that as an only child who happened to be a daughter she must have decided that she had disappointed her father's dream of producing an academically successful son, a dream I hope he never gave her reason to think he actually nurtured. At some level of her consciousness those ridiculous novels about public school allowed her to imagine such a life for her own son.

My unexpected rejection by Leeds was therefore far more of a blow to her than it was to me. Outwardly at least, my father was less concerned. A younger son at a time and from a class when it was taken for granted that money could be found only for the education of the first-born, assuming that to be a boy, my father, like my mother, finished with school at an early age, and from then on was expected to make his own way of the world. If he ever felt any resentment at this he was careful to keep it from us. He got on well with his older, better educated brother, and I think he simply accepted that the world was the way it was and you couldn't do much to change it.

For my mother's sake, I made a show of some distress at Leeds' unexplained decision. But secretly I was relieved. When I had been summoned for interview I claimed an interest in forestry. But that was pure hokum. It wasn't forestry that interested me but being a forester. Having at some time in the previous year read *Walden*, I had managed to persuade myself, all evidence to the contrary, that a geography degree with forestry as a special interest would infallibly lead to the life of a solitary, that as such I could live in a hut in a forest clearing, and that there I would be in the perfect position for "woodsheddin". This was the accepted term for the hours of practice required of aspiring jazz musicians, though in point of fact such hours were less often spent in the silence of forests (what forests?) let alone the shed at the bottom of the garden (what garden?), than in attics or basements, or shut inside airing cupboards. Years later, I was told of an East Anglian cornet player who managed daily practice while steering his tractor over the lone and level ploughlands of Lincolnshire.

How I thought I could square the life of a solitary with the necessary camaraderie of a jazz group I now have no way of telling, but anyway, not long before I applied to Leeds the dream of being a musician began to slacken its grip. Luckily the one that now took hold could just as well be nurtured by the solitude I persuaded myself went with a career in forestry. Browsing through the dictionary one day early in 1955 I came across the word *scripturient*: a. and n. "desire to write", "having a passion for writing or authorship". "A person with a passion for writing." The shock of recognition was as powerful as my meeting with "The Unpredicted". Scripturient. Yes, that was me. From early childhood I had written: short stories, plays (one about Bessie Bunter, which was mostly stolen from a Girls' Annual, introduced me to the word "incorrigible"), brief essays, either facetious or purple-in-the-prose nature notes, letters to friends, and poems. These last, which I more or less abandoned writing as soon as I got to Hampton, were heavily influenced by two anthologies my mother had inherited from her father, and which I still have on my shelves: the 1930 edition of *Poems of Today*, originally published in 1915 and primarily intended for children, and the Poetry Bookshop's *Georgian Poetry, 1920-1922*, edited by Harold Monro. Looking through their contents now, and reading the anonymous preface to *Poems of Today*, with its insistence that "there is no arbitrary isolation of one theme from another; they mingle and interpenetrate throughout, to the music of Pan's flute, and of Love's viol, and the bugle-call of Endeavour, and the passing-bell of Death", I try to imagine what it was that attracted the eight or nine year-old Lucas to them. Many of the poems must surely have passed over my head. But Walter de la Mare entered. "Nod" is in *Poems of Today*, and from "The Moth", in Monro's anthology, I can recall lifting the words "glooming" and "tryst"; and I got by heart Ralph Hodgson's "Time, You Old Gipsy Man", which I associated with the word "quaint", the meaning of which I learnt not long before I first read the poem. There must have been others, though I can't now be sure which.

I can, however, be certain that from about the age of eight my *need* to write had the kind of persistence that never left me, an actual physical ache which, when it came, could only be assuaged by putting pencil, later pen, to paper. There was no virtue in this. It simply happened. I do, though, think that it may have been connected to and part-prompted by my experiences at the hands of a teacher called Mrs Levett, under whom I suffered in my 3rd year at Junior school in Burbage. I was, I am, left-handed, incorrigibly so. But Mrs Levett was determined to make me right-handed. She knew that the brains of left-handed people develop on the right side, right-handed people vice-versa. Produce an ambidextrous person and you have a genius in your charge. Mrs Levett made me sit on my left hand and grip the pen in my right. "Now," she said, "write a few sentences. Take your time." Of course I couldn't do it. In those days children were issued with steel-nibbed pens which we had frequently to dip in the ink-wells slotted into holes at the front of our desks. The page on which I was made to write was soon an impasto of Rorscharch blobs and Taschiste scrawls, as though a drunken spider, having fallen into the inkwell, had managed to scramble out and was now doing its erratic best to make a getaway. Mrs Levitt decided I was trying deliberately to thwart her hopes. I was dragged in front of the class, my ears were cuffed, a ruler cracked down on my ink-stained fingers. I was offered for scornful inspection as an idiot, my head gripped and pressed up against her green-and-white candy striped blouse.

I wasn't alone. All over England teachers were taking out their frustration on children who refused to become geniuses. They included that excellent poet and jazz musician, Roy Fisher, a few years older than me and living out his put-upon boyhood in the West Midlands. I don't know whether Roy adopted the distorted style of penmanship that used to be common among cack-handers of my generation: elbow up, hand moving crab-like round and above the page in order to avoid any chance of smudging still-wet ink as the letters formed. Old habits die hard. The coming of biro and instant-drying ink put paid to the need for so contorted a manner of writing, yet it remains a life-time habit for many. Spotting it is a bit like recognising a Freemason's handshake. It makes us part of a cenacle, a fronde: us against the world. Not that I ever learnt to take this particular form of evasive action. I sometimes try to tell myself that heroic recalcitrance must have been involved in my refusal to adopt this way of staying out of trouble, but the probable truth is that it didn't occur to me. I dipped and wrote, dipped and wrote, and the pages of my exercise books acquired the appearance of *Bleak House*'s Chesney Wold: "alternately a lead-coloured view and a view in Indian ink." I could have used pencil. I should have used pencil. Occasionally, I was *made* to use pencil. But I loved the smell of ink, just as later I would come to love the chattering sound of a typewriter. Both smell and sound were inextricably linked with the act of writing. They were, to use a word I think I may have coined, tokens of scripturience.

* * *

Like me, Pete had passed his A Levels with the required grades and yet failed to get into the university of his choice. Reading was at that time one of two universities that offered a four-year honours course in Fine Art. He had applied, been conditionally accepted, but then rejected. Why? No more than me did he get an explanation. Goldsmith's, the other institution to which he had applied, accepted him, but their offer came with a condition. He had first to do his National Service. He hated the thought of that, but he hated still more the prospect of staying at school while he re-applied for an art degree elsewhere; so he left. Unfortunately, while school provided a shelter against conscription, once you had turned eighteen and were out in the world you were legally required to offer yourself to her majesty's armed forces for two years. There were dodges for failing your medical. Pretend deafness, lay claim to flat feet. Not easy to bring off, although stories abounded of some who had successfully clumped their way into rejection. (Escapees included the gentleman cricketer, Colin Cowdrey, whose flat-footedness did not prevent him from playing for Kent and England.) You could also present yourself as a "tick-tock man", that is, one who walked with an arm swinging in time with the near leg, as a result of which you obviously couldn't march. But tick-tocking was devilishly difficult. Some sixth-formers I knew practised assiduously, but I don't think any of them succeeded in keeping it up for more than a few strides. A preferred alternative was to swallow the albumen of half-a-dozen eggs the night before medical inspection. This was said to give your blood the appearance of pernicious anaemia, and there were, as always, rumours that several boys from Hampton had got away with it. But Pete, who anyway quite enjoyed treating himself as the persecuted artist, couldn't be bothered. Instead, while he waited for his call to arms, he created a studio in a lock-up garage in Twickenham he had somehow come by and for which he was charged a minimal rent; and he now spent his days there, painting obsessively.

I was determined that come what might I wasn't going to do my National Service. I therefore accepted Hampton as my shield until I landed a university place. Geography was no longer desirable. Leafing through university prospectuses I came across a combined honours course at Reading for Economics and Social Psychology, went for interview, and was given a place to start the following autumn, 1956. I was a happy man.

But Pete was appalled. "What in heaven's name made you choose such a course?" he wanted to know when we met for a drink soon after my letter of acceptance had come through. "You must be mad."

"Not at all," I said. "Economics will help me to understand how capitalism works, and social psychology ought to give me an insight into how people learn to live with it, or are affected by it."

Even to myself it didn't sound especially convincing and Pete was derisive. "In the first place," he said, not unreasonably, "you don't know anything about economics. I'm amazed they took you on given that you haven't done A Level maths."

"What's maths got to do with economics?"

He stared at me, aghast. "Economics *is* maths," he said. "It may not be *all* maths, but you can't expect to cope at university level without knowing a damned sight more than *you* know." And he explained that on several recent occasions he'd chatted with a former Hamptonian, now at the LSE, who drank in a Twickenham pub Pete frequented and who, himself a student of economics, had confessed to Pete that he was finding the maths now required of him by far the most difficult part of his course. "And Paul got a good grade for A Level maths," Pete added.

"Well," I said, "not all courses are the same." It was the best I could manage.

* * *

As soon as written confirmation of my acceptance from Reading came through I planned to quit school. The idea was to take casual work, save money, read, and, most important, write. As it happened though I stayed on for the whole of the autumn term and some way into the New Year. I was free now to read whatever I wanted and besides there were the parties.

Someone had discovered that Jessie Matthews lived not far from school in a large house with grounds that included a barn-cum-stable which she let out for social occasions. A former musical comedy star turned radio actor, she was still beautiful, with large, dark eyes and a wide, generous mouth. A few of us were allowed into her carpeted entrance hall to discuss the rental for what we had to promise would be a "quiet" party. On the walls were publicity photographs that showed her in her hey-day as a long-legged *danseuse*, others of film and stage actors, all of them signed.

"You can bring drink, of course," she said, "though I won't tolerate drunken behaviour. And I assume there will be girls? Well," seeing our nods, "you are to behave yourselves. And that means," she said by way of settling the matter, "nobody is to piss in the goldfish pond." Was this a recherché, theatrical phrase for sexual shenanigans? But no. She really did have a goldfish pond.

As to girls. Next door to Hampton was, as I've said, The Lady Eleanor Holles School for girls. The schools were divided one from another by wire netting and we were forbidden to stray within 20 feet of our side of the fence. Punishment for being detected in no man's land was severe, although few of the prefects assigned to patrol the perimeter fence bothered to report infringements.

174

It wasn't merely contact between the sexes that was sternly forbidden. On my first day at Hampton we first-formers were given a lecture on the reason for the existence of the two outside lavatories, one for boys up to the 3rd form, the other for "senior boys". Except that no reason for separating juniors and seniors was provided. "If one of you ever sees a senior boy in the junior lavatory you are to report the incident immediately. And if a junior boy is found in the senior lavatory he will be expelled." None of us had a clue what it all meant, and as no member of staff ever enlightened us it seemed to us newcomers the oddest, most arcane, of Hampton's many rules. By the time I got to the sixth form I was aware that one or two boys were, as we said, "that way inclined", and we had our suspicions about at least one master, but I don't recall any attempt at bullying or intimidation.

Yet for all that homosexuality was never mentioned, at least by members of staff, the subject was much discussed among the boys, especially after what became known as the "Montagu Affair". Early in 1954 a sensational trial made the national headlines. Three men, a peer of the realm, Lord Montagu of Beaulieu, the journalist Peter Wildeblood, and a Major Michael Pitt-Rivers, were accused of having "procured" some National Service men for immoral purposes at a private house party held in the grounds of Montagu's house. They were all found guilty and sent to prison. But I think I am right in saying that most people, or at all events a sizeable number, were disgusted, not by the "crimes" of which the men were found guilty, but by the hypocritical vengefulness of the law and of certain newspapers, especially the *Daily Express* and *Daily Mail*. Wildeblood had been a leading reporter for the *Mail*, which as soon as the trial result was announced sacked him. Most of us admired him because during the trial he openly declared his homosexuality, and while he was in prison he wrote a book called *Against the Law*, published in 1955, a clear-eyed account of his life up to and including his trial and imprisonment. It was widely read at school and we wanted to debate the issues it raised. (Naturally, the debate wasn't allowed.) I'm not suggesting that Hampton was free of homophobia — the idiot teacher who banged on about the school lavatories was clearly on the side of all that is "pure and manly" (he even warned against older and younger boys walking to or from school together let alone any boy being seen "in close proximity to another person"); but I'm confident that it didn't count for much. Which isn't to say that some boys could escape the misery of knowing that what they did or wanted to do was against the law, a state of affairs that lasted another decade and the effect of which I was to become aware soon after I got to Reading.

For now, though, girls. A very few of my contemporaries had girlfriends at the school next door. But the majority favoured Twickenham Grammar School for Girls, and it was a select group of these who were invited to the parties at Jessie Matthews. Once started, these occupied most Friday nights during the period I was seeing out school. They weren't especially wild occasions and I doubt that the Matthews goldfish were ever under threat. In those days, drink was largely confined to bottles of ale and cider. Occasionally a ghastly white wine would turn up, though nobody ever pleaded guilty to having brought it. The label proclaimed it to be *Spanish Graves* and it tasted like sugar water mixed with paraffin oil. As an alternative, at least for the inner *cadre*, a hip-flask of whisky was passed around, but in the main we got by on the beer and cider which, together with lemonade and chopped apple, were mixed in a large plastic bowl. "Punch" the drink was optimistically referred to, though Pete, who came once and once only, pronounced it toothless. He also said the parties lacked bite.

Still, they went on. The accoutrements of the frowsty barn included a record player which could be plugged into an extension lead running from the Matthews house, and there was a pile of records to hand, mostly 78s, including Jessie Matthews herself singing "Over My Shoulder", a pretty, vividly syncopated number. ("Over my shoulder goes one care,/over my shoulder go two cares".) But we preferred to bring our own. My jazz LPs didn't meet with approval, although one featuring the Benny Goodman Quartet minus Benny Goodman was tolerated, partly because "Moonglow" could be danced clingingly to (nobody remarked on Teddy Wilson's ravishing solo), but the favourites were American crooners such as Guy Mitchell, Tennessee Ernie Ford, Frankie Lane, and the weepily dreadful Johnny Ray. Oh, and England's very own Dickie Valentine, who had left the Ted Heath Orchestra, a genuinely good swing band, in order, as the *Melody Maker* put it, "to pursue a solo career", and whose sentimental ballad "All the Time and Everywhere" was the signal for the already dim lights to be further lowered while the dancing turned to a suspenseful rocking to and fro and, briefly for us boys, "the wonderful feel of girls", as we inhaled the frail, applewood scent of their fresh-washed hair. It all ended peaceably at 10.30pm. After we had tidied the place, reclaimed and re-sleeved our records, one or two couples might wander off into the night, holding hands; the rest of us got on our bicycles and headed for home through silent lanes or wider, straighter roads where, apart from the occasional dim patch of light coming from an upstairs window, all was dark.

* * *

But the Friday nights began to pall. The routine was unvarying, so, too, the conversations, such as they were. Nobody was interested in the subjects I wanted to talk about and if I so much as mentioned art or poetry I was sure to be met with a mock-quizzical look and very probably a cry of "ooh, 'ark at 'im" or, more earnestly, a request to "give over. We're here to enjoy ourselves." So to the disappointment of nobody, I stopped going. London, however, called with increased urgency. At least once a week I took the train to Waterloo, either with Pete or on my own. The thrill of arrival never lessened. There was the walk past Topolski's studio built into an arch of the railway viaduct that connected Waterloo to Charing Cross, to my right the Festival Hall and the National Film Theatre, which I had begun to attend, its hard wooden forms seemingly essential to the experience of watching such films as *Earth* and *The Battleship Potemkin.* There was the walk over Hungerford Bridge, the grey swirling Thames thronged with tugs and coal barges, as though, I fancifully told myself, Whistler might be expected to show up at any moment; there was the waterfront towards which I walked, the white stacked tower of the Shell Building, other towers and spires stretching beyond and behind it, on my left the incessant clatter of the green-painted electric trains of Southern Rail, then the steps down to Villiers Street with its pubs and small shops, most notably one whose window was stuffed with a forbidding array of prosthetic limbs and what looked like plaster-of-Paris corsets and out of or into the unlit interior of which men would scurry, coat collars turned up, hats pulled low over their foreheads; then the Strand and — Pete's discovery, this — a tiny café called The Soup Kitchen, in what seemed no more than a hole in the wall of Duncannon Street, where for very little you could get a large bowl of minestrone soup ladled from a metal tureen that sat on a permanently-lit gas jet and, to go with it, a hunk of new-baked granary bread. After that, it was into the National Gallery or, increasingly, a prowl through bookshops on the Charing Cross Road before I or we headed for the Bond Street galleries.

I bought few books, for the simple reason that without the meagre income jazz gigs had gained me I lacked funds. But magazines, yes, especially second-hand magazines, which were often bundled up and sold as job lots. *The Adelphi, London Mercury, Glass, Poetry Review, Cornhill, Argosy* (short stories only), *Contemporary Review, the Nineteenth Century* (still bearing the name it was given at its founding over a hundred years earlier), the *London Magazine....* From substantial quarterlies to the flimsiest of badly-printed, saddle-stitched, fly-by-night ventures, I bought and hoarded. And I began to write pieces I thought might be suit-able for any magazine whose contents I had studied and send them off to the given editorial address. That was to be the last I saw of them, scarcely surprising given that I had no access to a typewriter and that, always supposing an editor managed to decipher my scrawl, he would have had no incentive to reply because nobody had told me that you were required to enclose a stamped, addressed envelope with your submission.

But then nobody could have told me. Nobody knew about my writing, not even Pete. I think I may have planned that when something of mine appeared in print I would casually let drop that I was now a published author; but as this never happened there was no need to say anything. However, I took note of how certain essayists came by their effects, how they developed arguments, how they made these vivid and particular, made them vivid by *being* particular, and then, or was it therefore, also and with great confidence moved to more general statements. I read everything that appeared under the name of V.S. Pritchett, whose essays were featured at regular intervals in the *New Statesman*. I also kept by me an issue of the *Statesman* from 1954 which contained a short piece by John Berger. It was about the artist Fernand Leger. I hadn't managed to see the exhibition on which Berger's essay was based, but repeated re-readings convinced me that this was a model of how to write expository prose and I took some pains to analyse the way he came by his effects. What was it made him so persuasive? Why did I feel sure he could be believed? Trying to answer these questions, I came to understand that Berger's air of authority sprang directly from the clarity of his vision. In addition, his way of writing made evident that he wanted to share with his reader a set of unopposable truths. He wasn't trying to push you into sharing unreasonable assertions. "Our productive, scientific abilities have outstripped our ethical and social conscience", the first sentence announced, and anyone in the mid-50s looking at the world around, and thinking for a moment of the newly-tested H-bomb, would be unlikely to disagree.

But what an opening! This was not to set art against or apart from the world. On the contrary, art was within the world, *our* world. "As an artist Leger is often accused of being crude, vulgar, impersonal. He is none of these things. It is his buoyant confidence that makes him seem crude to the diffident. It is his admiration of industrial techniques and therefore of the industrial worker that makes him seem vulgar to the privileged; and his belief in human solidarity that makes him seem impersonal to the isolated." From state of the world to state of the artist in a few, swift, epigrammatic sentences. And then, equally terse and every bit as vivid, a rapid résumé of Leger's effects. "Look at his bicycles, and his girls in their sports clothes, and his holiday straw hats, and his cows with their comic camouflage dapples, and his steeplejacks and acrobats each knowing what the other takes, and his trees like sprigs you put into a jam jar, and his machinery as gay as the youth who plans to paint his motorbike, and his nudes as familiar as wives... and his compasses and keys painted as though they were emblems on flags to celebrate their usefulness — does his work seem mechanical and cold?" Leger's use of cubism, Berger adds, is different from either Picasso or Braque. For Leger, cubism made possible the depiction of the solid machine object: first in and of itself, then "he saw that the machine had made labour collective.... From that moment everything ceased to be a celebration of the mechanical industrial world as it is, and became a celebration of the richer human world to which industrialisation would eventually lead. He painted Adam and Eve and made them a French worker and his girl granted Leisure. He painted bicycles as a symbol of the machine available to the working class which could convey them to where they wished." After which, and following the remark that Leger is the only modern European painter to have created an heroic style, comes the summing-up. "The current vision of the genius is almost synonymous with that of the mysterious, misunderstood outcast; Leger's vision of the genius was of a man with an imagination so in tune with his time and therefore so easily understandable, that he could become almost anonymous — his work as easy and yet sharp to the eye as popular proverbs to the ear." The ability to blend Marxist generalisations with such acute, detailed observation that the two seemed to interpenetrate and reinforce each other, was what made Berger so admired and so influential to those of us who read him at the time. And for what it is worth, I will add that for me and I suspect countless others of my generation as well as younger readers, this remains the case. In a recent collection of essays, *Hold Everything Dear*, Berger justly reprises the opening of his Leger review when, in a short piece on Pasolini, he remarks that "it is not only animal and plant species which are being destroyed or made extinct today, but also set after set of our human priorities. The latter are systematically sprayed, not with pesticides, but with ethicides — agents that kill ethics and therefore any notion of history and justice." That same implacable voice, though now with a newly-coined word to identify the human enemy. I count myself lucky that I encountered so many of Berger's early essays as and when they first came out.

* * *

Early in 1956 I saw some paintings by Ivon Hitchens, semi-abstract landscapes. I loved the generous sweeps of colour, the over-layerings of paint that suggested mysterious depths, recessions of light, of gaps and thickenings. I tried to write a Berger-like essay on Hitchins, beginning with a statement about the hidden desire of people living in post-war England for a now lost, innocent, pre-war world. Having read *Coming Up For Air* I made some sort of comparison between George Bowling's despairing search for the Lower Binfield of his childhood and Hitchens's landscapes. I wanted to mention this to Pete when we met for a drink one evening at the White Swan, a Twickenham riverside pub we especially favoured. But he was in a melancholy mood, the rope of black hair half-screening his pale face as he sat hunched over his drink. He had by now received his call-up papers, including a railway pass and instructions to report the next day for basic training, and he was looking forward

181

neither to square bashing nor to the mind-numbing routine of soldiering. He knew — we all knew — that regulars loathed National Servicemen, and as a natural rebel against authority he must have feared that he would be a target for the brutal venom of any NCO he came up against. As we parted, he said, "well, enjoy freedom." Then, "why bother staying on at that bloody school. You should be out and about."

"I've already left," I told him. I had, too.

"Good."

"Let me know how you can get on," I said as we shook hands. Sombrely, he nodded, then turned away and slumped off home while I headed for the train to take me back to Ashford. A week later I was on another train, rucksack crammed with clothes, books and notepads, this time heading north.

Chapter 11
Going North

TO THE NORTH the Motorway signs say and no matter how far north you go they continue to say it. In 1956 there were no motorways and apart from my interview at Leeds the only time I'd headed north had been with Michael Hill and his French pen friend. We drove up the Great North Road, and because I was stuck in the back among piles of camping gear and much of the journey was through rain, I saw little of it. I saw even less of Leeds when I was called for interview, because on my one visit the city was drowning in tides of thick yellow fog. All I knew of the north was what I read in *The Road to Wigan Pier*. Intrepid traveller that I was, I decided to see it for myself and I had a plan to combine seeing and writing. I bought a one-way ticket to Newcastle and with the micro-scopically small sum of money I had managed to save I planned to visit some of the cities whose football teams made them famous: Newcastle United, Bolton Wanderers, Preston North End, Burnley, Manchester United and Manchester City, Blackpool, and perhaps back down south by way of Wolverhampton Wanderers and Birmingham's Aston Villa. As I travelled from place to place I would record my meetings with "ordinary" people, note any features of city architecture that seemed worthy of comment, and — this, I told myself was the selling-point — I would produce reports on all the football matches I went to. Surely somebody, somewhere, would want to read about these, even if they weren't interested in my other observations? Ivon Hitchens would have to wait.

So, one wet Thursday in late March 1956 I went to London and took the Edinburgh-bound train. For a while I shared my compartment with a middle-aged man who, as soon as he joined the train — at Peterborough, I think — removed and carefully folded his heavy woollen, dark-blue overcoat, which he placed on the rack above his head, having first hoisted up a sizeable suitcase he took some time to adjust so that it wouldn't tumble down. Then, having pulled straight the points of the waistcoat of his dapper green suit, flicked some invisible specks of dust off a pair of brown, brightly-shined shoes, he settled himself in the seat opposite and, giving my grey gabardines and sports-coat the once over, asked "pleasure or business?"

I must have looked startled because he said again, his voice now less peremptory, "pleasure or business? Why are you on the train?"

"I'm going to Newcastle," I said.

"Same here," he said, "and as nobody in his senses goes to Newcastle for pleasure you'll be going there on business. Right?"

"Well..." I was wondering how to answer, but he swept my hesitant beginning aside.

"Guess what line of business I'm in. Bet you can't, can you. No." He smiled, moved his head vigorously from side to side.

"Hairbrushes, that's me. Look at my hair. Straight parting, no sign of receding is there, and nice and flat on my head. Set an example to the gentlemen and their good ladies." As he spoke he again swivelled his head from side to side and at one point almost turned back to front in his determination I should register his impeccable coiffure.

"Only the best brushes, mind. They're in the suitcase. I'd show you but it would mean unwrapping them. Tortoiseshell or Mother-of-Pearl backed, finest quality bristles. Nothing to damage the follicles."

"Follicles?"

"You take all that baldness there is nowadays. People put it down to bad diet or too much how's your father. But it's over-use of the wrong bristle and that's a fact."

He looked hard at my hair. "You ever use a hairbrush? No, I shouldn't think you do. You'll be bald by the time you're thirty, I'm telling you. A good vigorous brushing, morning and night, that'll save you any future embarrassment. You're no use to the ladies without hair, you know. Take a tip from me. A proper hairbrush is an investment."

I decided that he wasn't so much making conversation as practising his doorstep patter, so merely nodded, and after a few moments he got up, said he was going to find the restaurant car in order "to fortify the inner man," and I didn't see him again until the train pulled into Newcastle.

As we clambered down from the carriage I wished him luck, but he was already marching down the platform in the early evening gloom, swinging his suitcase with an air of confidence. Within a few minutes of leaving the station I found a cheap B & B, went out for a stroll about the strange, dark, cold streets, and as the rain came heavily on ducked into a pub where I could make out little of the conversation beyond the fact that on the coming Saturday Newcastle United would be in London. Idiot that I was, it hadn't occurred to me to check the football programme before I left home, but there now seemed little point in staying in the city that had taken me all day to reach. So the next morning, after a breakfast of cornflakes and badly-fried egg and bacon, seated at a communal table with middle-aged men who all seemed to know each other, who were all commercial travellers, and who took no notice of me except for the occasional request to pass the sauce or teapot, I went back to the station and bought a ticket for Carlisle. From there I could catch a train to any of the Lancashire towns that were on my itinerary.

Blackpool, perhaps? Why not. At Carlisle I boarded a stopping train and stared out at a landscape I could hardly see through curtains of rain. When we pulled into Blackpool I saw at once that I'd made a mistake. The rain soused unrelentingly down, most of the B & Bs were shut and the one that offered to take me in stank so appallingly of boiled cabbage and stale cigarette smoke that I turned down the landlady's promise of a "clean" bed and breakfast. "1s and 6d extra for fried" the scribbled sign pinned to the door said. She didn't seem disappointed, merely shrugged and, without removing from her mouth a cigarette stained with dribble, told me I wouldn't get a better offer elsewhere. I decided to believe her. Wet through and cold, I plodded back to the station. A train for Preston would be leaving in twenty minutes. Very well, I would go to Preston.

Preston was even worse than Blackpool. Rain sluiced the pavements, the gutters overflowed, the air was chokingly foul with smoke from industrial chimneys, people huddled along, head down, not speaking even when they bashed into you, as frequently happened, and, though I hadn't yet read *Hard Times*, a brief acquaintance with the place was enough to make me believe that Preston was indeed "a town of machinery and tall chimneys, out of which interminable serpents of smoke coiled themselves for ever and ever, and never got uncoiled... It contained several large streets all very like one another, and many small streets still more like one another, inhabited by people equally like one another, who all went in and out at the same hours, with the same sound upon the same pavements..." Unfair, of course, as even my brief stay there brought me to realise, but my introduction to the town really did make it seem as though it belonged to a circle of Hell Dante forgot to invent.

Eventually I found a bed above a small, backstreet pub, where I was given for evening meal a plate of slithery fried egg and bacon huddled pinkly in grease. The bar was draughty, the gapped, splintery floorboards half hidden under a dark green lino barely redeemed by decorative explosions of white and pink flowers. The few locals in that night, all of them men, stood steaming in raincoats and caps, talking or rather grumbling among themselves, although from time to time one would turn to stare at where I sat in a corner near the door, wrapped in both my sweaters and unable to keep warm. I'll write about this, I thought. Next morning, after a repeat of the previous night's meal, plus a slice of charred toast and stewed tea served by the landlord who, having silently provided the food for his only lodger, stood, one elbow propped against the bar while he coughed round a Woodbine and scanned the back page of his newspaper, I asked for directions to the public library.

"Library," he asked, startled, jerking his head up and staring at me, then away. "What you want the library for? It's all books, you know." Then, shaking his head to indicate that I must be mad, he told me.

Through streets that looked even drabber under the morning's grey skies than the previous evening's gloom, I found my way to the library, settled at a table, and took out my notebook. "Down and Out in Newcastle, Blackpool and Preston", I wrote at the top of the first clean page. What next? What of the pub where I had left my rucksack and clothes still damp from my arrival. Which words best summed it up? Disconsolate? Morose? It occurred to me to consult a dictionary. Excusing myself as I squeezed past the other occupant of the table where I sat, an old man who was listlessly turning over the pages of a journal and whose startling baldness suggested that he was paying the price for a lifetime's application of the wrong bristles, I fetched a dictionary, opened it at morose and read: "deliberate, scrupulous", 17c. But that wasn't what I meant at all. And then I remembered that some time previously I had come across the phrase "morose Ben Jonson." I'd assumed that Jonson was being accused of anti-social behaviour and, having glanced through Drummond of Hawthornden's accounts of his conversations with the great man, "morose" seemed an apt term to describe someone who claimed that among other things "he did beat Marston and took his pistol from him." Now, though, it became apparent that Jonson's moroseness could be seen as a very different attribute. Far from implying criticism, it was intended as compliment. I think this was the first time I grasped that through the course of centuries words can radically change their meanings. Well, to borrow Larkin's phrase, "useful to get that learnt." I read on. "Of a person, a mood, sullen, gloomy, unsocial. Of a thing, and idea, heavy, ponderous, oppressive." Better. In fact, spot on. "Sullen, gloomy, unsocial" skewered not only the pub where I had found temporary anchorage but its inmates.

Over the years friends and I have sometimes compared stories of the worst pub we have ever encountered. That

Preston pub remains for me Malebolge, pure anticopacetic, ahead even of The Shires, the station bar at the unreconstructed St Pancras where the only thing older and more decrepit than the regulars and the furnishings were, as someone remarked, the pork pies. Yet even The Shires, appalling though it was, lagged behind one I was told about in Clay Cross, Derbyshire, where, during the dreadful winter of 1947 an acquaintance, an older man, found himself stranded one evening. He had been due to take a WEA class in the town, but by the time he arrived from Nottingham, his train having been delayed by the weather conditions — "points iced over, mate" — such members of the class as might have ventured out had long since returned home and it was made plain to him that there would be no more trains until the following morning. He would therefore have to find a bed in Clay Cross. But how? The town seemed quite shut up apart from one pub near the station, which, when he decided to try it, proved to be empty except for the barman who stood at the far end of the bar glumly wiping beer tankards with what looked like a grime-caked handkerchief and who didn't so much as glance at the newcomer, let alone nod a greeting. Nor did he speak when my acquaintance asked for a scotch. He merely sighed, laid down his handkerchief, produced the whisky glass, and then returned to his task of smearing tankards.

"Could I get a bed here for the night?"

No answer.

The man from Nottingham tried again. "Does this pub do bed and breakfast?"

Tankard in hand the barman came over to where my acquaintance stood and looked him slowly up and down. "Where d'yo fookin' think yo fookin' are," he said. "Fookin' Buxton?"

* * *

Sitting in Preston's library I wrote perhaps a page about the pub where I was staying before I suddenly realised that I knew nothing of the men I had just categorised as "naturally belonging there". How could I possibly know that? The answer of course was that I couldn't. Orwell had been a *plongeur* in Paris. If I was to write about the underside of English industrial cities I ought at least to get a taste of what life was like for working men. I shut my notebook, put on my coat and left the library. A nearby newsagents' window was badged with small adverts for cleaners, odd-job men, carpenters. Someone needed gardening work. I made a note of the address, asked directions, and half-an-hour later was walking up the drive to a substantial brick-built house on the outskirts of the town.

The clangorous bell brought a middle-aged woman to the door. She wore a white, ruffled blouse and pleated, grey skirt, and her carefully made-up face suggested that, as my father would have said, "she wasn't short of a bob or two." The expectant smile on her face was at once switched off when she saw me on her doorstep. It was replaced by a puzzled frown.

"I've come about the advert," I said. And, when she stared at me as though I might be mad, added "gardening. You know."

"Ah. I was expecting someone else."

"You mean the job's already taken?"

"No, no," she said, smiling faintly. "To tell you the truth, I'd rather forgotten about that advert." I thought I detected the faintest sign of a blush. Then she said, as though by way of an explanation, "The men who do this work are usually, well, older. Mill casualties or war-wounded. Still, as you're here..." A pause. "Go round to the back of the house. I'll see you there." And she shut the door.

But when, after a few moments, she stepped out from her back door, pulling it to behind her, she was friendlier, pointing to a long lawn with, to either side, bushes and flower beds. She gestured to the end of the garden where I could see a wooden summerhouse with what looked like stained glass windows. "My husband and I enjoy sitting there in the summer," she said, following my gaze. "Do you know much about gardens? Flowers? Plants in general?"

189

"Not really."

Her nod suggested she had expected this answer. "Well, never mind. For the moment it's a matter of general tidying up. Some weeding, edging the lawn, sweeping the paths. Let me show you."

I followed her past a substantial conservatory to a wooden shed, its door ajar. "You'll find all you need in here," she said, "anyway, enough to get you started."

Peering in, I saw a wheelbarrow, beyond it a workbench, gardening tools neatly racked on the sides, an old canvas chair and, beneath it, a pair of Wellington boots. "I don't know whether those boots will fit you" she said, "but you may as well try them. No point in ruining your own..." she was going to say shoes, but then, seeing my rain-splashed suede boots, she left the sentence unfinished. She looked at me again, more closely now. "What's your name?"

I told her.

"And what do you do?"

"I'm waiting to go to university."

"You're not from 'oop North', are you?" The satiric edge she gave to the words implied that neither was she, a matter she confirmed by adding, "I used to wish I was back in Gloucestershire, but now I've come to quite like this place. When can you start?"

"Now, if you like."

"Then now it shall be. Oh, and as to money. Thirty shillings a day for a full day's work. Alright? I'll pay you at the end of the week." She turned to go, then turned back. "I may be rather busy today" — the blush returned — "but I'll leave a flask of tea and some biscuits outside the back door."

"That'll be fine," I said.

I put in three days, by the end of which I had finished all the work she had asked me to do, and then by mutual agreement I left. She needed someone who understood far more about flowers and shrubs than I did, and for my part I could hardly pretend that trimming grass verges and stirring into flame low bonfires of twigs and leaves amounted to the down and out experience I was meant to be seeking. The nearest I came to that was when, the second afternoon, I was summoned to help push start a car, a large black saloon which was parked outside her house. The driver, a man with sleeked-back hair and a heavy black overcoat, sat at the wheel, staring straight ahead, and after I had spent minutes straining to get the car to move it jerked forward a few yards, the engine growled, hiccuped and started into life, and the car disappeared round a bend in the road. When I turned back I noticed that she, too, had disappeared inside her house.

Sometime later she brought a cup of tea into the shed where I was cleaning mud off the tines of a fork. "That car of your husband's, it's a Humber Hawk, isn't it?" I asked, genuinely curious. She looked startled, then blushed and turned away. "If you say so," she said. And then of course I knew that the man wasn't her husband at all and that it was the same man, presumably a lover, she must have been expecting when on the previous day I had rang her doorbell.

I stayed one more night in Preston, splashing out some of the money I'd earned on an unsatisfactory helping of fish and chips followed by a seat in the stalls of an unheated, near-empty cinema, where I watched a dreadful film starring Debbie Reynolds, of which I remember nothing except its garish colours and the theme song, "Hold My Hand" ("Pass through the portal now, We'll be immortal now, Hold my Hand") sung by a crooner called Don Cherry who didn't appear in the film. The following morning, one of predictable low-slung clouds and drizzle, I paid for my bed and board and made to leave.

As though stung into involuntary candour, my host suddenly said, looking not at me but at the ochreous ceiling, "Who'd run a pub, eh? Tell me that."

I couldn't, nor could the ceiling, but I muttered something about there being worse jobs, or so I supposed.

"Not that I know of," he said. And that was all.

Not much later I caught a train heading south, and as we lurched away from Preston I made a vow never to return to the place.

But years later I did. Coming back from a few days in Edinburgh, the express I was travelling by stopped wontedly at Preston station. Hence the following:

The train from Edinburgh, that *soigné* town
This time took the western route: right down
To Carlisle I slept off a whisky night,
Woke to a gleam of visionary Lakelight,

Then slept again until we slid beneath
A station-roof's arced gleam. "Good God, Preston!
I worked here once, it felt like a slow death"
I groaned to my travelling companion —

At which a man rose promptly, hefting his case
From off the rack, scooped up a rainproof hat,
And then announced, eyes blow-torching my face,
"Some of us like it here, you southern prat."

Later still, I was talking to that excellent poet, Jim Burns, who was born and brought up in Preston, about my experiences in his home town. "But then I was an outsider," I said, "I imagine the locals will have seen it very differently." To my surprise, Jim had few fond memories of the place. Prestonians, so he said — or anyway implied — were dedicated to rejecting any but the most obvious pleasures, of beer, fags and football, and they typically scorned any attempt to lighten the darkness. By way of illustrating what he came to dislike about the place, he told me a story which, with his permission, I used at the beginning of a poem called "Tales of the (English) Jazz Age":

Spud Murphy, Preston's first known jazzman,
Stood by his feisty, green-stockinged wife
In your dad's good-for-men-only local

ordering pints to a jaw-clenched
silent riff of "Poof, weirdo,
Red."

Provincial England in the 1950s could, no doubt about it, be that philistine, that devotedly joyless. I don't want to side with Lawrence's despair when, in *Lady Chatterley's Lover*, he has Connie wonder as she drives through a mining

192

village, "what could possibly become of such people, in whom the intuitive living faculty was dead as nails," but more than twenty years after he wrote those words the England in which I grew up could at different times and places exhibit, even revel in, a kind of dedicated joylessness. But that's not the whole story.

Chapter 12
Heading South

Back at Ashford I found a brief note from Pete telling me that army life was even less fun than he'd expected and that he'd been transferred to Portsmouth. "Can't say more," he concluded, mysteriously. Why Portsmouth? Surely he couldn't be planning to join the navy. By my reckoning he had so far completed no more than half of his basic training. I knew that during this period all newcomers were confined to barracks, which meant we'd no chance of meeting for several more weeks. I spent a few days at home writing up my experiences of Preston, then, having sent the resulting article to a magazine, this time making sure to enclose an sae, I once again set out on my travels.

This time I headed south, though without my scheme for turning whatever I encountered into prose. It was early May and after the rain and gloom of Preston I was in search of sun. I took the train to Torquay, where my father's parents lived and where I could base myself while I searched for work. Almost at once I found what I was looking for. One of the local newspapers carried a notice stating that The Devon Coast Country Club wished to take on "Seasonal Workers": waiters, handymen, kitchen staff, gardeners.

"That's a Paignton number," my grandfather said, peering over my shoulder. I phoned, was asked to come for interview, and the following morning, having taken the short train journey from Torquay past several halt stations, found myself walking up an incline out of the seaside town of Paignton until I arrived at the entrance to what looked like a replica of the Pontin's Holiday Camp I had just passed. A low brick and wood building fronted the entrance gate. OFFICE, a sign painted above the door said. And, on the door itself, *Reception. Please Enter.* I entered.

Behind a desk facing the door sat two young women of about my own age, one copper-haired, the other with wild, ginger curls, green or were they blue eyes, and freckles spreading across her face. There was even a scattering on the bridge of her nose which looked at though it might at one time have been broken. Both women stared in friendly enough fashion at me, the freckly one adding a lop-sided grin that at once put me at ease.

"I've come to be interviewed for a job," I said to her. "A Mr Porter asked to see me."

"He's just gone out," she said, "but he'll be back very soon."

"Her voice was full of money," Nick Carraway thinks of Daisy Buchanan. *This* voice was full of laughter. "Why not sit down" — she gestured towards a chair by the far wall — "and we can get you a drink, if you'd like. This is Barbara, by the way, and I'm Jackie."

I nodded to each of them, said I'd do without the drink, and told them my own name.

Jackie looked down at a notepad that was open on the desk. "Ah," she said, "well, in that case you're early. Mr Porter wasn't expecting you for another half hour."

"Might he be back before then?"

They looked at each other. "Doubt it," Barbara said. Her deftly modulated voice suggested she'd been to elocution lessons and she spoke through lips that moved very little, as though she was anxious not to fracture her carefully-applied lipstick.

"He'll be busy," Jackie said, turning to Barbara for confirmation, then as the other girl looked swiftly away she went off into hoots of laughter which she had some difficulty in controlling. I would later learn that when Tony Porter was "busy" that was because he was with his mistress, a woman called Mrs Simpson — I never learnt her Christian name — whose official function was manageress, and who habitually dressed in a black-and-white check skirt and crisp green blouse that crackled as she moved and did nothing to hide a bust of which Mrs Merdle would have been proud.

195

"This Country Club," I asked Jackie, once she had stopped laughing. "It's a holiday camp, isn't it?"

"Well, it will be when guests start to arrive," she said, the laughter bubbling up again. "Until then it's holiday time for the staff."

"No, Jackie, that's not *quite* true," Barbara said, perhaps in reproof. "People are busy all the time. The place has to be got spick and span. Ernie and his crew are here at all hours, hammering away. Ernie Simmons," she added, "chief carpenter and works manager."

"Ably assisted by Sheila Fox," Jackie said. "Sheila looks after laundry."

"And bedding," Barbara said.

"I'll say." This time Jackie only stopped laughing when a large, silver-haired man in a grey suit appeared through the office's front door.

"Mr Porter," Barbara said. "This is the young man you asked to come for interview. His name is..." and she peered at the notepad.

"Lucas," he said, looking me over. "Good." Was he complimenting me on my dress or my promptitude? "Come through."

Twenty minutes later I had been given work as a general handyman, duties to include grass-cutting, creosoting wood fences — "You'll be taking orders from Mr Simmons for all those jobs" — and bar work. "Nothing demanding," he added, noting my expression. "I'll put you in the 'Pirate's Snug', not the main bar. Keith, the head barman there, will tell you what's needed. Changing barrels, bottling up at the end of the evening and always, *always*, keeping tables clear of filled ashtrays and empty glasses. Overalls for outside work will be provided, but you'll be expected to supply your own white shirt and black bow tie for the Snug. Understood." It wasn't so much a question as an order. "Right then," he said, "you'll be starting tomorrow. Eight a.m. sharp. You'll be expected to live in, of course. All meals provided. Get one of the girls to tell you about eating arrangements and to show you to your accommodation."

Back in the outer office I told Jackie and Barbara I was now on the payroll.

"Lucky you," Jackie said, and though the remark was playfully ironic the following six weeks were on the whole not merely happy but often riotously comic.

Not that the accommodation was up to much. Jackie took me from the office up a grass slope past rows of identical, white painted chalets, through the gap in a wattle fence, and then pointed to a huddle of wooden huts that looked like the old army barracks they in fact were. "This was requisitioned during the war," Jackie said. "Now it's where the workers of the world live." She looked at the key she'd grabbed from a shelf behind the office desk. "This way." She led us to a hut at the rear and stepped through a door, warped and battered by what looked like a steady application of army boots.

The corridor we entered ran down the hut's entire length. I counted six doors off to the left, six to the right. Two open doors on either side gave onto a bathroom and toilet, the rest were closed.

"No kitchen, then," I said, as I followed her along the corridor, admiring the swing of her hips through the blue, pleated skirt she wore below a dark blue jumper. "Nowhere to make a cup of tea."

"I should think not," she said over her shoulder. "Old Porter wouldn't want anyone running up a gas or electricity bill he couldn't control. Now, here we are."

We stopped outside the last door on the right and, having unlocked it, she handed me the key. "All yours," she said.

Apart from a double bunk bed on the inside wall the room was bare. No mat on the wooden floorboards, not so much as a rag of curtain at the window. Well, at least the two beds were made up. I pressed down on the upper bunk and through the coarse blanket came a rusty squeak of springs.

"Luxury," I said.

"Don't speak too soon," Jackie said, "you'll probably have to share."

We backed out of the room, I locked the door, and as I turned found myself face to face with a much older man who was filling the doorway of the room across from mine. He was wearing a stained, long-sleeved vest and a pair of old, baggy grey trousers, from the waistband of which braces dangled. Wisps of matted grey hair hung over his ears and ashen, unshaved face. When he yawned, hugely, I saw he had no teeth.

"Whasa fuckin' time," he said.

I looked at my watch. "Just gone midday." He blinked at me as though I was speaking a foreign language.

"Tell you one thing for free," he said, "fuckin' scrumpy's no fuckin' good for a working man. Pardon my French, love."

"George," Jackie said, "it's a good job you're not on kitchen duty until this evening." Then, shaking her head, "if I were you I'd keep out of Mr Porter's way until you've tidied yourself up. I'm afraid he's on the war path as far as you're concerned."

"Don't I fuckin' know it," the man called after her as she turned away, "not that he's been nearer a fuckin' war than Dover."

Outside the hut, Jackie paused and said, "You'll probably have trouble with him. He's nice enough when he's sober, but with a skinful inside him he can be an absolute terror. Threatening to fight any and everyone, Porter especially. He was in the first war — in France. If you ask me he still suffers from shell shock. Slam a door when he's nearby or drop something heavy and he screams fit to knock the place down."

The following night, after a first, back-breaking day spent cutting grass which had grown thickly under the chalets, I was lying exhausted in bed when I heard George come blundering down the corridor. Outside my door he paused, then began to kick it violently.

"Come on out, you fuckin' bastard," he yelled. "Come on, I'll fuckin' kill you." The door shook in its frame and I gave serious thought to making my escape through the uncurtained window. But then the kicks and yells dwindled away and I heard him fumble at his own door. He must finally have managed to open it because I heard it slam shut. There came a thump which had to be that of a falling body; this was followed by a depleted groan and, soon enough, muffled but unmistakable, the sounds of heavy snoring drifted through the plywood wall.

Next morning, as I bent over the cracked, grey-rimmed basin in the bareboard bathroom, I became aware of a pair of torn, black trousers at the basin next to mine. I looked warily toward where George loomed and watched as he tried to strop a razor-blade on a piece of mirror he held, none too steadily, in his left hand.

"Good morning," I said, ready to sprint for the door.

But, having slowly ratcheted his head in my direction, he peered at me as though he'd never seen me before.

"Seems like a right fucker to me," he said. "What you got on today, then."

"More grass cutting," I said, guessing he wasn't interested in what I might be choosing to wear. I dabbed my face dry with the coarse, yellowing towel that hung from a nail beside the wash basin. It bore the legend, printed in red, *Property of the Devon Coast Country Club. If Found Please Return.* "How about you?"

George rasped a slow hand across his chin. "Cleanin' the fuckin' ovens," he said. "I'd sooner roast that bastard Porter in one, I'll tell you that for nowt."

Which is apparently what he tried to do.

That evening, after another day of grass cutting which was brought to an abrupt end when I sliced through a gas pipe underneath one of the chalets and as a result was told to creosote fencing — "now let's see how long it takes you to flatten every bloody fence" Ernie Simmons said sardonically as he handed me brush and pail of tarry substance — I went for a drink with Jackie to the *Pirate's Snug*, empty apart from the two of us and Keith the barman, who took time off from stock-checking the better to hear Jackie's story.

The version she had came from one of the trainee kitchen staff, a PE student who had watched the incident with appalled fascination. Apparently George had been on hands and knees scrubbing away at one of the vast ovens when

Porter entered, as he did every morning, this time to check that preparations were in hand for next week's grand opening. He bent to look into the oven at which George was working, pointed to what he said were still unclean areas of the interior, and demanded that George go over them again. George, enraged, straightened up, grabbed Porter by the lapels of his coat and tried to force him into the oven. "I gather his language was a bit choice," Jackie said, hooting with laughter, "but not much damage was done before some of the staff dragged George off. But that was him done for, of course. Paid off, marching orders, out the door. Poor old chap."

"Why did he have it in for Porter?" I asked. "As bosses go, Porter seems alright."

"George probably sees him as a brass-hat," Keith said. "One of those who sent him over the top, ordered him into action, invited him to stop a bullet. I don't know. He survived the Somme, but Porter was more than he could stomach. Poor sod."

"He wasn't badly hurt, so I was told, though a bit shaken. More a matter of injured pride," Jackie said.

"Not Porter. George."

"Oh, sorry," Jackie said. "Yes, poor George. Well I expect he'll find other work easily enough. Pontin's may take him on. And if not, there are plenty of other holiday camps around."

Which was true. The mid 1950s was still the hey-day of such camps. Billy Butlin had started his first at Skegness in 1936, but it was in the post-war years that they spread right around the English coast. There was even a film, inevitably called *Holiday Camp*, a sentimental comedy which featured a family called the Huggets, who for a while became the epitome of a kind of Englishness: ordinary, uncomplaining, warm-hearted, with stereotypical roles for mother (played by Kathleen Harrison), father (Jack Warner) and in this instance the adolescent Petula Clark as their 12 year-old daughter. The film was hugely popular and must have done wonders for the camps themselves. For some reason I missed it, though my parents saw it. But I remember watching documentary footage of a holiday camp, shot, I think, in 1946, in which professional men, doctors, bank managers, mingled in fellowship with working class revellers and were shown taking to a platform with trousers legs rolled up for the knobbly knees competition. Everyone ate the same food at trestle tables, each night there would be dancing supplied by good bands, there were singers, comedians, fancy dress parades, beauty competitions, "fun for the kiddies"; and as well as cooks, cleaners, creosote daubers, sparkies and chippies, each camp had its front-of-house staff (in Butlin's case the "Red Coats") to organise activities throughout the day and evening.

It was all very democratic and inevitably this soon led to some entrepreneurs claiming superior status for the holidays they provided. Hence, the Devon Coast Country Club, which affected to look down its nose at down-the-road Pontin's, though I imagine their clientèle were distinguished only by the fact that those who chose the Country Club had to pay more for the privilege of being further away from the beach. Most of the campers were northerners. They arrived by train or charabanc and, each Saturday, change-over day, we all were required to go "tear-arse", in Ernie Simmons' phrase. As Keith's assistant in the Pirate's Snug, one of my duties was to serve men who, fresh off their coach journeys from Birmingham, Blackburn or Bolton, left their wives and children to sort out the chalets they'd been assigned while they themselves came straight to the bar, ordered pints, and, while they were paying, handed over £10 notes with their names pinned to them. These were to be kept behind the bar and drawn on for all future drinks. "Anything left over at the week's end," I was told, "goes to you and your mate." Of course, the £10 was usually gone well before the end of the week (few campers stayed for a fortnight); but even so we did pretty well from instructions to "keep the change", and just occasionally we would clean up from men who, perhaps to maintain appearances, left their £10 on arrival and then, for the rest of the week, steered clear of the Snug.

Waiters did even better, paid in kind by some of the young women who habitually arrived at the Club in pairs. One waiter in particular, a blond, slim man who bore a close resemblance to a then famous young film actor called Hardy Kruger, seemed endlessly in and out of different chalets. At the end of each night he would turn up at the Snug, waiting duties over, and sit at the bar while Keith cashed up and I mopped tables, emptied ashtrays and pushed a broom over the floor. "Hard life, this," he would say, sipping his gin and tonic and drawing on a Capstan Full Strength.

"Way you're going, you'll be lucky to reach thirty," Keith said, nodding towards the open cigarette packet. "How many do you get through in a day? Twenty?"

"No," the waiter said, laughing, "never shag more than half-a-dozen in any day, mate. Haven't got the time."

Then there was Michael. An Oxford undergraduate, he joined the staff as waiter some two weeks after the season had begun, and Sheila Fox at once took a shine to him. Michael was the kind of man my father would have called "nattily attired". He wore a hound's-tooth jacket, his grey flannel trousers were always impeccably creased, he had highly polished brogues, and I don't think I ever saw him without a rolled umbrella. On even the hottest of days he would swing his brolly as he sauntered about the place — he was an expert saunterer. He also had a cut-glass accent which it took me some time to realise was pure pose, as was his dress. He was in fact, a louche, witty Londoner, and he often turned up at the Snug after hours when Keith had a lock-in for a few favoured fellow workers. Michael called people by a rich variety of soubriquets and camp terms of affection. Keith was "mine host," I was either "young feller me lad" — I was two years younger at most — or "Marx minor". (He had once come upon me reading the *New Statesman*.) Porter was "He Who Must Be Obeyed", or "Crewe" (an oblique reference to Marie Lloyd's famous song appealing to "Mr Porter" to tell her how to get to that station), "Sweetie Pie" — because, Michael told us, he had once overhead Mrs Simpson so address Porter, or Herr

Kommandant. As for Mrs Simpson, she was "the bosom companion".

On occasions he brought Sheila Fox with him. A few years older than him, Sheila was a plump woman with a pretty face, large brown eyes, and she plainly adored Michael. Unfortunately, she was supposed to be Ernie Simmons's lady, which explained why, as Keith muttered to me one evening, "that Ernie, he's like a bear with a sore head. There's bound to be trouble, and I hope it ain't here."

But it was. That particular evening Keith had as usual locked the bar's outside doors before setting up our drinks, but Ernie had keys to every building on the site. He was, after all, works manager. It was now late June, and at my suggestion Laurie, who had finished his first year at Bristol University as a student of Electrical Engineering, hot footed it to the Club, where I had negotiated work for him as a storeman and arranged for him to have the other bunk bed in my room. Laurie duly arrived, complete with his double-bass and my trumpet which I'd asked him to collect from home, and that evening we took our instruments over to the Snug where we were joined by a waiter called Nick, a medical student who sometimes came to the lock-ins and who played reasonable jazz piano on the Snug's battered upright. A jam session of sorts had been under way for about half an hour, and our audience, consisting of Keith, one or two student waiters and Michael, with Sheila sitting on his knee and nuzzling his ear, was in a state that might best be described as one of rapt indifference, when Ernie appeared.

At first I didn't notice him, not surprisingly, because I had my eyes shut. "Keep playing," Nick said, and I opened my eyes to see Ernie marching across to Sheila and Michael. It would be good to report that the visions of a 1920s Chicago speakeasy came to mind: that we were the Ben Pollock Trio and here came Dutch Schultz to confront Legs Diamond over the moll whom Legs had inadvisably stolen from Dutch. But no: despite Nick's urgent advice, we stopped playing and Ernie didn't reach for a shooter. In fact, it was a dreadful anti-climax.

Ernie began by shouting at Sheila in his thick Devon brogue that she was a whore — "whooer" — and that she belonged to *him*, Ernie Simmons, and not this poncey stuck-up bastard.

"What about your wife," Sheila said, coolly. "Doesn't *she* belong to you? Don't you belong to her?"

"Don't bring my wife into this," Ernie yelled. "She's a decent woman, worth twenty of your kind."

"Then go home to her," Sheila said, and turned back to Michael who sat face half averted, a slight, puzzled smile suggesting that he had no idea what was going on, but that whatever it was it had nothing to do with him. As, to be fair, it didn't. It was Sheila who had made the running, and Jackie later told me that she had been tired of Ernie's attentions long before Michael hove in view.

I doubt that this would have been how Ernie saw the end to his affair. He was William to Michael's Ganymede, though Sheila, I have to add, was no Audrey. She was attractive, able to turn a neat phrase — I once heard her tell Barbara that Mrs Simpson had all the charm of a stone bolster — and from what I knew of her seemed genuinely warm hearted.

But her public rejection of Ernie inevitably felt like an act of cruelty. Poor man, he could do nothing except glare round at us all, then turn his back and walk away. There was unbroken silence as we watched him go. It was like a Western showdown in reverse: Wilson retreating before Shane's implacable gaze. He didn't even slam the door behind him.

The manner of his going, his humiliation, put a damper on the evening, and almost immediately afterwards Keith shut the bar. The next day Michael left and soon after that Sheila was gone, too, though whether to join Michael I've no idea. Barbara thought possibly yes, Jackie said no, absolutely not, he had a girlfriend waiting for him in London. How she knew this she didn't say, but she was definite.

"A girlfriend," I said, "well, she won't be too happy if she knows what's gone on here."

"Why should she," Jackie said, "what the eye doesn't see.... Anyway, it was a holiday romance."

As I suppose it was. And looking back it occurs to me that as no doubt in common with other such places, the slightly febrile atmosphere of the Devon Coast Country Club made possible not merely brief romances but sexual liaisons of an uninhibited variety that knocks on the head Larkin's contention that sexual intercourse only got going in 1963. But then Larkin never booked in for a week at Billy Butlin's or any other less celebrated holiday camp.

Not that the Devon Coast was without its "celebrities". One weekend the Max Jaffa trio played for tea-dances. The trio was formed from the Palm Court Orchestra which regularly broadcast what were called "light classics" as part of the BBC's Sunday evening programme, and as with most of those who were required to dole out musical pap they were classically trained, expert instrumentalists. I enjoyed talking to the three of them and was impressed by their lack of cynicism. "The public pays for what we play, so no messing" was their attitude, as it was of the various "guest" comedians and singers, "names" but never really "stars", who were usually booked in for a week at a time. They came, they performed twice nightly, they took their wages and they left. This week Paignton, next week Filey, the week after that Skegness. Do your best, take the money, smile and be grateful.

Only one entertainer stayed all summer, the resident comedian and compère, stage name "Alex Henry". He had hard features, a professional smile that never reached his pale blue eyes, wore well-pressed grey flannels with a powder-blue blazer over white shirt and carefully knotted red tie, and he was a dab hand at most pub and club games: darts, billiards, dominoes, bar skittles. I knew this because he'd occasionally show up at the Snug after hours, never to drink but for a chat and the chance to win a few bob at the billiards table or on the darts board. He took on all comers and I don't recall him ever being beaten. He hailed from somewhere "up north", he said, so knew and understood the ways of most of the paying guests, and he quickly established a professional camaraderie with each new intake. I noticed that when Billy Liddell brought his family for a week to the Devon Coast, Alex Henry spent a good deal of time with him and that Liddell seemed genuinely to enjoy his respectful but never fawning behaviour.

Liddell was by then in the late stages of his career as Scottish international footballer and wing forward with Liverpool. A tall, straight-backed man with neatly-combed black hair, he always appeared in public in his Liverpool blazer with an open-necked white shirt, was affable, never without wife and children, and he modestly declined the chance to take part in an impromptu football match which had been organised for his benefit, though he agreed to referee. I got his signature, intending to pass it on to my father, but to my chagrin I somehow mislaid the piece of paper when I left the Country Club.

Despite his occasional bouts of friendly behaviour, Henry was essentially a loner. From time to time a woman, guest or staff, would make it plain that she fancied him, but I never heard that any of them got him into bed. "Never mix business and pleasure, it's not professional", was his only comment when he joined the discussion in the Snug the night after Ernie's humiliation, and he never did. I once stood at the back of the camp theatre where he was on and off stage throughout a two-hour show. He introduced each act with just the right build up, his patter was routine but flawless, and in his own ten-minute slot, which came just before the interval, he told and sometimes acted out jokes that made the audience laugh but not so much that whoever was top of the bill that night would feel challenged about their own reception. Although I didn't much like him — what, after all, was there to like — I admired his profession-alism.

* * *

All over England at that time other "Alex Henrys" were working night after night during summer seasons to earn not very good money. They were among the last of those entertainers John Osborne would soon turn into a kind of symbol for a fading England. By the summer of 1956, Osborne's *Look Back in Anger* had become not merely a hugely successful play but, even for those of us who hadn't yet seen it, a rallying point or cry. Twelve years later, when I was a visiting Professor at the University of Maryland, I was amazed by the overnight transformation of blond, muscular youths into hunched Dustin Hoffman look-alikes as the release of Mike Nichols' film *The Graduate* became absorbed into and even helped shape the ethos of young Americans protesting against Vietnam and various insufficiencies of the white American Dream. *Look Back in Anger* didn't quite have that impact, not, though, because of Jimmy Porter's claim that there were no great causes left. It was more that "anger" was typically the stance of those whose class circumstances privileged them to display it. Peter Hennessy says that soon after Osborne's play opened in May, 1956, *The Times* coined the phrase "angry young men", and "The Angry Young Men" became the title for a series of articles run by the *Daily Express*. I doubt the phrase had much currency among readers of the *Daily Mirror*. Spokesmen for the angries included Lindsay Anderson and Tony Richardson, both Oxford educated, and rather as the following year political radicalism would become focussed on the Oxbridge-based *Universities and Left Review*, so those who were most vocal in promoting "the angry generation" were undoubtedly making shrewd career moves.

Still, anger was in the air. It disturbed even the tranquil atmosphere of the Devon Coast Country Club. It wasn't merely the inchoate, forgiveable rage of poor George, nor the less excusable anger of Ernie Simmons. Discontent with Porter's increased high-handedness was growing among us workers. As one or another member of staff left, and they were doing so in increasing numbers, most of them fed up with the poor wages and long working hours, so Porter, without enquiring into our own skills or preferences, would demand we take over the chores of those who had gone. Replacement staff were apparently difficult to come by —

"better pay and conditions elsewhere, that's why" we muttered — with the result that you might find yourself ordered to help in the kitchens, say, or wait at table, even though you had just finished a full day's work as pool attendant or gardener. The grumbling grew and in the early hours of one Saturday morning anger finally had its way.

Keith had as usual arranged a lock-in, there was the nightly jam session, and afterwards a few of us, carrying bottles of beer, made our way down to the open-air pool, where we sprawled under the stars, talking and laughing. Suddenly Porter appeared. We were disturbing guests, he said, we should be in bed, and anyway we must know that the pool was out of bounds to working staff.

One of us stood up to argue with Porter. He was a student whom I will call Alan. In the winter Alan played lock-forward for a leading rugger club, a position he also occupied in England's XV. At six foot two and all muscle he was not a man to be taken lightly, so I'd have thought. But Porter was used to issuing orders and unused to being opposed.

"You will go to bed at once," he said. "All of you."

By way of an answer, Alan simply picked Porter up, carried him to the shallow end of the pool — rather considerate in the circumstances — and dropped him in. Then, while the owner of the Devon Coast Country Club scrambled soggily out of the water, Alan went back to his beer.

The next morning, and no doubt a few seconds before we could be sacked, we all queued up for the wages due to us. These were handed over by a silent Mrs Simpson, Porter being nowhere in sight. Then we left.

Chapter 13
London to Reading

Almost as soon as I was back in Ashford, Pete phoned. He'd wanted to ask my parents for my Paignton address and was caught off-guard when he heard my voice.

Equally surprised, I asked him where he was speaking from.

"Home."

"I thought you were supposed to be in the army. Why are you home?"

"Why are *you* home?"

Early that evening we met at the White Swan. Pete looked more haggard than ever, shoulders bent as though in submission to some invisible, haptic load, the rope of hair, unwashed and unkempt, black against white face, his strained, anxious eyes.

"I've been discharged," he said at once, as we stood at the bar ordering our beers. At this hour the place was still more or less empty, but Pete spoke in not much more than a whisper, looking over his shoulder as though anxious that his remark might be overheard.

"Is that good or bad?"

"Good, I suppose." He shook his head as though trying to clear it. "Though it doesn't feel that way."

We carried our drinks over to a far corner of the room and, after we had settled into our seats, he added, "I had what the army are choosing to call a breakdown. Making me 'Unfit for Further Military Service'."

There was a pause during which we sipped our beers and Pete, hunched and disconsolate, stared gloomily at the round wooden table in front of us. And then he told me that after the first few weeks of square-bashing, which, if allowances were made for the usual pettifogging stupidities of barrack life, had passed off uneventfully, he had come up against a more than average bully of a sergeant. The man did his best to make Pete crack, insulting and humiliating him at every turn, hoping of course to make his victim answer back or, better still lash out. Pete could then be put on a charge of insubordination. Even so, he had more or less coped. "I was being the good soldier," he said, allowing himself the merest flicker of a smile.

I nodded, registering the allusion. Earlier that year I had bought the Penguin edition of Jaroslav Hasek's *The Good Soldier Schweik*, a novel that at once became for us both a model of how to cope with authority. (Joseph Heller's *Catch-22* takes more from Hasek than either he or any of his commentators have wanted to admit.) Schweik's cheerful agreement with authority's contempt for him seemed the perfect way to outwit brass necks. We would quote to each other the snatch of dialogue which begins with the lieu-tenant telling Schweik, "The Chaplain recommended you as a champion idiot, and I'm inclined to think he wasn't far wrong." To which Schweik replies, "Beg to report, sir, the Chaplain as a matter of fact wasn't far wrong. When I was doing my regular service, I was discharged as feeble-minded, a chronic case, too."

"You mean you acted out being a chronic case of idiocy?" I asked Pete.

Yes, he said, he had, but in the end the act took on the force of reality. He lost the power of speech, found himself in defiance of regulations wandering around camp dressed only in singlet and shorts with — a bizarre touch, this — a rugger ball tucked under his arm, and was at that point whisked off to army hospital in Portsmouth where he was placed under "observation." Two weeks later, he was discharged from the army. The telling of this tale, which was uncharacteristi-cally full of stops and hesitancies, took some time, but once he had completed it, Pete relaxed. "Tell you what," he said, "let's walk down to the Barmy Arms, have one there. I want to show you something on Eel Pie Island."

"I've been there," I said, "plenty of times."

I had too. The island was an eyot in the river, one of the

largest or at least longest of several such islands that interrupted the flow of the Thames between Staines and Richmond. It was well-known as a place where a shifting population of artists and jovial eccentrics had built their own often crazily dilapidated sheds and living quarters, garishly painted, the tiny front gardens sprouting metal and wood sculptures among undisciplined crowds of flowers and vegetables, its banks ringed by narrow boats, home to equally eccentric escapees from the routines of daily life. One May morning, between my inglorious return from Preston and departure for Devon, I had cycled along the riverbank from Sunbury, stopping when I came to the chain ferry that served to connect Eel Pie Island to the tow-path and mainland life. The Penguin edition of Hopkins had recently become a prized possession, and without having to summon them up, phrases from "Spring" arrived in my head. "When weeds, in wheels, shoot long and lovely and lush", thrush's eggs "little low heavens", and perhaps most piercingly, blue "all in a rush, With richness." Kingsley Amis says that at some moment in his young life any Englishman seriously interested in poetry is bound to think Keats the greatest of all poets. Substitute Hopkins for Keats and I agree. Hopkins out-Keats Keats in sheer intensity, linguistic and rhythmic exuberance, and when you are young your senses aren't so much new-peeled as not yet crusted with habit, so that there feels to be no barrier, no kind of mediation between the in-here and out-there. I suspect that poets who for whatever reason come to either Keats or Hopkins later in life will feel that the famed sensuousness is all a bit embarrassing. But at eighteen you don't have to apologise for your emotions.

Whether I would have mentioned this mildly epiphanic moment to Pete I don't know, but as we strolled down the tow-path to the Barmy Arms I became aware that an unusually heavy press of people, mostly our own age or slightly older, were all going in our direction. "Off to the island," Pete said.

"Why?"

"You'll see."

We turned into a pub forecourt, a small, paved-over area, separated from the tow-path by low, green painted metal railings — more a decorative border — about which were scattered metal tables and chairs, also painted green, and pushed through the crowd of art students and their look-alikes in order to gain the bar. Standing shoulder to shoulder, we downed our pints, scarcely able to hear each other's words above the general, good-humoured hubbub.

"Right." Pete took my empty glass and plonked it, with his own, onto the bar. "Onward and upward. Prepare for pleasure." His earlier gloom, which I had taken to be settled on him, had now quite lifted.

We left the pub and walked the few yards to the chain ferry where a long queue had formed, everybody dressed pretty much alike, cords, lumberjack shirts, raggedy pullovers, tweed jackets, the women in dirndl skirts and white blouses, their hair worn long, looking as though they might have stepped out of an Augustus John painting.

We crowded onto the ferry and a minute later stepped off it, this time onto the island, the two of us borne along by fellow-revellers, though I still had no inkling of what the revels might be. But there was a feeling of carnival in the air. The path along which we shuffled was leading us to an old ramshackle hotel that stood on the far side of the island, hard up against the more rapidly flowing stream of the divided Thames. I had walked past this hotel on previous occasions. It looked shut up and on the verge of collapse, surrounded by river on one side and, on the other, ragged, unkempt bushes and shrubs which might once have formed the hotel's grounds, though they had long since run to seed, like the hotel itself. Surely Pete couldn't be leading me there? But he was.

If dance halls were in their hey-day during the 1950s, the great good places where people of my parents' generation could go to spin away the hours, to enjoy both themselves and the company of others, it would be good to report that jazz clubs performed a similar function for their offspring. In a way they did. I imagine that by the mid-1950s most English towns had such a club, though in practice this usually meant the once-a-week hire of a church hall, civic function room, back or upstairs room of a pub. Outside London there were few clubs whose be-and-end-all was jazz, and even in the metropolis drinks licences were hard to come by. Jazz was widely regarded as the devil's music, especially by those in authority: police, magistrates, the press. One intrepid reporter from a popular Sunday newspaper claimed to have "penetrated" Cy Laurie's Club where he found a young woman lying unconscious beneath the grand piano. To prove his point, the paper carried a photograph of a grand piano from under which, sure enough, a pair of stockinged legs poked out. Debauchery ruining the nation's young. The fact that the club owned no such piano didn't lessen the frisson of horror. Even Humphrey Lyttelton's 100 Club in Oxford Street ("Humph's" as it was popularly known) had for some time to make do with a Soft Drinks Only licence.

But the hotel on Eel Pie Island was something else. At the entrance, a heavily-bearded man, pipe clenched in all-but hidden teeth and dressed in ragged blue sweater, equally ragged grey trousers and open-toed sandals through which his bare toes protruded, collected our entrance fee. As I handed over some money, he grabbed my hand, turned it over, and with a rubber stamp pressed a blue sign, blur really, onto my wrist. I looked to Pete for an explanation. "It's your passport," he said, "so you can go out and come in again without being challenged."

I went out only once, for a breath of evening air. It was charged with the sweet, heavy scent of a substance then called "hash", "viper", or "rope." The scent came from the shrubbery, as did various sounds: giggles, whisperings, susurrations, grunts, the audible evidence of what were known as knee-tremblers. People went and came at regular intervals, but for the most part I stayed inside, leaning on the well-stocked bar which ran the entire length of the ball-room, happy to listen to the jazz.

That first night, the music was, to be sure, pretty mediocre. The band playing was the then virtually unknown Acker Bilk's. A few years later a smart publicity man turned the outfit into "Mr Acker Bilk and his Paramount Jazz Band", complete with striped waistcoats and bowler hats, a phenomenon captured both wittily and with a kind of wry affection by the poet John Gohorry:

> The snazzy silk waistcoats are gaudy as deckchairs
> set fluttering all the way along the striped sand
> as the New Hippodrome Management proudly presents
> Mr Acker Bilk and his Paramount Jazz Band
> on whose sleeve notes Teutonic upper case Incipits
> augment a diction that's pure Brobdingnag aureate:
> *Herein the Ensemble's Titular Head executes*
> *Effusions so far Unparalleled upon the Clarionett.*

And yet, although the band itself was no great shakes, the atmosphere was so thrilling, so heady with a sense of *liberation*, that the musical inadequacies didn't matter. At one point in the evening I wandered over to the far side of the rackety old ballroom, my back to the whirl of bodies, the jeans and check shirts, dirndl skirts, flying beads and pony tails, and looked from a smeared window as light faded above elms and, below, the Thames, glistening in oblongs of light cast by the hotel, made its way toward London. Behind me, the sprung floor shook and thumped to a number that may have been "Muskrat Ramble". *New Orleans on Thames* I thought. And on later occasions, when on a packed sweaty Saturday night I heard Sandy Brown's band in full cry, the thought turned to something like ecstasy.

Ah, that band. It was one of Brown's routines to begin the evening's final set with an up-tempo blues, though the word routine does no credit to the actual music. Brown not only played the blues better than any other UK musician, his clarinet was unique in its intonation, able to encompass the savage, the lyrical, the melancholy-sweet, the joyous. He himself composed several memorable blues numbers, mostly in the key of C: among them "Saved by the Blues", a slow, haunting tune, the more upbeat "Bad Day at Black Rock", "Those Blues", "Fifty-Fifty Blues" and, one of my personal favourites, "Nothing Blues", on which he sang, his voice gravelly with scotch, cigarette smoke and a feeling for the music which as he said, for he was not a modest man, made him a far better singer of the blues than George Melly.

He was also far and away the most original British clarinettist of his time. His tone was by turns lyrical and edgily aggressive. Glassiands and swoops that arced through octaves were interspersed with notes that seemed to have been bitten off in sudden anger, and he brought great inventiveness and power to his music. Unlike other bands he wasn't interested in sounding like, say, King Oliver, or Jelly Roll Morton, or Kid Ory. And when he began the last session, as he often did, riffing on Ellington's "Swinging the Blues", Al Fairweather playing trumpet catch-up, holding onto and then leaping over his leader's phrases, the music swelled with such exuberance that you felt it was straining to untether itself from earth, from any gravitational pull against joy. It became the thing itself.

Following my first experience of the Brown band on Eel Pie Island I did my best to get to every one of their gigs in the London area. They were rarely able to play farther afield because Brown was tied by his contract as a BBC acoustician. A pity, because it led to the band gradually falling apart. Musicians must live, and other bands offered more and no doubt better-paid work. Perhaps the band would anyway soon have come to the end of its natural life. Brown composed an anthem for the newly created Ghana ("Go Ghana"), and wrote other music that showed an interest in Afro-Caribbean rhythms which, Fairweather always apart, the others probably didn't share. But while they were at their peak, which they certainly were in 1956, they were far and away the best band in the land. Not so much on record, it has to be said. Recording studios were bound to damp the fire of their live performances, and the four or five minutes allotted to each track, fine as many are, inevitably curtailed those rolling, swelling climaxes they built to when they were playing for live audiences: especially, *uniquely*, I want to say, when they were on stage at Eel Pie Island.

* * *

215

The man who brought jazz to Eel Pie Island, the bearded ur-hippy who stamped my wrist on that first evening in May, was, I now know, Arthur Chisnell. According to his obituarist in the *Independent*, Chisnell, who died in 2006, was a devotee of jazz who "organised a few jazz concerts while serving in the Army in the Second World War". Afterwards, he ran a junk shop in Kingston, where he began to realise that his love of the music was shared by plenty of others, especially those of student age. And so, the obituarist reports, "Chisnell convinced Michael Snapper, who owned the dilapidated hotel on Eel Pie Island, to let him put on trad-jazz bands there at weekends. Built in the 1830s, the Eel Pie Hotel had hosted tea dances during the Twenties and Thirties and, although it had lost its grandeur, it still retained a large dance hall and a bar with a licence." The first ever gig was on April 20th, 1956. Trust Pete to be on to it almost immediately. He never said anything much to me about Chisnell, but reading the obituary I can see that the junk-shop owner would have appealed to my friend's sardonic distrust of authority. "Chisnell," the obituary goes on, "was mostly attracting jazzers, beatniks, and eventually mods and rhythm'n'blues fans keen to dance, drink beer and enjoy themselves away from their parents..." He was, in fact, "a kind of outreach social worker, before there was such a thing.... He became well-known for his radical, informal approach to sociology and welcomed journalists and researchers studying this new post-war phenomenon the teenager, and what would subsequently be called youth culture." Not surprisingly, "the police often turned up in response to complaints from other residents about weekend crowds of up to 500." On one occasion, in 1967, "a raid found three teenagers without a membership card and Chisnell had to pay a £10 fine. 'Our major crime was to teach people to think for themselves, an unforgivable sin,' Chisnell reflected."

The cards, or passports to Eelpiland, weren't in existence at the time I went there. Nor do I ever recall a police raid. Both came later. But Eel Pie Island itself remains for me one of the great, good places of the earth, and all honour to

Arthur Chisnell for making it so. I wish I had known about him when I wrote some verses for the poet-clarinettist John Mole's sixtieth birthday, in which I imagine the bailey bridge which was slung from tow-path to island in 1957 as leading us to "Preservation Hall [while] magical/Sounds washed down the summer Thames — /The Brown band in a land of dreams."

The 1950s a grey decade? I think not. I do, though, think that free spirits like Arthur Chisnell might have found it harder to survive in later, more knowing, decades. He managed on precious little and he seems to have been indifferent to money, even in the days when the Rolling Stones were playing at the island's hotel. But then the bands he persuaded to come to Eel Pie Island took on the gigs for very little cash *and* they had to hump all their own gear across to the island. I have met other men and women like Chisnell and I don't claim that what unites them is the fact that they all flourished in the 1950s. I am, however, certain that the 1950s made it far easier for such people to find expression in ways of living that were remarkable for their undeclarative decency.

* * *

In 1957 the hotel on Eel Pie Island was the same as it had been the year before, the crowds larger, the music just as wonderful (or not, depending on which band was featured). And the feeling, amounting to conviction, that as soon as you stepped onto the island's grassy verge you were entering a kind of untroubled utopia was as intense: the scufflings in the bushes, the reek of wacky-backy, the Thames gliding at its own sweet will, the jostling, good-humoured crowds, above all, of course, the music. I was there often, both in term-time Reading and during the summer. But a year further on, when I went one Saturday evening, I found that the stage had been switched to the ballroom's far end, the ceiling was painted blue with stars — how silly can you get? — the Brown band had more or less broken up, the crowds were younger, edgier, or so it seemed, and Pete had lost interest. We continued to meet at our two riverside pubs, The White Swan and The Barmy Arms, but though Eel Pie Island was still there, we did not go to it any longer.

Of course in 1956 the world was only thirty years on from the recording of numbers that had in the intervening years emerged from the mists of time, so it felt, to become jazz classics, and some of the musicians who had featured on the original recordings were still alive, were indeed, still playing, or after years of neglect were kitted out with new instruments and, in the case of New Orleans trumpeter Bunk Johnson, new teeth, and put back on the road. Among them were Kid Ory, George Lewis and, supremely, Louis Armstrong. And in the jazz summer of 1956 I saw and heard Armstrong perform, live in London. For the previous twenty years the Musicians' Union had maintained a protectionist rule which forbade foreign groups from playing in the UK. Individual musicians, including jazz musicians, were free to accept work here, but on condition that they agreed to be accompanied by home-grown musicians. This gave some fine opportunities to British jazzmen. When in 1938 Fats Waller toured, he was on occasions joined by the outstandingly good young Scottish trombonist, George Chisholm. It was Chisholm's anecdote of how, when given a BBC regulation stool to sit on, Fats turned round to his vast bum and enquired, "Is y'all on, Fats," that gave me the idea for "Fats at the BBC". "Death soon got him down. He was on a train/going nowhere much when the cold stilled his voice./But no. I pile all of him on again/and again, he spins, Fats lives, and I rejoice."

I did and I still do rejoice at that irrepressible ebullience, that rhythmic power, the dexterity and delicacy of his right-hand playing, together with his seemingly inexhaustible melodic inventiveness. Fats Waller was the most enchanting of all jazz musicians. By 1956, though, he was long dead, even if his records span on. He died, as John Wain once pointed out, at the same age, thirty-nine, as that other exuberant maker, Dylan Thomas.

But in 1956 Armstrong was very much alive. Moreover, his name summoned a unique degree of reverence. So when, in 1956, the MU finally lifted its ban on foreign bands and groups, it was scarcely surprising that the first band to be invited over was the Louis Armstrong All Stars. Nor, looking back, is it surprising that the organisers of the tour were uncertain how to package the band. I had a ticket, courtesy of my father, for opening night at the Empress Hall, a vast, entirely unsuitable venue, with revolving stage and muddy acoustics. Proceedings commenced with half an hour from a big band, the Vic Lewis Orchestra. They played a sort of poor-man's version of Woody Herman. Not bad, but not what we wanted to hear. When they finished they received muted applause as did the act that followed, Peg-Leg Bates, an astoundingly agile tap-dancer, who on other occasions would have been treated to a standing ovation. But we weren't there for him. Nor were we there for a girl singer who followed Peg-Leg and who, through no fault of her own, had her last songs more or less drowned out by the persistent, swelling sound of slow handclaps and boos.

Then, and only then, did the Armstrong sidemen appear, coming one by one up the steps to the vast open stage: Barrett Deems, the drummer, pianist Billy Kyle, Arville Shaw on bass, Trummy Young, trombone, and on clarinet Edmund Hall. And then, finally, off-stage to the right, the sound we had waited for. Even before he came into view, Armstrong was playing the first notes of "Sleepy Time Down South". Years later, I read George Melly's account of that moment in his memoir, *Owning Up*. It was, he said, "the most moving sound I ever heard in my life.... How after all those years a man of his age could blow with such freshness, excitement and invention, and at the same time impose on every note his authority, is beyond explanation." Fair enough, although for me the excitement, the sense of Armstrong's unchallengeable authority, came from the combination of intensity and power with which he invested every note in "Sleepy Time Down South", so that I found myself on my feet, quite without knowing how I had got there, drawn upward by the silver keenness — that needle of white light — lancing through me.

The rest was anti-climactic. Too much singing, especially from the band's vocalist, Velma Middleton, who as Melly notes, "made up in bulk what she lacked in swing", too much of Barrett Deems' graceless, thunder-fist off-beats, too many of Trummy Young's cliché-haunted rasping growls, too little from those excellent musicians Kyle and Ed Hall (although the latter did manage a virtuoso up-beat feature on "Indiana"), and too little of Armstrong's own trumpet playing. Besides, soon, far too soon, it was all over.

Yet, cheated though most of us who went to the Empress Hall must have felt, it somehow didn't matter. We had at least heard for ourselves the sounds made by that small man — and Armstrong did look surprisingly small — whose name and genius, as though in defiance of his physical stature as of his colour, had travelled round the world, and who, up from near slavery, was without doubt the greatest exponent of a music which we felt was ours, courtesy of him, and the shared love of which linked us all.

* * *

From one form of celebration to another. July 14th, Bastille Day, was an occasion then still marked by socialists. Pete suggested that we go to a rally to be held at St Pancras Town Hall where the MP, Barbara Castle, was to be one of the speakers. Also speaking was a Spaniard who, twenty years previously, had fought against and escaped from Franco's clutches, and in addition someone I'd never heard of, a tall, handsome man with extraordinary rhetorical energy and a ferocious manner of delivery made the more emphatic by the regularity with which he thumped the table behind which the speakers sat and from which they arose to address the packed hall. The man, we were informed, was E.P. Thompson, a Marxist who the previous year had published an important book about William Morris. I can't remember much of what Thompson said, though I do recall his insistence that each generation had to find the right tools with which to fight oppression and that in our time we needed to be on the watch for anyone who used the word Liberty as a way of justifying any form of repression. I'm pretty sure it was on this occasion that Thompson quoted Milton's *Areopagitica* as a rallying cry to all who understood the importance of resisting the unjust power of the state. This would no doubt help to explain why, later that year, when Russia invaded Hungary, he chose to resign from the CPGB. But on July 14th he and the other speakers had in their sights the perfidy of Western Liberalism, of colonialism and imperialism, and the Spaniard was hugely cheered by the crowd when he spoke of the hypocritical uselessness of the Anglo-French non-interventionist policy which had enabled Franco, Hitler and Mussolini to destroy millions. Moreover, Franco, we were reminded, was still alive, still free to oppress his fellow countrymen. The oration was in Spanish, but an older man sitting beside me, who was wearing a beret with a red-star badge pinned to it, interpreted. He had been in Spain in the late 1930s fighting for the International Brigade, and indeed all round the hall banners and flags loyal to the Republican cause were being held aloft. At the end, when we stood to sing the Internationale and the Red Flag — the latter to the tune, as I knew, of the jazz march "Maryland, My Maryland" — the flags fluttered above us all. The moment linked us with a time when to be Communist made good political as moral sense. Those would-be savants like Clive James who curl the lip in wise disillusion at the idealism which led thousands of the young in the 1930s to join the CPGB are not only ignorant of history, they are forced to invent it. Hence, James's contention that most of those who became Communists in the "low, dishonest decade" were public-school products of the gentry. Try telling that to all who took part in the battle of Cable Street or who volunteered in droves to fight against Franco. Besides, it wasn't their idealism that betrayed these mostly working class men and women, nor was it socialism itself. The betrayers were those who used the ideals they inherited and claimed to abide by as a means to gain and maintain power.

* * *

In that same summer Pete and I walked one warm evening up Shaftsbury Avenue to the Palace Theatre. We were on our way to a production by the Berliner Ensemble of *Trumpets and Drums*, Brecht's adaptation of a Restoration comedy by George Farquhar. The ensemble was in London for a short season during which it would be performing three plays — I think the others were *Mother Courage* and *The Caucasian Chalk Circle* — for neither of which could we get tickets. As we came close to the theatre, we passed, sitting on some railings that must have protected an as-yet uncleared bomb-site, at least twenty men and women, all in light-blue "boiler suits". The ensemble, what else could it be, proclaiming itself as a collective of actors and technicians. No stars, no underlings.

The production itself was a revelation. (The cliché feels for once justifiable.) At the back of the stage a costume rail supplied all the clothes the actors would need as they came on and, in full view, donned military uniform, swords, maids' caps, dressing gowns, whatever. If someone needed to enter by means of a door, the frame itself was carried on, the actor stepped through and the frame was carried off. For anyone used to "realistic" box sets and to actors in full fig costume and make up, as I certainly was and as I suspect were most of those who made up the audiences during that season, the effect was at first unsettling and then exhilarating. The mystique of drama was being stripped bare, before, as Arthur Askey would say, our very eyes.

The play was in German, but I had taken the precaution of reading Farquhar's original beforehand — my introduction to what Hazlitt with good reason called "the artificial comedies of the last century" — and I thought I understood what drew Brecht to a play in which the brutal realities of money and social power lay not far below the surface farce. Soon after seeing the Ensemble I must have bought the special number of the self-styled *International Review, Adam and Encore* devoted to *Bertolt Brecht: 1898-1956*.

Unlike nearly all the small magazines I was then buying — always excepting the issue of *Stand* which carried "The Unpredicted" — I managed not to lose that number of *Adam*. Looking through it now, I see that among the several contributions is one by John Fernald (who must have been a stage director) which reassures "English interpreters of Brecht that there is certainly no need to have any knowledge of the theories. The plays speak for themselves." But Fernald adds that Brecht's method, whatever that is — Fernald doesn't explain — arises "from the fact that his plays seem designed for an audience of a wider range of mentality than that usually found in a Western theatre. They must entertain the simple minded manual worker: they must also tickle the palate of the intellectual..." I am pleased to note that in the margin beside these sentences, the nineteen-year-old Lucas has written "bloody snob: why must workers be simple minded!"

A far better piece by Eric Bentley, "The Stagecraft of Brecht", touches on the dramatist's use of "alienation": the denial of "intimacy" between actor and audience, his insistence on destroying any illusion that the play is "reality" in order to show the dramatist as "making an analysis of society, not portraits of individuals. He saw the audience as active, inquisitive, non-contemplative, in the spirit of our pragmatic, non-metaphysical age." Best of all, there was a short piece by Brecht himself, "The Fourth Wall of China", in which he lays down the generalisation that Chinese theatre establishes a principle of "disillusion". A Chinese actor "does not play as if a fourth wall existed apart from the three that surround him on the stage. *He makes it quite clear that he knows he is being observed.* I could see the sense in this, especially for someone intent on destroying the illusion of the self-enclosed world of "realist" drama. Whether it occurred me to that Shakespeare's soliloquisers had already gone some if not most of the way to pushing down the fourth wall, I can't say. Probably not.

A little later on in his piece Brecht insists that "The actor wishes to appear strange and even unfamiliar to his audience.

He succeeds in doing so by looking on himself and his performance as if both were unfamiliar to him." I didn't really know how to respond to this. How can an actor seem to be unfamiliar with his role. By forgetting his lines? By standing in the wrong place? By wearing inappropriate dress? I could imagine that once in every performance, in contravention of Noël Coward's advice to the budding thespian to "learn your lines and avoid bumping into the furniture", an actor might pretend not to know them or to bump inadvertently into another actor or clap on a maid's mob cap rather than an army helmet (say): but surely too much of this would become merely tiresome. The example Brecht himself gave of how to achieve this effect baffled me. "This style of acting," he says, "lifts ordinary matters out of the rut into which they are apt to sink," and then goes on to instance "A young woman, the daughter of a fisherman [who] is shown standing and rowing an imaginary boat. To steer it she uses an oar which barely reaches to her knees. The current becomes faster; she finds it more difficult to keep her balance. Then the boat comes into a creek, and she rows more quietly. Now this is the way to row a boat; but this sequence has something historical about it, as if it had been sung in many a ballad and was common knowledge."

Years later when I saw a performance of the Peking Opera Company, and watched a young girl on an entirely bare stage step into a non-existence punt and guide herself over a non-existent fast-flowing river to join a non-existent lover waiting on the non-existent far bank — each ripple and change of current made palpable by the extraordinary skill of her mime — I thought of Brecht's fourth wall. But actually, the actress so convincingly inhabited the role she played that I doubt anyone in the audience felt she was hoping to persuade us that she regarded what she was doing as unfamiliar to herself. What *is* true, and here I think Brecht's theatre became hugely important for English drama in the following years, is that acts of ordinary, working behaviour became treated with the kind of scrupulous attention that had previously been reserved for the speeches of kings. And so, to take one example, the actors in David Storey's *The Changing Room*, performed at the Royal Court in the early 70s, did look, walk, or sit in slumped dejection, for all the world as though they were professional rugby league players. When they stripped to shower, their bodies were pasty, imperfectly muscled and sag-bellied, and when they were once more dressed they wore their clothes without any actorliness. Similarly, a wonderful production of D.H. Lawrence's *The Collier's Friday Night* at Nottingham Playhouse, set in a miner's kitchen, included an entirely convincing display of the art of mixing, kneading, and then rolling out pastry, all managed while the mother doing the work talked and listened to those around her in a manner which undeniably "had something historical about it".

Our exposure to Brecht made the two of us judge other productions we saw that summer by the standards of the Berliner Ensemble's *Trumpets and Drums*. I think it must have been then that we saw a quite dreadful play called *The Strong are Lonely*, about Jesuits in 17th century South America, made even more dreadful by the old-style ham acting of Ernest Milton and Donald Wolfit, both of whom spent the entire evening trying to up-stage each other in order to bellow their lines with the kind of random claim to authority which suggested a reconstruction of the Nuremberg Rally. For some weeks afterwards we took to greeting each other in cod RADA voices. "'Tis thee, I do believe." "Indeed, brother-in-God, 'tis indeed, so 'tis. So very 'tis, indeed."

* * *

"Alienation" was a concept, or at least a term, much used in connection with Brecht. It seemed to mean both a technique of acting and production — a refusal to endorse the illusions of the well-made play — and a world view. Alienation explained the divorce between men and the world they lived and worked in. Brecht was a Marxist. So, too, was Jean Paul Sartre. We had come across Existentialism as a philosophical (or was it political?) ideology, though at this distance I can't remember how. I suppose it was "in the air", and people used the term much as a later generation used the terms "écriture" and "jouissance", with a kind of weary familiarity often accompanied by a slight smile, really no more than a down-turn of the lips, as though they admired but at the same time were becoming a little disillusioned by possibilities that the rest of us were only now beginning to discern.

Paris, the Left Bank, Gauloises, Juliette Greco, black berets, black sweaters, jazz, coffee-bars, talk. Existence as preceding essence. We are left alone with our day and must choose what to be, how to act. From time to time I invoked Marx's apophthegm "we are not what we are, but what we do". Existentialism, we told each other, had its merits. It also had one novel, Camus's *The Outsider*, which, in its account of the *acte gratuit*, seemed to revisit *Crime and Punishment* in order to rebut Dostoyevsky's Christianity. And in Camus's essay, "The Myth of Sisyphus", Existentialism, at least in the mix-and-match way we treated it, also provided a metaphor for the absurd world we must live in and, despite the absence of metaphysical answers to the overwhelming question WHY, endure. "Shall we go?" "Yes, let's go". *They do not move.* The ending of *Waiting for Godot* seemed perfectly to exemplify the mood I detected drifting to me from the Left Bank. So, too, did Giacometti's emaciated figures, examples of which Pete and I had seen the previous year in an Arts Council exhibition, and which, in the inconsolable suffering and isolation they embodied or at least suggested — as though they were abandoned in a world that had lost all means of communication — seemed to articulate the angst of an existential position from which the last chance of comfort had been removed.

* * *

And then it was the beginning of October, and I packed my bags for Reading.

Chapter 14
Being There

I arrived at Reading in a golden autumn. The sky, seen through a screen of reddening leaves that hung from tall maples and chestnuts lining the town's avenues, was unfailingly blue, and as the warmth of each day dwindled toward late afternoon, it would be met by an expectant tang of frost that sharpened the air with a promise of keener pleasures to come. The weather was an augury. Eight years later, married, with a young son and heavily pregnant wife, I left for a teaching post at Nottingham University. In between, first as student, then postgraduate and, finally, assistant lecturer, I came as close as anyone has the right to expect to what seemed to me then, as it does now, an earthly paradise. Somewhere proper to grow wise in.

This may seem to exalt the place unduly, especially to those who know Reading only after its transformation into a concrete-and-glass product of London's "Silicon Valley": soulless, anonymous. But this process of what in the end amounted to a transmogrification began in the late 1960s. Reading in the mid-fifties was very different, a small, redbrick Berkshire market town, of no great architectural distinction, although with attractive features. There was, for example, the wide, cobbled London Street, which tilted down to the main street and, across, the market square, taking in an arched bridge under which ran the Kennet-Avon canal. Beside the bridge was a square-built two-storey pub called the Lower Ship, and, slightly above it and on the opposite side of the road, a double-fronted bookshop, William Smith, whose upstairs held infinite possibilities of finds among its vast stock of second-hand and antiquarian books. Broad Street, the town's principal thoroughfare, into which London Street ran, housed a splendid old coaching house, The George, a large store called Heelas, and a charming arcade in which was a tobacconist who, in addition to the usual brands of cigarettes, of cigars and pipe tobacco held in deep jars, stocked a range of more exotic goods, including heavily-perfumed Egyptian cigarettes, oval shaped, which came in pretty cardboard boxes on whose pale green background were superimposed pyramids and, in one instance, a sphinx's head. As for the cobbled market square itself, it had on one side a large Henecky's pub featuring the same kind of pews as distinguished London's Cheshire Cheese, home from home to the Rhymers Club, Yeats, Dowson, Johnson, Symons, and the rest of them. To order a drink you had to press a bell button on the wood-panelled wall above your banquette, which in due course summoned a white-coated waiter. On the other side of the square was the town library with generous gallery space, where I once saw an exhibition by that great, eccentric and compelling typographer, William McCance, held to coincide with his retirement from the University. In the middle of the square, incongruously guarding the entrance to public urinals, stood an obelisk designed by Sir John Soane. This faced across to an entirely predictable statue of Victoria, erected after she had been made empress of India, holding in her outstretched hand a globe, which most mornings was embellished with a lavatory brush.

The redbrick gaol, outside which a group of us stood one beer-fuelled night, demanding the release of Oscar Wilde, squatted on the edge of town hard by Abbey Gardens, whose ruined walls guarded the famous "Summer is a comen in" inscribed by medieval monks. And if you went the opposite way out of Reading you came at once to the Huntley and Palmers biscuit factory. Sutton Seeds were further out still, near Sonning. As for Reading's own brewery, Symonds, it can fairly be said that both its sign (a gold Hop Leaf on a scarlet background) and the pubs it had built in and around Reading, each of which featured a rusticated porch entry, were far more attractive than the actual product. Biscuits, seeds and beer provided work for a large percentage of Reading's population. Others were employed by the Royal Berkshire Hospital, a grandly imposing, grey stone building on the London Road. And I suppose the University increasingly found work for others.

The University buildings were also on the London Road, a stone's throw from the hospital. The main entrance was through a brick porch and then by way of a slabbed, covered walkway to the porter's lodge, with, on both sides, walls on which baize boards and a few glass-covered cases — they bore at the top the names of societies picked out in gold lettering (Rowing Club, Rifle Club, Drama Society) — were encrusted with printed or handwritten posters advertising meetings, talks, social occasions. The walkway opened out into a small square. From the right, stairs led to the offices of bursar, registrar and vice-chancellor and also some lecture rooms, all of them housed in a two-storey Georgian building the University had taken over. To the left another covered but now open-sided walkway conducted you to music rooms and, I would later discover, a vast magnolia tree which screened a rather handsome house containing the senior common room. Ahead, a further open-sided walkway led to the body of the University.

Reading University College had been created at the end of the 19th century as an extension college of Christ Church, Oxford, a place to send all those Jude Fawleys who didn't qualify for Christminster. Hence, the fact that the architecture combined features of an Oxford college with Arts and Crafts functionalism. Hence, too, the construction of the University round three stone-slabbed walkways or cloisters — the back was left open — off which, at right-angles, ran the various single-storey departments: art (including, when I arrived, those Arts and Crafts specialities tapestry and typography), physics, chemistry, botany .... The cloisters surrounded a green space in the centre of which stood the three-storey library. The library was thus positioned as the college's centre of learning. And whatever severity might be implied by the strict arrangement of the buildings was more than off-set by the warm, red Berkshire brick of which they were built. This was not civic, imposing red brick. The ambience of the place not only implied that it was hospitable to knowledge and to learning but that its modest scale provided a model of what the King of Navarre calls "a little academe," though Reading certainly wasn't "Still and contemplative in living art". On the contrary, for all the sleepiness of the town, the University as I found it in 1956 was alive with debate, with an intellectual energy stoked-up by but in no sense dependent on visiting lecturers from the worlds of Fine Art, Letters, Philosophy and Natural Sciences, who seemed to pass through so regularly and often that it sometimes felt as though every night of the week brought with it the promise of intellectual excitement.

Moreover, unlike Navarre, staff and students at Reading weren't confined to a few male members of a privileged social set. This was only partly because a large number of students were recruited from the families of farming folk, both home-grown and abroad. The University was well known for its expertise in matters agricultural. One result of this was its outstandingly good Museum of Rural Life. Another was the yearly arrival of students who, coming from far and near, had chosen Reading because they wanted, or anyway their parents wanted them, to learn about farming. Among them were wealthy sons of Indian and Singhalese tea-planters, others who were the offspring of white South African and Rhodesian tobacco planters, a Jewish student from a kibbutz, and one, a hapless, gawky young man with retroussé chin, always dressed in a brightly-checked hacking jacket, cavalry twills and suede brogues, whose mother was a missionary in northern Africa and who spent most days and nights devoting himself to the task of becoming spectacularly and at the last rigidly drunk. On one occasion when a visit from his mother was imminent, three of us managed to retrieve him from under a rhododendron bush and dunk him in a cold bath in order that he might be in something approaching a fit state to receive "the dragon", as he called her. She turned out to be elderly, mild mannered, and sweetly innocent of her son's fondness for the bottle. I was told by a friend who witnessed her discovery of him in bed and groaning faintly, that she ascribed his condition to "nerves". A number of equally innocent young men arrived from Welsh hill farms, mostly short of funds and amazed to be so far from home. Among this gallimaufry were loathsomely arrogant white supremacists, several of whom had enough money to buy cars, and one of whom objected to being on the same floor in his hall of residence as a black student from Nigeria. He was, I am glad to say, told that if he didn't like the arrangements he should pack his bags and leave.

Virtually all these students played rugger for one of the several university XVs, and on Monday mornings they would appear in public, some of them limping badly, others with blackened eyes and cut or scraped faces. I once asked one of them, a Welsh youth, whether he didn't mind being endlessly injured. He looked at me in amazement. "It's all part of the game," he said in his soft lilt. "It's for the honour of Reading." There was no point in asking him what kind of honour he had in mind.

I don't want to sentimentalise. Quite apart from the Hooray Henries and their lady friends, most of whom had been to public school, and the male versions of which had invariably undergone National Service — as officer-material of course — Reading attracted a large number of huntin', shootin' and fishin' types, who typically registered for degrees in Geography and History. (Their public school lady friends tended towards Classics or Modern Languages.) Most left with 3rd class degrees and no regrets. As far as I could see, their purpose in life was to play rugger in winter, golf in summer, and each evening drink themselves into a stupor. For the rest of us they had unbounded contempt. Students studying science subjects were "oiks". Students on arts degrees were "pseudo intellectuals". I once asked one of them whether he had ever met a genuine intellectual. "Impossible," he said, "there are none." Most of the men wore tweed suits or jackets with cavalry twill trousers, Van Heusen shirts and cravats or tartan ties; the women came in twin-sets and pearls, and underneath their pleated skirts were, so a spy in one women's hall told me, spectacularly ragged and holed underwear. By contrast, grammar-school girls fresh from home came armoured against vice in brand-new bras and knickers.

It was the presence of women at Reading which finally dispelled any idea that the University could be Navarre. Navarre was not only all-male, but its members had to promise to "war against" desires of the flesh. In the Humanities departments at Reading women students were in the majority, sometimes by as many as ten to one. This being the 1950s, desires of the flesh were to be monitored and, if at all possible, suppressed. Reading, like all other universities at that time, stood *in loco parentis*. Women's halls of residence were barred to men after 7pm and women had to be out of mens' by 10pm. Infringement of the rules automatically led to severe punishment. A male student found with a woman in his room after hours could be sent down for a term. A woman student guilty of the same sin had her university career terminated. Of course, the rules were broken, and by and large hall wardens, while not entirely avoiding their responsibilities, took a lenient view of offenders who acted with discretion. Only one, the warden of Mansfield Hall for women, was prompt to enact the letter of the law. In her comparatively brief reign of terror she sent several women students on their way. But then, to everyone's joy, she was hauled up in Reading Crown Court on a charge of adulterous relations with a local doctor. Having been found guilty and earned themselves headlines in the national press — the relevant pages were pinned up all round the University — the couple disappeared to run a hotel somewhere in Cornwall.

The hall of residence to which I had been assigned was called Wantage. (It was named for a small Berkshire town between Reading and Oxford where, though I didn't then know it, John Betjeman sometimes lived, and whose Lord had given money towards the hall's construction.) A two-storey building of red brick, it began life in 1908, and was intended to look like a model Oxford College. For all I know, it may have been an actual imitation of one. The front entrance was through a gated doorway set in a tall-crenellated clock tower and guarded by a porter's lodge which gave onto a gravelled walk surrounding a rectangular, well-maintained lawn. Further doorways, spaced at regular intervals on the two sides, led to student rooms, and a flight of stone steps took you to the upper storey. The rooms themselves were a delight. Each had a truckle bed, handsome, dark wood table and bent-wood chair of the type known as "carver's", plus a leather easy chair, wardrobe and chest of drawers. Heating was by gas fire, for which you had to pay. The rooms were genuinely comfortable as well as elegant, and, what I liked best, their mullioned windows let in a soft light filtered in spring and summer by chestnut trees that grew around the hall. When you threw your window open, birdsong and the smell of fresh-cut grass entered like some guarantee of delight. As autumn and then winter drew on, you could close the dark green curtains at an early hour and feel yourself to be in a scholar's cell, alone with your books and thoughts.

Opposite the entrance to Wantage, enclosing the hall's fourth side, was a large common room with plenty of easy chairs. Above was the dining hall, complete with raised high table, an oak-beamed ceiling, parquet floor, and tables and benches at each of which eight diners could be accommodated. Obligatory portraits in oils of various benefactors and dignitaries hung in chains from the walls. The food was infallibly awful. Breakfast: cereals, soggy toast, very occasionally a piece of what was optimistically identified as ham; lunch: boiled potatoes, splotched blue and green, fibrous cabbage, carrots all wood, stewing meat all gristle: dinner, (for which we were required to wear our gowns and which was preceded by grace uttered by the hall warden or his appointed deputy) same as lunch, though with brown Windsor or red soup to start, and, to finish, sponge pudding as hard as cobblestone. The only exceptions to these culinary routines came on Fridays, when we were treated to fish — boiled haddock, I imagine the stolid mess to have been, although potatoes, carrots and cabbage continued unabated and woefully identifiable — and Sundays, when, breakfast apart, we had to forage for ourselves.

* * *

On my second or third day at Reading I fell into lively conversation with a woman art student who, like me, was a newcomer. She wanted to be a sculptor. Barbara Hepworth was mentioned. She had recently seen some of Hepworth's new work and spoke enthusiastically about it and the work of other contemporary sculptors. Perhaps Elizabeth Frink's name came into the conversation. I was impressed both by her knowledge and her excitement at being at Reading. "I'm going to enjoy being here," she said. Yes, I thought, so am I. But when she asked me what I was studying, I havered. I ought to have been able to talk about Economics or Social Psychology, but really I knew nothing about either. Instead, I talked about poetry and lent her my Penguin Hopkins.

Two weeks later, having gone to some introductory lectures on economics and realised that I hadn't understood a word, I decided I would have to change my degree course. Pete had been right. What on earth had made me think I could cope with Economics? Psychology was fine. But the economics lectures, given by a man who mouthed nothing but statistics, left me befogged. I was like Satan gazing on Pandemonium. I consulted the hall warden, a dour Scotsman who, apart from his pastoral duties, lectured on agricultural matters. "Ask Gordon," was his terse suggestion. Who was Gordon?

"Professor Gordon. Dean of Arts. He's also Professor of English."

I made an appointment. The office was in the Georgian building that fronted onto the London Road. I arrived at the appointed hour and, dressed as required in gown, knocked, was bidden to enter, and did so. A small, dapper man in a grey Harris-tweed jacket and dark blue trousers over highly polished brogues was sitting, legs folded, in a dove-grey wing chair beside the lit gas fire. Swarthily-complexioned, with longer than usual dark hair, he looked somehow Italianate, although I would come to learn that he prided himself on his wholly Scottish ancestry. But what most took my attention were his large, berry-bright eyes and pudgy white hands, one holding a smouldering cigarette. Beside him, on a low table stacked high with books and papers, was an open box of Players Navy Cut. He gestured to me to draw up one of the hard-back chairs arranged about the heavily book-lined walls, the gesture at once casual and grandly theatrical.

As I did so, I realised I had seen him at high table in Wantage, and, at an awkward sherry reception for freshmen on my first or second night, had spoken to him about the Camden School of Art, although goodness knows how the topic came up. "Are you aware of Sickert's Venetian paintings?" he had enquired. I wasn't. "A very different palette," he murmured, "*very* different." The words, like his hand gestures, were both casual and grand. Now, he said, "Ah, the young man who likes art, but who" — and here he glanced at the letter I had written him — "does not like Economics."

"I don't understand it," I said.

"Then you had better come and read English." It was that easy.

He might have given me a reading list, but that wasn't Gordon's way. Instead, he told me to "acquaint" myself with all of Jane Austen and George Eliot, the two novelists we would be studying that term, and attend classes on practical criticism. "Otherwise known as How to Read a Poem". Without difficulty he managed to indicate the capital letters. The following term would be devoted to Marlowe and Restoration drama. "Tiresome stuff, the latter, but a colleague wishes to persuade the world otherwise." This was followed by a downturn of his mouth, a throwaway smile. "And there will be further classes on poetry and criticism."

As there seemed no more to say, I rose to leave, but he waved me back down. "What are your other subjects?" Reading's system, unlike most universities, followed Oxford's to the extent that during the first year every student in the arts faculty was required to follow three major branches of knowledge. Only after passing in all three were you allowed to proceed to your preferred subject. Apart from Economics I had of course embarked on first-year studies in Psychology, and I had also opted for Philosophy. My version of PPE.

I listed the other two subjects.

"And are you enjoying them?"

"Yes," I said, I was, which was the truth.

"So I should hope," he said. "Both Professor Vernon and dear Hodges are eminent scholars. *Most* eminent."

I didn't yet realise that eminence in scholarship was no guarantee of competence in teaching, but in fact both Maggie Vernon, whose work on the psychology of perception put her among the first rank of contemporary theorists, and Hodges, were excellent lecturers. Hodges in particular enthralled me. It was one of his lectures that I was due to attend as soon as my interview with Gordon was over. The Philosophy department was further along the corridor from Gordon's room, and Hodges' lectures were given in a queer, dusty attic you climbed up to by a set of teetering wooden stairs. Montaigne's tower, or where Il Pensero's Platonist toiled on. Well, not quite, perhaps, but classes in Philosophy did undoubtedly make you feel you were in a world apart. One more instance of the little academe. On the otherwise bare walls of the lecture room hung black and white portraits of, among others, Hobbes, Hume, Kant and John Stuart Mill, the glass of some cracked, others almost hidden behind curtains of cobwebby dust.

Perhaps as many as a dozen of us gathered for lectures on the History of Philosophy, and an Introduction to Ethics, for which I was now bound. There was also a course on Aesthetics, which first-year students of Fine Art as well as English and Philosophy were required to take and which had to be given in a lecture room elsewhere, the one reserved for philosophy being too small for the purpose. All these courses were conducted by Hodges. It was some time before I discovered that the Philosophy department consisted of him, a Leibniz specialist, Dr Parkinson, a shy man with whom I would later become friendly (among his passions were jazz and cricket), and a young woman from Oxford with a convulsive manner of disposing of cigarettes and sherry. She later disappeared into a convent. Hodges lectured without notes, although from time to time he would draw from the pocket of his grey suit jacket a postcard and study it before pushing it back. He had a nervous, high stepping movement and a scrawn of grey hair over large blue eyes and a high, aquiline nose, which between them gave him a close resemblance to some long-legged water fowl.

But he was a wonderfully good lecturer, utterly lucid, and passionate in his belief that Kant was the greatest philosopher who had ever lived. He himself had made his name by producing the authoritative edition of and commentary on the German idealist and follower of Kant, Dilthey, but Dilthey didn't come up in any of Hodges' lectures. The History of Philosophy began with the pre-Socratics (subject of an excellent little book by W.K.C. Guthrie, which we were recommended to buy), continued with Plato/ Socrates — *The Republic* and *The Symposium*, took in Aristotle (who also of course featured in the course on Aesthetics), skipped the Romans, apart from a brief detour via Democritus and Epicurus, then travelled through the Church fathers (A.E. Copplestone allowed to be the best commentary on Aquinas and Duns Scotus), before entering the broad highway of modern times, although we bypassed detailed study of French and British philosophers. These were to be left to those continuing with the subject beyond the first year. For Hodges, all roads led to Kant. Not only the short and, despite its title, comparatively graspable *Fundamental Principles of the Metaphysics of Ethics* (for the course in Ethics), but *The Critique of Pure Reason*, which I don't think I ever fully understood, any more than I did *The Critique of Pure Judgement* (required reading for the course on Aesthetics), although the distinction Kant drew between the mathematical and dynamic sublime proved useful when I came to the Romantics. So did Ruskin, Bergson and Collingwood, whom we read for the Aesthetics course. I once startled the young woman from Oxford, who was briefly my tutor, by quoting more or less verbatim the passage from *Modern Painters* in which Ruskin compares Claude unfavourably to Cimabue — I think I can still do it — and, when I began to study the 19th century in earnest, Mill's *Utilitarianism* and *On Liberty* proved equally useful.

I mention these names not merely to indicate what a first-year course in Philosophy at Reading then was, but because so much of what I read fifty years ago has stayed with me, and that it has done so is in large measure thanks to Hodges. He was a fairly remote bird. But the eagerness with which he lectured — as it were picking and pecking his way among ideas — transmitted itself to us. No doubt the transmission was faulty, but enough got through the ether for most of us to pursue the subject in out-of-hours conversations in the buttery or, occasionally, the pub. There was also the stimulus of the Philosophy Society, run by second and third-year students, who regularly brought outside speakers to Reading. Not all of these were as lucid as Hodges, but some were good value. There was, for example, Stuart Hampshire on Empiricism, there was Ernest Gellner, whose reputation as a kind of belated *enfant terrible* seemed justified when he arrived with a rucksack out of which he drew and drank a bottle of milk as well as the manuscript of his latest book. There was also S. Korner — that was how he was introduced and how his name appeared on the cover of his Penguin study of Kant, by then in circulation. I still have several of those Penguin studies, including the ones on Berkeley, Hume, and Locke, monographs which, with the best will in the world, I can't imagine being published today.

I remember especially the occasion of a talk Hodges gave to the combined Philosophy and Literary Societies, on Blake's possible debt to Boehme. The talk, which took place late in the spring term of my first year, was remarkable for the thoroughness with which Hodges trounced the claims of Blakeians who argued for Boehme's influence. After he had finished, he left the room, rather than, as was the custom, taking questions. He had a good excuse — a train to catch — but the large audience he left behind might have felt cheated. As it was, however, discussions broke out all around, until one voice stilled them by booming, "So much for Boehme, plainly. But what of Swedenborg?"

As Coleridge more or less said of Wordsworth, I would have known that voice anywhere. It belonged to a lecturer fresh to the English department, Ian Fletcher. He had been appointed to replace John Wain, when Wain left to pursue a career as full-time writer. I had already attended some of his lectures on Poetry and Criticism and Restoration Comedy, occasions which hovered between high seriousness and low farce, and which always threatened — or promised — to dissolve into unstoppable laughter. What I didn't then know was that he had no degree. This lack, so I would discover, had caused much consternation among the more convention-ally-minded of Reading academics when Gordon insisted on appointing him. But Gordon, who had no love for such conventionality, and who had received assurances from Wain as to Ian's suitability, went ahead. His confidence in Ian would have been boosted by the approval of Frank Kermode, at that time a lecturer in the department. (He had earlier been a research student of Gordon's at Liverpool.) Probably through Wain, Kermode met Ian in London, where he passed his days as a children's librarian in Lewisham Public Library. Nights were devoted to writing poetry, to increasing his already massive store-house of knowledge about literature, and to being a kind of litterateur-about-town. Honour to all involved that, despite the opposition of the mean-minded and mediocre, Fletcher came to Reading.

Ian was one of a generation of writers and intellectuals whose careers had been interrupted, even severed, by the war. Of those who broke off college life to join the armed forces many chose not to return to education but, with the coming of peace, found their way to London and the hand-to-mouth world of literary journalism. Among those I myself came to know well were the Marxist poet and magazine editor Arnold Rattenbury, who eventually and none-too securely earned a crust as a wonderfully original exhibition designer, and the poet and novelist Ernest Frost. Although I had heard about Ernest from Ian, I only met him when in 1977 I took the chair of the newly-established Department of English at Loughborough University. Ernest was among a group of lecturers who had been gathered in from the old College of Education. Before coming to Loughborough he had racketed about London publishing poems and several novels, for some of which John Minton supplied the cover designs, and he knew everyone, including George Fraser, who some 20 years earlier had given up a freelance life for a lectureship at Leicester University. It was inevitable that in the small world of literary London Ernest and Ian should meet, though not inevitable that Ian would admire Ernest's poems. But admire them he did and when he talked to me of them he was characteristically eloquent about their virtues. Eloquence was Ian's forte.

In his memoir, *Not Entitled*, Kermode says that when Ian was interviewed for the post at Reading, he was for once struck silent — presumably with nerves — and so he, Kermode, was himself sent for and interviewed on Ian's behalf. The interview was successful and Ian was appointed. "Soon he was roaring and booming about the place as if he had never for a single moment been short of words. I regard this as probably my finest academic achievement." There will be more, much more, to say about Ian, whom I didn't really get to know during my first months at Reading, whereas Gordon, whose lectures on Jane Austen I now began to attend, became a familiar presence, both in the lecture room and at Wantage, where he would occasionally invite me to his rooms in hall for a drink.

The lectures were, I almost want to say literally, spell-binding. Gown falling from one shoulder, Gordon wandered back and forth in front of the raked lecture room, his voice sometimes descending to an almost inaudible whisper, at other times fluting with excitement, *rs* rolled with unmistakable relish — "the irrrron law of chastity" — and whole phrases seemingly uttered on an indrawn breath so that I found myself wondering whether, like Tommy Dorsey, he was capable of circular breathing. Meanwhile, his hands conducted their own

240

baroque commentary, stabbing at the words on the page, lifting as though in priestly supplication in order to emphasise a point, waving aside the benighted comments of some critic or other — David Cecil was repeatedly invoked in order to be dismissed — one hand, the right, very occasionally held high, fingers extended as though in blessing. Many years later, when in the course of reading Frances Yates' *The Art of Memory* I came to the passage where she identifies one of the Ciceronian requirements for rhetoric, pronunciation — by which was meant expressive gesture, a meaning we still retain when, for example, we speak of someone having a "pronounced stoop" — it occurred to me that Gordon, a Renaissance scholar who was intimate with many of the Warburgians, and who was very friendly with Yates — might, unconsciously at least, have put into practice some form of gestural vocabulary.

But probably not. Though studied, his effects were unlike any others I have ever come across. They were integral to an effect, no, a quality in him, which was as unforced as it was deep-rooted. You couldn't be in Gordon's company for five minutes without becoming aware of his passion for litera-ture, ideas, art. Music alone he had no time for, being, as he sadly admitted, tone deaf. Kermode says that you approached familiarity with Gordon through scholarship. But there was more to it than that. Kermode wasn't inter-ested in teaching. His lectures on George Eliot, though perfectly intelligible, were unremarkable. "I like George Eliot, but I do not love her," he said at the end of one lecture. But Gordon loved Jane Austen. This bare statement can make him look soppy, a "Janeite". But he wasn't like that, at all. He quoted Auden: "You could not shock her more than she shocks me,/Beside her Joyce seems innocent as grass." He referred approvingly to D.W. Harding's phrase "regu-lated hatred" as a key to an understanding of the novels. He also took delight in unwrapping them as *made* objects: their structuring, the control of narrative, the fact that key moments are craftily engineered as *social* moments.

There were times in the years I knew Gordon when I was angered by him, other occasions when he baffled me. But I never wavered in my veneration for him. That he was a great scholar, there's not much doubt. He was also a great teacher. Most important of all, he assumed you were as interested as he was in the subjects he cared about. In this he was the opposite of Kermode, who never bothered to conceal his belief that undergraduates were the unwashed and that he intended to give us all a wide berth. In our second year, a group of us attended seminars Kermode was required to give on Milton. At one of these he asked a friend of mine to read a passage from Book IV of *Paradise Lost*. The man, a keen student who had great love for Milton, but who was made nervous by the circumstances in which he was now called on to perform, read none too well. "Thank you," Kermode said icily, as the reading ended. "I think I can say that betrays very little understanding of the text." Gordon would never have said anything so calculatedly belittling.

I remember a visiting American student telling me once, in amazement and admiration, "the thing about Gordon is that he treats you as though you're in on the game." He meant that in conversation Gordon seemed to make no distinction between undergraduates and the numerous eminent scholars he brought to Reading. All were addressed as though they were equally serious, equally knowledgeable, equally avid for learning. This could lead to awkwardnesses. One evening, not long after my switch to English, Gordon drifted into the English seminar room which doubled as a common room and collapsed into an easy chair among a few of us. He invariably fell backwards into chairs rather than lowering himself and this, too, could lead to moments of awkwardness, even unintended comedy, as on the occasion when a chair he dropped into shot suddenly backwards with Gordon waving his legs in the air rather like the metamorphosed Gregor Samsa. On the occasion I have in mind, however, the chair remained unmoved. Not so our group, when Gordon, not waiting to discover our topic of conversation, announced as he fell backwards, "I think we have heard *quite* enough about narcissi for the moment."

I have no idea what we'd been talking about when Gordon arrived, but it certainly wouldn't have been narcissi, a subject on which I suspect most of us would, as Empson said of death, have prepared to be blank. However, inferring that Gordon must be interested in flower gardens — which proved to be the case — I murmured something no doubt inane about rhododendrons being pleasant enough. Gordon looked round, his smile one of mischievous amusement. "Don't talk to *me* about rhododendrons," he said, thus plunging us into definitive silence.

He wouldn't have meant this to happen. "Don't talk to *me* about ..." was, peculiar though it must seem, his way of inviting talk, the jemmy that would, so he hoped, pry open the window to conversation, and I think he was always genuinely puzzled when it failed to work. Once, in the early 60s, by which time I had become an assistant lecturer at Reading, Gordon and I together interviewed a prospective student for the department. What would he like to talk about, Gordon asked him. The candidate elected to discuss Wordsworth, a poet Gordon revered. "Then tell us something about Lyrical Ballads. Do you find the Preface a helpful way into the poems?"

"Well," the understandably apprehensive young man began, "the statement about 'the real language of men'..." and got no further.

"Don't talk to *me* about the real language of men," Gordon said, which, as this was precisely what the candidate had been invited to do, not surprisingly flummoxed him so badly that he became lock-jawed with terror.

Loneliness no doubt played its part in Gordon's sometimes bizarre and perhaps even desperate attempts at conversation. Kermode says that Gordon was "alone and lonely". There was undoubtedly a deep, inner loneliness about him, but he was by no means always alone, at least in the obvious sense that he enjoyed company, even though he wasn't very good at sociability. What he *was* good at, wonderfully so, was sharing his intellectual excitements. And although he could from time to time be tiresomely snobbish, especially when a

Name or a Title was in the offing, he was deeply democratic in his assumption that you didn't need to possess either name or title to care about those things he himself cared about: especially art, architecture, and above all literature. This was what made him a great teacher. It wasn't so much what he taught, though he could be a dazzler, as the intensity of his regard, and I revered him, as did others, because he took for granted that we would be as committed as he was to the subjects he held dear. This meant that he was frequently disappointed, as someone fell away or turned his or her back on the possibilities Gordon had opened up. But at least in the years I knew him, when his passion for the Renaissance was becoming largely supplanted by new interests — Yeats, in particular — he never lost his desire for intellectual quest and mastery of a subject, nor his habit of involving others, of behaving as if the quality of their excitement would at least come near to matching his own. And when you are young, a first-generation undergraduate from a home with no great pretension to intellectual interests, to be treated as though you are an equal in such a quest, even when both of you know that you are no such thing, is not merely flattering, it is profoundly enabling, though the words barely do justice to the depth of my gratitude to Gordon, a gratitude which has lasted throughout my life. If, as I have been told by contemporaries who were at other universities, their undergraduate days were for the most part forgotten boredoms or had dust strewn over them by remote and ineffectual dons, I can only say that mine were ones the memory of which I bless.

Chapter 15
The Larger World

It was largely because of Gordon that Reading became a place where scarcely a week went by without some distinguished outsider appearing as a guest lecturer on campus. Many of these came from the Warburg Institute with which, through his spectacularly original work on Masque, Gordon had close connections. In that first autumn term alone, I recall Ernst Gombrich coming fairly regularly to talk — nominally to art students but in fact to students and interested members of staff from all disciplines. Professors of Chemistry, Physics, Botany, Classics, were regular attendees, so, too, students from across the entire range of disciplines. The little Academe grown large. And more than one local town resident, who wasn't part of the official University scene, might turn up. Chief among this group was a poet, so anyway he styled himself, who wore a ginger-coloured corduroy suit and red polka-dot bow-tie, claimed to have a considerable reputation in Italy although woefully overlooked nearer to home, and who answered to the name of P.O. Fitzgerald Moore. He published one poem in the University's literary magazine, which included lines about towers that "invade /Staining the heat of evening /With the effortless selection of a cellulose knob." As Ian said when told of the poet's Italian success, "no doubt the language barrier helps."

Gombrich's method of dealing with his chosen subject was intriguingly like that of a great detective. A picture would be shown, often featuring "Ze Wirgin", a pictorial oddity or seemingly inexplicable feature pointed out — "Vy is zat angel hidink its eyes" — and an hour later we would have been led step by journeying step to the answer, taking in as we went iconographic enquiry into Greek and/or Roman and/or Egyptian statuary and writings, plus texts of the early Church fathers and commentaries on the ancients by mythographers, among whom Isadore of Seville appeared to be *primus inter pares*. And if it wasn't Gombrich it would be Ettlinger pursuing the same line of enquiry and, like Gombrich, occasionally interrupting his narrative flow in order to make clear his contempt for some modern artist. Mondrian in particular was liable to be flayed by the Ettlinger gutturals.

After these lectures, which began at 5 o'clock, presumably so that students could be in time for hall dinner, several of us would cram into The Turk's Head, a low-ceilinged pub diagonally opposite the University, where we would discuss all we had heard. Gombrich, a large, avuncular figure, never joined us there. I suspect he went off to dine with Gordon. But from time to time Ettlinger would show up, always, or so memory insists, with a different woman meekly in tow. Each of these women would be introduced as a colleague, though they plainly were not there out of collegial loyalty. Short, dapper, tending to bow-ties and dark-grey suits, and with a swart, crumpled face which made him look froglike but which did not lessen his attraction for women, Ettlinger would sip a gin-and-tonic while accepting the praise and diffident questioning of the circle that gathered round him. There was a testing moment once, when a part-time tutor in sculpture, David Kellaway, took exception to what he had interpreted as a slighting reference to Rembrandt. Kellaway began hotly to defend what he called Rembrandt's tragic realism, but by the time he finished Ettlinger had somehow managed to disappear with that week's female colleague, and Kellaway was left to make do with the sympathetic attention of P.O. Fitzgerald Moore, who had been much struck by the phrase "tragic realism", an effect which, if he might make so bold as to mention, sympathetic readers had sometimes registered as integral to his own work.

Other visiting lecturers on art I heard soon after my arrival at Reading included Alan Bowness, who gave a dull talk about Cezanne, and Peter Murray, far more lively on Tiepolo. All were invited by Gordon, who sat in attendance in the front row, occasionally murmuring to himself entirely audible remarks among which "I *don't* think so" and a magnificently expressive and infinitely extensible "hmmm-mmmm" featured regularly, whereas I don't recall seeing the Professor of Fine Art at any of them. Anthony J. Betts had been a student of Sickert's and the staff he gathered around him seemed for the most part low key and, even, drab. Betts himself was very short and fat, with a goatee beard, and in public he always wore a cape over a silver-grey suit, carried a silver-topped cane, and his head was crowned by a wide-brimmed black hat worn with undeniable élan, although overall the impression he gave scarcely avoided affectation. This was intensified by his manner of speech, which at first sounded like genteel cockney, but which he almost certainly created as a mark of singularity. I once heard him ask a student about the whereabouts of another because "Aye event seen anythin' of 'im lately."

It may be that with his invitations to the many art historians who were plainly friends and acquaintances of his, Gordon had put Betts's nose out of joint. "Perhaps it wouldn't be impossible to point to equally impressive groups in some modern common or combination rooms, but it might be harder to represent them as normally in easy, serious talk," Kermode says, recalling his Reading days and the seemingly endless stream of academics and writers Gordon invited to lecture and talk. True, but what was most notable for students was that Gordon intended that the easy, serious talk shouldn't be exclusive to the senior common room. Of course, his very presence, his mannerisms, that fluting voice and his smile of seeming contempt for whatever you said, could inhibit, even prevent conversation. In *Clearances*, her witty, sharply observant and affecting memoir, the second edition of which I had the privilege of publishing in 2007 under the Shoestring Press imprint, the poet and novelist Mairi MacInnes reports that, soon after John Wain became a lecturer at Reading, she went there to meet him and was "introduced to the professor of English, Donald Gordon, who was about to go off to Italy, a man with a fine self-regard who laughed at me, because of my crude verses perhaps."

Gordon was undoubtedly arrogant. But the arrogance was intimately connected to what Kermode calls the purity of his scholarly ambitions. Toward his students he could be and usually was forgiving of errors. With those who set themselves up as *savants* it was a very different matter. On one occasion a then famous American academic, W.K. Wimsatt was touring UK universities, bringing with him a new interpretation of Aristotle's Poetics. Wimsatt was known for his book, *The Verbal Ikon*, a full-length, remorselessly tedious study of poetry which elaborated on the "Intentionalist Fallacy" he and his fellow-American Monroe K. Beardsley had exposed, and partly as a result of which what was called the New Criticism — of rigorous attention to the text itself and nothing but the text — had assumed dominance in English departments everywhere. Everywhere but Reading, perhaps, because Gordon often wondered aloud what *was* the history of which these "gentlemen" were so scared, leaving us to draw the inevitable conclusion that for him at least the New Criticism was a product of Cold War politics. But it wasn't that which caused him to voice public displeasure at Wimsatt's lecture. The lecture seemed to go on for a long time, and as Wimsatt had his head bent over the lectern in order to read out the prepared text he was bound to miss the signs of Gordon's increased displeasure, the roll of shoulders, the shifting from one haunch to the other, the glances round at the audience, eyebrow raised in disdainful wonder.

As soon as Wimsatt sat down to the regulation round of applause, Gordon stood up. "Mr Wimsatt, may I ask, do you read Greek?" Wimsatt admitted that he didn't. Gordon then launched into what seemed a five-minute quotation from Aristotle in classical Greek, at the conclusion of which he said, "I recommend you employ a reputable scholar to explain to you what that means", and made for the exit, leaving the six foot plus Wimsatt a wreck, holed below the waterline and sinking fast.

Some who were at the lecture held that Gordon was being discourteous to a distinguished visitor. I disagree. He was

248

exposing pretension. As an undergraduate at Edinburgh University, he had studied under the Shakespeare scholar, John Dover Wilson, and it was Wilson who recommended Gordon as a research student to Cambridge. Trinity College took him in and I believe E.M.W. Tillyard, probably the most famous Renaissance scholar of his time in England, became the initial supervisor of Gordon's doctoral thesis — the putative influence of Commedia del Arte on Elizabethan comedies. But Gordon was indifferent to what he saw as Tillyard's mediocre attainments, and soon he was on his way to Italy, specifically Vicenza. After a year there, where, despite some personal difficulties he was for the most part extremely happy, he returned to England in order to continue his studies under Fritz Saxl, the director of the Warburg Institute, then newly installed in London after escaping from Hitler's Germany — most of the Warburgians were Jewish. From Saxl Gordon learnt the importance of scrupulous scholarship, of wide learning, of what he himself called "rigorous enquiry" and accuracy. On an occasion when I mentioned to him that I had read admiringly Edgar Wind's *Pagan Mysteries in the Renaissance*, he murmured only "his quotations, my dear Lucas, are *by no means* reliable", and the gravity of that emphasis made clear the depth of his disapproval for a scholar who failed the standards he himself had learnt from Saxl and those of whom Saxl approved.

As to Saxl. Nine years after his early death in 1948 a collection of his essays, *A Heritage of Images,* was published with an introduction by Gombrich, and in the same year Gordon edited a collection of essays on his hero which contains an introductory essay by Gertrud Bing, another Warburgian. Toward the end of her piece, Bing quotes Saxl's own words in which he reports that although he was trained as an art historian in Vienna and Berlin, he had come to think of himself as more of "a wanderer through the museums and libraries of Europe, at times a labourer tilling the soil on the borderstrip between art history, literature, science and religion." I don't think of Gordon in those terms, although his own contribution to the book is an essay entitled "Giannotti, Michelangelo and the Cult of Brutus", which breathtakingly combines most of the disciplines Saxl enlisted in his own work and, incidentally, provides a perfect example of Gordonian scholarship when, in a footnote, he remarks that "We are gravely handicapped by the lack of lives and studies of the *fuorusceti*. There is no full life of Giannotti, no modern edition of his works and no edition of his letters..." This was a favourite Gordon formulation. "We" were always being frustrated in scholarly enquiries by gaps and insufficiencies. Either an edition didn't exist, or editorial inadequacies meant that it was in all likelihood not to be trusted.

Hence, his disapproval of Wimsatt's pretensions. The man was ignorant of what he was most assured. As I say, I think Gordon's response on that occasion was perfectly justifiable. But he could certainly be socially maladroit. He tried to cover up his slips by displays of old-fashioned courtesies which invariably made an already awkward moment worse, as when he required that in the presence of an invited guest you obey some complicated forms of etiquette which he alone understood. When to stand up or sit down, when to speak, when to light a cigarette, when not to accept a drink.... It sounds a form of social torture, and sometimes it came close to that. But once I realised that his peremptory hisses and nods came about because of his own lack of ease, I could cope with them. And I suspect that the laughter which Mairi MacInnes thought was occasioned by her verses was in fact Gordon's attempt to conceal his discomfort at finding himself in the presence of a young and attractive woman.

Yet against this, it needs to be said that he had close friendships with several women, including Frances Yates and Getrud Bing. And he did more than most at that time to appoint women lecturers at Reading. As he once said, "If the girls are cleverer than the boys, you appoint the girls", and by the early sixties, and I guess well ahead of its time, Reading's English department included a number of brilliant young women lecturers, including Anthea Hume,

Juliet Mitchell and Margaret Walters. Gordon was also very fond of the two women lecturers who formed part of his tiny department in 1956. One of them, Bridget Wilsher, married a physicist called Henisch and they soon went off to America, where, after he had hosted at Reading a ground-breaking conference on semi-conductors, Henisch was offered a top post at some prestigious institution. The other, Jean Young, had been *in situ* when Gordon himself arrived. She may indeed have been appointed by Edith Morley whose suffragette activities didn't prevent her from becoming in 1908 the first woman professor in the UK, although for some years no male academic was prepared or allowed to work under her. Jean was a sweet person, Reader in Anglo-Saxon and old English, author of an edition of the Prose Edda, and utterly devoted to her students. In 1956 she must have been in her mid-fifties but she looked not so much older than her years as an image of the period she taught, so that I more than once fancied her to have just stepped from some illustrated edition of *Hereward the Wake*. Under long grey skirts she wore thick brown woollen stockings, her feet were encased in leather sandals, her soft blue or lilac sweaters looked hand-woven, as did the full-length, grey woollen tunic she wore in winter. She had iron grey hair cut pudding-bowl fashion, and her round, cheerful face, which featured grey-blue eyes and a small hooked nose, suggested a cross between an owl without hunting instincts and a reed-cutter of the Norfolk broads. I liked her very much, we all did, and Gordon not only liked her, he admired her. "One of Jane Harrison's 'girls'" he said, referring to the great Cambridge anthropologist who had been the inspiration for setting several young women in the 1920s on an academic path.

But though I liked Jean, I didn't much take to Anglo-Saxon or medieval English. Or perhaps it's truer to say that I didn't want to give up my philosophical studies. It was part of the formal requirement for passing first year exams that I should successfully complete the course Jean directed, which included Chaucer, taught by an ex-tea planter, or so I was told, who went on to be a Professor of Chaucer studies at Cambridge and whose Saturday morning classes were a form of living death. Chaucer I could read for myself. The rest I was ready to let go. And so by the end of my first term I was committed to pursuing a joint-honours degree in Philosophy and English Literature. When, as required, I went to the dean's office to announce my decision, Gordon, in his chair by the gas fire, lit a cigarette, inhaled deeply, and told me not to expect a good degree. "Nobody, my dear Lucas, comes well out of *that* course." A smile, which became more of a grimace, a pursing of the lips followed by their down-turn, and a sudden hoot of indrawn laughter. "However, if that is your decision, let us at least hope that it brings you some personal satisfaction."

And with that I had to be content.

* * *

At the very end of October, 1956, the UK, together with France and Israel, invaded Egypt. I was working in the library when news of the invasion began to filter through. I hurried across to the buttery and found it in turmoil. An impromptu meeting had been set up by Tory students, one of whom was standing on a table, shouting to make himself heard over a growing volume of noisy opposition. He was a large, burly and bone-headed history student, son of a wealthy Yorkshire farmer, and as I arrived he was yelling that anyone who opposed the war ought to be denounced as a traitor. "These bloody Egyptians are going to be taught a lesson," he bellowed, "and about bloody time, too." In the audience were several Egyptians, most of them at Reading to study agriculture. Not surprisingly, they began to shout back. "Imperialist lacky," "The Canal is ours", "Long live Nasser" — that kind of thing. Friends of the history student, rugger buggers from the shires and South Africa, picked up one of the Egyptians and threw him through a window. Further mayhem was prevented by the arrival of a couple of porters.

Too upset to continue with work, I hurried back to the library to gather up my books and then ran most of the way

252

up Redlands Road to Wantage. Among my newly-made friends were some who, having done their National Service, might for all I knew be once more summoned to arms. And what of the rest of us? If this *was* war, might a general conscription be ordered? I was determined not to fight. I'd far rather go to prison than take an active part in so ridiculous, so indefensible a cause. The newspapers had of late been reporting Eden's growing conviction that Nasser must be toppled, that his "illegal" nationalising of the Suez Canal threatened world stability and the peaceful commerce of nations, that bullies must be confronted, and all the rest of the claptrap suggesting that the Prime Minister was on the look-out for some sort of a "showdown".

I found Geoffrey Creigh in his room and with him a huddle of other students, all talking about the invasion. Geoffrey, otherwise known as "Brumas", had spent two years service in the RAF, mostly at a small radar centre in Norfolk where he had done little but read, smoke, drink — he ingested prodigious quantities of both tobacco and alcohol — and spend afternoons in bed with the station commander's wife, the commander himself being, according to Geoffrey's own account, "a man who preferred a round of golf." He had also learnt the extremely useful skill of dismantling gas meters and re-assembling them so that the gas bypassed the mechanism which registered supply and, therefore, due payment. Because of Geoffrey's dexterity with a pair of tweezers, several of us got our gas more or less free, though we would occasionally lob a shilling into the meters "to keep the fraud detectors happy", as Geoffrey put it.

A pacific Tory, who when sober maintained an air of dignified, slightly olde-worlde manners — drunk, he was an altogether more anarchic and sometimes fearsome person — Geoffrey was appalled by Eden's decision and yet, he said, if recalled to the colours, he felt he would have to go. Mike Robson, a droll, insouciant and brilliant student of agricultural botany, who had also spent two years in the RAF, was inclined to think that hostilities would soon be over.

"And suppose they aren't?" I asked.

Mike shrugged. "I'll think of something," he said.

Another friend, Don Graham, hadn't done his National Service, but was vulnerable because, having left school at sixteen, he had worked at Harwell for two years before coming to Reading to study physics. Don, also a brilliant student, was a wry fatalist. The work he did at Harwell was sufficiently hush-hush for him to be required to sign the Official Secrets Act, a precaution he thought a farce. The place leaked like a sieve, he said, security was hopelessly inefficient — and indeed, to prove his point he later got me into the grounds without anyone checking up on my right to be there — and if the war turned nuclear we'd all be finished. No need to go to war, the war would come to us.

He spoke with an almost cheerful grin, but his words chilled me. Not long ago I heard an earnest radio discussion about the need, felt apparently by US presidents of recent vintage, to test themselves in war. Not by fighting in one, you understand, but by presiding over it. The same, it was suggested, applied to prime ministers. And for them all, Churchill was the figure of lonely excellence to which they aspired. At the moment the war to "liberate" Iraq began, Bush asked Blair to lend him the bust of Churchill that habitually stands in Number 10. Naturally, Blair acceded to the request. Eden always stood under the fobbed, impendent figure of Churchill. Suez was almost certainly his way of becoming Churchillian, even though Churchill himself was appalled by the destructive power of nuclear weapons and did his best to prevent their spread. No such fears for those who consider themselves his successors. To appease the vanity of such idiots, millions may have to die.

In the event, few died in the Suez debacle. It was in truth a farce. A jazz clarinettist I later came to know in Nottingham told me that at the end of October, 1956, he was in darkest Suffolk as a National Serviceman training for jungle warfare. As far as I remember, this required him and others to wade in full kit through a succession of farmyard ponds. Then, quite suddenly, they were airlifted to Aden. When they arrived, they were put into a lorry which was

254

supposed to join up with other troops advancing toward the canal. But the lorry crashed into a flagpole while trying to negotiate its way out of the base camp and, as no replacement engine could be found, they sat out the few days the war lasted doing nothing more active than drinking the mess canteen dry. No doubt the story gained in the telling, but it illustrates the subsequent English response to Eden's war: one of contemptuous laughter. At the time, however, people felt very differently, felt anger and a sense of humiliation at what was being done in their name.

Even those who, however inwardly dismayed, outwardly supported the war, were appalled at an immediate tragic consequence. By the time the troops were withdrawn, on November 4th in fact, the Soviet Union had invaded Hungary. As Peter Hennessy says, "The invasion of Suez was a boon for Khrushchev and Bulganin." The rising in Budapest was soon put down, though at a cost of some 20,000 Hungarian lives. I remember, as I have no doubt do most of the generation to which I belong, listening to the BBC as it relayed messages from Radio Free Hungary, begging the outside world to come to the aid of the Hungarian people. But "they could not look for help, and no help came." What possible moral grounds could the UK stand on? I now know that many Hungarians were as frightened of the possible return of fascists to power in their country as they were by the arrival of Russian tanks, but my own feeling at that ghastly time, one shared by most of my friends at Reading, was a combination of disgust, loathing, and shame. Disgust that men could so easily and apparently willingly kill civilians, whether in Port Said or Budapest, loathing for the brutality of power, for the uses to which it was put, whether clothed in Savile Row suits or Russian broadcloth, and shame, not merely that the old Imperialism was still kicking (I didn't, I think, realise that this was more the twitch of a soon-to-be corpse), but that Khrushchev and Bulganin, whom some of us thought might return the Soviet Union to the kind of idealistic communism Stalin had destroyed, were now showing themselves to be every bit as ruthless as the monster Khrushchev had earlier that year denounced.

Hungary was bound to be a turning point for many socialists of my age. We wanted to remain loyal to the cause, but the boot-faced thugs who ordered the destruction of the Hungarian uprising were ugly beyond redemption. Where now the hopes, the elation of the summer? Of Armstrong's music, Brecht's theatre, the Bastille Day celebration at St Pancras town hall? By November I knew — how or why I can't remember — that the St Pancras branch of the CPGB was an unusually lively and active one and that its being so must have contributed to the ebullience of the meeting Pete and I had attended. What I didn't know was that the invasion of Hungary persuaded E.P. Thompson, along with thousands of other members, to leave the party. Out of that decision a new radical energy would emerge, including Thompson's own brief-lived journal, *The New Reasoner*, and then CND.

* * *

But in the last weeks of 1956, the shocks of Suez and Hungary, though their immediate effects soon died, made for a sense of political bewilderment. It seemed a time when, even if the best did not lack conviction, it was the worst who were full of passionate intensity. This may be a partial explanation of why the discovery at the tail-end of the year of *New Lines* meant so much to me. I perhaps came across a review of Robert Conquest's anthology in *The Listener*, to which I subscribed, although the famous review, identifying the nine poets whose work Conquest chose to represent as "The Movement", appeared in *The Spectator*, which I made a point of not reading. But however I was led to it, and while it would be pretentious to use the words John Stuart Mill found for his discovery of Wordsworth's poems —"in them I seemed to draw from a source of inward joy, of sympathetic and imaginative pleasure" — the discovery of *New Lines* was all-important. Or rather, the discovery of Larkin was. As far as I recall, I enjoyed reading most of the other poets, but Larkin was in a class apart. One stanza in particular, from "Lines on a Young Lady's Photograph Album", struck deep.

> But O, photography, as no art is,
> Faithful and disappointing! That records
> Dull days as dull, and hold-it smiles as frauds,
> And will not censor blemishes
> Like washing-lines, and Hall's Distemper boards.

Rather more than ten years later, when as a visiting professor at the University of Indiana I taught Larkin to some willing MA students, I realised that virtually every line of his required footnoting, especially for people unaware, of what the Four Aways were, or why, in the context of "Mr Bleaney's Room" — which isn't in *New Lines* — Stoke made such a richly comic rhyme, or why, in "Toads" — which is — the thought of people who live "up lanes", eating "windfalls and tinned sardines", has such lugubrious, outrageous wit. And I imagine that in early twenty-first century England a rapidly diminishing number of people will know about Hall's Distemper boards. The reference is to what in post-war England seemed an ingenious and original form of advertising. Two larger than life-size figures, cut out of wood, their white overalls indicating that they are painters and decorators, shoulder a scaffolding board on which is painted in bold letters, *Hall's Distemper*. What made the figures instantly memorable was that they were often placed alongside railway lines, most frequently in fields across which, as the train sped by, they seemed to be cheerily striding.

With my discovery of Heath-Stubbs' "The Unpredicted", poetry entered my world. With the discovery of Larkin, my world entered poetry. I bought *The Less Deceived* and soon found I had several poems by heart and that whole stanzas of others were secure in my memory. The entrancement was so great that I didn't mind — I'm not sure I even noticed — the occasional syntactical inversion for the sake of a rhyme, nor that these rhymes could sometimes be not merely clumsy, but desperate. In the final stanza of "Church Going", which almost miraculously unwinds its syntax towards conclusion, Larkin rhymes "surprising" with "wise in". Yet I have quoted that stanza to more than one poet friend who has confessed that until I drew their attention to it they had never noticed the awkwardness of that particular rhyme. And of course it scarcely matters. "Church Going" remains a great poem. As for the last lines of "At Grass", "Only the groom and the groom's boy /With bridles in the evening come", the inversion is an essential part of the poem's emotional force, the denial until the very last of a word which signifies the approach of death. When I think of that, I think, too, of Browning's great "A Toccata of Galuppi's" and its "commiserating sevenths: life might last. We can but try", followed by "the dominant's persistence till it must be answered to!" Larkin's ordering of the closing lines of "At Grass" allowed for both the commiserating sevenths and the dominant's persistence.

* * *

One morning, close to the end of term, I was waiting with others to gain entrance to the lecture room where Kermode was due to lecture on *Middlemarch*. We lounged about on the asphalt path outside the building, smoking, chatting, and, in my case, gazing across every expanse of grass that stretched from where we stood outside the lecture block to the library. Suddenly, a young woman stepped out from the throng of students and walked across the grass to inspect a rain gauge, noted down some measurement or other and then, looking neither to right or left, returned to the anonymity of the crowd.

Whatever Kermode had to say that morning passed me by. All I saw was that girl. Not, however, her actual presence, because after scanning the heads in front and to either side, I realised she must be sitting somewhere behind me. What I saw therefore was image upon image of her: the swift, almost abrupt grace of her walk, the curtain of dark hair that fell across her face as she bent to the rain-gauge, the oval pallor of her face, and her eyes, their extraordinary, dark lustre.

When the lecture ended, I looked round, but she was already leaving the lecture room and all I saw was the pale yellow raincoat as it disappeared through a door at the back. Who was she? I had to know.

> "No, I have never found
> The place where I could say
> *This is my proper ground*
> *Here I shall stay;"*

Larkin wrote in "Places, Loved Ones," one of the poems of *The Less Deceived* I had by heart, adding,

> "Nor met that special one
> Who has an instant claim
> On everything I own
> Down to my name"

Not long before reading those lines I had become acquainted with the moment in *Emma* when Jane Austen's heroine "touched — she admitted — she acknowledged the whole truth", one that "darted through her, with the speed of an arrow". Physical feeling — touch — leading to a new self-awareness — admission — and so inexorably to intellectual awakening, acknowledgement, that comes arrow fast and brings with it the understanding that "Mr Knightley must marry no one but herself," or, as I would have said had I then known of Goethe's concept, that their relationship was less a matter of choice than one of elective affinity.

By the end of term I knew that the girl in the yellow raincoat was called, unusually and intriguingly, Pauline van Meeteren, that she was studying art and roomed in St Andrew's Hall, a women's hall of residence. Formerly a private red-brick mansion built in the late nineteenth-century, St Andrew's stood directly behind the University. This, which was little enough, was as much as I had managed to discover, but it would have to do until the new year brought us back to Reading.

Chapter 16
Summer's divisions

Love found a way and the way was jazz. As with just about every university in the UK at that time Reading had its own student jazz band. In fact, it had two. This was because it had two trombonists. Given that only one was needed for any group playing traditional jazz, the two trombonists formed separate outfits. I played trumpet in one of these, but badly. Having decided that I no longer had an interest in trying to be a professional jazz musician, I had given up serious, regular practice, my lip had gone soft and the valves on the cheap instrument I used clanked, wheezed and quite often stuck. The other band, led by an agriculture student who sported a trilby, perhaps in the forlorn hope that looking like Vic Dickinson might lead to sounding like him, included a promising cornet player, Don Richards, who was studying art, and an outstanding bassist, John Taylor, now justly famous in the jazz world as pianist and composer.

Not long after I first met John, which was at the beginning of 1957, I called to see him at St Patrick's, the hall of residence where he had a room. It was awash with the sound of a woman jazz singer whose recorded voice seemed to be coming from all directions. As it was. In advance of the days of stereophonic sound John had fixed up speakers high in each corner of his room, and he himself sat in the centre as though in determination to miss nothing of the all-embracing, wrap-around voice. Spectrally thin, eyes large and fixed in his gaunt face as though the intensity he brought to his playing was eating him away, he was obviously not to be distracted into conversation until the track finished.

When it did, he asked abruptly, "Who was that, then?"

"No idea."

"But is she good?"

"Yes," I said, sensing I was being challenged, my view not so much sought as being put to the test. "I'd say she's a top American singer."

John smiled triumphantly. "Cleo Laine," he said.

For most of us in 1957 British women jazz singers meant Ottilie Patterson or Beryl Bryden. John was streets ahead not merely in what already then seemed his vast knowledge of jazz, but in his musical expertise. I had dropped in to ask whether he would agree to play bass in the band we were forming to take part in the Universities' Jazz Band Competition, which that year was to be held at Oxford Town Hall. Don would play cornet and I would "take the drummer's stool" to use the *Melody Maker* lingo of that time. I wasn't much of a drummer but I knew my way round the traps and was at least a steady time keeper. John accepted, saying only that it would be a good idea to make time for some serious rehearsal work.

In the event, we put together a reasonably competent band although the winners, from Cambridge, and the runners-up, a smart Dixieland style group from Loughborough Colleges, were altogether more disciplined. John was quite rightly singled out for mention by the chair of the judges, an excellent jazz pianist from Wales called Dill Jones, who in his summing up made the useful distinction between playing happy jazz and having fun.

I don't know whether I was having fun that early spring afternoon in Oxford, but I do know that I was happy, though jazz had nothing to do with it. A few days earlier I had suggested to Pauline van Meeteren, with whom I had by now managed to engineer the odd conversation as I found myself sitting beside her in a lecture room — good lord, what a coincidence, you again — that if she had nothing better to do on competition day, she might like to come with me and the coach full of Reading musicians and followers to Oxford, and she agreed. So I wasn't as disappointed as I might otherwise have been at the failure of our band to come first or second. In fact, I wasn't disappointed at all. And by the time we returned from Oxford late that day I knew that my life had yet again changed and that, as with the discovery of poetry, so this was going to be permanent. When I came back from Oxford there was magic in my eyes.

* * *

That spring, the University began the long, slow progress of changing sites. Hitherto, nearly all teaching had been at what were called the old Red Buildings on the London Road. But some time earlier Reading had acquired Whiteknights Park, an estate on the outskirts of town, and at the beginning of spring term, 1957, with the first buildings ready to house students, Physics and Letters moved into their new quarters. I didn't think much of either two-storey building. They were of a pale, sand-coloured brick rather than the lovely Berkshire red, the green copper roofs looked cheap and nasty (and soon enough a rumour, probably well-founded, had it that run-off was poisoning fish in the local lake); and inside neither air conditioning nor heating worked especially well.

But the park itself was a delight. It had originally belonged to the Blount family, friends of, among others, Pope, who had dedicated his second moral essay, "On the Characters of Women", to Martha Blount. One summer afternoon in 1957 Pauline and I hired a rowing skiff from the foot of Caversham Bridge, under which the Thames flowed past the town, and, rowing upstream, we came to Mapledurham, a tiny hamlet of a few houses with a water mill on our right-hand bank, its roofs and the tops of house walls glimpsed behind willows and tawny stands of grass. We tied up and began to wander along an overgrown pathway and then, through a straggling hedge, found ourselves staring at what looked to be an abandoned grand house. On the far side, in front of the house, we could make out a gravelled curve on which stood a few cars. Presumably the house was let out as flats. But nobody bothered about the garden. We pushed through the waving grasses, found ourselves at the base of a ha-ha, clambered up it and now stood on what had once been a formal garden with, among tangles of shrub and grass, neo-classical statues, among whom I recognised Ceres with her sheaf of corn, Diana, still with a sickle moon cresting her forehead, bow in her right hand and sheaf of arrows strapped to her side, and either Amphititre or, perhaps, a river Goddess.

We had the place entirely to ourselves. The only sounds were of bird song, the soft drone of insects, and the hollow knock of water from the nearby mill-race. Above the elms and poplars and beyond an occasional bloom of white cloud, the late-afternoon sky was still intensely blue, and it seemed as though the cottages, which we could see among bursts of green hedge, were aglow in the steady sun. "As though waiting for Stanley Spencer," Pauline said, whom earlier in the year she had seen at Cookham, a few miles away, pushing his pram load of artist's materials along a narrow lane there.

Mapledurham, we later learnt, was also Blount property. But Whiteknights was on an altogether larger scale. The several acres of land which lay in front of the house itself had been at one point taken over by Huntley and Palmers and now served as the University sports grounds, although as the biscuit manufacturers

were Quakers you weren't supposed to play games on the Sabbath. This led to fearful shouting matches between those of us who played kick-about football and the choleric groundsman, a Gabriel Varden type whose determination to make us obey the rules we baffled by speaking to him in French. He was even more baffled when, on weekdays, we addressed him in English.

Take away the two raw-looking buildings now ready for occupation and the park must have looked much as it did in its hey-day. The back of the charmingly rusticated family house, which for some years had been in use as a men's hall of residence, led down to a lake, while in front was a parterre and, spreading beyond that, a formal garden dominated by a huge cedar. The wide, curving driveway that led to the house was screened by an avenue of lime trees. And if you tramped far enough beyond the house, through what must have been kitchen gardens and then outer lawn, you came at length to a grotto, where for all I know the Blounts, alert to the fashionable antiquarianism of the time, hired a holy man to sit in eremitic contemplation. A few years after the University took over, the cedar was uproooted and the garden buried under concrete for a new library; as for the limes, they bowed down to a huge administrative block.

Ichabod, Ichabod. Students who arrived at the University after the mid-1950s will never know the beauty been. I am glad I saw Whiteknights Park before the philistine depredations of university planners laid waste its loveliness, just as I am glad I experienced Reading when it was still a charming, small market town and not the soulless horror it has since become. At the top end of the sports ground was a cluster of wooden huts, built by the army during the Second World War and presumably intended as some sort of training camp. When I was an undergraduate a few mature students lived in the huts, others camped in dilapidated caravans which were strewn among them. Whether these students had established squatters' rights or lived there with the University's blessing I've really no idea; but the place seemed a colony for bohemians, not dissimilar from Eel Pie Island.

I would come to know the inhabitants of this encampment well, especially as it made an ideal place for parties. But for all the glories of Whiteknights Park, I felt an initial resentment at having to attend lectures in the new Letters Faculty, when the library, where I spent long hours, was still down the hill at what I thought of as the "proper" university. So was the buttery where many of my friends and acquaintances met, including arts students and, therefore, Pauline. That January was one of deep and persistent frosts. Walking down Redlands Road in the morning my feet would crack on leaves crisp as biscuits. The sharp sounds, the sting of cold air on my skin, the pungencies of wood and coal smoke — all became part of the atmosphere: an exuberant delight so overpoweringly strong that I had sometimes to pause in my stride, for fear that I might lose my balance and pitch uncontrollably forward. "It was a time of rapture", Wordsworth says of a frosty season during his boyhood spent skating. I know that at all times during my life I have exulted in physical activity; but the walk down Redlands Road was a delight not merely in itself but because of what I was striding towards.

> what happiness to live
> When every hour brings palpable access
> Of knowledge, when all knowledge is delight
> And sorrow is not there.

Wordsworth again. Access to knowledge waited for me in the library. It also waited for me in the buttery or across the road in The Turk's Head where I would meet friends to discuss current affairs, the films and art exhibitions we had seen or planned to see, the books we were reading, radio programmes we had heard and the records we listened to and shared out among us... Becket, Bergman, Bacon, Bratby, de Beauvoir, Bach, Broonzy, Brubeck... "Pseudo-intellectuals" the boneheads called us, but looking back what I recall is the unembarrassed if sometimes self-conscious because embattled delight in serious, occasionally heated talk. Whether we met in buttery or Turk's Head, or, having wandered down to William Smith's and rooted among its stacks we then compared buys over pints of Younger's Scotch Ale at The George, or whether, after an evening's study, a few of us, invariably including Geoffrey Creigh, would hurry for a last pint to the pub nearest to Wantage Hall, called The Queen's Head, known to habitués as "The Nob", our compulsions blent in the serious space we created for ourselves.

* * *

Pauline wasn't always with me on these occasions. As an art student she was expected to put in a full day's studio work except when she had to attend lectures, and then there was her Catholicism, a commitment which she took seriously and which I tried not to think about, although the church required her presence at what seemed to me an unusually demanding number of ceremonies and calendar events. Fifty years ago religion had a presence in student life which is now unimaginable. Among its various denominated societies Reading included Anglican, Methodist, Congregationalist and Baptist, all of them apparently thriving, all meeting socially at least once a week, and this was quite apart from attendance at church and chapel. Ministers and chaplains, some actually on campus, were assigned to all these societies, and for the well-attended Jewish society a rabbi was on hand. The Catholics were especially diligent in monitoring attendance at church, the upshot of which was that Pauline wasn't always free to come with me to social occasions. But we went together to a party to which I'd been invited one evening towards the end of the spring term.

My invitation had come from a second-year woman student who was editor of the University's literary magazine, *Tamesis*. Would I write for the magazine, she asked. I didn't much like her. Her Home Counties' drawl — "oh, ya", she would say, "oh, ya" — her twin-set jumper and cardigan of an especially bilious green, her unvoiced but evident conviction that not everyone she was obliged to know at Reading could be thought "top-drawer", and a nose which seemed permanently on guard against unseemly smells, all provided reasons for non-attendance. But then other possible contributors would be there, so she promised, and one or two lecturers might turn up. One was certain to do so. The editor-to-be lodged with a lecturer in Italian, Luigi Meneghello, who like so much that was important about Reading had been brought to the university by Gordon, and whose responsibility it was to teach aspects of the Italian Renaissance in the English department. Meneghello also taught Italian as a beginner's language, and Pauline was one of his students. So I said yes.

We arrived later than most at Meneghello's handsome house. The large, square entrance hall floor, which was tiled in black and white, reminded me of the set of an Italianate production of *The Country Wife* I had just seen in London, with Terence Morgan — a minor film star — as Horner, and a wide staircase led up to the first-floor drawing room, inside which we found some twenty people, among them Gordon who in his grey jacket, dark-blue trousers and suede shoes was reclining in an easy chair, smoking while he stared at the ceiling. The apparent absorption of his gaze suggested that he was entirely abstracted from whatever signs of life went on around him. There weren't many. The talk was subdued, scarcely more than mutterings, and students, most of whom I recognised but few of whom I knew, stood in list-less groups of three or four, glasses of what turned out to be viciously acidic red wine in their hands, a few smoking. One classics student, who had a curly-stemmed pipe in his mouth and whose reddened cheeks suggested that he was being semi-throttled by a yellow and black polka-dot bow tie, looked like a forlorn parody of the academic he no doubt aspired to be.

Meneghello came across to talk to us. He was small, dapper, had dark, bright eyes, an olive complexion, and was instantly friendly. His courteous attention put us both at ease. Then he called his wife over and made us all introduce ourselves. Katia was about the same size as her husband, but more generously built, with a beautiful, wide, Jewish face. I would learn from Gordon that she was a survivor of Auschwitz, although in my presence at least she never talked about that experience. And from the same source I would discover that Meneghello had fought with the Italian partisans, and, according to the obituary of him in the *Guardian,* in 1943 "set up a partisan group under the aegis of the liberal socialist and anti-fascist Partito d'Azione". I think that by 1957 he must have already begun work on the book which, published in 1963 under the title *Liero nos a malo*, made him famous in Italy, and which, according to the *Guardian* obituarist, is "an extraordinary accomplishment, one of the most important Italian works of the last five decades. The title page calls it a novel (romanzo) but it belongs to no traditional genre and is simultaneously an autobiography, an essay about the life and culture of his village, and a reflection on literature, language, and thought." Though it hasn't been translated into English, the work which followed a year later has. *I piccolo maestri,* published in the UK as *The Outlaws,* is "one of the few non-rhetorical, and therefore all the more effective, memoirs of the Italian resistance, which is true in every detail."

I knew nothing of Meneghello's writing when he and I shook hands on that spring evening of 1957. What I do remember is that he spent some time telling Pauline and me that the problem with the English was their northern coldness, their restraint, their lack of sexual candour. He sounded rather like a more articulate version of Forster's Gino and after some ten minutes of what would have been an harangue but for its being delivered smilingly and as though in rueful acceptance that this state of affairs could never change, I began to get irritated. I excused myself and went over to talk to Gordon who, I noticed, apart from having slid further down in his chair so that a good half of his body looked to be precariously poised above the carpet, continued to stare at the ceiling while he smoked, eyes almost closed, in the boredom of isolation, no doubt.

But then a voice smote upon my most amazed ear.

"Oh, Luigi, taunting the innocent young with tales of continental lubricity."

Ian Fletcher, or Iain as he then liked to style himself! Although I wasn't a regular attender of his lectures on practical criticism — too long, bolstered and basted by lengthy quotations from literary critics such as Cleanth Brooks, I.A. Richards and R.P. Blackmur, their prose a kind of verbal treacle — I turned up for all those he was now giving on Restoration Drama. These wildly comic occasions required Ian to deliver prolonged, enthusiastic readings of the most *risqué* scenes, finding *doubles-entendres* where no-one else would have spotted them, and, with the exception of *The Country Wife,* made notable by the lecturer's obvious preference for the little-known over the famous. As to Wycherley's bawdy masterpiece, the mere title was enough to send Ian off into his version of a giggle. This was a sniffle, an intake of at least four rising breaths through the nose, his lips twisted in the rictus of a smile. "My purfled lips," he once called them, when he and I were looking at the portrait bust of the younger Fletcher made by a sculptor friend at a time when Ian still had hair, and which he kept on his desk. "The face of a ruined archangel," he added, aligning himself with one of his favourite poets of the 1890s, Lionel Johnson perhaps, or Ernest Downson. Sniffle, sniffle.

It ought to have been grotesque, that combination of sniffle and leer, and perhaps it was. But, coupled with his lean, stooped figure, ill-fitting grey suit, tie never quite worn straight, and, most of all, his balding crown above a white face half-hidden by horn-rimmed glasses, the effect was that of someone playing a disreputable vicar in a Whitehall farce. What made it the more so was his voice. Ian's voice was unique, a thing of wonder. It had greater range and volume than any other voice I have known. As nobody who ever met him can be unaware, at his loudest he could make enough noise to awaken the dead and the fox from its lair in the morning. He was highly amused when one of the women who served coffee in the common room at Whiteknights, speaking out of Gordon's hearing, said that she always assumed that Ian was the professor of English and Gordon a mere lecturer in the department. Really? Why? "Well," she said, "You boom and Gordon hoots". Nobody boomed like Ian. But he could also flute. His Dame Edith Evans as Lady Bracknell was a party speciality. And then, in a trice, he would drop his voice to the merest whisper, though one that lost none of its resonance. "I could read aloud from the London Telephone directory and make it sound like poetry," he said with pardonable exaggeration on one beer-filled occasion.

That was in the 60s, by which time I was a young lecturer at Reading and he and I had become close friends. The words were at once self-knowingly absurd and yet true. When I first got to know him, I thought Ian might be unaware of the effect he produced. But in a letter to me of a much later date, the poet and critic Philip Hobsbaum recalled an occasion in

50s London when Ian stopped a potentially ugly quarrel in George Fraser's flat by a memorable reading of a poem by Lord Herbert, and Alan Brownjohn has told me that he can remember London literary occasions when Ian's combination of obscure and obscene vocabulary reduced everyone to helpless laughter. He knew exactly what he was doing, though he must have been delighted to find at Reading a tame audience for his performances. Gifted with a quite extraordinarily retentive memory, he made it his business to truffle through dictionaries for the most recherché words, rather as he combed the British Library and elsewhere for the most fugitive of writers, poets especially, whose causes he would then advance at the expense of better-known writers. I once tried to catch him out by letting drop the name of Edward Coote Pinkney, a selection of whose poems I had come across in an excellent two-volume collection of *American Life in Literature.* (I found the books, which had been issued to all U.S. combat troops in the Second World War, in a junk shop in rural Maryland.) "Ah, yes," Ian said, "1802-1828". 'Look out upon the stars my love, And shame them with thine eyes,' The influence of Byron doesn't help." After that I gave up.

Few of Ian's talents were on open display during that evening at the Meneghellos, which anyway ended not long afterwards. It was Gordon who, unwittingly I'm sure, brought the entertainment to a close. Someone may have offered to refill his glass because suddenly we heard his voice soar above the desultory conversation. "I really *cannot* drink any *more* of that *wine*," was all he said, but it was enough to still our own voices. This was good insofar as it meant I did not have to pretend an interest in the tedious monologue of some research student in the department, a prize bore dressed *à la* Colin Wilson in horn-rimmed glasses, roll-neck sweater, brown cords and hairy jacket, who wanted to tell me about a night he had spent alone on the canal towpath and how it had made him understand the difficulty of achieving authenticity. I was irked, though, that I hadn't found a chance to make Ian's better acquaintance.

* * *

But a few days later I met him again. This time it was in the
upper rooms of William Smith's. His back was towards me
as he bent short-sightedly to inspect what turned out to be
an early edition of Swinburne's *Songs Before Sunrise*.
Swinburne, predictably enough, was a favourite poet, one he
loved as much as he loathed Hopkins — "All that inspissated
nature-worship". For similar reasons he disliked Edward
Thomas, "author of *The Rose Piddle Papers*" as he put it. I
wondered whether I should greet him but as I made to speak
he turned slowly round, stared at me uncertainly for a few
moments and then, the rictus settling into place, said, "Ah,
the young ginnilman with the charming doxy. We met at
Luigi's. Fancy a snifter?"

"I'd love one," I said, guessing that Ian was inviting me for
a drink.

"I'll pay for these, then," he said, "and we'll be on our
way."

"These" turned out to be a large pile of books. Ian now
went through a complicated ritual of hauling out collections
of coins from various pockets, studying them closely as
though in the dark of his flannel trousers base metal might
have turned to gold, and finally, and slowly, oh, so slowly,
counting out the amount he owed. Then, with a compliment
on the shop's extensive stock to the man who took his money,
he drew an old army beret from his jacket pocket, settled it
on his head, accepted my offer to carry his books for him, and
we were off in the direction of The Turk's Head.

He had a most peculiar manner of walking. Stoop-
shouldered, head thrust forward like a tortoise newly emerged
from wintry sleep, he needed to hard-wrinkle his snub nose in
order to prevent his glasses from sliding off, and this, together
with a frown of concentration no doubt intended to help him
overcome chronic short-sightedness, had the effect of raising
his upper lip into what was bound to strike any oncomer as a
sneer of cold command. Meanwhile his arms moved backward
and forward in a kind of dog-paddle, hands clawing at the air

as though it was a resistant medium through which he must force his difficult way.

In the pub he repeated the ritual of excavating his pockets for signs of money, though this time the outcome was different. "I seem to be somewhat short of the readies," he announced, peering uncertainly at the few coins that lay in his by-no-means open palm. So I bought our drinks.

I also provided the cigarettes, "snouts" as Ian called them. In those days I smoked a brand called Guards. Filter-tipped, they came in a smart white packet with broad vertical red and black stripes. We spent a few brief minutes in discussion of cigarette brands. Ian professed himself indifferent as to what he smoked, which in time I came to understand meant that as he never bought any himself he was obliged to accept whatever he was offered. Guards were the best of the cheap cigarettes, I told him. For a short while Players' Bristol compared favourably, but they soon reverted to type. As with most new brands at the bottom end of the market, the manufacturers began an advertising campaign to attract smokers, kept the quality of tobacco reasonably good for some months, then began to fill the cigarettes with inferior stuff in the hope that nobody would notice. Of course, they did. The brand was then withdrawn and another one took its place. Few such brands lasted more than a couple of years. Some disappeared almost as soon as they arrived. Strand, for example. The advertising campaign was stunning. A poster of a man in raincoat and trilby leaning against a street lamp, collar turned up against wind and rain, smoke issuing from his lips. *You're never alone with a Strand.* Oh, but you were.

Ian told me that he sometimes smoked a pipe but that pipe tobacco was "damned expensive stuff". All in all, he'd rather spend what few coins he had on books. I began to study the titles of the perhaps dozen or so that were piled on the round table in front of us. It was midday, we had settled into the snug — a small area of the front bar partitioned off from the rest by wooden half-walls — and as yet we had the pub more or less to ourselves. Rather more than two hours later, by which time customers had been for their lunchtime pints and plates of egg, ham and chips (the pub's speciality) and had departed, we were still there. Only the landlord's request for us to "drink up" brought an end to our talk. I say "our", but in truth Ian did most of the talking. There were tales of his time in the Middle East on semi-active service with the army, although he told me that so poor was his eyesight that, what with an almost complete lack of hand and eye co-ordination, he was never allowed to hold a loaded rifle or revolver, for fear of what he might do to friend, let alone foe. He mentioned meetings in Cairo with Lawrence Durrell, Bernard Spencer, Terence Tiller, Reggie Smith and others, George Fraser especially. The two had become close friends, working together on magazines and publishing projects in post-war literary London, "although George has a finer critical mind, I tag along, a foot-soldier carrying a spear for him when necessary". This was a reference to the in-fighting that went on between rival authors and their cliques. There were hints of his passion for the 1890s, "a crepuscular decade, bound to the aesthetics of failure", which had a deep attraction for him; there were allusions to his own poetry, of a collection which "Tambi" had belatedly brought out — and of which, at a future hour, he would give me a signed copy. *Orisons, Picaresque & Metaphysical*, the author's name being given as Iain Fletcher, was published in 1947 by Editions Poetry London. There was even brief mention of a magazine he himself had started. *Colonnade* it was called and ran for a single issue. Although I don't remember all I heard on that first, extraordinary occasion, I do know that Ian held me with his glittering talk. I was entranced.

Only once did I stem the flow. It was when I told him that I'd been in Smiths to collect a book I'd ordered. *Mavericks* was an anthology of contemporary poets edited by Howard Sergeant and Dannie Abse, newly published in cheap paperback by Editions Poetry and Poverty, and intended as a riposte to *New Lines*. I wanted to discover whether it really could be a genuine alternative to Robert Conquest's anthology.

"No," Ian assured me. "The second eleven." He also told me that some years earlier, in 1953 in fact, he and "old George" had produced their own, more inclusive anthology of contemporary poets called *Springtime*, in which most of the poets who made up the now rival anthologies had been given an airing. "But Conquest has the pick of them." This was chastening. I knew that Silkin was one of the Mavericks, and ever since my fortuitous encounter with the editor of *Stand* I had been on the look-out for his poems, some of which turned up in magazines I bought. I approved Silkin's avoidance of the iambic thud on which so many poets relied, I admired the way he varied line-lengths, his use of loose-limbed rhythms, learnt, I assumed, from Lawrence, though in due course Silkin told me that Rosenberg was a more powerful influence. He built his poems by the paragraph rather than the line, or so it seemed to me; and I warmed to though I didn't fully understand a vocabulary that some-times felt over-ambitious in its determination to avoid ordinariness.

I put some of this to Ian. "Well," he said, "I shall be inter-ested to hear what John Wain has to say about your views." He smiled as though he could anticipate Wain's response, and that it wouldn't be a friendly one.

"I don't know John Wain," I said.

"I can set up a meeting, if you like." This was said casu-ally, as Ian leafed through my copy of *Mavericks*. "John Smith. Ha. The new proletarianism. Poets these days are all called Tom Hughes and Ted Gunn. This man was once C. Busby Smith. George used to say 'C. Busby Smith and die.' Who else have we got?"

Who else included two poets I many years later published under the Shoestring Press imprint. J.C. Hall, whose *Long Shadows: Poems 1938-2002* I brought out in 2003, and Vernon Scannell. I published Vernon's excellent last full collection, *Behind the Lines*, in 2004 and then his final pamphlet-length collection, *Last Post*, three years later, the year of his death. At the time, though, their names meant nothing to me. Nor did the others, David Wright, W. Price

Turner, Anthony Cronin, Abse himself, and Michael Hamburger. Ian told me that Hamburger was at Reading, a lecturer in the German department. "We are a nest of singing birds," he added, "though some sing more sweetly than others," by which I understood him to mean that he didn't think much of Hamburger's poetry.

Nor, when I had a chance to read it, did I. It seemed dull, tame, enervate even. But Hamburger's poem "A Poet's Progress" was of interest, less for its own worth, which was minimal, than because it was one of at least four meditations on poets, poetry and the act of creation in what was a remarkably slender anthology. The others, by Wright ("A Visit to a Poet"), Cronin ("Writing"), and Scannell ("The Unsuccessful Poet") were much of a muchness, although the last did at least benefit from a sceptical look at claims for poetic genius. Scannell's imagined poet may blame the age in which he lives, "where all standards are debased", but "Do not judge when he goes quietly to his hovel /To put his head in the oven or write a novel."

Scannell, as a note at the end of the anthology told me, had already published two novels; and at least four of the contributors to *New Lines* — Amis, Enright, Larkin and Wain — had done the same. Perhaps, then, writing a novel wasn't so much a refusal to rage against the dying of the light as an acceptance of writerly professionalism?

Elsewhere in *Mavericks* a kind of Thomas-like vaticism boomed hollowly. Poets were clearly Important People. Hence Dannie Abse's "Master", in which the speaker asks dolefully

Why did You choose me as Your instrument?
from pole to pole my hanging mind is rent
in two, a torn page nailed upon Your Cross,
a blankness for you to write in blood across.

Who was "You?" An apostle? Christ? But as an earlier stanza has it, "You wind the clockwork up and I perform /with this unearthly voice that is not mine", and the implication is that poets are chosen, have no alternative but to give utterance to the voice that speaks through them. Poets may be born but they are also made by the inner compulsion to bear witness, even if nobody listens. Poems welled up from the depths. This, coupled with a vague appeal to Jungian archetypes, gave a thousand gambits for plainly lousy verse to be respected for its sub-, pre-, or unconscious truths. Away with "mere" intelligence. That was arid reason, unanointed by the muse. Down with the flame-resistant timbers of "mere" craft. No real poems could be built from such material. True poets were about their Master's business of revealing truths. For them the dove flew, as it did not fly for others. In one way this was a recovery of the idea of the natural genius which had at an earlier time been of assistance to great poets like Burns and Clare. But it also gave the thumbs up to poems that didn't so much rest in mystery as wallow in rant.

It wouldn't be fair to blame Thomas for all of this, nor to suggest that Abse always succumbed to such mush, but Thomas's kitbag of ohs and ahs, his reliance on words such as holy, cross, saviour, and most of all his sensational death, which in 1957 was still recent and the subject of much rumour and hagiographical speculation, was certainly taken by some to signify the sacrifice of genius on the altar of art. A lonely impulse rather than whisky had driven him to his last goodnight. He was in a sense the messiah whom other poets had waited for. I realised this when, sometime later, I came on Wrey Gardiner's autobiography, with its suitably neo-Romantic title, *The Dark Thorn*. Thorns featured in much English art of the immediate post-war period. Lucian Freud, Graham Sutherland and Michael Ayrton all use thorns as symbols of pain, physical, psychological, metaphysical. *The Dark Thorn* has much to say about the war, whose chief offence seems to be that it interfered with Gardiner's work as poet, editor of *Poetry Quarterly* and publisher of the Grey Walls Press. A journal entry from 1943 will give a sufficient taste of the whole. The author is walking along the pavement by the British Museum when,

"The cold air of wisdom grips. It is only to be found in art. The lights of holy days glimmer in the night of empty streets. There is nothing at the end of them but the upright corpses ambling towards an unknown end. A word thrown on air but no illumination, no burning pestle in the dead of dream. There are one or two here and there….who walk the streets looking for the word, the animated ghosts of all the flowers they once saw blowing on the mountains of the past. The petty temporary scene is a witches' cauldron of disaster and despair mocked by the passing bell of compromise with the dawn."

After a page or two of this — there are well over two hundred — you begin to feel that there's something to be said for J.B. Priestley.

Of course, it was Ian who told me about Gardiner, and to be fair, Grey Walls Press, which he seems to have financed himself, produced some handsome books. They include selections from then forgotten or neglected poets, and in the 1950s could still be found on the shelves of second-hand bookshops, which is where I found the Grey Walls selections of, among others, Bloomfield, Crabbe, Skelton and Dunbar, issued as part of what Gardiner called his "Crown Classics", all under the general editorship of Sean Jennett and each supplied with an elegantly designed dust jacket.

* * *

I don't think Gardiner's name came up at that first meeting in The Turk's Head but I did gain the impression that Ian was more than a little drawn to the idea of artists as chosen by malignant deities who used them for their sport. Either then or soon afterwards he told me of Hemingway's meeting with a young man who introduced himself to "Papa" by claiming that he, too, was a writer. "Show me your wound," Hemingway was supposed to have said. And on more than one occasion Ian referred to Edmund Wilson's *The Wound and the Bow* in which Wilson famously read the story of Philoctetes as a metaphor of the artist. His suppurating, stinking wound, occasioned by a serpent's bite, and his endless shrieks of pain, cause Agamemnon to cast him ashore on the uninhabited island of Lemnos, only to recall him at Achilles' insistence when the Greeks are up against it at Troy. For Philoctetes has in his possession the gift of Hercules' bow, and with this he is able to kill Paris and so bring about the defeat of the Trojans. The artist, however reviled he may be, and no matter that he is an outcast, possesses a wisdom without which civilisation cannot survive.

I was once standing outside Ian's departmental office, waiting for him to finish a tutorial — we were due to go for a drink at The Nob — when I heard him start on the subject of Philoctetes and his wound. On and on he went, and after what seemed an age, and was certainly long after the hour's tutorial should have ceased, there came the unmistakable sounds of a woman sobbing. I put my head round the door. Ian was in full flow, tilted back in his chair as he stared unseeingly at the ceiling, while the solitary student, who had presumably given up hope of release from this immuration, sat, head bowed, sobbing into a crumpled handkerchief. Ian stopped when he saw me, then shifted his gaze to the student's hunched, weeping form, of which he was suddenly and it seemed newly aware. There was an apple on his desk. "Here," he said, lobbing it toward her, "bite on this."

As I write these words, I begin to realise why it would be impossible to find, even to imagine, an Ian Fletcher in any university English department today. (So much the worse for those departments, of course.) Leave aside the fact that he had no first degree — though, fulfilling the condition under which Gordon had been able to hire him, he did eventually gain a Ph.D for his work on little magazines of the 19th Century — his teaching would nowadays soon cause complaints. His tutorial method, for instance.... But Ian had no method. In order to honour the topic which he and his tutees had agreed on beforehand he would undertake a considerable amount of reading to add to his already huge store of knowledge, and then, come the allotted hour, begin to talk. And talk. Sometimes the talk would stay close to the subject meant to be under discussion. More often, it would fly off like an untethered falcon making increasingly wide sweeps of the circumambient air as it spotted some distant quarry. I recall an occasion, one among many, when as so often we were due to go for a drink, and I stood listening outside his office while he orated. This time it was on the Impossibilia Topos. At one point, while he drew breath, I heard a student hesitantly remind him that they were meant to be discussing *Macbeth*.

"Ah, yes," Ian said, coming briefly to earth, "a great play. Now, the Impossibilia Topos…" And off he soared.

Perhaps out of anxiety, he prepared his lectures almost too carefully, over which, despite their innocence of such latter-day pre-requisites as bullet points and aims and objectives, he took great pains, typing them out on an old, heavy Remington portable. He would then add notes and afterthoughts, with the result that they nearly always exceeded their allotted length and students would drift away to other classes as the due finishing time approached and then receded. It wasn't at all unusual for one of these lectures to go on for an hour and a half, sometimes even longer, so that by the time it came to an end Ian would be lecturing to a virtually empty room. "Like the Third Programme," he said to me, after one such lecture, "I am not to be constrained by anything so vulgar as a schedule."

He was a regular contributor to the programme, and I doubt that his producers there ever thought of scissoring his scripts, any more than they did those of other contributors. In the early 60s he even gave a talk on the cricket team he captained, cricket being a life-long passion of his. Fletcher's Particulars started life as a team made up of students, fellow lecturers and drinking chums, and for a while had fixtures all over Berkshire and even beyond. The talk, scheduled to last for 20 minutes, went on for the best part of an hour. But then timing on the Third Programme was at best approximate. A talk advertised to begin at 9pm and finish at 9.30 was quite likely to start at 9.15 and end some three-quarters of an hour later. I don't suppose any of us who listened much minded, the rewards were so great. The same went for Ian's lectures and, far more, tutorials. But university departments nowadays are run from "the centre", by administrators who, being almost entirely graduates of Business Studies, have sternly repressed any sense they may once have possessed of the education guaranteed by freedoms from which Ian, and therefore his students, immeasurably gained. As one of those students said — I thought it was me but this has been disputed — if you stood close enough to Ian a great deal of literature rubbed off on you.

But standing close would not now be allowed. And there is no doubt that Ian's attitude to women students would be subject to official reproof. Ian was *sui generis*. I have never known anyone like him, though I have come across several academics who wrongly fancied themselves to possess his gifts: a combination of richly heterogeneous vocabulary — that kaleidoscopic mixture of slang, French, Italian and Latin tags, and, as he himself said, the *disjecta membra* of some cloistered cenacle — his louche manners and his massive, wayward, endlessly surprising erudition. He was of his time in that at least during his early years at Reading he didn't expect to make much money from his employment. After all, most people in the literary and academic words got by on precious little.

Nor did Ian crave an academic reputation, though he eventually and deservedly gained one as an unrivalled authority on the highways and byways (especially those) of the late nineteenth century. He also produced an important collection of essays on Yeats and his contemporaries. Almost without intending to, he became a scholar, a scholar manqué perhaps, but one who knew more and wrote better than most of that often self-promoting kind. In addition, he was a poet of real talent whose *Collected Poems*, which I published through Shoestring Press, contains an affectionate, acute introduction by his friend Peter Porter — Ian had championed Peter's early work — in which he commends Ian's prodigious "word hoard" as well as his technical expertise and the comic exuberance of his best work.

But above all, Ian was a bookman, through and through. I am more glad than I can say that I knew him at a period when an abundance of second-hand bookshops and street barrows (all long gone), and of course Gordon's generous spirit, made it possible for him to flourish, though I'm not certain he would thank me for that word. Wedded as he was to what he called the aesthetics of failure, the poets to whom he was most drawn included not merely the much failing Lionel Johnson, Ernest Dowson and the increasingly mad Arthur Symons, but such latter-day equivalents as John Gawsworth, about whom he wrote a great essay and to whom, in Gawsworth's last, desperate alcohol-wrecked days, he behaved more than honourably. And there was Paul Potts, a heavily bearded down-and-out poet I once met in the French Pub when I was with Ian and whom I instantly recognised from earlier occasions, when I had been discovering London with Pete and he had stung us for a drink. He did the same now, and, Ian being unable to locate money in any of his pockets, I paid.

* * *

After that initial meeting at The Turk's Head I began to see rather more of Ian. Sometimes the two of us went for a drink, on occasions Pauline would be with me, or he might turn up at The Nob, where I, Geoffrey Creigh and another friend, David Howard, also studying Philosophy and Literature, would gather for a brief half hour before time was called. Like Geoffrey, David had done his National Service in the RAF, although in most other respects they were sharply dissimilar. Where Geoffrey was tall and comfortably all a shamble, David came in at rather less than medium height, was brisk in manner, neat, sharp, witty, and liable to convulsive explosions of laughter prompted by comic anecdotes he especially wanted to relate. We were all four of us standing by the bar one evening, when Kermode came in. He nodded tersely, asked for a half-pint bottle of beer — to take away — and, as he turned to leave, Ian said,

"Oh, Frank, I have another dancer poem for you." Kermode's *Romantic Image* had just appeared and it was known that he was now working on an extended essay about the image of the dancer in the 1890s. "Thank you," Kermode said, "I now know where to come when I need further such information." And he left.

In *Not Entitled*, Kermode says that "Fletcher's talk was of use to me, for I was working on a book which had to do with Arthur Symons and also with dancers and music-hall personalities." But on that chilling occasion, Ian's talk certainly wasn't allowed to register as being of use. It was instead treated as a piece of impertinence, the more so, it seemed to Geoffrey, David and me, because it had been in front of those whom Kermode plainly regarded as the untouchables. I was therefore taken aback when, some evenings later, Gordon suggested that I really ought to gather some fellow students and invite Kermode to accompany us for a drink. "He complains that he never meets undergraduates." Perhaps what I had taken to be a disdainful brush-off was gaucheness on Kermode's part or, could it be, envy of Ian's unmonied ease? Perhaps he wanted to make reparations for what he realised had been his less than civil behaviour to a colleague?

But the planned drink with Kermode never took place. It was Gordon himself who, admittedly without realising, put paid to it. From time to time when I returned from an evening with Pauline, he would come to my room and invite me for a drink at the flat he then occupied in Wantage. It was a suite of ground-floor rooms of which I recall the entrance lobby with some Ruskin water-colour studies of leaves, stones and running water, and a large, square lounge, where he entertained. This had a dove-grey carpet, floor-to-ceiling white-painted bookshelves, all of them crammed, many with what I came to understand was a priceless collection of folio-size works dating from the Renaissance, and several paintings, including a flamboyant one of himself in profile, dressed in blue jacket, hair long and curling at the collar, white handkerchief falling from his breast pocket, his swarthily complexioned face above a yellow shirt that accentuated the brightness of his eye.

"Harry Weinberger," he said, when he caught me looking at the picture on the first occasion I went to his flat. "Absurdly romantic, of course." But he was clearly flattered by it. The room also contained a number of elegant, wing-back chairs, one of them by a table on which, as in his departmental office, stood a pile of books and an over-flowing ashtray.

"There is an open bottle of wine in the kitchen," he said, sinking into his chair. "And you will find a glass. I shall drink gin."

Obediently, I went to the kitchen, found an open bottle of red wine on the cluttered draining board, rinsed out a used glass and returned to the room I had just left. Gordon sat humming to himself, eyes closed, a cigarette smouldering dangerously in the ashtray.

Hearing me come in, he opened his eyes and stared at me. He was plainly startled by my appearance.

"Lucas," he said, "why are you here?" And then, recovering himself, "ah, yes, we have matters to discuss."

But what these might have been I didn't find out. I did, however, realise that he was very drunk. Soon afterwards, his eyes again closed, his head drooped, and he began to breathe deeply. I waited a moment or two, then tiptoed out.

A few days later, as though he had no recollection of the previous occasion, he told me that he required my presence the following evening. This was the very evening some of us had finally agreed to invite Kermode for a drink.

"Come at no earlier than 9 o'clock. I shall need you to help dispense drinks. I am entertaining a *very* serious scholar and his wife to dinner." He looked me up and down. "And *do, please*, make sure that you are presentable. Clean nails, a tie."

Promptly at 9 o'clock the next evening, having excused myself from the evening with Kermode and found a clean shirt to go with my one tie, I knocked on Gordon's door. He called out that I would find the door open. I went through to the lounge where I found him sitting in his chair opposite a large, oval-faced man in a grey suit, with white hair and the kind of horn-rimmed glasses and heavy-soled brown shoes I recognised as a uniform for American academics. Beside him sat a woman of the same, late-middle age, small, in a dark grey, two piece and with crimped hair surmounting a pretty, faded face.

"*This*," Gordon said grandly to me, "is Professor Bentley. Professor *G.E.* Bentley." He waved me over to the couple and the man stood to shake hands.

"Glad to meet you," he said, his voice courteous, "are you doing research here, maybe?"

Gordon hooted. "Lucas is a first year undergraduate," he said, and whatever dim light of interest there may have been in Bentley's eyes faded to nothing.

I don't remember much of the subsequent, desultory talk, in which I took no part. Exchanges of information about such and such a scholar, of books with undeserved reputation, of Shakespeare productions, of learned conferences, of the dimness of that *wretched* Tillyard with his *absurd* belief in a World Picture, "as though *everyone* in Elizabethan England walked about thinking *exactly* the same thoughts and sharing *exactly* the same belief in God *and* art *and* music. Well, *really*." They were at one in their conviction that Tillyard's book had done more harm than good to Renaissance studies, and they were in accord over other matters, too, including the importance of someone called Sternfeld, whose work on the music of Shakespeare's plays was, all things considered, "one of the *few* advances in recent years". So Gordon observed magisterially, and Bentley, murmuring, "oh, quite", treated himself to a very slight nod of agreement, as though to offer more would be a failure of scholarly decorum.

All this was mildly interesting, but I noticed that the longer the evening dragged on, the odder Gordon's behaviour and manner of speech, loosened no doubt by drink, became. There were mentions of *dear* Peter, *dear* Nicholas, *dear* James, and as he spoke, not always in unambiguous approval of those to whom he applied the term of endearment, Gordon increasingly took to fluttering his hands above his head as though in dismissal of those of whose work he especially deprecated — any mention of Tillyard caused a butterfly tsunami — made extravagant *moues*, writhed in his chair or shuddered in tacit approval of Bentley's not very barbed comments, falling back with a cry of *"Don't* talk to *me* about..."* X or Y.

When, with a show of reluctance that was almost certainly more genuine on the husband's side, the couple eventually rose to leave, Gordon made me go with them to the door.

"And remember to shake hands," he said, in a stage whisper. "With *both* of them."

Awkwardly, I did so. Awkwardly, they looked half away as they said goodnight.

I shut the door and went back to find Gordon walking unsteadily round the room, pouring wine over various potted plants that stood on shelves and the window sill.

"I thought that went rather well," he said.

* * *

Later, back in my own room, I came to two conclusions about the evening. One was that Gordon's drinking habits were beginning to get out of control. The other, that he must be homosexual. If his "theatrical" behaviour hadn't been sufficient clue there was no mistaking the import of the departing Bentley's averted gaze. They thought I was... well, his Antinous, maybe. That *was* a shock, and an unwelcome one. I wanted to believe that Gordon's various kindnesses to me — his lending me books, eager discussions of art, listening for the most part patiently to my views on politics and culture — were without a sexual basis. And the more I thought about it, the more certain I was that I hadn't misunderstood him. In addition, and this came as something of a relief, I was now ready to see that he was attracted to a certain kind of young man of whom there were several examples in Wantage: stocky, broad-shouldered, fair-haired. I had noticed his eyes straying to such youths whenever he left his flat before dinner to wander round the hall quadrangle. Some years later, he told me that his favourite film star was Alan Ladd, "though *not* the appalling films he allows himself to appear in." I suppose the Housmanic name may itself have helped.

But this was 1957. Gordon was a man with a reputation to maintain. A professor, a Dean, he must have been terrified at the possibility of exposure and, should that ever occur, the inevitable disgrace of prison. Already that year two waiters at Wantage Hall had been found guilty of soliciting — the public lavatories in the town's market square were apparently a known venue for cottaging — and both had disappeared into Reading gaol. One of them, a sweet-tempered, ageing Irishman, was popular with many of us. But when we got up a petition on his behalf, requesting the University to give him his job back once he was freed from prison, quite a few students refused to sign. I encountered more homophobia at Reading than I ever had at Hampton. "Shoot 'em all," was one response, and another, "soft on shirt-lifters? Why, are you a nancy boy?"

In order to *épater* the bone-heads who made such remarks, Geoffrey and I decided to go to a fancy-dress party as Oscar Wilde and Lord Alfred Douglas, parading through the dining hall to hisses and boos before we took ourselves off to what proved a desperately dull affair. Still, I'm glad that we did it.

Whether Gordon's increased drinking was connected to the misery his sexual longings must have caused him I don't know, but I do know that the fear — no, terror — of exposure would have been real. I want to exonerate the 1950s from many of the crimes of which it is pronounced guilty by people who see the decade through a fog of clichés and misapprehensions. But the treatment of homosexual men was quite simply a disgrace. I have often wondered whether the Wolfenden Committee's recommendation that homosexual acts should no longer be criminalised, released in the summer of 1957, may have been in part prompted by its

286

chairman's recognition that one of the most brilliant professors at the university, where Wolfendon was vice-chancellor, was himself homosexual. For Wolfendon was a great admirer of Gordon; he could appreciate at least something of the intellectual distinction Gordon brought to his devotion to ideas, art, to literature. And he could see, too, how deeply Gordon was admired even by those who didn't much like him, who feared his scorn for what he saw as the second-rate, wherever it showed itself.

The Report wasn't adopted. Even before it was debated in Parliament its findings were so vehemently attacked in the tabloid press that rejection was an inevitability. I cut out and kept a piece by John Gordon, which appeared in the issue of the *Sunday Express* dated September 8, 1957. I have it by my elbow as I write. This is how Gordon begins: "After three years of expensive cogitation, Sir John Wolfendon's investigating committee produces 'The Pansies Charter'." He goes on to claim that the main proposal "is so repugnant to the moral standards of the majority of people of Britain that no Parliament is likely to accept it in our lifetime." Then, with a wonderful show of magnanimity, he adds: "There are it is true a few physiological misfits who cannot control their leanings towards perversion. We can deal with their problem, without altering the law." (How, he doesn't tell us: castration, perhaps?) But the majority of homosexuals "glory in it... They seek converts assiduously and pervasively. Their evil power runs deep and strongly in many walks of life." And so on. Well, good to know that the *Sunday Express* was to be proved wrong about legislation. A little more than a decade after the Wolfendon Committee's recommendation was turned down, a Labour government de-criminalized homosexual behaviour.

But I can't agree with Hennessy that after 1957 what R.A. Butler, then Home Secretary, called the loosening of "Victorian stays", applied to homosexuality. I was still at Reading in the early 1960s, by then a young assistant lecturer in the English department, when a lecturer in the department of French was arrested for "soliciting for sex" on a train. He had been set up by a plain-clothes policeman giving him the eye. This was a well-known device for catching "deviants" and no doubt an easy way to earn some stripes or a pay rise. The lecturer was sentenced to nine months in jail. After his release he returned to his post, though not for long. He must have felt that in the eyes of others he was the tainted wether of the flock. This is how Gordon would have been made to feel. And this is why I use the word homosexual of him, not gay. It is daft to think you can retrospectively apply the word "gay" to men whose lives were in fact made a misery by the criminal law, and I sometimes find myself getting angry with younger acquaintances, themselves gay, who have no sense of how difficult life was for homosexual men before 1968, of how they were habitually forced to conceal their sexual nature. You knew about it and yet you didn't know. I don't think I knew that Forster, whose novels I loved and about whom I will write more in the last chapter of this book, was homosexual. And yet I *did* know. At all events, there was something decidedly odd about his descriptions of heterosexual encounters. But not knowing was a defence mechanism, a way, odd as it perhaps now seems, of keeping people you admired on the right side of the law. And as I revered Gordon, I wanted him to be safe, too, not to fall victim to the thugs and philistines who formed his foul namesake's snarling, vindictive constituency, and who would have taken delight in bringing him down.

* * *

As the year wore on so my involvement with Pauline deepened. I was enchanted by her. "Enchantment", the *O.E.D.* says, "great charm or fascination; the property of delighting; an enraptured condition." The bicycle rides we took to outlying villages that lay seemingly hidden at the end of rutted lanes among wood and heathland and where we could usually find a pub, including some whose neglected, frowsty look made them seem as though nothing had been disturbed since the last visitors left to fight in the Great War; occasions when we rowed up the broad, slow flowing, willow-screened Thames, walks to the favoured hamlet of Sonning, all thatch and cottage gardens and home to Edward Hudson, the founder of *Country Life*, whose riverside house, Deanery Garden, had been built for him by the doyen of Edwardian architects, Edwin Lutyens; visits to London art galleries; the Saturday evening I took her to hear the Brown band at Eel Pie Island and, even before we got to the bridge that would take us onto the island, could hear the sound of that unique, urgent clarinet cutting through the summer air — all was enchantment.

There was just one problem: her Catholicism. For a while I tried not to let this bother me. Simply being with her was wonder enough. But over the months it swelled until like the Bad Thing in a poem of John Wain's, "it blocked the sun." It led to rows, reconciliation, further rows. The tension between us grew until it was almost unbearable.

* * *

One evening at the very end of the summer term as I was mooching disconsolately in the quad after an evening of fruitless argument with Pauline, Gordon came out from his flat to take the night air. Seeing me, he walked across and asked me if anything was the matter. No, I said, I was alright, merely feeling a bit low, perhaps because the academic year was about to end.

Gordon looked at me as though he half guessed my problem. "Never mistake pity for love," he said and turned away.

But pity wasn't the problem. Love was.

Chapter 17
Lost Love's Labour

In the spring of 1957 my parents moved to a new house. It was one of a pair of small semi-detacheds erected on a patch of ground beside a winding by-road that ran from Staines to the little village of Laleham, and although not on the river itself you could reach the Thames by a short gravel path that led out onto the tow-path. Once there, it was a twenty minute stroll along the river to Staines Bridge and thence into town. By the time I arrived home at the beginning of July, the raw, claggy soil surrounding the house had been transformed into neat gardens, front and back. The ground at the back had been levelled off and turfed, regularly watered, rolled and cut, there were flower beds, a shed where new garden implements were housed, a small green-house where my mother grew potted plants, including tomatoes and the beginnings of a peach tree; and in front, too, there was a lawn, some rose bushes and, at the low wall dividing garden from pavement, aubrietia frothed purple, as it did virtually every other frontage up and down the road.

My parents called the house and garden "manageable" and were intensely proud of it. It was the visible evidence of a new phase in their lives, a step up into (very) modest afflu-ence. The kitchen had a number of gadgets bought from Saturday morning ventures into Staines. These included a wall tin-opener which my father had painstakingly attached to the inside of the back door, an electric egg timer that could be set to ping the moment your boiled egg was done to a nicety; there was even a metal cutter for removing the top of the egg. A cross between midget-sized shears and a pair of pliers, the "dratted thing," as my mother called it, invariably crunched the eggs into a gooey mess.

Still, my parents delighted in attending to their gardens, and where I saw only conformity with the tastes of others, they saw achievement. This was perhaps especially notice-able as far as the front garden was concerned. The waves of aubrietia that swept over chains hanging between short wooden, glossily-white painted square posts positioned at regular intervals along the knee-high, grey brick wall, the wrought-iron gate, the flagged path up the front door, the stone troughs in the porch that held trailing greenery, the carefully-tended rose bushes, these and all the other features indicated not so much imitation of the neighbours as the satisfaction of arrival. In his fascinating if appallingly-titled biography of Brian Clough, *Provided You Don't Kiss Me*, Duncan Hamilton remarks that Clough recalled with pride how his "mam's" front door step was the whitest of any of the terraced houses along their street in working class Middlesbrough. My guess is that this claim would have been disputed not merely by the rest of the street but by the rest of working class England. *Everyone's* front door step was the whitest. Daily whitening marked not only a defiance of the industrial dirt against which working class people had to contend, but a show of pride in the house, behind the front door of which there was usually little enough money to lash out on clothes, let alone fripperies, and often scarcely sufficient food to put on the table.

My parents' front garden was a show of pride. And when they called it and all else "manageable", they meant that they could control it, that it wouldn't get "out of hand". I can understand why Blake thought the bones of the people — villagers — were "bent and low". I understand Lawrence's rage against "bungalow culture" and the "small man's" dream of modest expectations. And, when I first came across it, I could understand and to some extent sympathise with Nietzsche's scorn of "littleness". But then I remember an old brandy colonel I saw on television. He was recalling the days immediately after the fall of Dunkirk when, having managed to get back to England, he was given the task of trying to stiffen the resolve of folk living along the south coast against the surely imminent Nazi invasion. "The people in the big houses didn't care," he said. "They thought they'd be able to cut a deal with the Germans. It was the *little* people who were ready to fight. They were poor but they were prepared to defend what they had. And that meant defending England." And I remember Forster's mildly expressed scorn of "great men", and how he always felt "a little man's pleasure when one came a cropper", and how, in its casual slanginess, the word "cropper" mischievously unhorses those who are riding too high. Above all, I remember Little Dorrit, that frail body with its "strong purpose", moving unflinchingly among the arrogant and the froward and the vain, all those "who fretted, and chafed, and made their usual uproar". The case for littleness is a strong one.

Of course, such people find the world a frightening place. My parents were averse from risk-taking. Like many of their generation, they knew all about risks, not because they went looking for them but because risks crowded about their lives, and nobody could feel safe from their looming, dark presence. The growing threat of war, the constant fear of unemployment, the humiliations that threatened to scald you every time you opened your mouth or by mischance wore the wrong clothes or "risked" (ha!) an opinion — risks were everywhere. Hence the delight, from which relief cannot have been absent, in a manageable house, one small enough to keep spotlessly clean and "tickety-boo" as they might have said. "Have you the visible means of support?" policemen were licensed to ask those they countered on the streets of pre-war England and whom they suspected of being vagrants. A show of four pence meant "yes". Enough to purchase a doss-house bed for the night. Whitened door steps and displays of aubrietia might not be proof of "means of support", but in their different ways they signalled a modest victory, a claim to be waving, not drowning. "We can manage". I sometimes think that even the preference for small dogs which my parents shared with many of their friends may well have been an unconscious expression of their desire to own something that would be manageable. Lap dogs, hearth dogs, dogs that could be brought to heel, that would obey your every call. "Cats," my mother once complained to me, "are so mysterious. You never know what they're thinking."

A few days after I had been home my father suggested one evening that we might go for a drink. Yes, I said, a good idea. Let's do that.

"Then put a tie on," my father said.

"I don't need to wear a tie."

"We can't go into a saloon bar if you're not properly dressed."

We could, but instead of pointing that out, I said, "Then let's use the public bar."

"I want to be in the saloon bar, where it's quiet," my father said.

"Well, I'm not going to wear a tie."

"Then I'm not going for a drink."

Looking back, I wish I'd done as he asked. I know I thought he was trying to manage me, to show the world, or as much of it as might be found on a Saturday evening in the saloon bar of a public house in Staines, that, despite my beard, I was his properly-dressed son. But so what. It was no great concession he was asking of me. My refusal to do as he asked hardly compared with any that Stephen Dedalus forced himself to make to *his* father. Besides, most men did then wear ties and they went on doing so until well into the 1960s. Look at early photographs of the Beatles, look at publicity stills of the Rolling Stones. They're wearing ties. I sometimes wore a tie. But on that summer evening of 1957 I wasn't prepared to offer my father the small satisfaction of dressing according to his code of what was proper.

What lay behind my inexcusable mulishness was a letter I had written earlier that day to Pauline. If it hadn't been for that I might have done his bidding. But the letter was, among other things, a protest against the right of parents to determine their children's lives. In it, I told her that, given her Catholicism, I couldn't see any future for us. Why did she let her parents control what she thought? Parents might manage their own lives, but they couldn't justifiably try to manage their children's. I probably didn't say all of that. In fact, beyond telling Pauline that I wanted to put an end to our relationship — which I didn't — I don't know what I said, but I do know that as soon as I had posted the letter I began to feel sick with anger and dejection. They were feelings that would last the entirety of the summer.

* * *

A few days later I reported for work at a small builders at Sunbury, a bicycle ride of some four or five miles from my parents' house. Gamblins, the builders were called, and the boss, Alan Gamblin, was a friend of my father's and a member of the same golf club, which was how I had come by the job. Not that I was to be shown any favours. On the contrary, I was told to be expect hard work, although I was pretty sure that it wouldn't be as exhausting, let alone dangerous, as a stint I'd put in two years previously at Staines Linoleum factory. There, I'd worked for three weeks on twelve-hour night shifts, and had seen something of the toll that such work could exact on non-unionised labour. (And nobody at that factory was protected by a union.) The broken and crushed limbs as immensely heavy rolls of lino fell on tired men, the breathing difficulties brought on by the foul stink of the chemicals required for the manufacture of the lino, even, so it was whispered, the unduly high levels of bowel cancer among those who'd worked in the factory for any length of time. By contrast, casual work on the Post was a doddle. But with increased union militancy, the hiring of part-time workers to assist with the delivery of Christmas mail was discouraged and by 1957 had virtually ceased. Anyway, this was the summer.

I doubt whether many small firms in the 1950s were subject to union rules and regulations. It was a time of full employment when, as I saw for myself, men and women could hop from job to job in the confident expectation of slightly improved work conditions and pay, or simply because they were bored and wanted a change. Much labour was casually taken up and as casually put down. The more skilled you were, the easier it was to find the work that suited you. In the building trade employers took care to look after their men well enough for them not to seek redress through the union, or to down tools and go elsewhere. Alan Gamblin certainly took good care of his small work force, and they were for the most part loyal to him. In fact, despite the pain of my break-up with Pauline, the six weeks I spent working for him were by and large a happy time. True, the work itself was in many ways dull, repetitive and undemanding. There's only so much satisfaction to be got from applying under-paint to wooden window and door frames, mixing mortar, stacking bricks, lifting roof tiles and digging holes. But the men I worked with or, more accurately, for, were a different matter.

* * *

On the morning I began life as a casual labourer I arrived at the yard, which was close to Sunbury Cross, prompt at 8am. My boss, in badly-fitting grey trousers and green, buttoned-up cardigan, was waiting for me at the door of his small, brick-built office half-way down the yard. Beyond, stretched a couple of lock-up garages and a large shed which I would later find housed the firm's carpenter, "Nogger" Newman. Facing these single-storey buildings was a brick stack, beside it a hillock of cement bags, then, at the bottom of the yard, a low, rough-cast wall with scaffolding poles and boards laid along, viewable over it the curved corrugated roofs of what, judging by the variety of feculent smells coming from that direction, had to be pig sties.

"Like shit in the jungle," Alan said, noticing my reaction to the smells. He spoke round the stub of a cigarette that glowed between his lips and which he now removed in order to light a new one — Capstan Full Strength. His voice was wheezily hoarse from long years of chain-smoking, so that at first I had some difficulty in understanding what he was telling me, particularly as in the middle of a sentence he suddenly doubled up in an explosion of coughing. While he was still trying to clear his throat, a small grey van turned into the yard, parked beside the office and a man hurried towards us.

"Malcolm," Alan wheezed, "he'll tell you," and once again doubled up, this time clutching his knees as he coughed, spat and coughed again.

Malcolm, the gaffer, the foreman, was a strongly-built man in early middle-age. He had greying hair, thick at the sides, thinner on top, which, together with his firm, clean-shaven jaw and hawk-like nose, gave him a distinguished look, rather like a lawyer in mufti. He wore grey flannel trousers whose cleanliness and sharp crease put his boss's to shame, grey shirt and a grey, sleeveless sweater. As we drove out of the yard, he told me that I'd be working with the firm's two brickies — Harry and Hector — on a boathouse that Gamblins were building at Shepperton.

"For a film star?" In those days Shepperton, a favoured village which stretched down to the Thames no more than a couple of miles from Sunbury, was home to a famous film studio, and in one or other of the pubs grouped round the village square you could see most nights of the week such then well-known actors as Dinah Sheridan, Kenneth More, Glynis Johns, John Grigson, Richard Todd, Donald Sinden, and the Bradens.

But no. The boathouse was being built for a Harley Street specialist who had recently acquired a grand riverside house which he was keen to make still grander.

"You won't see him," Malcolm told me, "but his house-keeper is always there. She'll keep you supplied with tea and coffee."

He had a slightly mannered way of speaking, as though he was guarding his vowels. "I need to pop back home before I take you down to join the others," he said. "Some plans I require for a house we're tenderin' for. I was studyin' them last night."

"Home" was a bungalow in a cul-de-sac of identikit bunga-lows. Malcolm manoeuvred his van between the concrete posts from which hung smartly-painted black wooden gates.

"Shan't be a jiff," he said, clambering out of the van.

While he was away I noted the bungalow's diamond-leaded windows, their ruched, flowered curtains, pebble-dash walls, and, guarding its privacy, the shaven, four-foot high hedges which enclosed a small front garden looking in its immaculate trimness — the squares of grass exactly finished off, the flower beds almost painfully short of weeds — as though each night it was gone over inch by inch, with nothing left to chance. A few years later, when I read Elizabeth Gaskell's description of Mrs Thornton's front parlour in *North and South* and of the effort required to "secure that effect of icy, snowy discomfort ....there was evidence of care and labour, but not care and labour to produce ease", I thought, incongruous as it may seem, of Malcolm's front garden, and I recalled my assumption that within his bungalow the amount of care and labour would have been as evident, and as discomforting.

"So," he said, as he rejoined me and we headed for Shepperton. "What are you studyin' at your university?"

I told him and he nodded but made no comment.

Before long we turned off the main road and bumped down a narrow, unsurfaced lane to the river. At the bottom of the lane Malcolm brought the van to a halt. "Here we are," he said, and for the first time allowed himself to look straight at me. "You'll find Harry and Hector" — he pronounced the aitches with careful emphasis — "a bit on the rough side, but I'm sure they'll make you welcome."

Malcolm, it seemed, wanted me to think of him as more my sort than theirs.

"I'll come over and introduce you," he said, as we left the van. He led the way through a gap in the hedge, starry with dog-rose, that ran to our right. To our left the Thames glittered in the morning sun. In front of half-built walls was the inevitable detritus of building work. Bricks, bags of cement, buckets, a mound of what, from its slithery gleam and the spade sticking from it, had to be fresh-mixed mortar.

"'arry," Malcolm called, aspirate momentarily forgotten.

"Over 'ere, mate."

We stepped through a door frame and there were the two men, standing on scaffold boards balanced between trestles. Their brown-overalled backs were toward us, though the taller one called over his shoulder, "'ard at it, Malcolm. We could do with some 'elp."

"Which I've brought you," Malcolm said, "name of John." Then, to me, he added, "You'll be alright. I'll leave you now, plenty to do elsewhere," and with that he went. It was only as I watched his van drive off that I realised that he hadn't actually collected the plans for which we'd ostensibly called in at his bungalow, and I sensed that he must have wanted me to see that he lived in a manner he might not have called "a cut above", but which for all that he thought of as superior to the rest of Gamblins' work force. And the van he drove, while belonging to the firm, nevertheless also separated him from the others, all of whom came to work by bicycle or bus.

The two brickies turned to watch me as I walked over to them. Both wore caps, both had collar and tie showing above their overalls, both had thin, rolled-up cigarettes between their lips

The man who had spoken to Malcolm spoke again. "I'm 'arry," he said, "so guess who's 'ector." And his smile, accentuated by his greying, Clark Gable moustache and keen blue eyes, held both challenge and the promise of welcome.

* * *

Later that summer, after I'd finished at Gamblins and was spending my days working through seventeenth century authors who were required reading for the autumn term, as well as trying to write up my experiences of six weeks as a general labourer, I met Pete for a drink at the White Swan. He seemed to be largely recovered from the nervous exhaustion of his army experience and ready to mock my enthusiastic tales of the men I'd recently worked with. "Idealising the working class," he said. "Heroic, horny-handed sons of toil. Remember I met some in khaki. They were bastards."

But I wasn't to be deflected from my view. "Perhaps that's what the army does to people," I said, "though if so it doesn't last." And I told him that all the men I met at Gamblins had fought in the war. "Except Hector, that is. He was in the army during the first war. In France, too."

"He's lucky to be here, then."

"Luckier than most. He told me he got away without a scratch."

Which Hector had indeed told me, laughing wryly as he did so. In the weeks I worked for Harry and Hector, the two of the them changed from an initial suspicion of me to a kind of genial tolerance, and the longer I was with them the more they were inclined to tell me something of their lives. These conversations happened at tea-breaks and during lunch hours. While they worked they said little, either to each other or to me, though from time to time Harry would deliver a gruff command for me to mix more mortar or to bring them further hodsful of bricks. I was also responsible for knocking on the doctor's back door promptly at 10.30am, under instructions to enquire — nudge, nudge — if I could spare the housekeeper the chore of bringing out our mid-morning coffee, a duty to be repeated at 3pm if by then our afternoon tea hadn't appeared. "Go on, Whiskers, you've got the voice for it. Ask her nicely and you might get more than you bargained for."

Fetching and carrying, my hands and shoulders at first rubbed raw and blistered by spade and hod — "piss on yer 'ands mate, that'll toughen them" — I watched as under their deft skills the boathouse grew around us. The unvarying rhythm of the work fascinated me. Trowel into the small heap of mortar held on a board in the left hand, flick excess of mortar off, then slap the remaining mortar on top of brick already in place, fit new brick on top, knock down with base of trowel handle, trim off excess mortar, reach for new brick, trowel into mortar, repeat actions. When they came to the end of a row and there was a gap too small to be plugged by a whole brick they would size up the amount needed and with a sharp blow sever a brick with such precision that the piece they held onto always fitted snugly into place. String and spirit level ensured that the walls were exact, both vertically and horizontally. They were unassuming masters of their craft and it was part of their mastery that at the end of the day they looked as neat as they did at its outset, their caps as exactly set, their ties unspotted by mortar or brick dust, their overalls remarkably clean. Only their hands were stained, fingers and nails encrusted with drying mortar, and at all breaks they plunged them into a bucket of water and dried them off with a rough towel brought for that purpose alone.

I had one other task. Each lunchtime Harry and Hector settled down to read the *Daily Express*. At first I couldn't understand this. After all they told me they voted Labour. "Expect you're a Tory," Harry had said, and seemed surprised when I replied that I certainly wasn't. Why on earth did he think that? Well, I was a student, so I must be from the upper class. Well, I said, he bought the *Daily Express*. Only for the racing column, he said. The best there was. Hector agreed.

Their faith seemed, however, misplaced. At all events, while I was working for them their devotion to the *Express*'s tipster failed to bring them much by way of luck. I once mentioned this but Harry wouldn't hear a word against him. "Can't always win," he said. "Otherwise nothing would ever get built, would it? We'd all be on the razzle." It was logic of a sort.

As they squatted below the scaffold boards to unwrap sandwiches and unscrew the flasks each brought in an army knapsack, they would begin to discuss the tipster's recommendations. After some minutes of this, Harry — it was always Harry — would take a stub of pencil and piece of paper from the top pocket of his overalls, and the two having agreed which "gee-gees" they were prepared to put money on, he would write down the details — names, racecourse, time of race, the amount of money to be placed on each horse, hand the paper and coins to me and say "on yer bike, Whiskers." They knew a bookies' runner who could be found at a nearby newsagents where he doubled as assistant, and it was my duty to cycle there and hand over both paper and cash. This had to be done discreetly because such transactions were illegal. If there was a customer in the shop I had to wait, if there were several I might lose most of my lunchtime. But Harry was unapologetic. "Excuses," he said, straight faced, if on return I complained that I'd been kept from my food. "Probably been in the Dog and Duck."

* * *

One Friday night, after Malcolm had brought our wages and was made to stand there while the two of them counted their money out, they asked me if I'd like to go for a drink with them. In those days pubs rarely opened before 6pm of an evening, and a glance at my watch showed only 5.30, but Harry said, "Don't worry Whiskers, we know a place."

Ten minutes later we were sitting in the front bar of a small pub midway between Shepperton and Sunbury. Harry and I sipped pints of bitter, while Hector had a black-and-tan, which in his case meant half bitter and half mild. They were unusually cheerful that evening, not only because it was Friday night, but because for once a horse of theirs, an outsider, had won, and each would be due a few quid. It was then that they told me something of their war experiences.

Hector had volunteered early in 1915, immediately after turning eighteen. "Could have gone sooner, but me mother wouldn't 'ear of it, not with me dad away, and me brother, too. By the end of the war she was a widder and I was an only child, but in a way I got off cheap. Plenty of blokes I went with never come back and those that did often 'ad to make do without an arm or a leg. And in those days that meant you couldn't get work for love nor money. So I was lucky, though a good many weren't. It were bad for thousands, especially if they 'ad wives and kiddies."

"And you didn't?"

"Nah. Too young before I went and when I come 'ome there was me mum to look after. Not much use bein' stuck with a war widder's pension. That wouldn't pay the bills. And of course, I 'ad to go out lookin' for work, which wasn't always there. But with a bit of luck and a follerin' wind I could usually get somethin' without goin' back on the land."

Stupidly, I'd assumed that Hector had always been a brickie.

"Not me. Left school at thirteen, worked as a ploughboy till I joined up in '15. 'Course, farmer were on at me to go. 'Do your bit for the country,' that kind of thing. And by the time I volunteered most of the 'orses 'ad been took." And then he began a litany of their names, ten, twelve, perhaps more, of which to my shame I can remember only two, Beauty and Blossom. In the intervening years I've often wished I'd written down the names Hector reeled off that evening. There was a natural poetry to the list, and his voice, while he spoke the names, took on a kind of rapt eloquence very different from his usual dry, mild shuffle of words. Hector was an essentially mild man. He liked jokes, but ones without edge, let alone venom. "Thames is runnin' low," he said to me one morning, nodding towards the river as it slid easily by. "See. Water's only comin' 'arf way up them ducks." And whenever he laughed, it was really no more than a slight convulsion of his shoulders, accompanied by a quick turn down of his mouth. But on that evening, when he spoke the names of horses that had gone from his farm, he was for those few minutes another person, and when I glanced towards him I saw that his eyes were bright with tears.

Many years later, when in the early 1980s I was teaching an evening course to a group of people in Bottesford, the memory of that moment came back to me. Bottesford is a small town on the rural Nottinghamshire-Lincolnshire border, and the course I had been asked to tutor was on the poetry of the First World War. On the final evening we took among other poems Edward Thomas's "As the team's head-brass" and for several minutes discussed the implications of the closing lines, where Thomas, seated on a fallen elm, watches as "The horses started and for the last time

/I watched the clods crumble and topple over /After the ploughshare and the stumbling team."

The last time for Thomas, the last time for the horses. The lines are a virtual threnody for a disappearing way of life. It seemed as good a way as any to bring the course to a close.

Afterwards a woman came up to me, one of those who rarely said anything in class, but who now wanted to speak. She told me that as a small girl in the Vale of Belvoir she remembered an old man — "well, I thought of him as old, I don't suppose he was" — who was regularly invited to the junior school she attended, as he was to others in the area, to talk about the effects of the war on life in the Vale. "And what I especially remember is that he stood in front of us and recited the names of all the horses he'd known when he was a boy working on the land, and all the time he was doing this the tears rolled down his cheeks. Nearly all the horses had been taken for the war, he said, and they'd been killed in France." Would I by any chance know how many horses in all were taken overseas in those years? I didn't but thought I'd seen a number as high as 500,000 quoted. "Poor things," she said.

Harry was a good deal more caustic than Hector, rougher-tongued, capable of abrasiveness in word and manner, though once I'd indignantly rejected the suggestion I might be a Tory he accepted me, albeit grudgingly. I don't think he ever quite believed my protestations of being a socialist. Socialism was for the working class and I wasn't working class. He himself was socialist through and through. He had read *News from Nowhere* and was all for making change happen, by violent means if necessary. As Hector took our glasses up to the bar for refills, Harry said, "See, Whiskers, the difference between old 'ector and me is that he can stand the bosses and I can't." And by the time his mate came back with full pints he was launched into an account of how his army experiences had sharpened his distrust, amounting to angry contempt, for "brass 'ats and bullshit." The only General he had any time for was "Monty", because he cared about ordinary soldiers. "The rest didn't give a bollock, they'd see you in 'ell so long as they saved their own skin."

Harry had fought in the desert, up through Italy and onto Berlin. He loathed the "teds" — German soldiers — but hardly more than he despised the officers he served under. He was a handsome man, Harry: tall, lean-faced, his small moustache giving him an almost rakish charm. But you could feel the anger that was never far from the surface ready to spurt out at any fancied slight or evidence of what he called "fart-arse Toryism." One afternoon as we worked on the boathouse, some young women on horse-back came clattering down the lane and turned onto the river path. "Oh, Fiona, isn't this *heavenly*," one called out as they rode below the spot where Harry was bent, squinting at the spirit level atop the row of bricks he'd just laid. Hector and I looked apprehensively at each other. Sure enough, Harry straightened up, glared over the rising wall at their retreating backs and shouted after them "'ope you break your bloody necks, you fat arses." Then, having spat, he turned to us, a slight smile on his lips as he said "No point in wastin' good words on the likes of them. They wouldn't understand."

What Harry understood, so he explained as he sipped the beer Hector had slid in front of him, was that he and those he was with in the war were fighting for a different England from the one they'd left. He told me that in the days leading up to the end of hostilities in Europe, and even more in the period after it and before they got home, the troops were endlessly ear-bashed by chinless wonders who were called in to give them lectures on how to vote in the next general election. "We were supposed to take part in debates. Put one point of view, then another. All bollocks. The only point of view they were interested in was good old Winnie and vote Tory. A mate of mine wanted to stand for the Reds. Not allowed. Those bastards thought they was too good for us, that we'd see things their way sooner or later. That was what one of them said." Harry mimicked an upper-class accent. "'Yorl see things more reasonably when you've reflected on what I've been trying to tell you.' Like we was too stupid to take it in at first. About all we reflected was that we wanted the lot of them locked away and us 'oldin' the key. They couldn't credit it when old Clem got in." Recalling the looks of disbelief on the faces of the "orficers" as the results of the 1945 election came through, Harry actually laughed with pleasure, a thing he very rarely did. "We were in charge. Put that in your bloody pipe, if you can find your way to your effin' mouth, and smoke it."

I wanted to ask how he explained 1951 and then 1955. The enemy once more running the country. But he swallowed his beer, stood and said, "Right, off for me tea, then me and the missus 'll be up the boozer for a pint or several. See you Monday, Whiskers." And with that he and Hector, who had hastily emptied his own glass, went.

* * *

As it happened, I didn't see Harry and Hector the following Monday. Instead, Malcolm was waiting for me when I arrived at the nearly-finished boathouse. I was to report to the yard, where "the boss" had other plans for me. These turned out to be underpainting some newly made window-frames and doors which were due for delivery at Shepperton. "I want that job finished by Friday," Alan Gamblin said round a smouldering Capstan. "Otherwise we get penalised for not finishing on time. I've got problems with Len" — the painter and decorator who was famous for never meeting deadlines — "I can't afford another fed-up customer."

So that day and the next I joined the firm's chippie, Nogger Newman, in his carpenter's shed, and spent long hours sloshing pink lead paint onto the wood he'd lovingly cut, chamfered, adzed, glued and fitted, one piece into another, by means of a whole variety of joints. Nogger was an artist, someone utterly absorbed in the work he did, and he loved the medium with which he worked. True, he would grumble about some of the wood he was brought. "Soft as buggery," he'd say, digging a thumbnail into a strip of pine. "Like that French cheese you're so fond of. And about as much stinking use." But for the most part he would crouch over his bench, eye half-closed in silent concentration and against the thin smoke that coiled from the roll-ups he had waiting for him in a tin box he kept at his elbow, measuring lengths of wood with a folding ruler he'd made himself, marking up, squinting along surfaces for signs of warp or other imperfections, reaching for a range of chisels which he repeatedly sharpened on the circular treadle whetstone that stood nearby, easing tiny flaws from the bevelling, sanding, planing and stroking the smooth-as-satin wood with fingers that were instantly alert to any last remaining roughness.

Why does he bother, I wondered, as I watched him. It's only doors and windows and skirting boards. But a look at that blue-overalled figure, his nose within an inch of the wood he was working on, seeming to think with his fingers, gave me the answer. As my friend Gurth Higgin said to me when he was explaining how he had spent weeks fitting gas lights in a cottage he owned in a part of Wales too remote for electricity to reach, "if a job's worth doing it's worth enjoying." And in his undemonstrative way, Nogger embodied Gurth's saying, its neat avoidance of cliché. It was only when I'd been working with him for a few days that I put the question that had been bothering me since I'd first shaken hands with him.

"Do you mind me asking," I said, as we sat sipping tea during our brief morning break, "if you used to catch the 216 bus." (Used to, because Nogger came to work on a bicycle).

He looked quizzically at me. "Yes, is the answer, and why, is the question. Why do you want to know?"

"Because," I said, "I think I used to see you, when I was coming home from school of an afternoon. You were with a younger couple, man and woman." After a moment, during which Nogger's gaze changed from the quizzical to the more openly enquiring, I added, "She was very pretty. I used to think she looked like June Allyson."

"My daughter," he said.

"And was the man her husband?"

"*Was* is about right. A wrong 'un. Took off soon after she found she was pregnant."

"I'm sorry," I said.

"Well," Nogger said, draining his cup and getting to his feet, "it came out alright in the wash. She's married now to a decent bloke and with two more kiddies. Could've been a lot worse. Come on, back to work."

Nogger was a stickler for work. Not so, Len. Len was a bodger. In *The Ragged Trousered Philanthropists*, Robert Tressell provides the definitive account of bodging. Never do properly the work you've been contracted to do. At all events, never do it more than bare-bones adequately. And make it last as long as you can, because while you work you're getting paid, but once the work is done you have no guarantee of further work. Tressell was writing about a time in Edwardian England when work was hard to come by, easy to lose, and when working men were exploited by employers who squeezed from them the maximum amount of labour and rewarded them with minimum pay. As I have already said, matters were different in the 1950s. Employment was easily come by and, as even Harry admitted, Alan Gamblin paid decent wages.

Not that this registered with Len. The firm's one painter and decorator, he caused endless problems for his boss. Dissatisfied customers would complain that Len had skimped with the paint so that old markings showed through, oil-painted wood surfaces hadn't been given any undercoating, dados were wonky; besides, he wasn't reliable, would go for days without showing up, or, if he did, might well arrive late and leave early. Nor was that all. Nogger let drop that Len was filching paint from the yard. Of course, at one time or another all of them took a certain amount of what Wemmick calls portable property. Harry, I knew, had carted off bricks and a bag of cement to make the base for a lean-to shed at the back of his house, Hector had built a brick bird bath, including pedestal and surround, with materials that came from Gamblins, and even Nogger had palmed screws and a length of batten for some purpose or other. But these were allowed for. Alan more or less gave them permission to take what they wanted as long as they didn't overstep the mark. A certain amount of portable property was no doubt reckoned into the contracts he tendered for.

But there was no reckoning with Len. He had a profitable side-line in liberating tins of paint which he then sold on to acquaintances. His pretence that he used them in his daily work fooled no-one. In addition, he moonlighted. He undertook work for his own customers which he completed during hours when he should have been working for Alan, and for such work he used materials Alan had paid for; as if that wasn't enough, he had what Nogger called "a fancy woman", with whom he reputedly spent most afternoons. Matters came to a head during the week I began work for Nogger. Mid-morning Thursday, as he and I sat drinking tea on an improvised bench of untreated wood, Malcolm appeared in the shed. "John," he said — he was the only one apart from Alan not to call me Whiskers — "I've got orders to take you off this work for the rest of the day. Get your coat."

In the van, he explained that I was to work with Len. "To be honest," he said, "we think he's not pullin' his weight. I'm not askin' you to keep an eye on him, but I'd like to think you can keep 'im up to the mark." Malcolm was full of a gaffer's anxious clichés. "If you're there he's more likely to put in the hours we pay him for."

We, indeed. Malcolm was the boss's man alright.

The house which Len was supposed to be painting turned out to be a semi-detached house down from Sunbury Cross toward the river, on the route the 216 took. As we pulled up outside, we could see Len's extension ladder propped up against a front bedroom window.

"Don't let that fool you," Malcolm said. "'e puts that up so that if I come by I'll think 'e's at work. But more than likely 'e'll be elsewhere." As he spoke, the white-overalled Len came round the side of the house, carrying a large pot of paint and brush. He saw us but beyond a cursory nod gave no greeting before he began to mount the ladder.

"Len, can you spare us a moment," Malcolm called.

"Can't you see I'm busy." Len made a great show of being put out by this request.

"And the moon is blue," Malcolm said, sotto-voce. Then, as Len clambered down the ladder and turned to face us, "Alan's worried this job is taking so long," Malcolm said. "That's why I've brought John to help. He can clean and scrape any old paintwork that still needs attendin' to, and 'e'll be alright at usin' a brush, if necessary. 'e's been workin' with Nogger on undercoatin'. John knows the basics."

Len sniffed derisively. "This isn't a job for a beginner," he said. "Anyway, he's not dressed proper." He ran his eye over my streaked, raggedy sweater, my old cords, the battered, down-at-heel shoes.

"I've got 'im some overalls," Malcolm said. "In the back of the van."

So that was that. A few minutes later, when I'd wriggled into the white overalls Malcolm had lobbed at me before driving off, Len told me to get up the ladder and begin painting. "Finish that winder frame with topcoat and if the old witch who's inside wants to know what you're doing here, tell her you're my assistant. That'll shut her up. I'll be back soon as I can. Got things to do."

He still hadn't returned when Malcolm's van once more appeared later that afternoon. By then I had top-coated the front upper windows and was making a start on the lower ones, aware of the scorch marks and notches left by Len's less than careful work with blow-torch and scraper.

"Where is 'e?" Malcolm was not in a good mood.

"He said he had things to do."

"Oh, 'e did, did 'e. How long's 'e been gone?"

This was difficult. I had no desire to make trouble for Len, which I almost certainly would have done if I'd told the truth — that he'd been away for over four hours — but it must have been obvious that work lagged. Fortunately, while I was still working out how to reply to Malcolm's question, Len materialised.

"Blimey, have I had a caper," he said, bustling up to us.

"How you been doing while I've had to dash off?" he asked me, winking so that Malcolm wouldn't see. Then, "soon have this lot finished," he said for the gaffer's benefit.

"I want to know where you've been, Len," Malcolm said, and he wasn't joking.

"Bit of trouble at home," Len said. "Missus needed some help."

It didn't sound convincing and Malcolm wasn't convinced. "Pull the other one," he said.

"You calling me a liar?"

"Among other things."

"Right, gimme me cards." Bluff or bluster.

To Len's obvious amazement, Malcolm took the buff national insurance card from his rear pocket, together with a brown envelope. "You'll find your card is stamped and wages are paid up to date," he said.

Without looking at either, Len pushed card and envelope into the top pocket of his overalls. "You always was a spineless creep," he said to Malcolm, who flushed and took a step forward.

Then, seeing Len flinch, he checked himself. "I wouldn't dirty my hands on scum like you," he said, "you just get off, now." He stood there, breathing heavily, opening and closing his fists, and after a few moments of being outstared Len turned silently away.

For the rest of the day I painted on my own and by Friday afternoon the job was done.

"If it'd been left to Len, we'd 'ave been here till Doomsday," Malcolm said, as he ran me back to the yard. "Anyway, 'e'll find other work easily enough." He was, I thought, trying to justify himself. Sacking Len made him the boss's man and though at some level he plainly wanted to be considered as apart from and superior to the rest of the firm — I couldn't forget that transparent ruse to let me see how he lived — at another he still wanted their trust, wanted to be one of them. By training an electrician, and so the firm's "sparks", Malcolm perhaps aspired to be his own boss. The confrontation with Len had forced on him the discovery that he couldn't easily straddle the gap between work mates and his role as foreman, and I'm pretty sure that the discovery was a genuinely painful one. Malcolm was a decent enough man. Had he not been, doing what amounted to Alan's dirty work wouldn't have bothered him. "He did his duty," Jarndyce says of Neckett, the debt collector in *Bleak House*. The words are intended as commendation. But Dickens knows that the duty Neckett does is bound to harm others. A similar knowledge made Malcolm uneasy. That's why I say that he was a decent man.

Chapter 18
Other Lives

The following Monday morning Malcolm drove me to a small industrial estate on the far side of Sunbury where the firm was demolishing a factory that had once made furniture for shops and offices but had now gone out of business. I would be working with two others. "It's dirty work," Malcolm had warned me when he dropped me off the previous Friday afternoon, "I'll get you some overalls, but wear your oldest clothes."

Now, as he led the way under early morning August sun across rubbled grass toward the open hangar-wide door of the factory building, swirls of black dust came from inside, soot presumably, stirred and dislodged by the hammering. As we stepped into the abandoned factory, I made out in the gloom a figure bent over what looked like a heap of desks, although when Malcolm called out "Ted", the answering cry came from the roof. A face poked through a hole that let in such a dazzle of light I could see nothing but the bare outline of head and shoulders.

"Malcolm? 'arf a mo'."

Seconds later a small man was scrabbling down the ladder that jutted through the hole. As he hurried across to us, wiping his hands on heavily stained blue overalls, I saw from his welcoming grin that he appeared to have no teeth. I also noticed that even in the factory gloom his black eyes shone, and when he shook hands he did so with a kind of unguarded friendliness.

"Bill," Malcolm called to the other man, "come over here. Meet John. 'e'll be working with the two of you while you finish off this job."

Bill when he hoved in view proved to be about my age. He wasn't in overalls. Instead, he wore a tight black singlet and pale blue jeans over winkle-picker shoes. His blond hair stood up in spikes. He looked unwaveringly at me.

"This is Spikey Bill," Malcolm said.

"And you're Whiskers," Bill said, his voice flat, unimpressed. "'eard about you. Nogger reckons you've always got your nose in a book. Fat lot of good readin' 'll do you on this job."

"Right," Malcolm said, seemingly relieved that, now the introductions had been made, he could be off. "I'll leave you to it, John. Ted here will show you the ropes. We're 'opin' to have this work completed by the middle of next week. Reckon you can manage that?"

"Like fallin' off a log," Ted said cheerfully.

"It'll take bloody big log," Bill said.

But Malcolm chose not to hear that last remark.

In the event we didn't finish until the end of the following week, and to achieve that we had to work flat out. But although it was the hardest work I did that summer, the dirtiest, the sweatiest — day after day of flawless skies and heat left us drained, whether we were on top of the roof lifting slates under Ted's expert supervision or sorting into piles the various desk parts, benches, sundeala boards and pieces of useless-looking machinery left over from an earlier auction of the factory's effects — when I look back at the time I spent as a labourer, it is those days I remember with the fondest feelings.

Bill was a teddy boy. He despised all authority, loved Bill Haley and Elvis Presley, whose songs he was always whistling or singing, and had a regular girlfriend called Suzie, though she wouldn't let him go all the way. "Not till we're married, anyhow. We're savin' for that. Soon 'ave as much as we need for down payment on a place we've got our eye on. Then watch me. Nothin' but a hound dog, Whiskers, ruttin' all the time."

Ted was married, with two small children, photographs of whom and of his wife he passed around at dinner hour as we sat on the grass outside the derelict building, chewing sandwiches which, no matter how much we rinsed out our mouths, tasted grittily of soot, before we lay back to sun ourselves and drift in and out of sleep.

"'ow about you Whiskers? You got anyone?"

No, I told them, I'd got no-one. For Pauline hadn't replied to my letter and though I cursed myself for my stupidity — why on earth had I written the damned thing — I couldn't think of any reason to write to her again. I could hardly say I'd changed my mind and planned to become a Catholic. Nor could I tell her that her Catholicism didn't matter, needn't come between us, because it did. The only way I could cope with the ache of lost love was not to think about it. But then images of her would start up in my mind.

"Wanna come night fishin' then?"

I rolled over and looked at Spikey Bill. He looked back, questioningly. "Well, you 'aven't got a bird, so you must 'ave evenin's free."

"I've got no fishing gear," I said.

"Don't matter," he said, "I've got enough for both."

"What about Suzie?"

Suzie, it seemed, would be away this coming weekend, visiting "some old aunt up north", and anyway Bill often reserved Friday nights for fishing. Nor did it matter that I knew nothing about the sport. He could teach me all I'd need to know.

So I said yes, and late that Friday evening we met by arrangement at Penton Hook Lock. The lock, beside an island the Thames near Staines swerves abruptly round, is ideal for fishing, so Bill told me. Different water levels and the fact that you got almost still pools and then, at the two weirs constructed on either side of the island, races, guaranteed several varieties of freshwater fish. Dace and roach were mentioned, barbel ("though you don't get 'em before early light"), others I can't recall.

As we pushed our bikes onto the island that Friday night and Bill led the way to a favourite spot where he proposed to set up camp, I asked what he was carrying in the crammed, heavy knapsack slung across his shoulders.

"All we'll need, Whiskers."

A few minutes later we were unpacking and erecting a

small tent, setting out hurricane lamp, primus stove, skillet, tin kettle, saucepan, can of beans, bacon wrapped in grease-proof paper, loaf of bread, and screw jars with tea, milk and sugar.

"Should see us right," Bill said. "You mash and I'll set the rod up."

"Don't I get a rod?"

"Nah, we'll take it in turns. Get some kip in between shifts."

Though in fact we both sat by the rod all night, talking, smoking, brewing tea, at which task Bill was far more expert than I was — "Don't teach you much at your college, do they, Whiskers" — in the early hours frying bacon and bread over the primus stove, and, very occasionally, lifting a fish which Bill would carefully unhook, study by the light of his hurricane lamp, and then return to the water.

A year or so later, when I came to that marvellous passage in *Fiesta* where Jake and his friend Bill go fishing and Hemingway lets us glimpse through their apparently desultory talk their feelings of friendship, I thought back to that night by the Thames. Not that Spikey Bill and I were friends. In the brief period we knew each other we weren't even especially close. But that Friday night had its own slow, shareable magic. Along the bank we could see the light of other lamps, at our feet the Thames flowed, scarcely visible apart from an occasional reflected gleam from our hurricane lamp but alive with the slap of tiny waves against the river bank, or, further out, splashes and gurgles, a sudden dry flurry among reeds — "water rat" Bill said, "after some chick or bird eggs" — the rush and hiss of water combing over the weir to our right, the creak of branches above our heads as an elm stirred in stray gusts of wind.

Early on Saturday morning, we packed up, stiff with cold and lack of sleep, but elated by the experience of our night's fishing. It was as though we had passed some sort of test.

"Time for breakfast," Bill said, as we pushed our bikes off the island onto the tow-path. "Fancy it, Whiskers?"

Together we biked to a transport café on the main Staines

to Sunbury road. At that hour there were few customers apart from a pale-faced group who, to judge from their dress, had come straight from an all-night party. They looked wearily at us as we came in, me in my cords, checked shirt and windcheater, Bill in his skin-tight jeans, bristly hair and, I noticed, shirt elaborately embroidered with black stitching which he wore under a velvet-collared drape jacket. Bill ordered "full breakfast" for himself, and I made do with a mug of tea and bacon sandwich.

"Won't keep you alive," Bill said, gesturing with his fork at my plate. His was piled with sausages, egg, fried potatoes, baked beans, tomatoes and fried bread. Then, "Friends of yours, are they, Whiskers?" nodding toward the group of wasted revellers who were staring lethargically at us.

I stared briefly back. "No," I said.

"Thank Christ for that. Wouldn't want to think of you bein' with that lot," Bill said contentedly, and drank his tea. He raised the empty mug to them in ironic celebration. "Cheers," he said, "to you and 'oorays everywhere."

* * *

Ted wanted to know how we'd got on, but he waited to ask the question until he and I were sitting in his house at lunchtime the following Monday. Over the weekend the hot spell had broken, the sky, now overcast, leaked fat, heavy drops of rain, and Ted had decided to go home for a hot meal, his house being only a few streets away from where we were working. "Bring your snap with you," he suggested to Bill and me, "the wife will make us a cuppa." But Bill preferred to go to a nearby pub and so, after Ted had climbed out of his soot-caked overalls and I had used my hands to bang the worst off my clothes, he and I cycled off together.

His house proved to be a small semi, one of a row of similar houses built, Ted told me, by a farmer who long since had sold them, so that they were now rented out by a local agency. "They're alright, as long as you keep up with the payments. Fall behind and the bailiffs are in before you can say 'knife'. I'm safe, though. I let Jean 'andle the money. She's good with figures."

Jean was his wife, to whom I was introduced once he'd steered the way round to the back door. A pretty, plump woman, neatly dressed in grey pleated skirt and green blouse, she was busying herself at the gas-stove, and glanced smilingly at Ted and then more uncertainly at me as I followed him into their kitchen.

"This is John," Ted said to her. "Whiskers to one and all. The weather's up the duff, so I told 'im to come and eat 'is sandwiches with us."

"Ted, you should have warned me," she said reproachfully. "I'd have got more than one chop."

"I couldn't, could I," he said. "I didn't know until an hour back that 'e'd be comin' with me." He waved me to a chair at the kitchen table, and sat down facing me, listening, arms folded, as Jean explained that she worked as a counter-assistant at a local chemist's, always came home during her lunch break, and on this occasion, knowing that her husband would also be coming back at dinner time — "we settled that before I went" Ted butted in, as thought I might not have guessed — had slipped into their local butcher's as soon as she'd left the chemist's.... They both seemed flustered, and even after I had assured Jean that a cup of tea was all I needed to go with my sandwiches, I saw them exchange glances that suggested they felt they had somehow failed in hospitality.

But once Jean had put Ted's meal in front of him and given us our mugs of tea, the tension eased.

"Aren't you eating," I asked Jean as she hung up her apron and prepared to leave the kitchen. But she'd had something before we arrived, she said, and now had to get back to work. She bent over and kissed the top of her husband's head, then mock grimaced.

"Pooh," she said, "it's like kissing the chimney."

He broke off from chewing, turned and made an affectionate grab for her but she was too quick for him. "Nice to meet you,

Mr...John," she said, smiling, and I thought how pretty she was.

"Whiskers," Ted shouted after her. A moment later, the front door was pulled shut.

"Your wife is a nice person," I said, meaning it. And Ted, entirely serious, said, "Jean's the best. Bloody wonderful mother, too, Whiskers."

Their two children, called Terry and Brenda, were both at school. "And they both take after Jean, thank gawd. Got 'er looks *and* 'er brains." He grinned happily.

I swallowed the remains of my tea. "Ted," I asked him, "do you mind telling me how you ended up with so few teeth?"

He looked at me, laughed, and opened his mouth so I could see his stained ivory stumps. "In a bit of a scrap."

"Really?" Ted seemed the least aggressive of men, his cheerfulness so unwavering that I couldn't imagine what force would be needed to disturb it.

"'appened when I come out the army. I'd spent the last year of the war in France and when I was demobbed I didn't fancy a nine to fiver, so I took up with a fair. Goin' all over."

"Wanderlust," I said, "like a gipsy", and suddenly realised that with his bright, black eyes, tanned, even perhaps tawny complexion, and small, wiry body, there was something of the Romany about Ted.

He grinned his gappy grin. "If you say so, Whiskers. Anyway, it suited me down to the ground, bein' a grafter. You know — bit of this, bit of that, sometimes a bit of the other. Ridin' dodgems to get the money, fixin' stalls up. That kind of thing. The money wasn't too good though, the bloody owners robbed you blind, so I thought I'd try me luck in the boxin' booth." He rolled himself a cigarette, stuck it in his mouth, lit a match and inhaled deeply. "I'd learnt a bit at a Lads' Club before the war. Reckon I could use me feet and fists to keep away from big trouble. And I did OK. Took on all comers. The deal was to stay on your feet for three rounds. If they knocked you down they took the dosh, otherwise you got to keep whatever was thrown into the ring. Plus your regular nightly pay-out. So, I was doin' alright. Few cuts and bruises, nothin' much, and the money was comin' in. But I got greedy. Someone told me of a fairground in another town, not far off, Leamington, where the bloke in the ring was reckoned to be able to see off any challenge. 'You want to take 'im on, Ted, could be a big pay night.' So off I goes, and when I get there's this big black geezer in the ring, well, more brown really. Lots of blokes there, all standin' round, but no-one about to challenge 'im. So muggins 'ere says I'd take 'im on." He drew in more smoke, shook his head at the memory. "Got given the gloves, off with me shirt, and thump! Got 'it so 'ard I thought I'd woken up in the middle of next week." Another pause. "Always reckon it could 'ave been Turpin."

"What, *Randolph*?"

Randolph Turpin had recently been middle weight world champion and was a national hero. He had beaten the famous Sugar Ray Robinson in London and according to most neutral commentators was cheated out of victory in the return fight in America when, at the end of a close-fought contest, the American judges — "nobbled" everyone in England was convinced — declared Sugar Ray the winner on points. And, it now came to me, I had read that in his early days Turpin was a fairground scrapper.

"Could 'ave been 'im. Tell you one thing for free, this bloke packed a wallop big as a shell from a Sherman tank. So after that it was Goodnight Vienna. Took a nice, steady job, met Jean, settled down and lived 'appily ever after."

Another grin as he stood. "Right, Whiskers, if you're done and dusted, we'd best be gettin' back. Don't want Malcolm blowin' a gasket."

In the following days, with the weather still blustery and the sky full of rain, Ted and I cycled each lunchtime to his house. Jean was always there with an offer to cook me a meal, but I insisted I was more than content to eat the sandwiches I'd brought with me. They were a loving couple — in fact Ted plainly adored Jean, his eyes followed her everywhere, his smile, which would from time to time broaden into a grin as he watched her about her business, was one of pure happiness; and they took great pride in telling me about their children's doings and progress at school. "Brenda, she's really goin' places," Ted said, "readin' this and readin' that and 'oh, dad, why can't you work out the sum I've given you.' She's tryin' to educate me, see. But not much sticks. It's Jean who's the brains."

"And you're the brawn," she said, teasing him.

He didn't mind. "Samson, that's me."

"Well, don't bring the factory crashing down until we're well clear of the place," I said. By then we had nearly finished our work there.

"You'll come and see us sometime in the future I hope," Jean said as I left their house for the last time.

I promised I would. And for several years I sent them cards at Christmas, and, when I was in the area, dropped in on them if I thought they'd be at home, which they usually were. Jean found better work as a secretary to a firm manufacturing plastic bags, Ted became a storeman in a factory specialising in gas appliances. "Bit more money, Whiskers, and it keeps you out of the cold," but they were always the same loving couple, hospitable, eager for conversation, keen to show me photographs of their now teenage children, whom I once or twice got to meet and who seemed as cheerful and friendly as their parents.

* * *

One morning during my last week at Gamblins, Malcolm, who was in charge while Alan took a week's holiday, asked Bill and me to prepare the footings for a new brick-built store that was to go at the top of the yard. We hadn't been long at our task — Bill using pickaxe to break up the ground, me shovelling away the resulting asphalt and soil — when behind us a female voice enquired "How do you know that you're not a clod of earth."

Mary. She and her husband, John, worked from one of the lock-ups further down the yard. He was a spot welder, a short, intense man, whose flaring blue eyes looked as though they were at one with the flame he was endlessly directing at pieces of metal it was his task to turn, join, adapt for parts of motor engines and whatever else he was brought to repair or create. John seldom spoke, though he occasionally grunted, and from time to time would make clicking noises at an Alsatian which each morning arrived in the back of their battered old van, and from which it was released only to be chained inside a metal cage John had made for it. It would then spend most of the day frustratedly gnawing on the cage's iron bars. There was a desperate, dangerous edge to both dog and owner, as though they longed to break loose and go on some killing spree. They made me uneasy and I tried never to look in their direction when I passed the lock-up.

By comparison with her husband Mary was voluble, but she seemed equally desperate, her close-set blue eyes, which glittered either side of her long, beaky nose, repeatedly shifting focus. You felt she was on the look out for answers to questions she was too scared to put. I also thought she looked a bit mad.

"How do you know that you're not a clod of earth?" She repeated the question almost as though she was stamping her foot.

We rested our implements and turned to look at her. Her eyes seemed even more glitteringly bright than usual. Perhaps she really was mad. I was nonplussed.

Not so Bill. "Easy, luv," he said. "See, I can put this pickaxe through a clod of earth, but a clod of earth can't put a pickaxe through me. That's your answer."

Mary stared at him, swung her glare in my direction, then without a word span round and walked briskly towards the lock-up.

"That 'ad 'er," Bill said. And he took up his pickaxe.

But it hadn't. In a very few minutes she was back, this time with a pamphlet for each of us. "I want you to read this," she said. "It will change your lives. Just as it changed ours."

I looked warningly at Bill but too late to stop him from saying, "well, it's never too late to change back," but she seemed not to notice.

"This is the science of the future," she said, "it will save us all."

I looked at the cover of the cheaply-printed pamphlet. In bold black lettering against a pale green background I saw the name L. Ron Hubbard and, below, *The Science of Dianetics Explained*. I read the words out.

"Ron Hubbard," Bill said. "Who's 'e when 'e's at 'ome? Old Mother Hubbard's bloke?"

"Mr Hubbard is a great man, a great prophet," Mary said. "He has written over fifty books. You should read them."

"I think I'll wait for the film," Bill said.

"There are septics everywhere," Mary said, "but soon even they will understand."

Poor Mary. The next morning their van didn't appear, nor did it show up the following day.

"Done a runner," Nogger told us, over coffee break. "They owed on the lock-up and on suppliers. We shan't see them again."

"Who's due the goods they've left," Ray Bindoff asked.

Nogger shrugged. "Doubt there's much in there, and what there is won't be worth anything."

"Pity," Ray said, "I could have found a home for most of it, no trouble."

Dear Ray. He rented the other lock-up, which he used as a store for the goods he was forever buying at what he reckoned were bargain rates, and from which he always expected to make not so much a profit as a small fortune. He never did. But no set-back ever dowsed the flame of his belief that the very next consignment would land him on Easy Street. "Mr and Mrs Bindoff's little Ray of Sunshine" he called himself. He even had business cards printed with those words on them, and I never once saw him downcast or even weary from the repeated failure of his hopes that *this* time he was certain to strike gold.

"Come and look at this little lot, Whiskers," he said one

322

morning, as he leapt from the orange-painted transit van he's swung into the yard, parping triumphantly on the horn as he came to a standstill. Dressed in the brown dustcoat he always wore, he hastened round to the back, dragged open the van doors and hauled out a large cardboard box. "Here." He prised the lid off and stood back so I could peer inside.

"Well, what do you reckon?"

"Calendars?"

"Correct, my son. Five hundred calendars at half price."

I looked more closely. "But Ray, they're last year's calendars."

"I know, I know," he said, "I wasn't born yesterday. But see, what I plan on is to rip off the old set of dates then staple on next year's. Good as new, they'll be. Then watch the money roll in."

The lock-up was crammed with other boxes intended to make Ray's fortune. There were biros with transparent plastic tops which, when you held them upside down, were supposed to make a tiny nude woman slide into view (she often didn't and anyway most of the pens wouldn't write); there were small, pink china pigs into the rectums of which you inserted a grey pellet and then applied a match, thereby causing the pellet to curl out as imitation pig shit, an item Ray was convinced would prove a winner until a leak in the roof turned the pellets into grey mush; there was a job-lot of shirts with only one sleeve, a matter which caused him much concern: should he halve his profit by cutting off the sleeve of every other shirt and sew them into place on the incomplete ones, or should he cut off all the sleeves and market the shirts as fashionably sleeveless; there were guaranteed copper toasting forks whose streaked appearance as well as the tines' tendency to bend when confronted by flame rather suggested that "copper" wasn't the material out of which they had been manufactured; there were what he called "canteens of cutlery" which were really odd-job supplies of knives and forks from abandoned cafeterias, plus huge spoons and ladles that must have come from army stores; and that was only the start of it.

323

I was never aware of him selling any of these items, and yet he must have done some business. "Rushed off me feet," was his standard reply to a polite, "Hello, Ray, how are you?" And he certainly gave the impression of always being, in Pancks's words, "at it". But unlike Pancks, Ray found being at it a pleasure. It wasn't only the dream of pennies cascading from heaven that sent him out in his van. I think that he was also excited by the thrill of the chase, by the thought of a "genuine bargain". "Can't stop," he once said to me when I asked whether he'd like to join Bill and me for our coffee break. "Just heard of a mattress sale at a Kingston warehouse." And sure enough, an hour later he came tooting into the yard with mattresses roped to the roof, mattresses piled inside the van, one even bent to fit into the passenger seat. "Look at that," he said, rubbing his hands, after we helped him pile the mattresses on the lock-up's floor. "Never been slept on."

"What's wrong with 'em, then?" Bill asked. "Must be somethin' dodgy."

Behind thick-rimmed glasses, Ray's brown eyes gleamed. "Nothing," he said. "Perfect. Well, supposed to be some missing springs. They're factory rejects, but who's going to bother with a little thing like that?"

"Out of the bent timber of humanity nothing straight can ever be made," Kant had written. Ray wasn't "bent". He probably sailed close to the wind, but while some of his goods may have been picked up from dubious sources he didn't fence them, and he certainly didn't make much money from them. But, as Hodges had remarked, Kant meant that no system which tries to make people conform to an ideal, however intensely beneficial, can ever succeed. I was a socialist, but I could see that Ray's view of the world was not so much that it was him against all others as that the world wasn't about to do him any favours and that he wasn't about to offer any. And as far as he was concerned, that, as he liked to say, "was fair dos". It made him, so he more than once told me, "a free agent. I don't ask much of others, Whiskers, and I don't expect much, either, and that's the way I prefer it. If you're in trouble and I like you, I'll give you a hand. Might even help an old lady across the street. But I don't go a bundle on that All for One crap. By my way of reckoning the money always ends up in some other bugger's pocket. No, pal, if I swing it'll be for my own mistakes."

* * *

At the end of the week I said my farewells. Biking to Gamblins that Friday morning I had worked myself into an exalted frame of mind, imagining that the final handshakes would come as moments of emotional significance for us all. But when the time came I had to realise that my going meant far more to me that it did to any of Arthur and Hector, Nogger or Malcolm or Bill, or, for that matter, Ray. Ted was on his holidays. I remember that I had planned to make each of the men I'd worked with a short and no doubt excruciatingly embarrassing speech about how much I'd enjoyed and profited from their company. But as I shook hands and noticed their at best perfunctory smiles, I had enough sense to realise that whatever words I found would have been impossibly misplaced. To them I was a casual labourer and such labourers came and went. Another week, another face. Later I would come across Arnold Bennett's great story, "The Death of Simon Fuge", about an artist who leaves the Five Towns to pursue his artistic life in London. After Fuge's death his southern friend, Loring, goes back to Fuge's birthplace, assuming that the Five Towns will recall the artist and want to talk about him. Instead, he finds himself faced with the question, "Who *was* Simon Fuge?" Art may be important, but Fuge's erstwhile townspeople have their own lives to get on with.

Only as I went to shake hands with Bill did I say "I'll miss you. I hope you and Suzie have a good life."

"Thanks, Whiskers," he said, and then, seeing my look of puzzlement as he extended his left hand, added, "the right hand's OK for most things but the fingers don't work proper. Come out the womb that way," he explained, as I began to stumble out words about not having noticed and how sorry I was…. He grinned. "Did me a favour. Meant I was registered unfit for National Service. Couldn't 'andle a gun." And the grin became a laugh. "Wedding tackle's all in order though." Then, turning away, he said over his shoulder, "look after yourself, Whiskers. And don't read too many books. They'll rot your brains."

Chapter 19
And Where You Love

Almost the first person I saw when I got back to Reading at the beginning of October was Pauline. She didn't see me, however, because as soon as I caught sight of her coming past the porter's lodge of the Old Red Building, presumably on her way to the art department, I ran back up the library steps I'd begun to descend and waited in the vestibule for some few minutes. Then I got away.

Only when I was back in Wantage could I bring myself to confront the pain brought on by that unexpected glimpse of the girl I had lost through my own stupidity. Had she replied to my letter I might — no, I *would* — have tried to amend its blunt words. But she didn't. As the weeks went by it occurred to me that perhaps she'd found another man. And there were moments during the summer when I tried to convince myself that, were this to happen, it would be for the best. Such an ephebe of magnanimity I was! Yet the merest glimpse of her and all my resolve was shredded. A god, a god our severance ruled, and between us now and for all time flowed the umplumbed, salt, estranging sea.

As it happened, and probably for my better health, I didn't see her again for the rest of term. A few days into that term, however, an event occurred which might have been not merely for my but everyone's worse health. Windscale blew up. That, anyway, was how it was put to me by a friend at breakfast on the morning of what must have been October 11th. Sometime on the previous day, so Hennessy says, "the graphite core in plutonium pile no 1 ...had caught fire." He recalls "watching cinema newsreels of milk pouring from churns into drains in Cumberland and Westmorland for fear that it had become contaminated with radioactive iodine." I, too, recall such a newsreel. A few days after the news of the averted disaster had been both reported and at the same

327

time and to few people's reassurance played down, I was sitting in a flea-pit on the edge of town with my physicist friend, Don Graham, waiting to watch what proved to be an amateurish but enjoyable English comedy called *The Green Man.* This featured Alistair Sim (as what English film of the period didn't?), George Cole as a vacuum salesman who becomes caught up in a murder perpetrated by Sim, and Terry Thomas as the inevitable "bounder" with a floosie.

In those days a full cinema programme began with what was called a B Feature film. Always made on a low budget, with cardboard scenery and plots that didn't so much creak as collapse about the ears of the actors, these films often "starred" an American-born crooner Paul Carpenter — until, that is, his death in a car crash with another non-acting American called Oscar Bonaventura Jnr. Carpenter had for a short period sung with the Ted Heath Orchestra. The films as often featured the invisible talents of a one-time boxing champion Freddie Mills, whose subsequent mysterious death from gunshot wounds — suicide or murder? — made for weeks of headline speculation. Freddie's performances were so flawlessly inept that among the cognoscenti they became collectors' items. Poor man, he spoke with leaden emphasis, each word given equal weight, as though he had just been handed his lines, which for all I know he had. We imitated him at breakfast, lunch and dinner. "Would You Pass The Salt Guv'nor?" "Right Ho Mate." The films invariably ended with a chase — cops after robbers — and a crook might die from falling off a fire escape. Why did they never simply run *away*?

Then came the interval. Lights up, couples easing apart, women rearranging their hair, men off to the ice-cream seller at the front of the stalls, lights dim, couples soldered together again, curtain up, feature film starts. But first, the newsreel. The voice-over reporting the explosion at Windscale, jovial, hearty, plummy, Mine-Hostish, went all out to reassure us that We Had Nothing To Fear. Much was made of the procedures that were "immediately" put into place by the safety-conscious workforce. We saw gallons of

328

milk swilling down drains, prompt action which, we were given to understand, ensured that nobody would suffer from the fire or explosion, or whatever it was. As for the "accident" itself, this was treated as a trifling mishap, the jolly voice letting us know that all was well and that we had absolutely nothing to worry about. If anything, we could congratulate ourselves on the calm foresight of those in authority.

This was not Don's view. "No fire without smoke" might have summed up his verdict. Contamination of the countryside around Windscale was, he said, inevitable. And besides, "where do they think all that bloody milk is going? Back into rivers and the Irish Sea, that's where. It doesn't just disappear." I thought of that when, some thirty years later, I heard Thatcher's initial response to the news of the disaster at Chernobyl, and of how the Russian authorities had tried to hush it up. "The kind of thing that could never happy in a free society," she fluted on that morning's BBC radio news. But the remark was screened out when her words were replayed on subsequent newscasts. Someone with a better memory had obviously told her of attempts to cover up what had gone on at Windscale, even though the official version of the incident was that no damage had been done. It must, then, have been mere coincidence that in the weeks following the Russian disaster, contamination from the Chernobyl fall-out was said to have been blown across Western Europe and fallen to earth in remarkably high quantities on the ground about Sellafield, as Windscale had been renamed in an effort to expunge memories of 1957. Contamination all the way from Chernobyl was also found around the particular area of North Wales which housed the nuclear plant Trawsfynydd.

But in October, 1957, the events at Windscale provided more evidence of the fact that we lived in a terrifyingly dangerous world and that nuclear power seemed far more of a curse than the blessing claimed for it by our political and military masters. The time had come to challenge repeated governmental assertions that the world needed such power and that Britain in particular couldn't do without its own atom bomb. What made the matter more urgent was the government's admission that, in the words of the Defence White Paper which were either quoted or summarised in newspapers I read: "It must be frankly recognised that there is at present no means of providing adequate protection for the people of this country against the consequences of an attack with nuclear weapons." In other words, if Windscale didn't get us, a bomb almost certainly would. So something had to be done. The question was, what? Or should we simply sit and wait for the inevitable, wait for a war which, according to William Golding's *The Lord of the Flies* — a novel much read at that time — would prove how helplessly weak the good are when faced by the will-to-power of the forces of evil.

* * *

"We are on each other's hands /who care. Both of our worlds unhanded us." I heard John Wain quote those words from Berryman's "Homage to Mistress Bradstreet" a little later in the term, at a crowded meeting of the Literary Society he addressed soon after he had returned from a trip to the USA. It was one of several such trips he was taking at the time. The link between the twentieth-century male poet and his seventeenth-century predecessor, "The Tenth Muse Lately Sprung up in America", seemed to me on that occasion less one hammered out by poetry than by a desire for Truth, although I later came to recognise that, like so many of his poetic contemporaries, Berryman was obsessed with his reputation and with the conviction that he lived and somehow suffered in a land where *plenty* spelled *philistinism*, a conviction which gave an extra *cachet* to the very idea of being a poet. The poet as lonely hero. Where had I come across that before? Why, in *Mavericks*. And for poets on both sides of the Atlantic, but perhaps especially still in America, Dylan Thomas was the exemplar of such heroism. The Rimbaud of Cwmdonkin Drive was also holy fool, scapegoat, victim, pleading trumpet tongued for the damnation of those who took him off. Though in another sense, taking Thomas off by pestering the poems with Ohs and Ahs and the rhetoric of secular religiosity was by no means dead, as the pages of many a poetry magazine made clear.

But Wain's talk threw open doors, for me and, I would guess, for others present that evening. My knowledge of contemporary American poetry was confined to a very few names, among them Frost, Ransom, Tate, Eberhart, and Jeffers. I think the only post-war poet I had heard of was Richard Wilbur. This was about to change. The four poets Wain talked about and read from were Berryman, Stanley Kunitz, Robert Lowell, and David Wagoner. "Not ever likely to be a great poet," he said of this last, "but a good *solid* poet." Wagoner was one of the North Western poets whose number I soon came to understand included Carolyn Kizer and Richard Hugo, all of whom saw themselves as under the inspirational protection of Theodore Roethke. In fact, given Wain's great regard for Roethke, into which I was later to have some insight, I'm surprised he didn't feature him in that evening's talk. But in the poets he read from there was more than enough to be going on with. Wain praised Kunitz for his "lyric grace", and among the poems he read were the charming "Benediction" ("God banish from your house /The fly, the roach, the mouse /That riots through your walls...") which he later put into his Hutchinson anthology of Modern Poetry, and "The Science of the Night," a love poem which includes the following lines:

> And even should I track you to your birth
> Through all the cities of your mortal trial,
> As in my jealous thought I try to do,
> You would escape me — from the brink of earth
> Take off to where the lawless auroras run,
> You with your wild and metaphysic heart.
> My touch is on you, who are light-years gone.

For days I walked about quoting those lines, applying them to the girl I longed to touch although she was now inaccessible, light-years gone, and I continued to quote them even though Ian sniffled with derisive laughter at the phrase "your wild and metaphysic heart".

But it was Wain's reading from Lowell, saved for the end, which struck deepest. He explained that Lowell's style had undergone a transformation from the "famous" early "A Quaker Graveyard in Nantucket" (of which I had never heard, although the few lines he recited, which came from the poem's ending he said, were so intensely thrilling, had such rhetorical grandeur, that I at once resolved to hunt the poem down). Lowell's new collection, *Life Studies*, was very different. And then Wain read "Skunk Hour". I'm pretty sure that our response to the poem was one of puzzlement. What on earth *was* this? Wain wasn't about to tell us. He simply said that the new work was personal and that its "rawness was tempered by art". The poem was certainly unlike anything I'd come across before. Was it even a poem? It seemed in one way too casual an assemblage of notes, jottings, random observations, to be called art. I have read essays aplenty in the intervening years which smoothly explain "Skunk Hour," but they all miss, are perhaps unaware of, the impression it made on most readers of the UK who were introduced to the poem soon after its appearance. What added to the intrigued bewilderment of those who heard it read at on that occasion was that we couldn't read it for ourselves, because Faber didn't publish the collection until 1959, and when they did someone (Eliot?) took the decision to omit the long prose sequence "91 Revere Street", which in my American edition, bought some ten years later, runs to thirty-five pages.

Wain's reading of "Skunk Hour", and he was an excellent reader as well as being one of the best proselytisers for poetry I've ever known, left me stirred, excited, but also frustrated. "My mind's not right." That line in particular, intimate, almost casual, shocking, suggested that Lowell was writing about a personal breakdown. Was the skunk with which the poem ends an image summoned up by an ill spirit, or was it meant as a symbol (fact?) of reassuring normality?

In The Nob afterwards David, Geoffrey, I and a few others, discussed what we could remember of the poem. We all felt that we had heard something entirely new that evening, though exactly what it amounted to we couldn't gauge. It did, however, feel to be yet another expression of that self-confident energy which we were enviously aware came from post-war America and which showed itself in all aspects of culture: music, film, art (a large show from New York's Museum of Modern Art had visited the Tate in 1956, and the names of the leading Abstract Expressionists — a form of art I wanted to resist — were now much touted), and literature. This last included drama, especially the plays of Arthur Miller, whose *Crucible*, which played at the Royal Court in 1955, we admired without necessarily having seen, because of what we understood to be its heroic stand against red-hunting Joseph MacCarthy. *Death of a Salesman,* first staged in England in 1949, we watched enthralled when a TV version featuring the American actor Lee J. Cobb was transmitted in the autumn of 1957. We were also discovering American novels, including *The Naked and the Dead, On the Road, The Adventures of Augie March* and *The Catcher in the Rye,* about which more later. And, now, poetry.

Neither Hennessy nor Robert Hewison, in his *In Anger: Culture in the Cold War, 1945-60*, part of his trilogy, *The Arts in Britain Since 1939*, has much to say about the impact of American culture on Britain in the 1950s. Yet it was huge. And however ambivalent we felt about this, we had to acknowledge that most of the energy of the new flowed in one direction — ours. Wain had brought back from his recent trip to the USA not merely the good news about the poets to whose work he had introduced us, but the fruits of his interviews with Lionel Trilling, Edmund Wilson and Arthur Miller, interviews which were now being run in the *Observer*. Imagine, we said, an American writer coming to England to carry out similar interviews. Who would he talk to? Who *could* he talk to? I suggested John Berger, Larkin and Angus Wilson. Other names were offered.

And then I had an idea. The university literary magazine wanted me to write for it. Why didn't I interview Wain? Ian could get me an introduction and I even had a ready-made question with which to open the interview. On the previous Sunday both the *Sunday Times* and the *Observer* had carried reviews of Lord David Cecil's recent collection of essays. In the *Sunday Times* Raymond Mortimer had praised Cecil for the very qualities which the *Observer* reviewer had dismissed as a form of gentleman's club amateurism. And who had been that reviewer? Why, none other than John Wain. I put my suggestion to Ian and some evenings later he and I were on our way to Brunswick Street, a stubby row of houses at the edge of town.

The flat in which Wain lived turned out to occupy one side of the ground-floor of a nondescript 30s building, set back from the street by no more than a few feet of asphalt. I had time to notice steel window frames and some drab-looking green curtains before in answer to our knock the black-painted, scuffed front door was yanked open and Wain stood staring out at us. He was wearing a fez.

Ian said, "Why are you wearing *that*?"

Wain, or John, as I may as well now begin to call him, stood aside to let us enter. "Because," he said in reply to Ian's question, "I've got a mad poet at work in my bedroom and I need to keep my brains cool when I deal with him." The language, poised between the dramatic and absurd, was typical. Events in John's life, even the simplest, always seemed to be on the verge of crisis or about to become or cause one. Once, when I was running water in order to fill a kettle, he clutched his head, groaned, and then muttered that for all we knew to the contrary we might be draining the Thames. His stare was equally dramatic and, if a stare can be called hyperbolic, then hyperbolic it was, although I later came to understand that it was partly due to detached retinas, a condition which caused endless difficulties and toward the end of his life required him to be registered as half-blind. Milton, as he never tired of saying, was blind and it did *his* poetry no harm. Emphasis was also much to John's taste.

Now, as we stood in his pokey front room, I could indeed hear the clacking of a typewriter from an adjoining room — the sound that, whether I heard it from behind a closed door or from an open window as I passed underneath a house, never failed to thrill me, associating it as I did with the physical process of writing. *Scripturience.* I looked quickly and as I hoped unobtrusively around. The room we were in had few creature comforts. A single bed with a green cover was pushed up against the wall opposite from where the now faltering, now rapid sounds of the typewriter came, and on the floor beside it was a Dansette record-player, a ten-inch LP sleeve of some Beethoven Late Quartets balanced on the turn-table. Beyond the bed and hard by an open door through which I caught a glimpse of a small kitchen area, a small plywood table held a portable typewriter together with piles of books and papers. Further books were heaped up on the floor among two or three upright chairs, and pushed back against the rear wall was one shabby easy chair through whose torn pink material a spring coiled up into the uncertain light of day. The room was shabby, unkempt, and the most desirable room I had ever been in. A writer's room.

John gestured Ian to the easy chair. "We'd better have the hard chairs," he said to me. "We're here to work." There was a kind of comic aggressiveness about him I found at once daunting and attractive. It came out in his explanation, such as it was, that he was feeling "winded", because he had just been to see the film, *A Face in the Crowd*, which the *Observer* wanted him to review. "Give me some leads," he said, "tell me what to say. The kind of phrases that film wallahs use. You know, 'Powerful but fragrant. Serious but fun-loving.' That kind of thing. Gimme." Then, when I hesitated, he said "Well, never mind, we'd better get down to the interview."

I scarcely had time to ask the first question before the door to his bedroom was thrown dramatically open and a tall, distinguished-looking man with a fringe of iron-grey hair and leonine, swarthy features, entered. He was wearing a well-cut grey suit and clutched a sheaf of papers.

"Kosta," Ian said. "I thought I recognised the way you addressed the typewriter keys. That Hellenic impulsiveness mastering a *soigné* diffidence."

I was introduced. Kosta was C.A. Trypanis, Professor of Byzantine Greek at Oxford and a then well-regarded poet, who must, I now reckon, have been putting together the poems of what would become his second Faber collection, *The Cocks of Hades*. I can't recall the poem he read to us, though I do remember his slightly guttural speech and that when he finished John nodded approvingly, causing the tassel of his fez to dance in front of his face like a demented spider. "Better," he said. And Trypanis disappeared back into the bedroom and once again the typewriter stuttered into life.

We recommenced the interview and, after nearly an hour, were done. I asked John whether he thought Cecil's prose style, which he had memorably characterised in his *Observer* piece as a series of half-hearted exclamations, pointless inversions, and a general air of twittering, fairly indicated his critical worth. For answer, John suddenly stood up and began an impromptu lecture in what he said was the manner of Cecil on "Dear Jane", "concentwating" on the "gwace" with which she disposed of unwanted tea-leaves and people; and then, as suddenly as he had started, stopped, his fingers aflutter as he stared in appalled fascination at nobody in particular, but as though, he said as he dropped back into his chair, Cecil had just become aware of a venomous insect crawling up the inside of his trouser leg. At one point the twenty-year old Lucas opined that Mortimer's criticism needn't detain us, an opinion with which John nodded agreement, and which he used as a reason to conclude the interview.

"For hark," he said, getting to his feet once again and cupping an ear, which action knocked his fez awry so that it slid off his head and toppled to the ground. "I do believe I heard the voice of beer calling sturdily to us." He stared conspiratorially from Ian back to me. "I suggest," he said, "we leave Kosta here while we sneak along to the Brunswick."

And suiting action to words, he put a finger elaborately to his lips to warn Ian into silence, buttoned himself into a long, black overcoat, then, having donned a straw hat and grabbed hold of a walking stick, he tiptoed to the door, beckoning us to follow.

Outside, he stood glaring up and down Brunswick Street. "I have enemies everywhere," he said to no-one in particular, then, to me: "Run along to the pub will you and peer in. If you recognise anyone, especially Donald Gordon, report back at *once*. I can't possibly go in if he's in residence. I've already seen him this week and I've used up *all* my conversational gambits." And in passable imitation of Gordon's manner of speaking, he added, "I have *nothing* to add."

I did as I was told and there, when I peered in the window of the small pub's front parlour, was Gordon, sitting at a table in front of a large glass of clear liquid.

"Oh well," John said, when I told him, "it can't be helped. We'll simply have to brave it. Courage, comrades. Ian, I suggest you enter first and engage Donald in seemly talk. We two will follow."

In fact, for all his show of reluctance to meet Gordon on this occasion, John liked and greatly admired him, and Gordon was fond of the younger man. Kermode, who has some shrewdly generous pages on John in *Not Entitled*, says that he was "abnormally quick-witted and far from mealy-mouthed; he used his wits to needle Gordon, who sensed in him a difficult rival." John, he adds, "cultivated a manner antithetical to his boss's, covering his naturally beautiful manners with a veneer of proletarian, beer-drinking coarseness. He was harsh, irreverent, and rode a motor-scooter, which he called, inaccurately, I think his hot rod." He could also be open-handed, though he covered this, too. On the evening when I met him for the first time, John explained away buying the first round — including a large gin for Gordon and beers for several bystanders — by telling us that the advance from his new novel, plus a story he had just sold to the American *Saturday Evening Post*, would be enough to finance not only a new motorbike (it turned out to be another scooter) but the "leathers" he insisted he would have to wear when "hurtling" across England. I could see that Gordon was as entertained by John's mad exuberance as Ian and I were; he certainly laughed unrestrainedly at John's account of meeting Arthur Miller but not Marilyn Monroe. She, so John said, "was locked up in the back somewhere, so she couldn't get at me." And Gordon complimented John on his interview with Trilling, which he pronounced "*very* astute".

I left soon after that. I needed to make sense of the notes I had taken of my interview. But we arranged that I would "drop by" as soon as I had transcribed them so that John could check for possible libellous remarks. "Anything that might get me clapt in jail," as he put it. All John's verbs tended to a kind of comic, violent extreme, as though the sensibility of Dick Swiveller was being strained through the vocabulary of Smollett. I thought about the wild exhilaration of John's manner on the way back to Wantage, thought also that before we next met that I really must get hold of a copy of *Hurry on Down*, which for some reason I had so far failed to read. And I would look again at the poems of his included in *New Lines*.

Both fiction and verse, and I take no pleasure in saying this, turned out to be something of a disappointment. Had I read *Hurry on Down* soon after it was first published I might have enjoyed it more than I now could. But by 1957 John's novel had been pushed into the shadows by the success of *Lucky Jim*. In fact, at the time I first met John, Amis's novel was being filmed, and although I didn't much like *Lucky Jim,* which, the opening episode apart, I found entirely unfunny, I couldn't pretend to myself that John's novel was any better. Besides, it didn't seem to be about anything, not really. To call *Hurry on Down* picaresque, as commentators did, was to admit that it was at best loosely plotted, and although one or two episodes were mildly entertaining, even the best of them lacked the comic energy, the exuberant inventiveness of the man himself. John Wain was a creation far more enthrallingly vivid than Charles Lumley, his novel's protagonist. Kermode says that having published

338

Hurry on Down, John advised his Reading colleagues to write novels, "it was so easy and so profitable". The words may well have been a concealed apologia for a book he must have known wasn't up to much.

I preferred the poems, although their dependence on fixed rhyme and metre sometimes threatened to become a straightjacket. Before I went to interview John, Ian had made me read "Ambiguous Gifts", John's brilliant early essay on William Empson, which appeared in 1950, in the very last issue of *Penguin New Writing*. John's disentangling of some of the more difficult poems of this most gnarled of poets, as well as his praise for Empson's handling of complex forms, undoubtedly brought Empson to the attention of a new generation of readers, and probably did more than any other piece of writing to point the direction English poetry would take in the 1950s. Here is John making good on his claim for Empson's "measured rhetoric": "it would be impossible to assess Empson's achievement without some reference to the slow, heavy fullness of his lines; they seem to me a miraculous blend of the colloquial immediacy of Donne and the immense weight of Hopkins; and in the middle of a quiet, meditative poem he will suddenly introduce lines of an enormous Marlovian grandeur: "Wait, to be fathered as was Bacchus once, /Through men's long lives, that image of time's end." I loved and have gone on loving what John's prose demonstrates in this essay: an accessible style, combined with a sure but unassuming authority. This seems to me as good as a certain kind of criticism can get. Knowledgeable, unshowy, acute, persuasive. "Talking turkey", to employ a phrase he himself liked to use.

I'm not sure, though, that his admiration for Empson helped his own poetry. Mairi MacInnes was clearly unimpressed. She met John soon after his first, early marriage broke up, which was almost as soon as it began, and was puzzled that his poems "contained no reference to his wife, nor to teaching in the university, nor to living in a bungalow in Reading, nor to riding a scooter. Nor were there any poems of feeling, except elegies for feeling. They were poems in tight form, tightly controlled, the resonance kept within bounds." Exactly how I felt about the poems of John's included in *New Lines*, so that even where lines do seem to be searching for or modestly acknowledging some half-hidden emotional resonance, what comes over is a donnish concoction: "So Nature from a simple recipe — /Rocks, water, mist, a sunlit winter's day — /Has brewed a cup whose strength has dizzied me." Still, that particular poem, "Reason for not Writing Orthodox Nature Poetry", ends with a line that has stayed. "And where you love you cannot break away." Others felt far less memorable, and, truth to tell, although they were better crafted than the novel, I wasn't greatly attracted to them.

When I took the typed-up text of our interview round to John's flat some days later I was therefore uneasy. Might he expect me to comment on his own writing? It would be unthinkable to imply I hadn't read any of it. If this was so, why in heaven's sake had I wanted to interview him, why had I been determined to seek out his views on other writers? And if I acknowledged that I *had* read his novel and his poetry, what next?

Fortunately, the question didn't come up. John was waiting, coat on, when I knocked at his door. I had come, he said, most timely upon my hour. All day he had been working on a new poem, which he proposed to try out on me as soon as we were safely settled in the pub. He managed to invest the word "safely" with the suggestion that between us and the pub, some twenty yards away, lay an ocean of unforeseeable troubles.

But we got there and once John had divested himself of his coat — "Lie there, my art" — we settled into our seats. John raised his pint. "Let's be lucky," he said, weightily, as though luck was in short supply. This was, I came to learn, his usual invocation to beer. The typescript of the interview he stowed away in an inside pocket of his jacket. Then, visibly relaxing, he looked about him and nodded to the three or four other occupants of the bar. "A tavern seat is the throne of felicity," he said, turning back to me as he quoted

Johnson, the author he adored above all others. A sudden hiccup of laughter. "Even a chair as torn as this one." The pub furniture was certainly in poor shape. Pub furniture in the fifties was rarely new, but at least pubs were places for talk, and in those far-off days before the dreadful admen and marketers of the 80s got to work in tearing down partitions and removing tables and chairs in order to create "vertical drinking experiences" — if you have to stand you will drink more — each had a range of rooms, Public for games (dominoes, shove-ha'penny, darts, table quoits, and so on), Saloon for talk, Snug for special guests. And there was no canned music.

John now took out a piece of paper, laid it on the table between us, smoothed it, and immediately began to read a poem which, when it appeared in his next full collection, *Weep Before God*, was called "Anecdote of 2am.". It begins

"Why was she lost?" my darling said aloud
With never a movement in her sleep. I lay
Awake and watched her sleep, remote and proud.

Four tercets later, after the idea of apartness has been perhaps too firmly planted, it ends:

This was our last night, if I could have known
But I remember still how in the dark
She dreamed her question and we lay alone.

What did I think of it?

I mumbled something about the poem's admirable concision, although I wasn't sure, I said, why the word "proud" was used. John nodded and promised to look again at that word. (If he did, he didn't alter it in the published version.) But, he added, he thought he was about finished with that way of writing. "It only takes you so far," he said. "I want something else now, something more open." He folded the poem away and from a different pocket took out another piece of paper and began with what I thought at first was a show of some difficulty to read what he'd typed. This time, I was far more engaged. The poem, called "Au Jardin des Plantes," also made it into *Weep Before God*, although

341

apparently it might not have done so. When he finished reading it, John told me that he'd not long since sent it to *The Listener* and back had come a cool letter from the literary editor — presumably J.R. Ackerley — saying that because it was by John the magazine would publish it, but implying that had it come from someone less well known the poem would have been rejected. "So I asked for it back and took another look at it, thinking that perhaps I'd better destroy it, but then I decided to try it on a fresh pair of eyes and ears before it went into the waste-paper basket."

This was unnerving. Was it up to me to decide the poem's fate? Fortunately not. John said that he'd already sent it to one or two poet friends, whose opinions he trusted, and "they waved it through. The fact is that I have difficulty liking people whose work I distrust or who distrust mine." Anyway, he added, the little episode showed him that there would always be those whose opinions you could safely do without, and these included literary editors and reviewers. "I never read reviews of my work. *Ever*."

I found this difficult to believe, but he was telling the truth. Some time later I sent him a congratulatory letter about the very warm notices that greeted the publication of *Sprightly Running*, his account of his early, formative years. His reply was tart and succinct. "Oddly enough, I meant what I said when I told you that I never read reviews of my own work." Which, I reflected, meant that he would have missed the irony of his third novel, *The Contenders*, being praised to the skies by, of all people, Raymond Mortimer. But then John's work was at this time regularly praised. Whether poetry, fiction — short stories as well as novels — or criticism (a collection of his critical writings, *Preliminary Essays,* came out at this time), he seemed able to take on any literary form and do it well, or well enough to gain favourable mention. "I'm a writer," he once said to me, "I don't think of myself as primarily a poet or novelist or critic. I want to turn my hand to anything that comes up."

It was a mistake, I see that now. Of John's contemporaries at Oxford, Larkin began by writing novels of which two were published; then he became a poet. Amis went in the opposite direction. John wanted to do it all. He even wanted to write plays, as had one of his heroes, Arnold Bennett, on whom when I first met him he'd recently completed a long and substantial essay which appeared in two parts in a journal called *The Twentieth Century*. (It was subsequently published as one of Columbia University's Pamphlet Series on Modern Writers.) In his flat he had some vividly evocative black-and-white photographs of the Potteries, taken in the place's Edwardian heyday, and John said he kept them hung above his work desk as a reminder of his roots. The last words of *Sprightly Running* are "Spirits of my unknown ancestors speak through me. Green hills of Staffordshire stand firm in my mind." John placed great value on Bennett's professionalism, his pride in being able to make a reasonable job of any task to which he turned his hand.

I have great sympathy with this, but it led John to over-estimate what he could do. He was quite wrong, I'm afraid, to think he had the necessary gifts to succeed as a dramatist. This became woefully apparent when, early in the 1960s, he asked me to direct a play he had just written. "Dynamite," he called it, and he wasn't referring to its title, which was *Spade*. A few years earlier he had been commissioned by John Osborne and Kenneth Tynan to write a play for the Royal Court. They turned his script down but he saw in the rejection a challenge to do better next time. When a Pirandello play I directed picked up a number of favourable reviews at the Edinburgh Fringe in 1961, John decided I was the right person to "knock into shape" his second play.

Well, no. *Spade* had an impossibly contorted as well as implausible plot. A group of Russian students come on a visit to London and while there drop into a Soho coffee house in order to meet a "People's Hero", the eponymous Spade. Based, so John confessed, on Christopher Logue, Spade, known for his denunciations of Western capitalism, falls in love with one of the Russian students. Will he then throw up his cushy life-style in order to join her in Moscow? Of course, not. He would far rather stay where he can denounce corruption while living off the money his celebrity brings him. In rehearsal we managed to smooth out some of the play's roughest edges but we remained dubious about its chances. Not so John. "I can smell the success of this," he announced at dress rehearsal.

If so, he was alone. Well before the end of opening night the various agents and scouts he had invited down from London — "wheels" he called them — had made their excuses and left. The play eventually became a not very good novel called *The Young Visitors*. I suspect that this second rejection of a play hurt John more than he let on. He sold the small house in Blackheath where he and his new wife had recently moved, and bought a cottage at Wolvercote, North Oxford, where he lived out the rest of his life.

I saw far less of him in those years and when we did meet I increasingly had the sense of someone who for all his bonhomie was a bit like an old trouper, keeping his spirits up but never sure where his next part might be coming from. People who only met him in those years will never know what magic he had as a young man, how endlessly funny he was, how bracing and enchanting a conversationalist, nor how generous of his time and advice. Being a knowledgeable aficionado of jazz, he gave me records, including some rare pressings of Billie Banks singing with Henry "Red" Allen's orchestra, he lent me books, he made sure I was present at various evenings when he was entertaining writer friends at the Brunswick Arms or further afield. He suggested to Routledge and Kegan Paul that they take my first critical work, written with two friends, David Howard and John Goode, a book which we rightly dedicated "To D.J. Gordon" and which, despite its lumbering title, *Tradition and Tolerance in Nineteenth Century Fiction*, gained for a few years some reputation in the academic world.

There are two other matters for which I remain hugely grateful to John. Not long after he had read to me in the Brunswick, we met, this time by chance, on the steps outside the university library, where, he said, he had been "scouring" the shelves for a quotation from one of Byron's letters he needed. It turned out to be for a piece he was writing for the *London Magazine*. "I want you to meet someone," he said, as though our own meeting had been planned. "At the Turk." So over to The Turk's Head we went, and there I was introduced to a grey-haired man with a beard whose name, William McCance, I recognised as that of someone recently retired from the Art Department, and who was spoken of with respect verging on veneration. But he looked harmless enough, and though our meeting was brief — McCance had a train to catch — I was thrilled to shake hands with the person who, with John's energetic assistance, set up the Reading University Press. The Press had published John's own early collection, *Mixed Feelings*. Now, with both of them gone from Reading, there were doubts as to whether it could continue. Ian, it was rumoured, might be interested in taking over editorial duties, and a young typographer in the Fine Art department called Michael Twyman, who had been partly trained by McCance, could perhaps handle the practical side of affairs. But Ian would probably need some help. John looked at me and said nothing. But the look was enough. I would ask Ian about the Press.

Either then or a little later John gave me a copy of a novel he had just reviewed and thought I would like. It was called *The Hosannah Man,* and though the name of the author, Philip Callow, meant nothing to me, John promised that "we'll be hearing more of him." This isn't the place to say much about a writer with whom, years later I was to become close, and whose last novel, *Black Rainbow*, I published under the Shoestring Press imprint, as I did his marvellous memoir, *Passage from Home*, as well as *Testimonies: New and Selected Poems*, and *Pastoral*, his final collection of verse. But it is to John's lasting credit that he picked Philip out as a writer of great talent. In most regards the two were very different. John was gregarious, outgoing, confident. Philip was shy, withdrawn, sometimes clinically depressed, though never, I think, in doubt about the deep, nourishing wellspring from which his writing was drawn. Where the two came closest was not so much in the fact that they were

345

native midlanders, John from Stoke, Philip from Coventry, as in their shared ability as biographers to invest the lives of the writers and, in Philip's case, artists, about whom they write with the kind of sympathetic, dispassionate but engaged insight that more conventional biographies quite lack, however much their facts are to be relied on. John's beautiful biography of Samuel Johnson forgets to mention his hero's honorary doctorate from Oxford, but I would far rather re-read his account than any number of the more lauded academic Lives of the Great Cham which line library shelves; and Philip's biographies of Van Gogh, of Whitman, and above all, his two-volume biography of Lawrence, are infinitely superior to most other, so-called "definitive" lives of the artists and writers he himself loved.

Love is the key. I don't mean the feel-good claims of empathy that "professional" biographers often protest for their hapless subjects. I mean the real attentiveness combined with understanding which John at his best had, and which is present in nearly all his critical writing, as it is in his account of Johnson and in his much-underrated *Dear Shadows*, a collection of memoirs about friends of his youth, both the famous and the unknown. If only he could have found a way to make use of these gifts in his poetry and prose fiction. But to do so would have meant spending a greater amount of time, and making more mistakes, than he was prepared to risk before he rushed onto the next commission, of which in those years there was never a lack. His pioneering, selfless and groundbreaking work for the Third Programme, where he presented a series of New Voices, made it almost inevitable that he would be asked to organise the Arts Council's venture into Poetry International Festivals, for which he chose the poets and organised many of the events. Then there was a television programme on Poets of the Great War for which he wrote the script and in preparation for which he suggested that I might like to accompany him to the Imperial War Museum. There, we watched silent film of soldiers going up to the line to death, an occasion that left us both in tears. He worked prodigiously

346

hard though with little apparent strain, he seemed to have read everything, to have an uncannily exact sense of which poet or novelist was about to deliver work "that will shiver their timbers" ("they" being the critics), and yet there would be regular evenings in the Brunswick or a London venue — the Salisbury Arms in St Martin's Lane was a favourite — where there would be someone "you might enjoy meeting". These included a silent Richard Murphy, a drunk and difficult Theodore Roethke, whom John handled with great tact and grace, and a jostle of other writers, some well known, others not. It wasn't "Sohoitis", but his hectic schedule did, I think, keep John from the work he might and should have done. Perhaps he was scared that if he put his writing more exhaustively to the test he would find himself unable to produce the work we all anticipated he must one day deliver. A review of his fifth and not very good novel, *Strike the Father Dead*, was ominously headed "Hurry on Up". But this is speculation. What I know for sure is that in the period from 1957 to 1963, when I knew him best, John not only possessed an extraordinary glow, he was able to shed at least some of it on those who came within his reach, so that, thinking of how he then was, I find myself murmuring the words that the American poet John Peale Bishop addressed to an admittedly far greater writer: "None had such promise in them, and none/Your scapegrace wit or your disarming grace."

Chapter 20
Commitments

The year turned into 1958 and soon after the start of the spring term the inevitable happened. I was invited to a party, arrived, and there she was, on the far side of the room, dancing with some man or other. Without allowing myself to think what I was doing I went over to them, waited for a suitable moment, cut in and took over from her male companion. He looked startled rather than resentful, shrugged and turned away. I had no words. I couldn't even bring myself to smile. I was so brimful that the slightest wrong movement and something in me would begin to spill and might never stop. Years later, when I came across John Montague's love poem, "All Legendary Obstacles", and read the lines about how the narrator meets his lover from the train in which she has been travelling and the two walk away "Kissing, still unable to speak", I thought, yes that's it, the words don't matter. Or rather, they matter so much that it's better to keep silent than to use them wrongly.

A few moments later life became social again. We talked to friends, we danced some more. But of course everything was changed. It was all rainbow, rainbow, rainbow. Time was away and she was here and when we left I could see no shadow of another parting from her.

* * *

There was, though, a shadow that hung over us all, that of the Bomb. As I've remarked earlier in this narrative, from early on I became aware of the menace of the age in which I was growing up, and the older I grew the more horrifically it loomed. One of its weirdest manifestations had come the previous year, when the Count Basie band released an LP which remains one of the greatest ever performances of big-band jazz, from the roaring, express-train power of "The Kid from Red Bank," through the mid-tempo bounce of "Splanky", to "Li'l Darling", an almost miraculous combination of restraint and lilting swing. I loved the record, played it over and over, but the cover sleeve left me aghast. *The Atomic Mr Basie* the LP was called, and behind the title and the legend $E = MC^2$ was the technicolour image of a nuclear explosion. How to stop worrying and learn to love the bomb. Ten years later, when I was a visiting professor at Maryland and then Indiana Universities, I noticed all around the campuses nuclear shelters — bunkers — fronted by steel doors through which people were supposed to escape to underground safety in the event of war.

But we in the UK had no shelters. The 1957 Defence White Paper had admitted as much. If bombs were to be dropped on the UK there was every chance that the entire population would be turned to ash. We were told on more than one occasion by those who sought to reassure us that our fears were "irrational". I have never seen anything in the least irrational about fearing death from nuclear explosion. The accident at Windscale intensified such fears. Don Graham told me that despite the apparent fool-proof security at Harwell it was very easy to gain access, and one night I went with him on his motorbike to the Atomic Research Centre, Don waved his pass to the man on the gate and in we went. The pass should have been surrendered the moment he stopped working at Harwell but he was never asked to return it. Besides, for all the guard knew, Don might have been waving a playing card or a KGB membership form. We drove around the place for half-an-hour and then left. The next day we reported our escapade to the *Daily Herald*, which duly ran a feature on the non-existent safety precautions at Harwell. Other newspapers took the story up, and for a few days there was a kind of brouhaha of which Claude Cockburn might have said, "small scandal at Reading. Not many involved." I was summoned to see the Vice-Chancellor, but Wolfendon took the view that as we hadn't "compromised" the University's reputation there would be no disciplinary action. He took a very different view when, two years later, *Tamesis* wanted to carry a poem by Christopher Logue which included the word "fuck". That would apparently guarantee opprobrium. Wolfendon therefore banned the editors from including the word, though he might have saved himself the bother because our printers had already declined to carry it. Logue's otherwise unremarkable poem, "The Road" finally appeared with expletive deleted.

As I left his office, Wolfendon advised me not to become entangled with reporters. "They will make up any story they please in order to satisfy their readers," he said. Fair enough. The next day a freelance reporter found his way to my room in Wantage. He wondered if I had a "personal" story to tell about our break-in. "It wasn't a break-in," I said, "that's the point."

"Right," he said, "I see what you mean." He looked about the room and saw a photograph of Pauline on my mantelpiece. "Your girl friend?" he asked. Sensing danger, I nodded. "Lovely looking girl," he said. "Where could I find her?"

"She's called Jane Brown," I said, "and she works for the Devon Coast Country Club. In Devon."

"Right," he said again, slipping a half-crown onto the mantelpiece. Obviously my information was worth big money. But at least he'd have to spend a great deal more in trying to run Jane Brown to earth.

Then a friend from Hampton days wrote to say that he had joined an activist group at Twickenham which was part of a new nation-wide Campaign For Nuclear Disarmament. What Don and I had done would be of use to them in their efforts to get others to join, he said, and asked whether I would care to drop over to see the group as soon as I was back from university that Easter. I did, and was both surprised and impressed to discover how many people crammed into a Twickenham church hall to hear J.B. Priestley support the cause of what almost at once became known as CND. I gathered that there was to be a march, held over the Easter weekend, which would start at

Trafalgar Square and end at Aldermaston. As I was within shouting distance of Reading I reckon get a number of home-based student acquaintance the march, even to offer overnight accommodati marchers who had come from afar. Correct on both cou As to the march itself, I enjoyed the camaraderie and th feeling that at last something was being done to oppose the licensed madness of nuclear armaments. At about that time Kingsley Amis came up with an advert he claimed he would like to see on hoardings. X's BEER MAKES YOU DRUNK. Mine would have read MARCHING IS GOOD FOR YOU.

* * *

Early in the summer term, Geoffrey Creigh, who had a rather grand girlfriend and the use of his father's equally grand, if dilapidated saloon car, a white Sunbeam Talbot, suggested that Pauline and I might like to drive down with Jean and him to Hardy country. We could visit Bockhampton, spend some time in Weymouth, and then have a meal in Dorchester before returning to Reading. The official academic view of Hardy the novelist in those days was adopted from Henry James's envious claim that with *Tess of the d'Urbevilles* the "good little Hardy" had achieved the success which always eluded James himself. As for the poetry, that, too, held a rustic charm which belonged to a gone world, one buried under the urban spread of modern times. Geoffrey was something of a pre-modern himself, the kind of character I imagined as belonging in a Ford Madox Ford novel, a mixture of elaborate courtliness and diffidence when sober, and, when drunk, which he frequently was, unpredictable and not always cherishable excess. He admired Hardy's novels as inordinately as I loved the poetry. The fact that Leavisites held Hardy in contempt no doubt helped, because the scorn they directed at writers we admired we directed at their obtuseness. From time to time a Leavisite would appear at Reading, led heaven knows how to this poor outpost of civilisation as a guest lecturer or invitee of the Literary Society, where he could be relied on to

of certain names with a knowing
ᴣ of the audience who were them-
ᴣge or who had been taught by one
espond with a titter. A few names
᛫ admiration and the mention of
at academic equivalent of obei-
ᶠ approval. Shelley, Tennyson,
⹁dy, Auden, Spender — titter.
⹁ued titter, but for Milton's admirers, a virtual
guffaw. Donne, Pope, George Eliot, Hopkins, James, Conrad,
grunt. And at the mere mention of Lawrence the grunters
cut loose, happy, as the vulgar phrase goes, "as pigs in shit".

Dickens was never mentioned. "Not for the mature mind,"
one young man who seemed scarcely out of short pants
assured us. And as if that weren't enough, we should
remember that Dickens found favour with the "metropolitan
literary establishment". Oh, quite. And — indrawn breath —
the same was true of T.S. Eliot. Eliot had once rated grunts
but those days were long gone and titters were the best he
could expect. He had spilled cigarette ash on Queenie
Leavis's carpet, recanted on Milton, and was lauded by all
those who united to "do dirt on life" — Lawrence's phrase for
Joyce, which the Leavisites liked to apply to everything of
which they disapproved. In their master's case this included
Tottenham Hotspur. So at least he averred when in the
early 60s he came to Reading to give a lecture in which he
announced that Dickens was after all a great writer but that
he, Leavis, had understandably been misled all these years
because of the dreadful reports on him issued by H. House
(Oxford) and Edmund Wilson (America). If *they* praised the
Inimitable, no wonder that F.R. Leavis could have no truck
with him. Anyway, he assured us, there could never be
another Dickens, "because this is the age of Telly and
Tottenham Hotspur."

From the standpoint of the early 21st century it's probably difficult if not impossible to understand Leavis's
influence on academic literary criticism during the 1950s. It
began earlier, with his journal *Scrutiny*, which he founded in

the 1930s as an attempt to bring "standards to
icism. The test was to prise the study of English
from the all-too slack grasp of the gentlemanly *régis*
whom knowing what was good and bad was a mat
"taste", "taste" being as certain and yet as ineffable as
"blood" identified by Hamlet's aunt in *David Copperfield*
"We see Blood in a nose, and we know it. We meet with it in
a chin, and we say, 'There it is. That's Blood!' It is an actual
matter of fact. We point it out. It admits of no doubt." Leavis
and his epigoni no doubt came like Cavafy's barbarians into
the precincts of first Oxbridge and then some of the dozier
places beyond. And the best of *Scrutiny* was without doubt a
kind of solution to the problem of how to write convincingly,
or at least argue the case, about works of literature.
Moreover, their habit of scornfully naming those fellow
academics of whom they disapproved, while weirdly rebar-
bative to anyone outside their immediate circle, may have
had its justification in the tiny world of academe. No doubt,
plenty of comparatively well-fed and housed tutors did
precious little to earn their money. But this was far less
likely to be the case in provincial universities, and it
certainly wasn't true of Reading. Besides, we were unlikely
to be impressed by critics offering to tell us that life was too
short to justify reading certain authors once it became
obvious that they hadn't read the authors they were
prepared to throw away. "The good little Hardy" indeed. So
off the four of us went to Dorset.

We left Reading in sun, but by the time we got to Max
Gate it was raining. An old lady who seemed to be in charge
of the ugly, gloom-laden house which Hardy had designed,
allowed us to wander about the place. "And him an archi-
tect!" Geoffrey's girl-friend spoke for us all. I can remember
of that visit only the old lady telling us that from time to
time a rook came to the back door and she would let it in and
scatter crumbs for it on the kitchen tiles. "But it never takes
any. It walks around, goes into one or two of the downstairs
rooms, then leaves. I believe it's Hardy's soul come to look
the place over." We made our excuses and left.

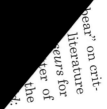

'ced along the deserted promenade.
v knows why, to go for a swim. The
ax Gate may have got into us. We
eds of tented chalets on the stony
rwear, dashed into the grey, cold,
ame back found that our clothes
e chalet by the one family which
ther and whose beach accommo-
...au invaded. As we shivered and dragged on our sopping, scrumpled clothes, a piper in full fig, including kilt and sporran, came marching along the beach, his bagpipe music in that deserted place making a weird, eldritch sound. It was like an emanation, a presence stepping from some Wordsworthian poem, the very emblem of resolution and independence. What was he doing there, we asked him. Weymouth Council had employed him for the summer, he told us, to entertain holiday makers who came to the beach.. But there *were* none, we pointed out, not that afternoon. "I do what I'm paid for," he said.

In Dorchester we found we lacked the funds for a meal and between us had barely enough money to buy a round of drinks in the hotel where Michael Henchard experienced his great reversals of fortune. We sat there for an uncomfortable hour then set off back to Reading which we finally reached about midnight, after an enforced stop to mend a puncture. We were tired, hungry, still damp, but strangely elated.

* * *

The 1950s was the great age of interpretation. Treading on the heels of the question, is this work any good, came another, what's it *about*, what does it *mean*? John Wain had edited a collection of critical essays called *Interpretations*, and although I think he was sceptical about the grander claims made for "archetypal" criticism, let alone symbolism — he would have agreed with Freud that sometimes a cigar is simply a cigar — he became friendly with the American critic turned sage, Marshall McLuhan, to whom he introduced me at about the time McLuhan published *The Gutenberg Galaxy*. This book, famous in its day but now, I imagine, forgotten, may not be about archetypes but it is certainly an attempt to systematise history, to see it in terms of vast movements, of "hot" and "cold" mediums of communication, and in this it echoes a work which, when published in 1957, and for a good while afterwards, had great influence over academia, and must have been anathema to the Leavisite camp. This was *Anatomy of Criticism*, by Northrop Frye. Like McLuhan, Frye was a Canadian and a fellow Catholic. His book is impossible to summarise in a few sentences, but it's certainly unlike McLuhan's work in being resolutely anti-historical. McLuhan's *Galaxy* implies a teleology, not so Frye's universe of permanent genres, unaffected, at a deep level anyway, by the moment at which any example of one is created. So *Hamlet* is more like *Oedipus Rex* than it is like *Measure for Measure*. And *Measure for Measure* is more like *The Birds* than it is like *Women Beware Women*.

I enjoyed reading Frye's work without ever believing it. But anyway it didn't much matter whether you believed it. The big questions, is this any good, what's it about, Frye left unanswered. But this wasn't the case with another work I read in the summer of 1958, Suzanne K. Langer's *Feeling and Form*. Subtitled "A Theory of Art", Langer's work, which I still greatly admire, performed miracles, it seemed to me, in identifying what she called the "Making of the Symbol", by which she meant expressive forms that allow us to know and make sense of the world. And what makes most sense has a fair claim to being called the best. I was hooked in particular on her discussion of "The Great Literary Forms", and "The Great Dramatic Forms" — "The Comic Rhythm" and "The Tragic Rhythm". These were compelling accounts of how to register the lives of community and of individuals, the cyclic propulsion of one, the forward momentum of the other, and when I later came on Valery's claim that verse "wanders around circuitously, winding back on itself, repeating similar gestures... and is not directed towards any single definite end," whereas prose, "has its own end always in view, and is often teleologically determined; it marches as straight as possible towards such an end", a claim that greatly helped me sort out my ideas on that masterwork, *Dombey and Son*, I thought of the French poet as working the same loaded rift as the American philosopher.

I talked excitedly to Gordon about all this and was miffed by his virtual dismissal of Langer's work. "She was not," he said — pettily, I thought — "Cassirer's favourite pupil." *Feeling and Form* is dedicated "to the happy memory of Ernst Cassirer", and Cassirer was, I knew, greatly admired by Gombrich and others of the Warburg. So why this put-down?

Not long after my excited reading of Langer I was in my room late at night when I found myself thinking about the Leibnizian monadology, on which my philosophy tutor, Harry Parkinson, had been lecturing for several weeks. Parkinson was a Leibniz expert and although something of a Marxist was prepared to recognise in the Catholic philosopher a great mind. (As Bertrand Russell did when he wrote about him in his *History of Western Philosophy*. Leibniz, the atheist socialist Russell said, "was one of the supreme intellects of all time".) The monadology was at once puzzling and intriguing, a way of fitting the individual into an overall scheme without making procrustean demands on either. It was in essence a philosophical argument for the benevolent universe close to the one Pope writes of in *The Essay on Man*, which I was also reading that summer. And of course Pope, like Leibniz, was a Catholic.

As I brooded over the Leibnizian thesis, it suddenly seemed to me that I held all my recent reading, of philosophy, poetry and critical theory, in a synthesis of radiant understanding. I left my room and went down into the deserted quad. For perhaps half an hour I walked round and round in a daze of joy which the startlit sky seemed to confirm. (Those were the days before light pollution dimmed the glittering brilliance of the night skies.) As near as I can recall I was in a state for which the words ecstatic wonderment, though dangerously exalted, nevertheless seem proper. Then it faded. I think I still know how to explain the monadology in intellectual terms, but I can't return to the imaginative grasp I then had of its meaning.

And anyway, soon afterwards, I began to see the fault-lines in Leibniz's argument, not only its dependence on logic rather than empirical understanding, but on what seemed to me a fatalism that took for granted that whatever is must be. Moreover, if this was the best of all possible worlds, how explain evil? And why, anyway, was a Catholic philosopher seemingly reluctant to confront this problem? How, more immediately, explain the development and threatening proliferation of nuclear arms which were coming under the control of people prepared to destroy the world supposed to be the best imaginable? What was lacking in Leibniz was a full look at the worst, as Voltaire was perhaps the first to suggest when he made Pangloss try to find something cheerful to say about the Lisbon earthquake, although the words are, of course, Hardy's.

And at that point I understood Gordon's irritation with Langer and the probable reason for Cassirer's doubts about her. Her philosophical arguments were in the last analysis either ahistorical or at all events insufficiently aware of history. Like McLuhan and Frye, I now decided, Langer lacked or anyway did without an awareness of the sheer horror of history, in particular the history of the 20th century, of the fascism which had forced Cassirer and his family, as with so many other Jews, to flee their native Germany. To be fair, this wasn't her concern. But then I could imagine Gordon sardonically asking, *why* wasn't it? Tragedy wasn't only what happened to individuals. It could happen to whole societies.

I think now that my brief attempt to come to terms with an essentially Catholic view of the universe may have been triggered by Pauline. Not by anything she said, far from it, but by my feeling at some level of consciousness that I couldn't afford to lose her again. Ironically, Pauline was now beginning to want to free herself from Catholicism's strong toil of Grace. And although I admired Pope's resourcefulness

357

in trying to make palatable his Leibnizian view of Man, I greatly preferred "The Rape of the Lock", his earlier, joyously Baroque masterpiece, whose sheer delight in making poetry managed to overcome its tiresome message. Avoid excess, the message pontificated. Love excess, the poem itself declared. "What a genius I had when I wrote that," Swift is said to have remarked when in old age he re-read that masterpiece of his youth, *The Tale of a Tub*. What a genius Pope had when, reducing the epic to microcosmic proportions and adapting Miltonic grandeur to the trivia of London society, he wrote about the new fashion for coffee-making as though describing a religious ceremony in some Eastern state:

> For lo! The Board with Cups and Spoons is crown'd,
> The Berries crackle, and the Mill turns round.
> On shining altars of *Japan* they raise
> The silver Lamp; the fiery Spirits Blaze.
> From silver Spouts the grateful Liquors glide,
> And *China's* Earth receives the smoking Tyde.

"Cheered by the grateful smell, old Ocean smiles," Milton had written in one of the great epic similes of *Paradise Lost*, and here was Pope matching him by elevating the act of pouring coffee to some vast natural force: "the smoking Tyde." It was simply dazzling.

* * *

My delight in Pope's poetry was given an extra fillip by the thought that at Whiteknights I was walking across lawns which he himself had probably trod. And then there was Mapledurham, its over-grown gardens and parterre a melancholy realisation of the lines in "The Use of Riches", where Pope had imagined how

> Another age shall see the golden ear
> Embrown the slope and nod on the parterre;
> Deep harvests bury all his pride has planned,
> And laughing Ceres re-assume the land.

Pope had in mind those who, stuffed with 'new' money, built themselves unnecessarily grand houses: Blenheim, Canons, and the like, many of which did indeed beggar their owners and not a few of which were demolished soon after completion. That wasn't Mapledurham's fate, and yet the house, while not the work of a "puny insect shivering at a breeze", symbolised in its all-but ruined demesne the lost certainties of Augustan values. Gordon had a penchant for those values, partly because he genuinely loved the art of landscape gardening and was a great admirer of "Capability" Brown, and partly because for all his democratic spirit he couldn't entirely escape a certain snobbishness; he rather liked being in the houses of grandees, at all events if the grandees had good libraries and serious works of art on their walls. He could be withering if they didn't. Some years later, not long after Pauline and I were installed in Nottingham, Gordon paid us a visit. I took him to see Belvoir Castle, where he tut-tutted his way from room to room. "So much money," he said loudly, "and such *complete* lack of taste." But he venerated the buildings of the better architects of the seventeenth and eighteenth centuries — Wren, Hawksmoor, Soane — to some extent, I think, because they recalled Augustan Rome, for him one of the greatest moments of Western civilisation.

But in the summer of 1958, reading *The Deserted Village*, I was made aware of the fact that in the cause of "improvement" and even more reprehensibly in order to accord with Brown's dictum that all nature should be a garden, cottages and indeed villages were knocked down so as to make possible the vistas which the great houses "needed". Chatsworth, often thought to be the origin of Mr Darcy's Pemberley, and thus doubly favoured by Gordon, was one great house whose owners had removed an entire village from their sight. And I read the Hammonds' account of the lives of village labourers and how these were endlessly subject to the whims of often absentee landlords who made and then took advantage of laws that deprived their tenants of land and livelihood. "Along the lawn, where scattered hamlets rose," Goldsmith wrote, "Unwieldy wealth and cumbrous pomp repose." I was stirred by the bitter wit of that rhyme. What once rose had been felled to make way for the ungainly show of those who, without lifting a finger in work, now owned the land. "Rose" suggested people getting up and out to their daily labour. There was a distich of Christopher Smart to which Donald Davie had drawn attention in his *Purity of Diction in English Verse.* "Strong Labour got up with his pipe in his mouth, /And stoutly strode over the Vale." In Goldsmith's poem, strong labour must make way for the "repose" of cumbrous wealth. Rose/Repose. Purposeful activity losing out to indolence. Thinking of this I saw the smug faces of the English establishment of the 1950s parting its lips just enough to squeeze out phrases from behind equine teeth, and I thought of Harry and Hector and Nogger and Spikey Bill and Ted. And I thought, too, of those smug-faced ones and their taken-for-granted assumption that art is above vulgar matters of the day. Right.

Some friends at Reading had started a little magazine called *Viewpoint.* I wrote a piece for it called "The Artist's Responsibility", in which I referred to the recently founded *Universities and Left Review,* soon to change its name to *New Left Review.* This had called in manifestoes from, among others, John Berger, Lindsay Anderson, Peter de Francia and Stuart Hall on the need for artists to Take Sides. I also brought into the reckoning a poem by Christopher Logue called "To My Fellow Artists", which had appeared in the *New Statesman.* It was then issued as a poster poem which I had on my wall. The poem invited writers "to work with your thoughts that never were contemptible". And I quoted Berger's contemptuous review of *Mavericks.* We live in bad times, Berger said. The responsibility of the artist is to confront this fact, not to seek escape in the privacy — for which read "privileged space" — of art. Had I known of Auden's "A Summer Night" I would have quoted:

> The creepered wall stands up to hide
> The gathering multitudes outside,
> Whose glances hunger worsens;

Concealing from their wretchedness
Our metaphysical distress,
Our kindness to ten persons....

Soon through the dykes of our content
The crumpling flood will force a rent,
And, taller than a tree,
Hold sudden death before our eyes
Whose river dreams long hide the size
And vigours of the sea.

Instead, I quoted Berger on the preciosity of poets who chose to write about small personal problems despite the "experience of recent years, when the world has been threatened with total destruction, saved, and threatened again."

Well, it was a start, a first sally into poetry's lousy leasehold and although, reading it now, I wince at its brash certainties, its hectoring carelessness, there are things in it I stand by, especially the assertion that art doesn't belong to those who by education and social position assume that they are the natural arbiters of taste and that the art they espouse justifies their lives. Everything else can be dismissed as not "true" art.

Another target now offered itself. The Literary Society held an annual garden party in the grounds of St Andrew's Hall. The party, at which people customarily stood around on the lone and level lawn, drinking the dubious wine on offer and trying to make polite conversation until cold or boredom drove them inside, took place towards the end of summer term, and one or two paid guests from the "real" world of writing were invited. There were also readings by student writers. Naturally, Ian was asked to supply the outside guests, and that summer he had secured the services of the Belfast-born poet, R.R.(Bertie) Rodgers, and a young prose writer none of us had heard of, called V.S. Naipaul. The weather being rainy, the party was moved inside to St Andrew's dining hall, from the dais of which Naipaul read a story about a lodging-house lady and her canary, Rodgers some unmemorable poems, and Ian declaimed, in full-throated ease, his recently-completed comic poem called

"Just a Pot-pourri from a Betjeman Slag-Heap", which begins

> A street lamp like a floating bruise,
> The lime-green light of evening fails,
> Lost in the Corporation Park
> The lovers tell illegal tales;
> Deep in the bosomy Engine Shed
> Dorinda slugs *The Prince of Wales*.

Then it was our turn. I had recently bought a Penguin anthology, *The Common Muse: Popular British Ballad Poetry from the 15th to the 20th Century*, whose editors were given as V. de Sola Pinto and A.E. Rodway. I persuaded Geoffrey, David Howard and an English student in her second year who, in figure at least, bore a striking resemblance to the singer Alma Cogan, to join me in a ten-minute programme of readings from the anthology. "Ars Proletaria" we called the programme, and we chose the bawdiest and most politically radical verses we could find — they included "A Lovely Lass to a Friar Came" and Ernest Jones's "The Song of the Lower Classes". Well before our time was up the organisers of the event asked us to kindly leave the stage. We were guilty of lowering the tone of the occasion, of introducing sex and politics into a literary evening. Naturally, we were delighted to have provoked such a response.

Next stop, therefore, our own magazine. *Engagé,* it was to be called. Ian, who had been amused by "Ars Proletaria" and who was pleased to make the acquaintance of "A Lovely Lass" as well as of the lovely lass who recited the ballad, offered us "Pot Pourri", which we could claim as a thrust at the poetry establishment. We also included some dreadful verses on "Cardiff Steel Works" by a research student, there was a short essay on Kierkegaard and Existentialism by John Dee, an art student who would go on to make a considerable reputation as a sculptor, David and Geoffrey in different ways considered the issues of Writing and Commitment, and I attacked Taschisme, the French art movement which was intended as Paris's new, improved

362

version of Abstract Expressionism and which I argued was a furthering of the decadent notion that the medium is the message.

In the case of *Engagé*, the message was more or less stifled by the medium. Problems began with the second-hand portable typewriter on which most of the contributions were typed up. I was passionately fond of the machine, which I had acquired for my 21st birthday, but its ribbon was old and some letters were missing, while certain keys refused to budge no matter how hard I struck them. Then there was the gestetner on which the magazine was to be printed. Battered, rusty, unstable, its action had all the steadiness of a drunk man in a gale, so that whole sentences were either lost or appeared as through a glass darkly. Others switched disconcertingly between splodged, furry blackness and a trail of diffident grey. The result was that hardly a page of *Engagé* proved legible. At the back of the magazine we apologised for difficulties which we anticipated potential readers might encounter and which we "tentatively trace to the idiosyncrasies of the machines." This humility was in steep contrast to the assertiveness of our Manifesto. "Commitment belongs to every sphere of life", we announced, and in future issues we therefore wanted to hear from "scientists and agriculturalists" as well as from writers and artists. As far as I can remember we heard from nobody, which may have had something to do with the fact that we only managed to have the magazine ready for distribution on the last day of the summer term and by then most students had disappeared. By far the best thing about *Engagé* was its cover, a lithograph Pauline designed, in which the magazine's name was spelt out in a spiky manner suggestive of struggle, imprisonment, *purpose*. If the rest had been as good we might have had the courage to continue. But the first issue of *Engagé* was also its last.

Chapter 21
Secrets

With term at an end, Geoffrey drove Pauline and me to
Bath, where we had lunch with his mother, an aged woman
living in a bungalow above the city. Both the narrow hallway
and dining room were stuffed with pieces of furniture
several times too large for the cramped spaces they occupied.
There were low, elaborately-carved mahogany tables with
elephants' feet for legs, a brass gong held within ivory tusks
glimmered on one such table, ivory chess pieces on another,
there were leather armchairs, and the dining table, which
took up at least half of the room it was in, had been shoved
into a right-angle of wall with the result that only two sides
were usable, though these could easily accommodate eight
diners. The bungalow seemed replete with the *disjecta
membra* of lost empire. At that period in post-war England
similar households will have been scattered about the
southern counties, their occupants minor civil servants from
the former colonies now sitting out their last years in a
disconsolate moping for a time of servants and, as here,
trying to convert the Quantocks and winding Avon into
vistas of distant mountains, high plains and jungles with
rock-strewn rivers. There was something about this in
Geoffrey himself, some sense of a life that he had once
hankered after but knew he approach only through his preference for Senior Service cigarettes, of which he smoked
many, his newspaper of choice, the *Daily Telegraph*, his
habit of appearing at breakfast in an old, paisley dressing
gown and scuffed, brown leather slippers, and the air of
gentle melancholy that never entirely left him. He rarely, if
ever, read contemporary novels, nor did he go to the cinema
except to watch Ealing comedies or re-runs of old black and
white films. It was easy to imagine him sprawled in one of
those shabby armchairs his parents had brought home from

Africa, glass of whisky at his elbow, wishing the world no harm, but on the whole hoping it would pass him by.

He and I had wanted to see some of the last day of the county match being played on the lovely cricket ground below Pulteney Bridge, but by the time we got there the match was over — the picturesque ground went with a wicket that spin bowlers would gladly roll up and take everywhere with them — and by mid-afternoon Pauline and I were in Bristol. We had arranged to stay for a couple of days with Laurie in the flat at Clifton he shared with a fellow-student and jazz pianist. Having now graduated, the two of them were about to leave the city in search of work. The basement flat was large and cluttered with musical instruments. Quite apart from Laurie's bass, a brass tuba leant against a kitchen wall, there were guitars on most seats, a drum-kit in the middle of the living room, and odds and ends such as maracas, tambourines, a treble recorder, besides a trumpet whose valves were, we discovered, stuck fast. Even so, the flat was comparatively tidy. No weeks-old newspapers, no empty beer bottles, no tins or bags of food in green corpuscence, and above all no fug of stale cigarette smoke. Neither Laurie nor his flat mate, Mick Short, smoked, nor did they encourage smoking on the premises. Well, it was a change.

Not for Laurie, though. He was used to keeping everything within bounds. Even his insistence on trim haircuts, his unscruffy clothes — grey pressed trousers, neatly ironed shirts, sober jackets —announced his self control, his cool disdain for excess of any kind. For so large a man — as well as being taller than me he was broader-shouldered by far — he moved with the stylish grace of the accomplished tennis player he was. I suspect that Mick, left to himself, would have reduced their flat to a tip. But there was never a chance of that. Chance, especially ill-chance, was to be guarded against, and when, despite Laurie's best efforts, it insisted on breaking through, it had to be contained. One evening at the Devon Coast Country Club, when he and I were in the room where we double bunked, I laughed so hard at something Laurie said that I fell off the top bunk and crashed into his bass. Laurie was far more concerned about the state of his bass than whether I'd hurt myself. After all, under the NHS I could get my head repaired for free. But to repair a fractured bass would cost hundreds.

How much of Laurie's reining-in of his emotional life was a response to his mother's suicide, which happened when he was ten, I have no idea. He never talked of it, and only once or twice did he say anything about her; but her death must have embodied ill-chance at its most violently, unforeseeably eruptive. After that, I suspect he did his best to guard against the unexpected. You couldn't imagine Laurie being surprised by joy. I think to a large extent our friendship was founded on each of us being an intriguing puzzle to the other, and also on our complementing the other's character and personality. At all events, I admired and perhaps envied Laurie's rational, sardonic refusal to endorse enthusiasms he thought in excess of the inherent worth of what was being enthused over. He was dazzlingly witty, but the wit was side-of-the-mouth put down or, if he was in a more relaxed, generous mood, a wry disclaimer. And I don't think I ever heard him raise his voice. It was inevitable that his favourite jazz should be the kind associated with various West Coast musicians. Horace Silver, Shorty Rogers, the early Gerry Mulligan quartet, Gil Evans, Stan Getz, Red Mitchell, that exemplary bassist who would later act as Laurie's tutor.

In his excellent history of *West Coast Jazz*, the pianist Ted Gioia, brother of the poet Dana who presented me with the copy I own, protests that what is still called West Coast jazz was always far more various than its critics maintained. "Too much of the debate surrounding West Coast jazz had focused on definitions." No doubt he is right to want to re-direct attention to the widely-disparate styles and approaches of the musicians who worked in California during the 1950s. But from the point of view of its aficionados in England at that time, West Coast jazz meant whatever wasn't wild, effervescent and, all too often, amateurish.

What I remember most vividly about the two days we spent in Bristol was my growing, gloomy realisation that in a year's time I would be in Laurie's position, newly graduated and looking for work. That his undergraduate years had come to an end didn't bother Laurie. For him, university was the necessary staging post from where he would journey onto a career. It wasn't that he hadn't enjoyed being at Bristol. But it had served its purpose and as far as I could tell he had no regrets in waving it goodbye. I, on the other hand, loved Reading. I loved the town, with its pubs, from the splendour of the old coaching-inn, The George, to the tumble-down conviviality of The Turk's Head. I loved the cobbled market square with the white-coated waiters of Henekey's, the town library and decent art gallery. I loved the occasional moments of shabby grandeur supplied by the town's Georgian past — the tall terraced houses of London Street, and, off the London Road, grey stone Eldon Crescent; I loved the surrounding countryside, the undulating downs and heathland, the small villages, their red-brick cottages with thatched roofs and luxuriant flower gardens half-hidden from lanes that ran through deep fields or by woods; I loved the winding reaches of the Thames, from medieval Dorchester through Hungerford with its many-arched bridge to the rocky steepness of Goring, the favoured waterside village of Pangbourne (where a few years later I would take all 10 wickets on a day of triumph for Mr Fletcher's Particulars); I loved the wide approach to Caversham Bridge with water-meadows on either side lined by handsome Edwardian villas below wooded escarpments. I especially loved the intellectual and literary life I found at the University, the hours of talk, of study in the library or in the quietness of my own room, the certain awareness that here at least it was quite alright to be serious about literature, art, music, ideas. Reading offered something I didn't want to leave behind but which I wasn't sure I could take with me. Above all, of course, it had Pauline.

* * *

367

We managed to see a good deal of each other over the summer vacation. I spent a week with her in Wolverhampton, where her parents had moved following her father's promotion to manage a branch of the Midland Bank, and where they lived in a late-Victorian semi-detached house made stylish by Pauline's mother.

One day we went to Birmingham, where, in the city art gallery, we witnessed a red-faced clergyman confronting one of Bacon's screaming Popes. "You are not ART," he screamed back. Then, spotting us, he came over. "Tell me that isn't art", he implored. He must have seen from our faces, which plainly suggested that *he*, not Bacon, was the cause of our consternation, that we were lost to all taste, because he shook his head in despair and wandered off. On another occasion we walked to Wightwick Manor, a red-brick mansion built in neo-Elizabethan style by William Morris's friend, Philip Webb. The place was now lived in by the Manders family, who had made their money from paint, and it was stuffed with pre-Raphaelite art and furnishings. As we left, a ground-floor window was flung open and a woman with a dreadful county accent called out, "Are you the *Reading* students?"

Having already signed the Visitors Book to that effect, we admitted that we were.

"Then come and drink a glass of sherry."

We went back inside and were ushered into the presence. The room we found ourselves now in was large, each square inch of wall seemed to be taken up by paintings or drawings, and tables were adrift with books and magazines. Lady Manders, back half turned, was pouring drink from a decanter into glasses that looked rather too big for sherry, although sherry was what it was. She motioned us to two high-backed chairs facing the chaise longue on which, having gestured to us to take our drinks, she now threw herself, one hand behind her head, the other reaching for a cigarette kept in a silver box on a small table beside her. She had faded blonde hair, a figure that I could imagine in her débutante days — now long past — would have been called petite, and wore a long, green, rather faded dress and high-heeled slippers of the kind and colour called camel.

"Tell, me," she said, having first inhaled and following with her eyes a trail of smoke as it lifted ceilingwards, "are you familiar with John Wain."

"I know him," I said.

She lowered her gaze to where I sat, although her eyes merely flickered across my face and then away. "Then perhaps you will tell me what the poor man can be thinking of to call this novel" — with an airy wave at the book open on the floor beside her — "*The Contenders*".

"Well," I said, at a loss as to what her objection could be. "It's about two brothers who have different ways of trying to get on in the world. And I suppose they're quite competitive."

"Oh, I know *that*," she said. "But *Contenders*. It's so fearfully vulgar. *Wrestlers* are *Contenders*."

I stored that up to tell John.

We were asked what we thought of the house and possessions. Dared I to say that I found them fearfully vulgar? Perhaps not. Sipping my glass of what Larkin would call washing sherry, I muttered that it was all too much to take in on one visit — so much for fearless commitment — Pauline murmured polite nothings, and not long afterwards we escaped.

When a few weeks later Pauline came to Staines, we made forays up to London, where we saw *La Strada*, a film I loved, and a matinée performance of *The Entertainer*, with Olivier as Archie Rice. You couldn't take your eyes off him, he commanded the stage, his every move, every word, were managed with an authority that only the greatest acting can achieve. An evening at Eel Pie Island was, however, a let down. No Brown band, the group that performed that night was at best routine, both in choice of numbers and performance — how many times can you bear to listen to Picou's solo on "High Society" played note for note, and *please* will the trombonist not try to imitate Ory's tail-gating rasp on "Muskrat Ramble". And the place, which was only half-full, lacked the rackety, sweaty excitement of its earlier days.

Soon, it would become a venue for rock and roll, though I didn't of course know that. I knew only that for me the magic had departed.

Towards the end of Pauline's stay I arranged for us to go to the small art-house cinema at Kingston, where we would be joined by Pete. He arrived, shambling, round-shouldered, dressed in his baggy tweed suit, his face pale as ever, the rope of hair hanging over his forehead, and presented Pauline with a box of chocolates he'd been sheltering inside his jacket. Was this an act of sardonic, pretend courtesy? But no, he seemed to mean it.

We watched the lovely, funny, ingenious *Lavender Hill Mob*, which among other things made me aware of how, unlike most nations, the English seemed positively to enjoy having as film heroes men whose "mild, knobby faces", to use Orwell's phrase, and lumpy bodies — though they could move them with surprising agility, even grace — made them very unlike American and continental concepts of the hero. The music hall tradition, I suppose. Dan Leno, Little Titch, Joe Elvin, Harry Tate, were loved by their audiences for *not* being better-looking or more "dashing" than those they were entertaining. Comedian and audience had a common enemy, their class superiors, the men who came from exclusive schools and belonged to exclusive clubs, and who looked down on ordinariness. For what else can "exclusive" mean? Charlie Chaplin, the archetypal "little man" who delighted in tripping up pomposity, was after all English. So, too, were Ian Carmichael and David Tomlinson, who played romantic leads but were "twerps" *à la* Wooster. Unthreatening, in a word. Not really "exclusive".

I tried this out on Pete, when, after the film, he, Pauline and I dropped in at a nearby pub for drinks. "And meanwhile," he said, "this country is still run by those who went to public school and come from the landed gentry. Tomlinson look-alikes control our lives, don't forget." As he spoke, the image of Selwyn Lloyd, Foreign Secretary at the time of Suez and now one of Macmillan's yes-man, came into my mind. Selwyn Lloyd undoubtedly looked rather like David

370

Tomlinson. It may be true that Lloyd came from a Liverpool professional middle class and non-conformist background, but he learnt to pass muster as a toff. But then even poor Len Hutton was given elocution lessons when in the early fifties he became England's first professional cricket captain. This led to a desperate, strangulated unintentionally comic — or heart-breaking — imitation of toff-speak. "Oh 'e 'as done orfully well," Hutton once said of that great bowler, Brian Statham. I love cricket, but as I grew up I came to loathe just about everything to do with its structure, especially its division of gentlemen and players, the former with their own gate through which they would walk from pavilion onto playing field, their own travel arrangements, and the fact that on score-cards their initials preceded their surnames, while those of professionals came after. You were Mr E.R. Dexter but you were Trueman, F.R. And so rigidly was this convention adhered to that on one occasion as the Middlesex and England spin-bowler Fred Titmus was walking out to bat at Lords, someone intoned over the loudspeaker, "For F.J. Titmus read Titmus, F.J."

Earlier in 1958 had come the Munich air crash in which many of Manchester United's team, agreed by most in the game to be on the verge of greatness, were killed. There's a photograph taken in the United changing room immediately after the first-leg victory against Red Star Belgrade, three weeks before the crash. Several United players are sitting on a bench, in the foreground a shirtless Duncan Edwards. Edwards was reputedly one of the finest players of his generation. He and the others in the picture all have short back and sides, their faces are almost expressionless, presumably because they are exhausted from their efforts, but what most strikes me is that these young men could be a group of miners just up from their shift. They are not yet "stars" as, a few years later, George Best, also of Manchester United, was to be. They may be working class heroes but they are anonymous, although Edwards is attempting a smile for the camera. The others are looking away. Yet they don't appear to resent the intrusion of the photographer into what ought surely to be a private moment. They know who is in control, and it isn't them.

As we sat over our drinks, Pete and Pauline talked art. He had just come from seeing some recent Henry Moore drawings about which he was enthusing. I was happy to see that my friend and the woman I loved enjoyed talking to each other. "Always we'd have the new friend meet the old," Yeats had written in his elegy for Major Robert Gregory, "And we are hurt if either friend seems cold." No coldness here. As we parted, Pauline and I to get a bus back to Staines, Pete to head for the station, I said to him, "why not come to see us at Reading some time."

He shrugged and his eyes slid away from mine. "Perhaps," he said. And for the first time it occurred to me that he wasn't happy. Or rather, because I didn't really think of Pete in terms of happiness, that he was somehow cut adrift. Had his experiences in the army affected him more deeply than I'd realised? Or was something else shaping the dark melancholy I suddenly sensed about him. But then he brisked up, shook hands with Pauline and, as he turned away, called over his shoulder, "Take care and keep in touch."

* * *

For the rest of the summer I spent long hours reading and writing and arguing with my father about the race riots of late August. These began in Nottingham, a city in which, to its shame, the blues singer Big Bill Broonzy had already been refused admission to the hotel where a room was reserved for him. "Sorry, I've got my reputation to think of," the hotelier reputedly said to Big Bill. Then over August's final weekend, when London was sweltering under a heat wave, there was serious rioting in Notting Hill. A man called Geoffrey Hamm demanded that recent immigrants be sent home and that further immigration be stopped. Blacks were over here to take our jobs and our women. A year later, when an absurd figure called Colin Jordan came to Reading we had fine fun with his argument that the presence of black men in England meant that white women would be "forced" to marry them. Laws would apparently be passed requiring this to happen. He was laughed out of countenance, as was the misguided woman member of the arts faculty who remonstrated with him because, she said, he was "corrupting these young people's minds."

But what happened in August, 1958, was no joke. In one of our arguments, my father remarked that he had for some time been told by the dockers whom he met whenever he went down to Wapping (he was there to oversee consignments of timber arriving from Canada) that they knew for sure that in-coming West Indians were being given preferential treatment over housing in the area as well as picking up work that ought by rights to go to Englishmen. It was obvious, he said, that as soon as someone like Geoffrey Hamm came on the scene he would be able to make trouble. "Stir the flames", was how he put it.

His words enraged me and I blurted out that if Hamm's dead body were to be found in some alley the world would thank whoever had got rid of him.

"I doubt the police would agree with you," my father said.

Rightly, of course, but his words provoked me to a further rant about the police being racists, which many probably were, and twisters of the law, which most probably weren't. Afterwards, I tried to write an Orwellian piece taking issue with his contention that the English were fundamentally a tolerant nation. Tolerance only counted, I said, when intolerance was a real alternative, and in my view whenever the English had the chance to be intolerant we not only took it but showed a real aptitude for it. It wasn't merely racism I had in mind; there was also homophobia. I didn't use that word, which I think wasn't then in existence. But John Gordon's *Sunday Express* article most certainly was, and I took aim at that, calling the columnist not only disgusting but probably terrified of his own sexual predilections.

Had I left it there, the piece might have been a reasonable polemic, even if unpublishable, but I then began to aim scattershot at a random list of pet hates — people who disliked jazz, people who liked the wrong kind of jazz, people who said that they didn't know anything about art but knew what they liked, people who said they liked art but who never went to art exhibitions, people who spoke the word "poetry" as though it was a life-threatening disease, people who spoke poetry as though it was the nine o'clock news. The essay became an incoherent charivari of dislikes and I abandoned it. And then it was once more time for Reading.

* * *

This time I returned with a sense of apprehension. The previous two years had provided not so much a temporary release from what my father and others called "the real world" as the entry into a new one. But now that world was coming to an end. In nine months time I would have a degree, probably the poor one that Gordon had warned me students of Philosophy and English Literature always ended up with, and, before I could even think of a life beyond, one which I still assumed or anyway hoped would be that of a free-lance writer, there was the prospect of two years in uniform. But no. I was determined that, come what may, I would *not* do my National Service. The problem was how to get out of it. I couldn't expect to be found unfit, and I wasn't at all sure that I could get away with registering as a conscientious objector. Leave the country then? But where would I go? Why? And what about Pauline? Once I'd gone, I wouldn't be able to return, not for years. There were rumours that National Service might soon be brought to a stop, that senior military men could see no point to it, that it did no good, or not enough good to justify its retention. But rumours were one thing, action to end National Service quite another. In the meantime friends and former student acquaintances were still reporting for their two years of submission to military rules and, perhaps, having no choice but to fight in wars they didn't believe in, as I certainly didn't believe we should be in Cyprus. Nor did I think we should try to persuade ourselves that we were still a great empire. Why not simply·

return the empire to those people whose land we had stolen and whose lives we had for so long controlled and harmed?

I voiced my loathing of National Service to Gordon when we were chatting at a departmental party thrown to welcome new students. "There is always research" he said. Research? What on earth did he mean? Didn't research involve devoting yourself to the crepitations of unread books in some dusty library corner, retreating into a world of "dried butterflies and tomes of casuistry"? I knew enough about myself to be certain that not only would I never be capable of Gordon's scholarly scrupulousness but anyway I didn't particularly want to follow his example. My passion for literature and ideas wasn't an especially scholarly one.

And yet. The University had one or two research scholarships — "though they are *very* competitive" Gordon said — and perhaps we should talk about the possibilities at some future date. I agreed. Two years research would buy me two further years of deferral from National Service, a point I put to Ian when, later that evening, I met him for a drink in The Turk's Head. "Well," Ian said, "the army never did me much good, although I did meet other writers, all as useless with guns as I was." There had been an incident at the end of the war when he and "old George" — Fraser — were sent out to repel a crowd of angry Egyptians demonstrating outside the British quarters in Cairo. " I was issued with a revolver which I waved with a certain élan. It proved rather more effective than George's plea that they might like to consider retreating. As well they didn't challenge me, though, there was no ammo in the damned thing."

Then he began to list some of those whom he'd knocked up against in the Middle East. These included Reggie Smith and his wife, Olivia Manning — "he was all for partying the night away, she took a dim view of it, not that her sourness wasn't justified." And he told me of an occasion when, late one night, he and George Fraser had been in the Smiths' flat. She had come in, said crossly, "Reggie I'm going to bed, and I'm hoping for a quiet night," and George, trying for a clumsy compliment, quoted "She walks in beauty like the

375

night," adding for her benefit, "Keats". "Byron, you fool," she said. Then there was the poet, Bernard Spencer, who worked for the British Council, as did another poet, Terance Tiller, and there was Lawrence Durrell, who floated in and out of Cairo and Alexandria. Also in Cairo at that time was a poet called Sir John Waller, "queer as a coot", who had stood to inherit a fortune if he produced a son. Waller arranged this through a marriage in which his wife and friend connived to do the needful....

At this point Ian broke off. "Oh, by the way," he said, "a chap called Parkinson has written to me from California, telling me he's bringing two young poets to England for a London reading in November." He fished the typed letter out of his pocket and squinted at the date. "He's hoping I might lend an ear but I'm otherwise engaged that evening. However, if you're free you might care to go. Parkinson sounds faintly amusing."

"How do you know him?" I asked, which seemed more tactful than asking him how Parkinson knew Ian. But in fact Ian's name was by no means unknown among American poets and academics. As he'd already told me, some years before coming to Reading and while he was still active in London literary life, he had decided to start his own magazine. It was to be called *Colonnade* and to give it some cachet Ian sought endorsements from various luminaries. The inevitable Sir Herbert Read and Stephen Spender wrote encouraging letters. So, rather more valuably, did Edwin Muir, T.S. Eliot, and, believe it or not, Wallace Stevens. These letters were nailed to the editorial masthead and Ian, perhaps realising things could hardly get any better, and in homage to the ener-vations of his favourite decade, the 1890s, made sure that the first issue of his magazine was also the last. Nevertheless, the one and only appearance *of Colonnade* gave him something of a reputation, even in the USA, and this, together with a number of essays on early Yeats as well as his editions of some of the more crepuscular poets of the decadence, was quite enough to explain the letter from Parkinson, a Yeats scholar as well as a poet. So "yes", I said, "I'll go."

The night of the reading was dank, cold, foggy, and I arrived at the venue, a hall adjacent to the Knightsbridge Road, only just in time. Parkinson, a huge man in a grey suit, stood at the door, to greet all who came in. I doubt there were more than thirty of us present when the first half began with readings by two English poets. Christopher Hampton, not the playwright but a rather good if little-known poet, read some angry political poems. He was followed by George MacBeth. In what I assume to have been a mock tribute to Larkin, MacBeth wore a belted mackintosh with cycle clips and read a poem about feeling guilty for having drowned a wasp in a jam-jar.

There was then an interval during which one of the two ageing gents who were organisers of the event passed among us with an offertory plate into which coins were lobbed while his partner played pieces of Schumann. Once the final note of the last of these had expired Parkinson loomed craggily up and announced that he himself would not on this occasion be reading. Instead, he proposed to leave the second half of the programme to the two poets he had brought with him. I had the impression that he saw them as his protégés, though he didn't use the word. He did however say that they represented something radically new in poetry. Well, he would say that, wouldn't he.

The first of the two poets, neither of whose names I had caught when Parkinson introduced them, was thin as a fish-bone, had a sallow complexion, dark, unwashed hair, horn-rimmed glasses, and wore blue jeans and a blue cord jacket over a dark blue or it may have been black shirt. He seemed the very image of an Ivy-Leaguer off duty, and I settled myself to listen to some clever, allusive, exquisitely-crafted verse. Then he began

I saw the best minds of my generation destroyed by madness, starving, hysterical, naked,
dragging themselves through the Negro streets at dawn looking for an angry fix.....

377

When he finished, some twenty minutes later, the audience sat in a kind of stunned bewilderment. There must have been a scattering of applause — we were far too polite to forget our manners — and then the second poet rose. Smaller than the first reader, this one had black jeans, crumpled white jacket, red shirt, and his wild hair and eyes, together with his swarthy skin, suggested that he had just stepped out of a painting by Caravaggio. He chanted a song about a Mad Yak, read of not wanting to make a bourgeois marriage, and then, suddenly, the evening was over, and we were free to head for the nearest pub.

Once in the Bodega, as I'm certain the pub was called, I found myself standing next to the poet in blue, whose name I now knew to be Allen Ginsberg, as I knew the name of the other poet to be Gregory Corso. Politely Ginsberg asked my name, politely I told him, and as though in response he said "I'm homosexual, Corso's bi-sexual. And Parkinson there, he's *tri-sexual*." Was he offering me a choice? Fortunately, I didn't need to reply because at that moment Corso, high on drink or drugs, or maybe both, clambered onto a table and began haranguing the entire bar-full of drinkers who, being English, looked on in bemused, tolerant silence as they — we — were accused of hating our poets.

"You killed Chatterton." (To be honest, I don't recall this particular accusation, perhaps because I was still engaged in conversation with Ginsberg, but Peter Porter, who was also in the audience on that occasion, told me that Chatterton definitely came first in Corso's litany.)

"You killed Keats."

Given that Keats died of TB and that his soul, despite Byron's sardonic speculation, was definitely not snuffed out by Lockhart's savage article, this seemed a tad unfair.

The next charge was even more unfair.

"You killed Shelley."

Shelley may have felt himself forced out of England but to some extent he had only himself to blame, and his death by drowning could certainly not be laid at the door of the nation. *Don Juan*, the yacht of which he had just taken possession and which he had insisted on having a hand in designing, proved remarkably unstable and capsized in storm winds that blew up as it was attempting to cross the Gulf of Spezia.

"You killed Byron."

Wrong again. Byron died of fever at Missolonghi while preparing to fight the Turks, though his death was admittedly hastened, and perhaps partly caused, by the doctor who, despite the poet's explicit instructions, insisted on bleeding him once Byron had lapsed from consciousness.

"You killed Dylan Thomas."

This was too much. "No," I shouted back, mindful of the way Americans had gladly fed the Welsh Rimbaud's drinking habits, "*You* killed Dylan Thomas."

At which point Ginsberg put his arm round my shoulders and nuzzled my cheek with his nose and tongue. "Love everyone, man," he said.

* * *

That was one of several memorable encounters of autumn, 1958. The next followed a few days later. I was coming out of the London Street bookshop when I saw striding toward me someone I'd known at school. He and I had played in the cricket 1st XI, and from time to time we bumped into each other at Reading, where he was studying Geography. Though in no sense friends, we had an affable enough relationship, and I was therefore stunned when he at first pretended not to see me, and then, when I insisted on saying hello, nodded curtly and brushed silently past me. I stared after his retreating figure. What on earth had I done to so upset him? I couldn't imagine it was anything I'd said, unless perhaps I'd unwittingly offended one of his friends? But as far as I was aware I didn't *know* any of his friends. What then? Time would perhaps untie a knot too hard for me.

And it did. That evening I found in my pigeon-hole a note from him. "Sorry about my behaviour this morning," it said,

"Can you meet me tomorrow, 2pm at —" and a pub at the far end of town, in a square called St Mary's Butts, was named. "Use the public bar." The note was unsigned. It all seemed very cloak and dagger, especially as I was warned neither to reply to his note nor tell anyone of it.

The following day I arrived at the pub at the appointed hour and as I went into the public bar I saw him standing at the far end, smoking, his grey raincoat pulled up to his ears so that had I not been familiar with his thin figure, pale, clean-shaven and somehow anonymous face, and the long, slightly greasy hair he seemed rarely to wash, I might have missed him.

"Pint?" he asked, as I touched his elbow. He ordered for us both and insisted on carrying our beers over to a small table by the back window. Silently, we raised our glasses and drank. Then, speaking slowly, unemphatically, and all the while watching the door through which people entered, he told me an extraordinary story. His father, he said, was a compulsive betting man and he himself had inherited the disorder (his word). Never too much at a time, but even so the gee-gees he backed rarely came home winners, and gradually his losses mounted up. So much so, that by the time he arrived back at Reading for his final year he was more than £300 in debt to a variety of bookies and their runners. Threats began to reach him. Notes pushed under the door of his room in hall. Letters.

"Saying what?"

"What you expect when you get in with the heavies. Promises of broken legs, of being done over, that sort of thing."

At last he decided to go and see his bank manager. Not that he had any real hope of being able to raise the wind by means of a bank loan, but what else was he to do? So he fixed a day and a time, went, to his surprise was sympathetically listened to, and told to come back in a few days. Which he did, and, scarcely able to believe his ears, was informed that he would be advanced the money to pay off his debts, that a further £200 was to be put into his account, and that from now on he was to steer well clear of all forms of gambling.

"Some people get all the luck," I said. £500 was in 1958 a huge sum of money, nearly £10 a week, more than the average wage.

"Not really."

"You mean an impecunious student get £500 stuffed into his pocket and it's no big deal. Either that or your bank manager's due for the funny farm."

"You haven't heard the rest of the story."

"Tell me."

And he did. A week after he had paid off the last of his debts, he went into his hall room after dinner and found two middle-aged men sitting side by side on his bed. At first he thought they must be race-course heavies, here to get their fingers into the pile of money he had come by. Because, as required, he'd paid off his debts in ready cash, and this had prompted a number of comments on his sudden wealth and guesses as to how he'd come by it. "Got yourself a tart, then?" or, "blimey, who's lost her glass beads." But then he realised the men looking at him weren't the type. These were better dressed, neat suits, Aquascutum raincoats, and when they spoke it was in cut-glass accents.

What they had to say was brief and to the point. They knew about his debts, they knew he had been cleared of them and that money had been put into his bank account. How did they know that, he might like to ask. Well, let's just say that there are ways and means. But those who had provided for him in his hour of need now required something in exchange. As a student he must come up against other students with all sorts of political views, including those who showed an unhealthy interest in communism, who might even be described as reds. Yes? He supposed that he nodded. Well, then, what they would like from him were names and details of any such students so that an eye could be kept on them. And when he had anything to offer he should leave a note at the newsagent on the corner of... and a road was named, though he didn't tell me what it was. The note was to be placed in a plain brown envelope, his name only written on the outside, and *For Collection*. That was all. Not much, is it, they said, but every little helps to guard against enemies of the state.

They took their leave then. But as they went out of the door, one of them turned and said, "We're trusting you to keep quiet about this. If anything leaks out, I imagine the bank would want all their money back, and fast." Then they were gone.

"So they've got me. I'm taking a big risk in letting you in on this." He took a lengthy pull on his beer. "You're the kind of student I'm expected to tell them about."

"And have you?"

He shook his head. "No, and I won't. But now you understand why I don't want to be seen in public talking to you. You never know who's watching." Then he added, "You leave first. I'll give it a quarter of an hour." He raised his near empty glass. "Cheers," he said, and when I looked at him I thought I'd never seen an unhappier face.

There were times in the months to come when we passed each other in the street. In a town as small as Reading then was you could hardly expect not to cross paths with most other students. But we never spoke again and I've no idea what happened to him after he got his degree and left. I hope he managed to get out of the malign grip of MI5, as I suppose his paymasters must have been. But in case he didn't and is still somewhere in earshot for the story's end, I have been careful not to give his name.

Chapter 22
The Best of Friends

It must have been at about the time of my meeting with the reluctant agent that Gordon suggested I might like to accompany him on a visit to a friend of his, someone who lived in a country house on the borders of Berkshire/Oxfordshire, and who cultivated what Gordon told me was "a remarkable garden". He also owned a house-full of "very important" pictures. We were apparently invited to take tea after we had inspected the house and its possessions. As soon as I accepted the offer Gordon began to fret about my table manners. I think he convinced himself that, either to show my contempt for the landed gentry or simply because I didn't know any better, I would pour tea into my saucer and/or use my tongue to lick my plate clean. Perhaps to offset such solecisms he invited the department's new senior lecturer, Philip Brockbank, to go with us.

Philip had replaced Kermode, who had gone off to be Professor at Manchester. George Hunter, a Renaissance scholar from whose tutorials I greatly benefited, had left at the same time and we now had a lecturer from Oxford called Brian Morris. Morris gave boring lectures on Wordsworth, to which I rarely went, while Philip, a clever, witty, if lazy man, lectured on Keats. Both were Renaissance specialists but in those days you were expected to know enough to teach any aspect of the course, something of which I entirely approve. We were still living in the blessed time before "field specialism" meant that a Dickens' scholar couldn't be expected to comment on George Eliot, say, let alone T.S.

On the way by taxi to our destination I told them of my encounter with Ginsberg. Philip laughed, Gordon, too, though he added, as by way of caution, "*not* a suitable subject for tea, I think." By the time we arrived the weather had become rainy and we were therefore spared a guided tour of the estate.

"Happily, Repton's influence has been *all* but erased," Gordon said in a stage whisper as, having paused to look at some misty meadows, we followed our host into the house.

I was taken aback by the pictures on display. Not simply by how many of them there were, but by the quality. After some initial pleasantries during which it became clear that Gordon and his host were genuinely fond of one another, we were set free to wander from room to room and to discover what most pleased each of us. In his essay, "A Mirror for Artists", to be found in *I'll Take My Stand*, that rank apologia for Confederate values, the Southern poet Donald Davidson drops one almost sensible remark into his ragbag of snobbish clichés. "What is a picture for," he asks, "if not to be put on one's own wall? But the principle of the art gallery requires me to think that a picture has some occult quality in itself and for itself that can only be appreciated on a quiet anonymous wall, utterly removed from the tumult of my private affairs." Some of us would argue that a picture on "a quiet anonymous wall" can at least be looked at by people who couldn't afford to buy it and who couldn't therefore put it on their own wall. And yet a personal collection can have a deep allure, the feel of something arrived at, assembled, improved, by interests that have nothing to do with the need to represent all shades of taste. It can also of course look ridiculous or second-rate. But for every Bowes Museum there is a Kettle's Yard. And there is also the house we strolled about that November afternoon in 1958.

I was bowled over by some early Turners, large, meticulous cityscapes of Oxford streets and alleyways, all of them empty of people. But then, as I had already realised, Turner couldn't draw or paint the human figure. Because, having thought about Gordon's suggestion that I might try for a research scholarship, I had begun to think a possible topic would be an investigation of nineteenth century illustrated books. This had let me to Turner's illustrations of *Paradise Lost*, which were almost comically inept. The one of Adam and Eve in Eden could have done service for any early "Wish You Were Here" card. The couple appear tinily and inexactly, at the very bottom of the picture, the real interest of which lies in lengthy, disappearing vistas of the earthly paradise. No, Turner couldn't manage figures.

When we adjourned for tea, I debated whether to bring the subject up, especially as I had spent so long absorbing the Turners on show here, before hastening on to look at other work, including a small, heart-breakingly lovely Watteau, one of those *fête-champêtres* where the figures, whose postures, faces and smiles at first seem radiant with pleasure, are, you realise, inhabiting a world on which tragedy encroaches. I later read that Watteau rarely primed his canvases correctly, with the result that over the years his colours, at first jewel-like in their brightness, began to crack and fade. That seemed entirely right, as though he was anticipating that the sunlit world he painted would shortly be wrecked by the thunder of revolution. But once we were grouped around the tea-table, Gordon insisted on doing most of the talking. He also noisily slurped his tea and, having pushed aside a half-eaten sandwich, immediately lit a cigarette which he then dunked into a cup of what I assume was splendid china. Perhaps this was how you had to behave among the gentry. At all events, our host seemed untroubled by such behaviour.

Going back to Reading in the taxi, Gordon said, as he so often did after an occasion which could be regarded as at best free of disaster, "that went rather well, I think." And fell asleep.

* * *

"Next Year Will be Better." I wrote that number in 1954 for the Towpath Ramblers skiffle group which we created from within the Vikings Jazz Band and which performed during intervals at various of our gigs. I can't claim that, walking through the town's quiet, pretty streets after leaving Gordon, I thought of how accurate a forecast the words had proved to be. But they had. I'd come a long way from the discontents of early 50's Ashford and Hampton to the present. So, *mutatis mutandis,* had many of my parents' and my own generation. What I couldn't know was that in some ways, at least, the following years might be worse. Not personally. But "The Swinging Sixties? Don't make me laugh./....A scattering of people in London/made it up. Everyone else just got along." Jim Burns's acidulous rejection of the journalistic view of what followed the 50s underrates at least one of its characteristics: the vigour with which it swung the wrecking ball. Had I been walking across Reading ten years later I would have seen very little of the town I'd grown to love. By the end of the sixties, and as was happening in towns and cities across the country, the demolition gangs had wiped out buildings and streets which, having survived Hitler's bombs, were now to be replaced by shopping malls and all that serviced them: inner ring-roads, multi-storey car parks, high-rise office developments. Civic architecture, once the guarantee of a town's individuality, was being replaced by the designs of anywheresville.

* * *

That evening Pauline and I were due at a party. A dull enough party, too, it was, until a student I had seen around but never before spoken to, came up and standing in front of me so we were almost toe-to-toe, said, "Excuse me, old man. I'm told you read books. What's your line on Stradlater?"

The question, asked in a manner that blended pretend deference with comic belligerence, at first threw me. Then I realised he was talking about the novel which at that time everyone seemed to be reading, even those who professed no interest in books. *The Lord of the Flies* and *Lucky Jim* were both hugely popular among students in the 1950s, and soon they would be joined by *On the Road. Sons and Lovers* was also widely read although I doubt it reached much beyond those who had a strong interest in literature. *The Catcher in the Rye* was in a different league. It was in a different world. No novel, before or since, has had such a strong or lasting impact on a whole generation of readers as Salinger's did on the generation which came of age in the 1950s. As I have earlier remarked, a decade later, when I was teaching for a year in America, I was astounded by the effect Mike Nichols' film *The Graduate* produced on male students at the University of Maryland. Overnight, it seemed, they changed from being tall, blond and athletic to short, dark, and bookish. There was good reason for this metamorphosis. Being tall and blond was part of an American dream, and early in 1968 a version of the dream was leading young men to Vietnam. General Westmoreland was tall and had once no doubt been blond. Dustin Hoffman's nay-saying attitude to his filmic parents, people who had bought into the dream, could be taken as metaphor of resistance to the draft. It was a rejection of no-questioning patriotism and, depending on your point of view, thrillingly liberating or wickedly seditious. When, in the final scene, the graduate gets his girl friend away from the altar where she is about to exchange vows with a blond hulk, the audience response — at least in the mid-town cinema in Washington DC where Pauline and I saw the film — was extraordinary. The older half were on their feet booing and calling out in protest; the other, younger half, were on their feet clapping and cheering.

In England, friends of ours who saw the film couldn't understand what all the fuss was about. *The Graduate* was a decent enough comedy — but *seditious*? You had to be in America at that particular time to understand its impact. In England in the 1950s, Holden Caulfield's belief that most of the adults in his life, and quite a few of his contemporaries, were "phonies", at the very least provided a useful word to point at those telling the young to grow up, love the bomb, and settle for a life of placid, unadventurous normality. And Holden's retreat into breakdown, his rejection of his girl-friend for being "a royal pain in the ass", and his certainty that the only person worth loving was his kid sister, Phoebe, could seem not only "authentic", a key word of the period, but a pointer to the next decade's devotion to "youth culture", to R.D. Laing's much favoured claim that the mad were the truly sane, that families were the problem rather than the answer to society's ills, and that to turn on, tune in and drop out, as Timothy Leary recommended, was preferable to any social arrangement lacking LOVE.

To make such claims is, of course, to verge on parody. And anyway, most English readers of *The Catcher in the Rye* settled sensibly enough for lives which the novel invited them to reject. The poet John Hartley Williams, who read it at the beginning of the 1960s, told me he detested the novel and couldn't understand why anyone would be attracted to what he saw as Holden's self-pitying wimpishness. Fair point. And certainly there's never any suggestion in the *Catcher* that anything can be done to confront the phonies. The only way out is the way back, which is no way at all. But as satire on certain conformist attitudes, the novel again and again hits the mark, and Stradlater, that all-body and no-brain sporting bully, the kind of cheesecake which, translated to the screen, became called Tab Hunter, say, or Rock Hudson, was well worth aiming at.

To my interlocutor, I said something along the lines of having come across English versions of Stradlater, that there were plenty to choose from at Reading, and that they should be avoided like the plague. "I think you *may* be implying that you are not an admirer of Stradlater," he said. "I wish in that case you'd put the point more plainly." He stared solemnly at me and, as I stared back, it occurred to me that there was something of an imagined Caulfield about the way he hunched his shoulders, as if he was on guard for possible blows from an unexpected quarter; the manner of his look, his dark, slightly bloodshot eyes, now fixed, now darting about, suggested a comic, self-conscious wariness; and his clothes, the dark blue sweater, cavalry twill trousers, seemed to insist that he was in disguise, though as and from what I couldn't guess. I asked his name and he said "Look here, old man, I perceive that you're trying to change the subject." Then, as though after hours of torture he was finally giving in to the Spanish inquisition, he mournfully confessed, "Carl Pigeon".

It was the work of several minutes to drag from him the information that he was in the same year as me, studying physics, but that his interests ranged wide, from cricket to classical music, from mountain climbing to architecture. Each of my questions produced a silence, followed by an answer that suggested he was giving it under threat of rack and screw. Before long his air of fraught solemnity, the sense he gave of having to guard a deadly secret before he dared reluctantly admit that yes, well, he did *quite* like beer or cricket or film but would be grateful if I didn't mention these preferences overmuch and especially not in mixed company because you never knew who might be wanting to take advantage of such confessions, reduced me to helpless laughter. He was effortlessly, endlessly funny. His language, as I would come to discover over the months and years ahead, was a unique melange of antiquated terms, slang, courtly periphrasis and an odd rag-bag of terms and phrases he'd picked up from his heterogeneous reading. On one occasion, when we were on a train going to London, he lent over the table at which we sat opposite each other and said, eyes locking forcefully onto mine, "I hope you don't mind my interrupting your thoughts, old man, but I think you should know that the kine out there are pretty well knee-deep in the sward and looking as though they mean business." He tapped with his forefinger on my book as though bringing an unruly brat to order, and said, "And I am *not* kidding."

On another occasion, when Pauline, he and I were drinking in The Turk's Head, Pauline mentioned that for years she had thought cows produced calves much as hens produced eggs, without the need of insemination. "My dear Pauline," Carl said, "allow me to be brutally frank. I think you should know that cows and bulls sleep together."

I remember too a party at which I arrived to find Carl in the kitchen, lying full-length with his head carefully cushioned inside an open oven. What on earth was he doing, I asked.

"Committing suicide," Carl said.

"You do know that's an electric oven?"

"My dear John," Carl said. "I'm not completely stupid."

Carl was attractive to women but his would-be affairs, while numerous, were rarely more than passing fancies that didn't so much end in disaster as refuse to begin. There was always some bar to progress. Invariably, the woman turned out not to be the paragon of beauty, taste, and intelligence he thought he had detected. One tapped her foot in time to Mozart, another laughed too loudly, the family of a third had high tea which featured sardines and strawberry jam. "On the same table, old man. Can you credit it?"

I never believed these excuses. They were a way of avoiding commitment, and although some of the women who fell for him were hurt by his quixotic rejection, they were at least spared the deeper wound of an abandonment that would soon enough have followed the start of a relationship. I sometimes imagined that the only women Carl felt safe with were those he could pine after in the certain knowledge that they were out of reach.

I doubt that it's possible to communicate a sense of Carl's charm, the effect he had on us all simply by appearing in a room. He seemed never to make an entry but suddenly, effortlessly, to materialise. One minute he wasn't there, the next he was. David Copperfield's words about Steerforth capture something of his effect: "in everything an indescribable lightness, a seeming impossibility of doing anything else, or doing anything better, which was so graceful, so natural, and agreeable...." But this leaves out the wit, the mixture of melancholy and gregariousness, the play-acting that could suddenly turn serious and as quickly return to a drama of known effects and means.

By the end of the Christmas term Carl and I were not only close friends but, in our shared determination not to do our National Service, had more or less decided that if we couldn't find research funding in England we would try our luck in Canada. My father could, he said, get us on board one of the freighters that brought timber over to London. The rest was up to us. But what about Pauline? I couldn't bear the thought of leaving her for two years. And with that unresolved and unresolvable dilemma to brood over I took myself back to Staines.

Chapter 23
Forster and Lawrence

On the first day of 1959, E.M. Forster turned eighty. The event was celebrated with a television Profile, interviews in the broadsheets, assessments in the literary press and, at Staines, a third-year undergraduate completed 47 typed pages of a projected critical study of Forster's pre-1914 novels.

For the past term I had been besotted with Forster. I read all the novels and everything else by him that I could get hold of, including the biography of his aunt, *Marianne Thornton*, notable for its eye-opening account of the evangelical Clapham Sect, those high-minded and for the most part joyless do-gooders who made it their purpose in life to oppress the poor with Christian virtue. There were the two collections of essays, *Abinger Harvest* and *Two Cheers for Democracy,* plus *Aspects of the Novel, Alexandria, Pharos and Pharillon* and *The Hill of Devi.* I scoured bookshops for copies of *The Celestial Omnibus* and *The Eternal Moment,* and, when I found and read them, tried not to admit that the stories they contained were a disappointment, though I was prepared to acknowledge that for all its good moments *The Longest Journey* was a failure. Forster's apparent preference for it over his other novels seemed as difficult to credit as his belief that Leonard Bast was a plausible creation. *Maurice* of course was unpublished and unknown to all but a few, Gordon included, who, taken aback by my intense admiration for Forster, assured me that the novel was "*far* too scandalous to see the light of day".

The remark puzzled me. If I had any criticism of Forster's fiction it was that for all his insistence on the sanctity of personal relationships, his description of such relationships seemed a little bloodless. Why, for example, should Margaret Schlegel be surprised when Henry Wilcox kisses her? They've just become engaged, for heaven's sake. And why, given the claim in *A Room With a View* that love is of the body, a claim with which I wholly agreed, was the relationship between Lucy Honeychurch and George Emerson so — so spectral?

The truth is, it never occurred to me that Forster was homosexual. Or if I did suspect it, I pushed the thought away. As, I imagine, did most readers at that time. And if this seems extraordinary, I can only say that unlike Auden and Isherwood, Forster had taken care to cover his tracks. The Greek poet Katerina Anghelaki-Rooke once said to me that she thought it both the curse and the blessing of the English language that it's the only one where a declaration of love in writing doesn't make evident whether the object of affection is male or female. "You" isn't gendered. But with Auden and Isherwood you knew, not merely because of the more explicit subject matter, but because of the way they wrote, the knowing campness of their vocabulary. Not so with Forster. In fact, even when the following year I paid him a fleeting visit, I still didn't realise.

The meeting came about because I had written him a fan letter saying how much I admired his writings and in reply he sent a friendly card suggesting that if I ever found myself in Cambridge I should call on him. So I did. Green as I was, I hadn't thought to make an appointment. I simply turned up early one afternoon at his rooms in King's. When he opened the door I saw he was shorter than I'd expected, though in all other respects looking exactly as he had in the television programme. Wispy hair, round face with spectacles and beaky nose, slight stoop, grey suit with green, woollen cardigan underneath the shapeless jacket. I stammered out my name and to my relief he appeared to remember the letter I had written some weeks previously. But, he explained, he was about to go out. Nevertheless, he stood aside to let me in to a room crammed with books and we talked for a few, feverish minutes, during which he told me that the original of the house Howard's End was called Rook's Nest House, and, in reply to my saying that I'd love to see it, he said he would write to the then occupier, the composer Elizabeth Poston. "And perhaps you should write as well," he said. "It can be an advantage to be fore-warned of someone's arrival." But there was no malice in this gentle rebuke.

So brief was my visit that I didn't have time to ask him much about his novels, and I certainly didn't dare tell him of the pages of typescript that now lay crammed into a folder in the bottom drawer of my desk. But to the mounting irritation of my family I spent most of Christmas 1959 banging away at my typewriter, trying to explain and justify my belief in Forster's importance. The novel on which I decided to rest this claim was not *A Passage to India*. Apart from Lionel Trilling, whose 1940s study of Forster I had found in a London bookshop and which very oddly and unpersuasively argued for the pre-eminence of *Howard's End*, most commentators were pretty well agreed that Forster's last novel was also his finest and the only one likely to stand the test of time.

But the other novels looked to be made of durable material, too. I had an especial fondness for *A Room with a View*, and decided that I would concentrate on this novel. I was certain that the structure and plot of *A Room with a View* ghosted another, Wagner's *Parsifal*. I had the whole thing worked out. Correspondence of characters, of story, of meaning. It's unnecessary to detail these here, though I may as well say that I was convinced Forster was inverting the Christian myth of the search for the Holy Grail. For him, evil lay not in the allure of the flesh, of Klingsor and his garden, but in renunciation. The church, in the figures of Mr Eager and Mr Beebe, and the governess, Miss Bartlett, standing "brown against the view" of Fiesole and its promise of a worldly Eden — these were the enemies. And the Emersons, with their working class energy and unashamed love of art and life, were the true heroes, though young George, like Parsifal, bore a death-in-life wound, in his case Lucy Honeychurch's renunciation of him. As for Lucy, who at one point sings the song "Taste not when the wine cup glistens", which is given to Lucy Ashton in Scott's *Bride of Lammermoor* and reproduced in Donizetti's opera, she has to move from the grey world of suburban middle class propriety into one of light and warmth, and, Forster rather coyly implies, of uninhibited sexual pleasure: a room with a view.

He had first pointed this contrast between the cold north and warm south in *Where Angels Fear to Tread*, but *A Room with a View* made for a more intricately-worked out novel as well as a more memorable one. So much so, in fact, that I think at one point I almost knew it by heart and I am still able to quote whole chunks of it. I can quote substantial bits of *Howard's End*, too, though here the interweavings of plot become so neatly symbolic that they lose contact with the messiness of earthly reality. The famous epigraph "Only Connect" requires more contrivance than is in the end good for the novel. Helen's affair with Leonard Bast and the resulting child who will inherit Howard's End itself — that symbol of country-house England scaled down to modest proportions — becomes the scaffolding for an edifice unlikely ever to be built, let alone stand. "We've got the bit, we've got the snaffle, but where's the bloody horse," as the contumacious poet Roy Campbell put it.

In the film of *Howard's End* the bloody horse is a far larger mansion than the one Forster intended. The elm tree has become a chestnut. And the house which had been in the English heartlands now stands on the south coast. This is inexcusably daft. Forster wanted not to aggrandise his liberal dream of reconciliation between classes and concerns. But dream is what it remains. I don't know how keenly I felt that when one Sunday in late 1960, Pauline, Carl, Gordon and I drove from Reading to Rook's Nest House near Stevenage in one of Carl's villainous old cars, but Gordon, although he wanted to see the house, brought with him an air of tart disbelief in the novel's symbolist gestures. In a photograph which Pauline took, he, Elizabeth Poston and I are standing outside the surprisingly small house, on the gravelled drive up which the Wilcoxes would have sped in their cars, and, though you can't see it, Gordon poses with a wisp of hay dangling from his hand. Hay fever is a conspicuous symbol in the novel. With the exception of Mrs Wilcox, the Wilcox family all suffer from it. They are not to inherit the house and land. They belong to the city, to business, to "the outer world of telegrams and anger." England — the land — belongs elsewhere, to those who know the importance of the "inner world" or personal relationships.

Gordon would have none of this, not so much because he didn't think it might be a worthwhile vision, but because, as someone who probably knew more about the tradition of the country house poem than anyone then alive, who had written about Jonson's "Penshurst", Marvell's "Upon Nun Appleton House", Carew's "To My Friend, G.N. From Wrest", and so on down to Pemberley and Donwell Abbey, he was well aware that the appeal to social harmony — "So all come in, the farmer and the clown" — by and large depended on habits of agreed deference which masked sterner agreements, indeed enforcements. The rich man in his castle, the poor man at his gate was a requirement made "natural" by the "ordered" estate, where order means both orderliness and compulsion. This was all to become familiar enough, but as with so much else Gordon was way ahead of the arguments advanced by Raymond Williams and others in the 1970s. And he also knew that Forster's dream of England was doomed. In fact, it was Gordon who made me read Dangerfield's *The Strange Death of Liberal England*. "That will disabuse you of your passion for *Howard's End*," he said.

But my passion for the novel didn't depend on being persuaded by its politics. Though the pig's teeth in the wych elm left at best faint indentations to show that Pan of Box Hill had passed this way, Foster's satiric view of the Wilcoxes was both exact and intensely liberating, worth any amount of teenage rant at phoniness. "You nearly did make a deadly mistake in glorifying those business people," Lawrence wrote to Forster some years later, "business is no good". How on earth Lawrence persuaded himself that Forster glorified Henry Wilcox defeats me. Yet this was quoted at me by more than one person I met in the late 50s whose preference for Lawrence over Forster usually went with either a Leavisite endorsement of the "passional life" Lawrence wrote about, or a desire to dress up straightforward sexual longings in the language to be found in *The Rainbow, Women in Love* and most of all *The Virgin and the Gipsy.* Male undergraduates tended to go on about cocksure men and hensure women. Women were less impressed. They knew where the talk was meant to lead. I read most of Lawrence, knew without much doubt that *Sons and Lovers* was a great novel, thought, as I still do, there were wonderful moments in the subsequent novels — *The Rainbow* is in essence an abacus of such moments, strung on a threadbare narrative — but couldn't stand the hectoring tone of much of the writing. "Oh, lord, I'm off on the preach again," Lawrence wrote apologetically to a girlfriend when he was telling her why he didn't like Pre-Raphaelite art. But this wry self-criticism didn't stop the preachiness of his novels.

This didn't bother his devotees. He was truth-teller, mage, guru, whose every word was to be accepted. Lawrence said that Joyce did dirt on life. Leavis quoted the words with apostolic fervour. No-one therefore should read Joyce. Lawrence said that Forster had glorified business people. Well, then, no-one should read Forster.

The hold Lawrence had in the late 1950s on large numbers of my generation has all but vanished now. It owed much to the fact that for the first time young men from the kind of background where the thought of going to university had hitherto been an impossible dream could now realise that dream. Lawrence was their spokesman. And his seriousness about sex undoubtedly helped. Maybe more of them read *The Catcher in the Rye,* but those who read Lawrence believed in him with an intensity and commitment that Salinger's novel couldn't begin to match. Lawrence was a lawgiver.

I was off to the side of this. I loved the poems that made up *Birds, Beasts and Flowers,* having bought and read through the three-volume *Collected Poems* while I was still at

Hampton, and some of the essays were magically good, especially those included in *Twilight in Italy*. Lawrence's account of a night at the opera was strikingly similar to Forster's accounts in his Italian novels. I warmed to the unruliness they both spoke of, the anecdotes of babies being passed around, of families arriving as for a picnic, of the noisy goodwill. I remembered what Forster and Lawrence had to say about this when in the 1980s I had my first experience of watching Greek tragedy in the open air theatre on Lesbos and found there the same joyous, carnivalesque atmosphere. But, having tried and failed to get far with *The Plumed Serpent*, I sympathised with Carl's response, which included from time to time hurling the book across the room and, having once more retrieved it and recommenced reading, tearing out and ripping up each page as he finished with it.

* * *

That unpluming of the serpent happened during the Easter vacation, while a group of us were staying in a barn belonging to the Nag's Head pub at Edale. The pub landlord was the stepfather of a student acquaintance of ours, an older woman studying art who lived in one of the caravans on the edge of Whiteknights — Bohemia-in-the-woods someone dubbed it. She was a friend of Pauline's. A hapless but kind-hearted person who smoked and drank more than was good for her, she repeatedly discovered ways of deferring her final examination. We formed the impression she might be at Reading forever, rather like one of Chekhov's eternal students. The group at Edale consisted of us four and two other women art students, like Pauline, in their third, penultimate year. Kath, elegant and sophisticated-looking, would go on to marry an academic, although in later years she left him for a musician and herself became a well-known jazz singer. Amy, who had a pretty, puppy-dog face, was involved with a talentless snob whom I will call Peewit. Peewit, having somehow managed to complete a Diploma in Art at Reading, was now a short-term commissioned officer in the army. While we were at Edale he obtained leave to visit Amy — compassionate leave for the rest of the army, one of us suggested — and brought with him an ex-public-school boy whose upper lip seemed unable to close over his teeth, and whom the snob, it was plain, intended to pair off with Kath. It was also plain that Kath didn't much welcome this though being a good sort she went along with it. As she said, it at least spared the four of us having to put up with Peewit's company. Sometime during that week Peewit and Amy got engaged. I thought of Graves's "A Slice of Wedding Cake": "Why have such scores of lovely, gifted girls /Married impossible men?.... Has God's supply of tolerable husbands /Fallen, in fact, so low?"

But on the whole it was a good week. The weather, bright, dry, windy, was ideal for walking, and when we weren't swinging over hills we visited various "great" houses: Hardwick, Bolsover, Haddon Hall, Chatsworth. The works of art held by these were of course wondrous; but being in them made me uneasy, and Chatsworth in particular I loathed. "A puny insect shivering at a breeze" I thought, looking at the vast building that dominated the landscape. This wasn't to consult the genius of the place, it was to coerce and so destroy it. "Still round and round the ghosts of rustics glide, /And haunt the places where their livings died". It wasn't difficult to imagine the cost in human suffering of achieving the stately home which could then be imagined as "natural", "rambling and irregular" as a hedgerow, to use the words by which Jane Austen assumed her readers would be reconciled to Donwell Abbey.

Pauline, who had lived for three years in Chesterfield, told us that she could recall the clatter of hob-nailed boots as miners went to and from the pits, and how amazed she was to see them squatting peaceably outside a pub waiting for opening hour. Squatting came easily to men who spent long hours each day hunched at the coal face. No wonder, as Orwell says, miners have "small pronounced buttocks and sinewy thighs," and that for anyone not used to the work, "the pain in your knees and thighs... becomes (I am not exaggerating) an unbearable agony." Agricultural labour brought its own agonies: being out in all weathers guaranteed physical pains. But the greatest of all agonies was surely dispossession, the fate that came to many of the small tenant farmers and agricultural labourers on the estates we visited. Their dwelings didn't apparently matter.

A few weeks earlier I had disagreed with both Gordon and Ian over the meaning of some lines in Yeats's elegy for Major Robert Gregory.

> We dreamed that a great painter had been born
> To cold grey rock, to Galway rock and thorn,
> To that stern colour and that delicate line,
> That are our secret discipline,
> Wherein the gazing heart doubles her might.

They insisted that Yeats was writing about visionary landscape and that the "secret discipline" referred to the tradition he claimed to find in Blake's disciples, Palmer and Calvert, a tradition which opposed and transcended the "natural" landscape painting of Constable and his followers. I suggested that Yeats was instead asserting the connection between imagination and place, and that the secret discipline which gave Gregory's work its especial quality (though "dreamed" suggests that Yeats was too canny to be taken in by what are in truth pretty inept daubs) is inextricably linked to his belonging to a particular spot of Ireland, in this instance Galway. This is "dwelling", a belief in the nourishing if demanding value of rootedness, much as Wordsworth claims Michael's dwelling in Grasmere Vale to be. I think I'm right about this, although I can see that my indifference to Yeats's remark that "I am deeply religious" led me to undervalue the symbolic value he saw, or anyway found, in all things. My excuse must be that I was in flight from all things religious.

* * *

And yet by the time of that Easter jaunt I had decided that if I was to undertake research it would be on a very minor but intriguing nineteenth century writer — novelist and polemicist — W.H. Mallock, who was constantly embroiled in political and religious controversy, especially against socialists and atheists. Perhaps it was the attraction of opposites. Mallock was an ultra-montane Tory and, though not a Catholic himself (at least until his death-bed conversion) wrote as a Catholic apologist. I was only incidentally drawn to him because he came from a family who inhabited Cockington Court, near Torquay, my father's birthplace. More to the point was the fact that in his first novel, *The New Republic*, published in 1877, he satirised most of the leading sages of his day, including the scientists Huxley, Tyndall and Clifford, plus Jowett, who had been his master at Balliol and whose Broad Church Anglicanism Mallock detested, Walter Pater ("Mr Rose"), whose languid prose is well caught, as is that of Mr Kidglove Cocksure himself, Matthew Arnold, who appears as "Mr Luke, the Apostle of Culture".

This last butt of Mallock's wit I especially relished. I had become irritated by Arnold, although it was perhaps less him than the stress laid by Brockbank in Leavisite mode on the "civilising" force of *Culture and Anarchy*. I particularly resented the claim that when Arnold voices his disdain for "Doing As One Likes" — which begins as an attack on those who rioted at Hyde Park in the 1860s — he had in his sights the uncivilised *hoi polloi* who, with no grasp of what makes for civilisation, needed to be kept under the control of enlightened leadership, the Governors. Without such leadership England would descend into anarchy.

As it happened, an example of that leadership presented itself to Reading in the spring term when Lord Hailsham came to address the student body at the invitation of the student Conservative Party. At a crowded meeting I challenged him on the government's nuclear policy and he called me a poor bloody fool who wasn't willing to think. Afterwards, Pete, who had finally acceded to my suggestion to come to Reading for a weekend, said "never boo a sermon or a comic turn".

"And which heading did Hailsham's speech come under?"

"Both," Pete said.

He had brought with him the Arden edition *of King Lear* and on Sunday we spent what seemed hours arguing over the play. Peter was unusually fierce in his conviction that Lear's claim that he was a man more sinned against than sinning held no water and he as fiercely stood up for Edmund. But then, gradually, he fell into silence. When it was time for him to leave he had become utterly distracted, although the French term *distrait* more accurately describes how he then seemed. "Until next time" I said, as I saw him off at the station, but he merely nodded and slouched into the booking hall. Back in my room, I found he had left behind him his
copy *of King Lear*. Perhaps he intended me to hand it over the next time we met.

But there was to be no next time. In the summer, home briefly from university, I tried to contact him, but telephone calls and then letters went unanswered. I got in touch with people who had known him at Hampton. Did they have any news of his whereabouts? Had he gone abroad? Temporarily buried himself in some anonymous place? Might he even have been taken back into mental hospital? Nobody could help me. For months that stretched into years I kept up my enquires, and even now, when I come across anyone who once knew him, I ask whether there's a sighting to report, a rumour of his continued existence. But there never is. Like Waring, like Weldon Kees, Pete gave us all the slip, vanished so thoroughly that I'm left to mourn the inexplicable loss of a dear friend, one to whom I owe so much.

Chapter 24
The Last Summer

A long, hot summer, and an exceptionally beautiful one. Days of almost flawless blue sky with just enough breeze to prevent the heat from becoming oppressive. Reading's red brick seemed to glow with a warmth that was more than physical, and elm, lime and chestnut trees provided not mere canopies of shade but a backdrop of luxuriant splendour. At Whiteknights Park students sprawled in somnolent talk on the grass or sauntered in twos and threes by the reed-fringed lake. It was all reprehensibly perfect. But exams were coming and after that my undergraduate life would be at an end and for all I knew I would have to leave this place I had come to love. Death is the mother of beauty, and in those weeks the prospect of expulsion from the scene seemed to whisper of an approaching death.

From the blur of that time I can call up only one image. It is morning and I am standing at the side of Redlands Road, looking up towards Christchurch Green, which is where Pauline has gone to buy the morning paper and cigarettes. I shade my eyes against the already dazzling light and see her walking down the road toward me. Wearing a dark-blue short-sleeve shirt-blouse, a striped, bell-shaped skirt of various colours that sway and ripple with her movements, her shoes gleaming blue-green (painted with nail varnish, they add to the sense of new-mintedness), she gives the appearance of having just stepped out of the sun.

Not long ago I read of how Humphrey Davy inhaled six quarts of nitrous oxide and "The pleasurable sensation was at first local... It gradually, however, diffused itself over the whole body, and in the middle of the experiment was for a moment so intense and pure as to absorb existence. At this moment, and not before, I lost consciousness..." The sensation I experienced that morning in early June, 1959 certainly absorbed existence. It was similar to but even more intense than a moment that had occurred at the very end of the Easter term, when Pauline and I went to an exhibition of modern Russian art at the R.A. One painting in particular caught my interest, though not, I suspect, as the artist intended. A night landscape. Agricultural labourers, men and women, in the rudest of health are working by the strong beams of a tractor's headlights, their brawny arms full of wheat sheaves, their cheerful faces expressing delighted love of their work. Bunkum.

Afterwards, we went to the Partisan coffee-bar which had recently been set up in Soho Square by the group round *Universities and Left Review*. It was full of earnest young men and women playing chess at low tables or crouched in solemn discussion. We looked at each other, bursting with silent laughter, and turned to leave. As we did so, the curve of Pauline's cheek was outlined against the wall beyond and for a moment I lost all sense of where I was. Then the world came back and we made our exit. God or whatever means the Good/Be praised that time can stop like this.

But the old gypsy man was soon summoning us to the examination hall. Again, I can recall only one moment from that period. The long room where we had to sit our papers was low-ceilinged and, for all that windows stood wide open, the heat built up so remorselessly that by the end of afternoon it seemed as though we were jammed into an oven. Geoffrey decided that something must be done. He scrutinised the rules for "the proper conduct of examinees", including attire. Male examinees were required to appear in tie and gown. Nothing however was said about other items of apparel. The next day Geoffrey presented himself in tie impeccably knotted round his bare neck from where it hung over a torso shielded from intrusive gaze by his gown. To complete the outfit he wore a pair of none-too clean white shorts and plimsolls.

"Where do you think *you're* going?" The examination invigilator that afternoon was a lecturer in the History department. Dressed in grey suit with black, stuff gown and

403

hood, stony-eyed, unsmiling, he was the very image of a gauleiter whose hour has come.

"To sit my exam," Geoffrey said.

"Not dressed like that."

Geoffrey looked down at the gauleiter. "I am fulfilling the University requirements," he said. "I am wearing a tie and gown."

"You are not going into an examination dressed like *that*." And the gauleiter held out an arm in order to block Geoffrey's further progress.

It was undoubtedly a mistake to address an ex-National Serviceman as though he was still an impudent schoolboy. It was even more of a mistake for someone who stood at most five foot six to attempt confrontational tactics with a powerfully-built young man of well over six feet. Geoffrey simply picked the gauleiter up by his lapels, moved him to one side and marched to his desk.

There were no repercussions.

* * *

Before exams began I had agreed to audition for the part of Arcite in *The Two Noble Kinsmen*. I needed something to do in the period between the ending of exams and the announcement of results. The play, an open air production, was to be staged first at Reading, after which it would go to Stratford. There, it would be one of three plays produced as part of a non-Shakespeare Renaissance Drama festival over a three week period in July. Oxford University Drama Society was first on with Dryden's version of *Antony and Cleopatra, All for Love,* then us, and finally Queen's Belfast would bring their production of Ford's *The Broken Heart*. For the Reading production of *Two Noble Kinsman* we used the formal garden in front of Whiteknights House, a large grassy area dominated by a vast cedar tree and edged by flower beds, all of which were due to be dug up as soon as the production was over. They were on the site earmarked for the University's new library. I thought the production might be fun and I was pleased when I succeeded in nailing the part for which I'd auditioned. I made no mention to the director of my former triumph as juvenile lead with Ashford Parish Players. Sometimes you can say too much.

Arcite is one of the two kinsmen — the other is Palamon — whose idealistic love for each other is wrecked by Emilia, the young noblewoman and innocent cause of their falling-out. This involves betrayal and, finally, the death of Arcite. I couldn't take the play entirely seriously, even though Gordon suggested that while it was credited to Fletcher alone he was certain that Shakespeare must have had a hand in some of the scenes, that he might indeed have written them in their entirety. A view now widely accepted, though few in 1959 agreed with him. But then Gordon was always ahead of the pack. Coleridge said that Beaumont and Fletcher's plays were like cut flowers stuck in sand, and the further we got into rehearsals the more that seemed the *mot juste* for *The Two Noble Kinsmen*. Quite apart from the main plot, which involves Theseus and an army as well as the lovers, the play features a jailor who isn't a million miles away from the porter of *Macbeth*, his Ophelia-like daughter driven melancholy mad by love, and a crowd of country bumpkins under the uncertain direction of a pedantic schoolmaster who have been hired to provide entertainment for Emilia's wedding to whichever of the noble kinsmen gains her hand. Remind you of anything?

Pauline had agreed to play one of the village maidens, so I willingly put up with the amateurish luvvieness of much that went on. The director, Max Maglashan, a lecturer in the Chemistry department who would in due time become a distinguished professor, had a deep, hammy voice and the habit of calling you darling if he especially disliked your interpretation of certain lines. He initially invited Kath to play the part of Emilia but they had a falling out — there were rumours that she had not welcomed his advances — so by the time I joined rehearsals Amy had replaced her. That this didn't lead to any coolness between the two women was more of a tribute to their good sense than Max's assumptions of his director's dues.

405

A couple of days before the opening I learned I had been awarded a starred first-class degree, which meant that my plans for research were now safe. Elated by this welcome news, I got drunk and forgot some crucial lines on opening night, though this proved less of a mishap than the unto-ward eruption of Theseus and his entire army of six into the middle of a tender domestic scene between the jailor and his daughter, supposedly taking place in a prison cell. In so vast an acting area, logistical snags were inevitable. Actors waiting to make their entrance as they hid behind the giant cedar or circumambient shrubbery were fed their cues by field telephone positioned at each point of entry, and these were controlled by an assistant stage manager propped on the lighting gantry at the back of the auditorium. Maglashan had made much of the need for prompt cues. Hence, the untoward arrival of the military in a prison cell, a contre-temps which Theseus, played by a jovial lecturer in Agricultural Economics, did his best to resolve by shouting "About turn, Gentlemen," and marching his army back to the rhododendrons. In the second half, the a.s.m. made up for his earlier over-eagerness by a number of late calls, as a result of which the executioner, who was supposed to be stopped at the very last second from cutting off the wrongly accused Palamon's head, had to raise his axe, lower it, raise it, lower it, raise it once more and then remain in a posture of frozen immobility while the messenger with the order of reprieve made his stately way across the grass, saying as he arrived at the executioner's side, "Hold, hold!" Pause. "O, hold, hold, hold!"

Afterwards, a few of us wondered why the messenger — stage direction "Enter Messenger in haste" — had been quite so relaxed about his movements, let alone the delivery of his order. "Well," he said, "I thought it would be undignified to walk any faster. Anyway, it's my one line. Why throw it away?"

There were fewer problems at Stratford. Unfortunately the first night of *All for Love*, which Pauline and I had gone to see, was a disaster. The area designated for the stage was a grassy stretch right on the bank of the Avon, a hundred yards or so along from the Memorial Theatre. Neville Coghill, who directed, planned for Dryden's piece to begin in spectacular fashion with the two lovers stepping ashore from a barge rowed up-river by slaves. The audience settled, the trumpets to announce the start of the play blew sturdily, and we waited. And waited. Minutes passed. The audience became restive. Finally, after what felt like an age and may have been as much as ten minutes, a pair of bedraggled actors clambered soggily up the river bank and, as Crabbe more or less says of mussels at Aldeburgh, sloped their slow passage to the acting place. The evening was not a success.

We later heard that some local Teds on the far bank, having seen the barge set off, decided to treat it as the flag-ship of an approaching armada which patriotism required them to repulse. Accordingly, they began to rake it with shot, or anyway lob stones at it, and as they did so at least one of the actors panicked, the barge began to sway, and everyone toppled into the water.

The next night Pauline and I managed to get tickets to see Olivier in *Coriolanus*. An evening of low, if unintended, farce, was followed by one of high tragedy. As with his performance in *The Entertainer*, Olivier dominated. I recall in particular the moment when, faint and weary from battle, Coriolanus suddenly brings to mind the poor host who, though helping his enemy Aufidius, "us'd me kindly." "I request you," he tells Comminius, "To give my poor host freedom." Comminius agrees and asks Coriolanus the man's name. Silence. His arms go out, fall uselessly by his sides. "By Jupiter, forgot!" It's a Roman soldier's attempt at humour, uneasy, embarrassing. He turns away, then back to the others, and now his face and voice are full of contrition and he makes an apology which even as he speaks it he knows is unworthy of him. "I am weary, yea, my memory is tired."

If I had to choose one moment to justify my belief that Olivier remains the greatest Shakespearian actor I have ever seen, that would be it. Pathos, yes, but far more telling, more harrowing, Coriolanus's sense of his own inadequacy, one which forbids self-exculpation. Great soldier he may be, but at this moment he knows he's failed a fellow human being, one who will almost certainly now be put to death. By comparison, the moment when he gives in to his mother, Volumnia, aware that it will lead to his own death, or when in a final blast of assertive hauteur he turns on Aufidius — "If you have writ your annals true, 'tis there... that like an eagle in a dovecote, I /Fluttered your Volscians in Corioli", electrifying though they were, came easily to Olivier and could have been — have been — perfectly well managed by lesser actors. But only Olivier could make you understand the depths of Coriolanus's anguish in those three words, "By Jupiter, forgot!" Aptly, of course. Jupiter *would* make Coriolanus forget. That's what war can do. The pity of war, an emotion that takes him by surprise and humanises him, is all in the gesture of weary despair.

I was so overwhelmed by Olivier's performance I scarcely noticed that the first Tribune was played by a young actor called Albert Finney. But the following year, when Finney became Arthur Seaton in the film version of *Saturday Night and Sunday Morning,* I would think of him as embodying the essence of that recalcitrant, stroppy vitality I associate with the 1950s. My 1950s.

Coda

In the autumn of 1959 the Conservatives were against expectation re-elected to office. On election night a distraught and drunken friend was briefly detailed by the Law on a charge of disturbing the peace — he had been found outside the local Conservative headquarters yelling an offer to punch anyone who dared to emerge. At more or less the same time National Service was brought to an end and Pauline and I got engaged. Having made the break with the Catholic church, she hoped to soften the blow for her parents by this public show of respectable conduct. Now, in her final year as a student of Fine Art, she carried on officially living in hall while Carl and I found a flat on the London Road no more than twenty yards from The Turk's Head. Carl brought with him his Dansette and a considerable supply of records. In the late 1950s record players of any sort were still in short supply. Pauline's friend at Bohemia-in-the-Woods had one, on which she played horridly scratchy recordings of Vivaldi's Double Violin Concerto, Schubert Leider, and Bruckner. But now I had a far wider choice, although one controlled by Carl's moods, which varied according to the state of his love affairs. Fast Forward or Stop. Fast Forward meant Mozart. Stop meant Beethoven. By the end of the year I had the Eroica note for note.

The flat was above a newly-established coffee bar called Café Olé, its décor comprising an anthology of then current coffee-house styles. Fishing nets with cork weights and plastic starfish were draped across the front windows, Chianti bottles into which candles had been jammed stood on the red-and-white check cloths at each table, and the walls were covered with posters advertising bullfights. On the outside wall above the café entrance a professional sign writer had been paid to announce in large lettering INTERESTING CONTINENTAL SANDWICHES. However, for whatever reason — lack of space or deficiency in the spelling line — CONTINENTAL came out as CONTENTAL.

I sometimes played with the idea of asking for a contental sandwich, though I never did.

The café was soon full each and every evening. Students and some of Reading's low-life rubbed shoulders as they vied to be in control of the juke-box. Though Tommy Steele was already passé, Cliff Richard proved popular, as did Billy Eckstein and Sarah Vaughan's "We Seem Like Passing Strangers Now", but the overwhelming favourite was Ella Fitzgerald's double-sided classic, "Every Time We Say Goodbye" and "Manhattan". This, rather than the various Elvis tracks on offer, turned out to be the preferred choice of Charlie, King of the Teds. A large, red-faced thug with psychopathic tendencies, Charlie was delivered to the café at ten o'clock each evening. At that precise hour a black Humber Snipe would pull up outside the café's glass door and as it did so a young man in dark suit and dark glasses would emerge from the passenger seat, tug open the door behind him, and, after a suspenseful pause, out slid Charlie. Naturally he wore a dark suit and dark glasses. The dark-suited and dark-spectacled driver would now leave the Humber, step onto the pavement, throw open the café door and stand aside so that Charlie could make his entry. The two henchmen following, Charlie would slowly walk the length of the café to the service counter where he stood immobile as the driver fed the jukebox and the minder delivered his one word order.

"Usual."

Three black coffees.

But Charlie didn't last long. He was arrested for hitting a policeman one Saturday lunchtime as the three left a pub in the town centre. We followed the case in the *Reading Mercury*. The prosecution claimed that Charlie had made an unprovoked, drunken attack on a police officer. Charlie's defence was that he had merely tapped the officer on the shoulder in order to ascertain the time and to his amazement the officer had fallen into the gutter.

Sentence: six months, to be served in Oxford Gaol.

Charlie's place was taken by Ken Spicer, the minder. A gentler man, he came to grief over love. Ken fell for a third

410

year student and pestered her with the offer of gifts. "Honest, Nancy, I'd do anything for you." On one occasion, desperate to be rid of him, she apparently said that she needed a new dress. The next evening Ken arrived with a bolt of cloth which he had freed from a draper's on the far side of town. He was followed in by two policemen.

"Evening, Ken, that your cloth, is it?"

Ken, too, disappeared into Oxford Gaol, having asked for several other thefts to be taken into consideration.

That left the driver. The driver passed. Or rather, he recommended that the person appointed to keep Charlie's seat warm should be a mutual friend, known as "Chick, the hardest man in Berkshire." Chick came, gazed around his stupendously bent nose at the café, voted it unworthy of his patronage — his actual words, as reported by a Mrs Gamp lookalike who served as manageress and was known to all as "Cookie", were, "bleedin' dump, I'm off"; and from then on the Café Olé reverted to being the preserve of students and the more adventurous of Reading's teenagers.

It was noisy but only in the evenings. During the day I could work there, though I preferred the library or Whiteknights, where, as a bona-fide research student, I now had a semi-monastic cell. Gordon was away. His drinking had become so badly out of control that as soon as the summer term ended he booked himself into a clinic specialising in curing alcoholics by a mixture of drugs and aversion therapy. After six weeks of what sounded like hell on earth — being given as much drink as he wanted and then left to crawl about in pools of his own vomit — he was granted a term's sabbatical and took himself off on a tour of parts of the Middle East before finally arriving in Greece, from where he sent a number of postcards to the flat. "'Look Back in Anger' at the National Theatre," one said. "It reminded me of you all. So I send a very angry object. I'm not angry but very peaceful, though worried by the Parthenon." On the reverse side was the image of a bronze Hercules. Another said only, "Am reading *The Long Revolution* and becoming MADDENED by Mr Williams's refusal to tell us exactly how and when the revolution will occur and what it will look like when it does." I think Gordon intended the remark as a jibe at me. I could have countered that my own socialist vision, indebted though I and so many of us were to Williams's earlier *Culture and Society*, a book for which Gordon professed considerable admiration, was Morrisian to the extent — a very considerable one — that I didn't think you could provide a blue-print for utopianism. That would be to pre-judge and therefore trammel the ways and means of its evolution. Five Year Plans were no guarantee of the kind of future we should want. If anything, they made it an impossibility. But I saved that up to discuss with Gordon for when he reappeared, which wouldn't be until after Christmas.

At the very end of the year I stayed for a few days with Ian and his mother in their cold, damp, dilapidated flat in Eltham. He and I were planning to write an extended essay on Yeats's "Meditations in Time of Civil War": "Vengeance on the murderers of Jacques Molay". That line from the seventh section of an intriguing and in some ways baffling poem had led me to De Quincey's book-length essay "Historico-Critical Inquiry into the Origin of the Rosicrucians and the Freemasons", and I had persuaded myself that the poem could be best approached through an investigation of Yeats's involvement with various occult sects, especially those linked to the Cathars. These were the bankers of mediaeval Europe, and included among their number was Jaques de Molay. Ian, who was endlessly fascinated by such sects, and who knew De Quincey's writings on the Essenes, needed very little persuading that therein lay the signature, if not the key, to all things Yeatsian.

The essay, however, made little progress. This was partly because I — and I suspect Ian — soon came to realise that our quest for understanding the poem through pursuit of the mustier by-ways of medieval heresies was taking us way off course. But anyway, I was a useful ally, and indeed fence, in Ian's far more compelling quest for books. Each morning we would leave the flat and set off to inspect second-hand bookshops across south London. I didn't mind this. The flat was so cold that even in shrill December weather I was glad to be outside. The only heating was provided by a stove of quite startling inefficiency, which required constant attention and gave back very little. Sheets and blankets, though perfectly clean, felt horridly damp, and I slept with difficulty. How Ian's mother coped, I've no idea. A tall, gaunt, craggy-faced woman clad always in black, she seemed a cross between Mrs Clenham and Wooster's Aunt Agatha. Deafness made her shout as though she was in an endless bad temper against the world and against Ian in particular.

This was, I came to realise, misleading. She was proud of him, once showing me some of his early poems in print and telling me that his talents were under-rated and exploited by others, which was true; and she was capable of small acts of generosity to his guests. But her life had not been a happy one. Soon after Ian, her only child, was born, her husband decamped to one of the more remote parts of Canada, where he made a living as a big-game hunter and from where he never returned, although in later years father and son contrived a meeting when Ian went to give a lecture in Vancouver. He had been invited there by Geoffrey Creigh, who was then a lecturer at Vancouver's university. Music was Mrs Fletcher's great solace. In earlier days she had been a more than competent pianist. But as deafness encroached, this solace was denied her.

Mother and son were, besides, hard up. She had a pension, but a poor one. University salaries were very low in the 1950s. I was startled when on one occasion Gordon, admittedly in his cups, said that nobody could afford to take a lectureship who hadn't a private income. He meant, I think, that without such means foreign travel would be difficult and the acquisition of a "working" library such as he possessed all but impossible. In this respect, at least, he was wrong. Second-hand bookshops abounded and books, even comparatively rare ones, were cheap. (While still a postgraduate I bought for a fiver Bishop Newton's great 3 volume illustrated edition of Milton's *Poetical Works*.) But once essentials were taken care of, a university salary didn't leave much for fripperies. At Reading we joked about Ian's stinginess. Typical Scotsman, we said. The man whose round rarely if ever came up. It was only when I stayed with him that I realised how little money he and his mother had between them. Which helps to explain Mrs Fletcher's stentorian complaints as yet another day out ended with an attempt to smuggle armfuls of books into the flat. If apprehended as we tiptoed indoors, Ian warned, I was to say that the books were mine. It never worked. The front door usually swung open while Ian was fumbling short-sightedly for his key.

"Ian, *what* are you doing with yet *more* books."

"Oh, mother, John bought these. For his research."

"Stuff and nonsense." And Mrs Fletcher's nigh-on forty-year-old son would be castigated for his profligacy, behaviour destined to bring them or at least his mother to the workhouse.

On my last evening she decided we would all go out to eat at a nearby restaurant, where cheap though nourishing food was to be found. I think this was her way of making up to me for previous episodes of short temper, as when she attempted to force onto a woman friend some old clothes she had rescued from the flat upstairs after the deaths of its occupants. (She had helped them in their last illnesses.) Ian accordingly became the owner of a heavy green three-piece suit. "What do you mean, it doesn't fit. *Of course* it fits. You need simply to hold your shoulders higher." Ian, who was very round-shouldered — he himself once described his batting stance as resembling that of a superannuated corkscrew — succumbed to the suit.

But the friend was made of sterner stuff, especially as money was involved.

Matters came to a head when Mrs Fletcher offered at knock-down price several pairs of button-over patent leather shoes which might have been fashionable in the early 1920s.

The friend made polite demurral.

Mrs Fletcher persisted.

"Oh, mother," Ian said, "you can see she doesn't want them."

414

"*You* keep out of this, Ian. *I* am trying to save us from the gutter."

Before we went out to eat, Mrs Fletcher decided to leave at home a five-pound note which she convinced herself would in a public place be filched from her purse. She therefore proposed to put the note inside one of Ian's books. The books, probably as many as ten thousand, were crammed onto shelves, heaped on tables and chairs, and spread in piles across the floor of the room we were standing in.

"Ian, kindly pay attention. I want you to remember which book I am putting this note into."

"Yes, mother." Ian, his back turned to her, was peering absorbedly at the binding of one of that day's bargains.

"Ian," she said, when we returned from our meal, "bring me the note."

"What note, mother?"

"The note I placed in that book before we left."

"Which book?"

"What do you mean, *which* book?" irritation modulated into ire, then into incredulity, then into despair. "Am I, at my time of life, to believe that you were *not* paying attention." Ian blinked at her.

We spent hours that evening and again the following morning in an increasingly ill-tempered search for the five-pound note, but without success.

* * *

A few days into the New Year, Carl, Pauline, and I held an impromptu party at the flat. Not many people were around but those that were drifted in, among them a student dressed in an odd assortment of clothes including jeans, a collarless shirt, knee-high boots and a thigh-length, camel-hair jacket. He was apparently studying art.

Sprawled on one of our kitchen chairs, he rolled himself a cigarette.

"It's a joint," he said, as I looked at it. "Want a drag?"

The 1960s had begun.

415

Other Works

John Lucas's many works of a critical, scholarly, and literary-historical kind include:

The Melancholy Man: A Study of Dickens's Fiction, Methuen, 1970; Harvester Press, 1980

Arnold Bennett, Methuen, 1974

The Literature of Change, Harvester Press, 1977

Modern English Poetry: Hardy to Hughes, Batsford, 1985

England and Englishness: Ideas of Nationhood in English Poetry, 1688-1900, Chatto & Windus, the Hogarth Press, 1989

The Radical Twenties: Writing, Politics, Culture, Five Leaves, 1997, Rutgers University Press, 1999

The Good That We Do, Greenwich Exchange, 2001

92 Acharnon Street, Eland, 2007

His latest poetry collection is *Things to Say,* Five Leaves, 2010

About the Author

John Lucas's *92 Achernon Street*, a gritty but affectionate portrait of Greece, won the Authors' Club Dolman Travel Book Award. His other books include critical works on England and Englishness, Dickens, Ivor Gurney, John Clare, Arnold Bennett and (from Five Leaves) *The Radical Twenties*.

He is a poet and translator, the current poetry editor of *Critical Survey* and former poetry reviewer of the *New Statesman*. His translations include *Egils Saga*, an Everyman Modern Classic. His eighth poetry collection, *Things to Say*, has just been published by Five Leaves.

John Lucas is Professor Emeritus at the Universities of Loughborough and Nottingham Trent. He has been the publisher of Shoestring Press since 1994, having previously been an editor at the Byron Press and Reading University Press. He lives in Nottingham and plays cornet with the Burgundy Street jazz group.